W9-CZZ-323

BEYOND PARIS

A touring guide to the French Provinces

A touring guide to the French Provinces

W • W • Norton & Company • Inc • New York •

BEYOND PARIS

BY LILLIAN AND PHILIP VAN DOREN STERN

FIRST EDITION

Library of Congress Catalog Card No. 65-13032

Published simultaneously in Canada by
George J. McLeod Limited, Toronto

All the photographs, except those credited to the
French Government Tourist Office, were taken by the authors.

Printed in the United States of America
1 2 3 4 5 6 7 8 9 0

Contents

INTRODUCTION 13

Part I *Traveling in France*

A NOTE ON THE SPELLING OF PLACE NAMES 22

1. PLANNING YOUR TRIP 23

HIGHLIGHT AREAS 24 · MAKING AN ITINERARY 24 · HOW TO PREPARE AN ITINERARY 26 · A SIMPLIFIED ITINERARY FORM 28 · TRAVEL AGENTS 29 · MAPS AND GUIDEBOOKS 30 · YOUR HEALTH 30 · YOUR PASSPORT 31 · INSURANCE 34

2. COSTS, CASH—AND THINGS TO ARRANGE BEFORE YOU GO 35

HOTELS 35 · FOOD 36 · CAR EXPENSES 36 · MISCELLANEOUS SMALL EXPENSES 36 · THE COST PER DAY 36 · MORE ABOUT EXPENSES 37 · BUDGET TRAVEL 37 · SAFEGUARDING YOUR FUNDS 38 · LETTERS OF CREDIT 39 · A BANK ACCOUNT IN FRANCE 40 · CARRYING CURRENCY 40 · CUSTOMS DUTY AND EXEMPTIONS 41 · RECENT CHANGES IN CUSTOMS LAWS 42 · YOUR CAR 45 · AUTOMOBILE INSURANCE 46 · BUYING, LEASING, OR RENTING A CAR 46

3. WHAT TO TAKE WITH YOU 49

TROUBLE-FREE PLANE TRAVEL 50 · WHAT TO BUY ABROAD 51 · LIGHTENING THE LOAD FOR THE RETURN FLIGHT 52 · YOUR CLOTHES 53 · SHOES, HATS, AND BEACHWEAR 54 · SMALL ITEMS 55 · WHEN YOU GO BY SHIP 56 · CAMERA GEAR 57 · PACKING 59 · A CHECKLIST OF THINGS TO REMEMBER 59

4. HOTELS AND *PENSIONS* 61

MAKING RESERVATIONS 62 · GARAGES AND PARKING 64 · TRAVELING WITHOUT HOTEL RESERVATIONS 65 · HOTEL AND RESTAURANT GUIDES 65 · GOVERNMENT HOTEL RATINGS 67 ODDS AND ENDS OF INFORMATION 68 · HOTEL NAMES 69 · *Pensions* 70 · CAMPS AND CAMPING 72

5. EATING YOUR WAY THROUGH FRANCE 73

THE CONTINENTAL BREAKFAST 73 · THE MIDDAY MEAL 74 FRENCH BREAD 74 · BUYING FOOD 76 · WATER 77 · *Pension* FOOD 77 · RESTAURANTS 79 · THE ALL-IMPORTANT MENU 79 · WHAT A FRENCH MEAL CONSISTS OF 80 · WHY FRENCH COOKING IS SO GOOD 82 · FRENCH TABLE MANNERS 84

6. THE WINES OF FRANCE 87

TABLE WINES 87 · WINE AND FOOD 88 · VINTAGE WINES 89 · BORDEAUX WINES 89 · BURGUNDY WINES 91 · CHAMPAGNE 92 · CÔTES DU RHÔNE 93 · ALSATIAN WINES 93 · WINES OF THE LOIRE VALLEY 94 · OTHER REGIONS 94 · LEARNING ABOUT WINES 95 · TIPS ABOUT WINE 96 · VINTAGE YEARS 97 · VISITING THE WINE REGIONS 98

7. DRIVING ON FRENCH ROADS 101

WORDS ON SIGNS 102 · THE DRIVER ON THE RIGHT HAS THE RIGHT OF WAY 103 · THE HIERARCHY OF THE ROAD 104 · THE FRENCH ATTITUDE TOWARD SPEED 105 · AVERAGE DAILY MILEAGE 106 · THREE TYPES OF FRENCH ROADS 106 SHIPPING YOUR CAR BY TRAIN 108 · LOCAL SPEED LIMITS 108 · FRENCH POLICE 109 · ACCIDENTS 110 · DRIVING AT NIGHT 112 · GASOLINE 112

8. THE COUNTRY AND THE PEOPLE 114

2000 YEARS OF BATTLE 115 · THE LAND 117 · FAULTS AND FAILINGS 118 · DEAD HANDS REACHING 120 · OTHER NUISANCES 122 · THE OLD ORDER CHANGETH 122 · NOT FAULTS BUT MISUNDERSTANDINGS 123 · TOURISM 124

9. SOME TIPS ABOUT TRAVELING IN FRANCE 126

READ ABOUT WHAT YOU ARE GOING TO SEE 127 · MEMORY AIDS 128 · INDIRECT REMINDERS 129 · MAPS AND PHOTO-

GRAPHS 130 · A HAPPY PHRASE 130 · FRENCH ARCHITECTURE AND HOW TO APPRECIATE IT 131 · GUIDES 135 · THE NEW FRANC 136

Part II *Places to Go*

A NOTE FOR FORGETFUL READERS AND FOR THOSE WHO SKIP 140

10. NORMANDY 141

WEATHER 142 · DRIVING FROM PARIS TO THE COAST 143 · ROUEN 144 · HONFLEUR 147 · DEAUVILLE AND TROUVILLE 148 · CABOURG AND DIVES 150 · THE INVASION BEACHES 152 · UTAH BEACH AND SAINTE-MÈRE-ÉGLISE 154 THE COTENTIN PENINSULA 156 · MONT-SAINT-MICHEL 158 THE INTERIOR 160 · ÉVREUX AND LISIEUX 161 · CAEN 162 · BAYEUX 162 · FALAISE 164 · HORSE COUNTRY 164 · FOOD IN NORMANDY 165

11. BRITTANY 167

A LAND OF TRADITIONS 168 · BRETON PLACE NAMES 170 MONT-DOL 171 · SAINT-MALO, DINARD, AND DINAN 171 · THE PINK GRANITE COAST 173 · MORLAIX AND BEYOND 175 THE CALVARIES 178 · OTHER RELIGIOUS ART 181 · THE WEST COAST 181 · HUELGOAT 184 · DOUARNENEZ 185 · THE POINTE DU RAZ 186 · QUIMPER 188 · CONCARNEAU AND PONT-AVEN 188 · QUIMPERLÉ AND PORT-LOUIS 190 · CARNAC 191 · MEGALITHS 191 · THE CARNAC ALIGNMENTS 195 · LOCMARIAQUER 197 · QUIBERON AND THE CÔTE SAUVAGE 198 · VISITING THE CÔTE SAUVAGE 199 · EXPLORING THE CARNAC COUNTRYSIDE 201 · THE GULF OF MORBIHAN 201 · AURAY 203 · LA BAULE 204 · NANTES 205 · FOOD AND WINE 207

A NOTE ON PROVINCES VS. DEPARTMENTS 208

12. THE CHÂTEAU COUNTRY 210

THE CHÂTEAUX IN TIME 210 · THE CHÂTEAUX IN SPACE 212 · A LIST OF CHÂTEAUX AND PLACES TO VISIT 214 · FOOD AND WINE 232

13. THE ATLANTIC COAST 235

POITIERS AND THE VENDÉE 236 · LES SABLES-D'OLONNE 237 · ROYAN 238 · COGNAC 240 · OTHER FRENCH BRANDIES 242 · VISITING COGNAC 243 · BEYOND COGNAC 243 BORDEAUX AND ITS WINES 244 · VISITING THE VINEYARDS 246 · THE LANDES 247 · HOSSEGOR 248 · BIARRITZ 249 WINES AND FOOD 251

14. PÉRIGORD 253

PÉRIGUEUX 256 · THE PREHISTORIC CAVES 256 · LES-EYZIES-DE-TAYAC 258 · PREHISTORIC SITES NEAR LES EYZIES 260 · BASTIDES 264 · SARLAT 267 · SOUILLAC 268 COUGNAC 269 · ROCAMADOUR 270 · THE CAUSSE COUNTRY 272 · CAHORS 279 · MONTAUBAN AND MOISSAC 280 · TOULOUSE AND ALBI 282 · FOOD AND WINE 284

15. THE PYRENEES 286

THE BASQUES 287 · SAINT-JEAN-PIED-DE-PORT 288 · LOURDES 291 · CAUTERETS AND THE CIRQUE DE GAVARNIE 292 · PREHISTORIC CAVES IN THE PYRENEES 294 · MONTSÉGUR 295 · LIMESTONE COUNTRY AND ITS CAVES 296 · TO AX-LES-THERMES AND BOURG-MADAME 297 · A LITTLE BIT OF SPAIN 299 · THE CERDAGNE 299 · BASQUE COOKING 300

16. ROUSSILLON, THE GORGES OF THE TARN, AND AUVERGNE 302

CARCASSONNE 303 · VIOLLET-LE-DUC 305 · CARCASSONNE AS IT IS TODAY 306 · BÉZIERS 307 · SÈTE AND MONTPELLIER 308 · MILLAU 310 · ROQUEFORT — TOWN AND CHEESE 310 · CHAOS AND CAVES 311 · THE GORGES OF THE TARN 311 · MENDE 312 · LE PUY 313 · IN STEVENSON'S FOOTSTEPS 314 · AUVERGNE 315 · CLERMONT-FERRAND AND THIERS 317 · VICHY 318 · FOOD AND WINE 320

17. PROVENCE 322

AIGUES-MORTES 323 · LES-SAINTES-MARIES-DE-LA-MER 324 · THE CAMARGUE 325 · ARLES 326 · LES BAUX 329 · SAINT-RÉMY AND GLANUM 330 · TARASCON AND

BEAUCAIRE 332 · NÎMES 333 · THE PONT-DU-GARD 334 · AVIGNON 335 · THE RHÔNE VALLEY 338 · ORANGE 339 · NYONS 340 · VAISON-LA-ROMAINE 341 · MONT VENTOUX 342 · THE FONTAINE DE VAUCLUSE 342 · EASTERN PROVENCE 343 · AIX-EN-PROVENCE 345 · THE FIELD OF THE DEAD 348 · MARSEILLE 348 · FOOD AND WINE 351

18. THE RIVIERA 353

BRITISH SUN SEEKERS 354 · THE RIVIERA CLIMATE 355 · WHERE TO STAY 356 · THE SHORE ROAD 356 · THE MAURES AND SAINT-TROPEZ 357 · THE ESTEREL 360 · LA NAPOULE 361 · CANNES 361 · ILES DE LÉRINS 362 · A VERY PRIVATE VILLAGE 363 · GRASSE 363 · VALLAURIS 364 · ANTIBES 365 · BIOT AND CAGNES 366 · SAINT-PAUL DE VENCE AND VENCE 368 · NICE 369 · THE THREE CORNICHES 372 · CAP FERRAT 373 · MONTE CARLO 375 · MONACO 376 · THE CASINO 377 · MENTON 379 · MOUNTAIN VILLAGES 380 · FOOD 380

19. CORSICA 382

WHEN TO GO 383 · GETTING AROUND 385 · NORTHERN CORSICA 386 · L'ILE-ROUSSE AND CALVI 389 · SOUTH TO AJACCIO 390 · AJACCIO 392 · PROPRIANO AND FILITOSA 393 · SARTÈNE AND ITS ANCIENT FEUDS 395 · BONIFACIO 396 · PORTO-VECCHIO 398 · THE OSPEDALE MOUNTAINS AND THE COL DE BAVELLA 398 · THE EAST COAST 399 · FOOD AND WINE 400

20. THE ALPS 402

ROUTES THROUGH THE ALPS 403 · GRENOBLE 404 · ANNECY AND TALLOIRES 406 · FISHING IN FRANCE 410 · EXCURSIONS FROM TALLOIRES 411 · MOUNT BLANC 412 · CHAMONIX AND THE COUNTRY AROUND IT 414 · THE MER DE GLACE 414 · THE BIONNASSAY GLACIER 415 · SUMMERTIME SKIING 416 · WALKING AROUND MOUNT BLANC 417 · THE MONT BLANC TUNNEL 418 · LAKE GENEVA RESORTS 419 · LE CHABLAIS 420 · FOOD AND WINE 421

21. BURGUNDY 422

PÉROUGES 423 · THE BEAUJOLAIS VINEYARDS 423 · SO-

LUTRÉ 424 · CLUNY 425 · TOURNUS 425 · THE CÔTE D'OR AND BEAUNE 426 · THE HOTEL-DIEU 428 · THE CÔTE D'OR 430 · DIJON 431 · AUTUN 432 · A CIRCLE TOUR OF NORTHERN BURGUNDY 433 · FONTENAY AND MONTRÉAL 434 · AVALLON 435 · A MEDIEVAL SONG LEADS TO A DISCOVERY 436 · VÉZELAY 437 · TREASURE AFTER TREASURE 439 · THE TRÉSOR DE VIX 440 · FOOD AND WINE 442

22. THE JURA, ALSACE, AND LORRAINE 444

THE JURA MOUNTAINS 445 · SAINT-CLAUDE 446 · ARC-ET-SENANS 447 · BESANÇON 448 · BELFORT 449 · ALSACE 450 · COLMAR 451 · THE STORKS OF ALSACE 452 · UNSPOILED ALSACE 453 · A GERMAN DEATH CAMP IN FRANCE 455 · STRASBOURG 456 · A ROSE-RED CATHEDRAL 459 · NANCY 461 · JOAN OF ARC AND DOMRÉMY 462 · A FORGOTTEN ROMAN CITY 463 · FOOD AND WINE 464

23. CHAMPAGNE AND THE BATTLEFIELDS OF THE FIRST WORLD WAR 466

BAR-LE-DUC AND THE VOIE SACRÉE 467 · SAINT-MIHIEL 467 · VERDUN 468 · THE BATTLEFIELDS AROUND REIMS 470 · REIMS 471 · CHAMPAGNE 474 · CHÂTEAU-THIERRY AND THE BELLEAU WOOD 475 · LAON 476 · THE BATTLEFIELDS OF THE SOMME 477 · AMIENS 478 · FOOD AND WINE 479

24. THE NORTH CHANNEL COAST 480

THE COAST ROAD 482 · LE TOUQUET-PARIS-PLAGE 482 · ÉTRETAT 483

L'ENVOI 486

BOOKS AND PAMPHLETS ABOUT TRAVELING IN FRANCE 487

BOOKS ABOUT FOOD AND WINE 489 · NORMANDY 490 · BRITTANY 490 · THE CHÂTEAU COUNTRY 491 · THE ATLANTIC COAST 491 · PÉRIGORD 491 · THE PYRENEES 492 · ROUSSILLON, THE GORGES OF THE TARN, AND AUVERGNE 492 · PROVENCE 493 · THE RIVIERA 493 · CORSICA 494 · THE ALPS 494 · BURGUNDY 495 · THE JURA, ALSACE, AND LORRAINE 495 · CHAMPAGNE AND THE BATTLEFIELDS OF THE FIRST WORLD WAR 495

A LIST OF RECOMMENDED HOTELS AND RESTAURANTS 497

RESTAURANTS 500 · NORMANDY 501 · BRITTANY 502 · THE CHÂTEAU COUNTRY 504 · THE ATLANTIC COAST 504 · PÉRIGORD 506 · THE PYRENEES 507 · ROUSSILLON, THE GORGES OF TARN, AND AUVERGNE 507 · PROVENCE 509 · THE RIVIERA 511 · CORSICA 513 · THE ALPS 514 · BURGUNDY 511 · THE JURA, ALSACE, AND LORRAINE 516 · CHAMPAGNE AND THE BATTLEFIELDS OF THE FIRST WORLD WAR 517 · THE NORTH CHANNEL COAST 518

INDEX 519

Acknowledgments

The authors want to thank Myron Clement of the French Government Tourist Office in New York for a careful reading of the manuscript, and Georges Normand of the Paris office for help, information, and advice in getting around France. For expert criticism on wine: Alexis Lichine, Frank Schoonmaker, Mme. Fernande Garvin, and Paul Chanson.

Introduction

This is a very personal book written by two people who love France, who have been going there since the 1920's, and who have visited nearly all of its 90 departments. We have not included Paris or its environs because we take it for granted that you know the city or will visit it before you begin your journey. The fact that we omit Paris does not mean that we don't like it; we love it dearly.

Beyond Paris lies the fair land that is fittingly the mother of so fair a city. Oddly enough, few people—even the French themselves—have thoroughly explored the rest of France. They are missing a great deal because this nation, although relatively small in area, is a traveler's paradise. It has beaches on two seas, the highest mountains in western Europe, broad stretches of carefully tended farms and vineyards, and vast barren plateaus through which industrious little rivers have cut deep gorges. Scattered across this widely varied land are thousands of villages, some of them hidden in isolated valleys or perched on steep hills. All these, together with numerous small towns and a few dozen not-too-large cities, make up the France that lies beyond Paris.

When we first explored this inexhaustibly interesting country we tried to go everywhere and see everything. We succeeded only in tiring ourselves. Then, one afternoon, we came across a quiet country hotel with a flowered terrace on which tables were set out under the trees. The accommodations proved to be good, the food and local wines excellent, and the prices reasonable. Best of all, the hotel was located in the center of an area where there was much to see and do. We stayed on. Every evening we returned to a base where everything was waiting for us, including a warm welcome. This was very different from the usual one-night stays we had made in city hotels or roadside taverns. Here we were regular guests, and our hosts and their staff wanted to please us so we would come back. We did—year after year.

We found, too, that by traveling in this way our days had a greater number of useful hours. When we had kept going from one town to another, we had had to stop early to seek quarters for the night. Now we could return at dusk, and when we arrived there was no unpacking to do. Lights glowed in the dining room where we could count on getting well-prepared food served with all the ceremony and skill that the French—even in small hotels—delight in.

We decided to try to find other places like this one. Unfortunately, it is not true that every French country hotel is good—or even fairly good. But much study of directories, personal recommendations, a lot of mileage, and an occasional bit of luck enabled us to locate enough pleasant bases for touring France by going from one to another with few barren areas between. Some of our finds were in historic châteaux, some were on the edges of cities, but most were simple establishments in the country.

But this book is intended to be far more than a hotel directory. Once the matter of comfortable quarters has been settled, you will want to know what there is of interest in the area. Most of the text is devoted to giving you this information.

We have tried to suggest a varied fare, for we know what a chore it can be to visit too many ecclesiastical monuments, minor museums, ancient market places, and streets lined with picturesque old houses—no matter how attractive they may be. We also know that too long a stay in one kind of region finally becomes tiresome, so we go from seashore to mountains, from hilltop villages and walled towns to modern resorts, from scenes of past war and violence to peaceful places where not much has ever happened except that people have lived there for centuries, tilled the land, built houses and castles, and perhaps left enduring works of handicraft or fine art.

France is larger than it seems to be on the map. And certain parts are far more interesting than others. We do not pretend to cover everything or to be impartial about the places we describe. We have avoided large cities, industrial areas, heavily traveled roads, and some over-commercialized resorts. In order to keep the book manageable we have concentrated on those sections of France which we think have the most to offer.

We include many much-visited places, for we have found that they owe their popularity to the fact that they are really worth seeing. People flock to the Riviera because it has the best climate and the most celebrated seaside resorts in France. They go to Chamonix because it is at the foot of Mont Blanc, the highest mountain in Europe—and one of the most beautiful. Its Mer de Glace is the most spectacular glacier they are ever likely to see at close range, for they can ride up to it in comfort on a train.

We include the popular places, but we also take you to areas where few tourists go. There is much of interest in remote corners of France where you can find the unexpected, the odd, and the bizarre.

We also tell you what to avoid. We have spent a lot of time and money exploring places that we found were worth only a brief visit or that could have been skipped entirely. France has so many treasures that you can afford to pick and choose only the best. Guidebooks don't tell you what to miss, for they are encyclopedic by nature and try to cover everything.

This volume is not intended to be a substitute for the standard guidebooks. We urge you to use them. We do ourselves and append a list of those we found most helpful. When good regional or local handbooks are available we mention them too.

Since we expect you to consult guidebooks for detailed information, we have kept our descriptions brief and informal. But when we think that something is truly wonderful, we say so and then usually devote a good bit of space to it. Lesser places get less attention, and so on down until some are only referred to or not even mentioned at all. You can't hope to see all of France. No one ever has. This book covers so much that it would take years to visit what it includes.

We think the best way to use it is to read it through, make up your mind which parts of France you want to see, and then re-read the regional chapters that describe them. On the first reading, skip the directions about roads and mileage. They mean little until you are on the spot and have to decide which way to go. You will find them very useful then.

Since we are great believers in marking up and annotating books that are intended to be of service, we hope you will read this one with a pencil in hand. We have provided both an analytical table of contents and a detailed index to enable you to locate anything you want to find, but if you add your own reference notes and emphasize things you consider important, you will make your copy of the book even more useful. Think of it as part of your traveling equipment and consider it as a tool rather than as a volume that is to be displayed on a living-room shelf.

Occasionally we point out certain things the guidebooks omit or barely mention, but what we add is usually of personal interest. Or we may draw your attention to something amusing. Formal guidebooks ignore such things; they will, for instance, tell you about the important retable of Issenheim in the Colmar Museum but ignore the elegantly mustached stone dog that sits in the garden on a pedestal dated 1544 in front and 1753 on

Colmar's mustached dog with two different dates

the side. We thought he was worth photographing from both angles.

Although we have based our book on a long circular tour that goes for thousands of miles around France, we do not expect you to follow all or even any part of such an itinerary literally. In fact, we often indicate alternate routes or hint that certain parts of the journey may be omitted. One of the joys of traveling in France is the unexpected discoveries you can make for yourselves. By all means strike out on your own and take full advantage of local information. French people and tourists you encounter along the way can tell about places we may have missed. Even if you are not going to make an extensive tour, we believe that what we have to say about the different areas will be of value if you want to explore France in depth.

We assume that you will travel by car, because you cannot get to some of the out-of-the-way places we describe unless you have your own transportation.

We lay special emphasis on the cultural background of France and say nothing about night clubs and very little about shopping for souvenirs. But we do tell you about the food and wine that can be had in each region.

France is rich in pleasant surprises that await you at every turn—a castle perched on a hill, a lichen-laden roadside cross, a canal boat moving placidly along an inland waterway, a church that can be anything from a fortified stronghold to a soaring cathedral lacy with colored light—all these and more will make your trip a constant delight.

As to the French people—we have heard complaints about them, but they have always been wonderful to us. We have never been robbed, cheated, or treated rudely anywhere in France, and this includes Paris and the Riviera, which tourists say are the worst. Perhaps our love for France and the French people shows, perhaps it radiates from us and brings out the best in those we meet. We have been well treated in most countries, but we have been treated very well indeed in France.

As to the language problem—well, it is obviously better to have some knowledge of French than to have none at all. Yet we have friends who have driven from one end of the country to the other without knowing a word of French. They communicated somehow and had a good time. Many hotels, restaurants, and shops, of course, have English-speaking employees.

In our case, our ability to get along with the French people does not come from having a perfect command of their language. We read French without trouble, understand it when it is pronounced clearly and slowly, but speak it only well enough to get by. We can handle any situation in French, but not gracefully—and not without grammatical errors. We have heard people say that unless you speak the language like a native, you will be sneered at and ignored. We have found this not to be true. We are often complimented on our French, inadequate as we know it to be.

Before each trip to France we spend months reading about the country. Some knowledge of its history, its famous people, its art, literature, and customs will make your visit more enjoyable because everything you encounter has a story behind it.

It is very easy to miss something you want very much to see along or near your projected route. We did until we began to make notes beforehand, jotting down the names of places that seemed especially interesting. We then organized them by areas so they would be easy to find when we were near them.

Travelers with special interests may want to visit factories, stores, and other places that are associated with what they do. Letters sent in advance will prepare the way and assure you of a welcome.

Readers who know France well are going to say that we have missed some of their favorite places. Undoubtedly we have. Over a period of six years we drove more than 17,000 miles back and forth across the country in an effort to see all there is to see, but it would take teams of scouts traveling in many cars to cover France thoroughly. We are only two people and have only one car, so this book is not exhaustive. Nevertheless, we think there is enough here to keep any ambitious traveler busy for a long time to come. And some of the places are surely worth visiting more than once. In fact, it is only when you go back to spend more time in a region you really liked that you learn to appreciate its full flavor.

You are about to visit a marvelous country. What you get from your journey depends on you. Bon voyage!

—The Authors

Part One ⚜ *Traveling in France*

A note on the spelling of place names

Since you will see nothing but French spelling on road signs and other directional marks while you are on your way, we have used it throughout the book except for a few long-Anglicized words like Normandy and Brittany.

When the pronunciation of a place name differs widely from what the printed word seems to indicate, we give a phonetically-spelled version. This applies particularly to the terminal consonant. French people themselves often don't know whether or not to pronounce the tricky last consonant of an unfamiliar name.

The proper pronunciation of a place name has its practical uses. Years ago we tried to buy a railroad ticket to Mons in Belgium. The man behind the window had never heard of "Moan," and it was not until a stranger helped us out that we got a ticket to "Mohnss." More recently, when we asked a road worker the way to the Leger Museum at Biot, we found out that the name of the town is *not* pronounced by the initial letters of Body Odor—as one might expect—but is called "Beeawtt" with the vowels quickly run together and with the accent placed on the last syllable.

1. *Planning your trip*

If you plan your trip carefully, you are likely to encounter better weather than if you don't plan it at all. Certain parts of France are warmer and sunnier than others. The Mediterranean coast, for instance, has less rain and higher temperatures than Northern France. It is therefore advisable to go from south to north if you begin your journey in the spring (and from north to south in the autumn), in order to follow warm weather.

May through September are the best months in France. April and October may or may not be warm in the north. November through March is the worst part of the year with some cold and rainy periods everywhere. Furthermore, many country hotels and restaurants are closed then. The Michelin red guide will tell you which ones. Museums and other places to visit may be closed entirely or open for only a few hours a week during the cold months. Unless you like winter sports, the best part of France to be in at this time is the Mediterranean coast, especially in sections sheltered from the famous mistral, a cold wind that comes down from the North. The stretch of coast between Nice and Menton is protected from it by a mountain range.

Americans have to realize that there are no really warm places anywhere in Europe during the winter. Nothing comparable to Florida, Arizona, or Southern California exists there. Europeans who seek good winter climate must go to other parts of the world. Even Corsica, Malta, and Majorca, are not truly warm then although the weather there is usually milder than on the mainland.

An ideally timed long trip through France would begin early in May and end late in September. A few extra weeks might be added at both ends of this five-month period.

For short trips, May and June or September and early October are fine for those who can get away then. But most people are more likely to be free during the summer months; actually, France is at its best then even though its resorts are crowded. Just make sure that you have confirmed hotel reservations; in August they are essential in the more popular places.

Highlight areas

Our love of France is so great that we enjoy exploring even its remotest corners, but we think that some areas are more interesting to tourists than others. If your time is limited to a highlight trip, we suggest that you visit one or more of the following regions:

1. Brittany
2. The Château Country, (easily combined with Brittany—especially southern Brittany)
3. Périgord
4. Provence
5. The Riviera (easily combined with Provence. If you are flying in, we suggest that you begin your trip at Nice instead of Paris.)
6. The Alps—concentrating on Lake Annecy, the French shore of Lake Geneva, and the area around Mont Blanc (You can fly to Geneva and get a car there.)
7. Burgundy

And perhaps Alsace and Corsica. If you go to Corsica, fly and then rent a car.

Making an itinerary

If you want to get mail and be available in case of emergency, you will need an itinerary. To prepare one you should ask yourself:

1. When you are traveling from place to place, how far do you expect to drive each day? We have seen people spoil a trip by trying to cover too much ground. From experience, we would say that an average of about 125 miles (200 kilometers) a day is enough. Chapter 8 gives our reasons for this.
2. Where do you want to go and how much time do you want to spend there? Allow some latitude; you may change your mind.

Your itinerary has to be built on a place-time structure. Instead of having letters sent to hotels, travel agencies, or banks, we usually prefer to use *Poste Restante* (General Delivery). Since you will need identification to pick up your mail, take your passport to the post office. There is a small charge for each letter received. For forwarding, for which there is also a small fee, ask for an *Ordre De Réexpedition, Numéro 755A,* which must be signed *on the back* to be valid. When we arrive at a town we have given as a mailing address, we don't fill out a forwarding order if we are going to be anywhere in the vicinity for a while. We return to the post office when we are ready to depart from the area, inquire about last-minute mail, and then leave the forwarding notice.

Except in cities, post offices are usually open from 8 to 12 A.M. and from 2 to 6:30 P.M. But there is no set rule about this. In some small towns they are open from 9 to 12 A.M. and from 3 to 6 P.M. They may close on Saturdays at 4 o'clock. One can never be sure; better check.

Large cities have more than one post office. If you don't give a special branch as an address, your mail will be sent to the main office. All post offices are closed on Sundays or holidays—a fact that may influence the making of your itinerary. Here is a list of the ten holidays when not only post offices but almost everything else in France is closed:

January 1 (New Years Day)
Easter Monday
May 1 (Labor Day)
Ascension Day (40 days after Easter)
Whit Monday (Pentecôte—50 days after Easter)
July 14 (Bastille Day)
August 15 (Assumption Day)
November 1 (All Saints' Day)
November 11 (Armistice Day)
December 25 (Christmas)

While we are on the subject of closings, note that nearly all barber shops and women's hairdressing parlors are not open on Mondays. Neither are most pharmacies, especially in summer, although they usually post notices giving the address of one in the neighborhood that will be open that day. And remember that in August, the popular month for French vacations, almost any kind of establishment may be closed.

In resorts the post office will be overtaxed in season, so you may have to wait in line for mail. All but the very smallest post offices have a special window for *Poste Restante,* so be sure you go to the right one.

Outside Paris, Nice and Geneva are the best places for overseas airmail because jet planes bring it there. Except for those two cities, however, we prefer to have *Poste Restante* mail sent to medium-sized or fairly small towns, largely because they are not crowded and are likely to have parking space near the post office.

How to prepare an itinerary

To prepare your itinerary you will need a map of France and the red Michelin guide, which gives distances between towns and tells you what departments they are in. You must have this information because the name of the department (placed inside parentheses), is an essential part of the mailing address. Michelin usually abbreviates the department names in its listings but spells them out in a table in the back of the book. Its plans of the larger towns show the location of the post office.

Here is a sample itinerary for a three-week trip through Brittany. Department names, which are needed for mailing addresses, are in parentheses.

MON. JUNE 22 Paris to Mont-Saint-Michel, 329 km. (204 m.)
TUES. JUNE 23 Mont-Saint-Michel (Manche)
WED. JUNE 24 Mont-Saint-Michel to *Perros-Guirec, 189 km. (117 m.)
THURS. JUNE 25 Perros-Guirec (Côtes-du-Nord)
FRI. JUNE 26 Perros-Guirec
SAT. JUNE 27 Perros-Guirec to *Huelgoat, 62 km. (39 m.)
SUN. JUNE 28 Huelgoat (Finistère)
MON. JUNE 29 Huelgoat
TUES. JUNE 30 Huelgoat to *Morgat, 74 km. (46 m.)
WED. JULY 1 Morgat (Finistère)
THURS. JULY 2 Morgat
FRI. JULY 3 Morgat to *La Forêt-Fouesnant, 80 km. (50 m.)
SAT. JULY 4 La Forêt-Fouesnant (Finistère)
SUN. JULY 5. La Forêt-Fouesnant
MON. JULY 6 La Forêt-Fouesnant to *Carnac, 97 km. (60 m.)
TUES. JULY 7 Carnac (Morbihan)
WED. JULY 8 Carnac
THURS. JULY 9 Carnac
FRI. JULY 10 Carnac to *Nantes (Loire-Atlantique), 168 km. (104 m.)
SAT. JULY 11 Nantes to *Chenonceaux (Indre-et Loire), 130 km. (81 m.)
SUN. JULY 12 Return to Paris, 213 km. (132 m.)

*Mail pickup points.

When you stay in the same place for several days you will obviously go to the post office more than once.

Aside from the fact that post offices are closed on Sundays and holidays, it is useful to know on what dates weekends occur because country hotels are more heavily booked then. Since museums and other places you may want to see are closed on Mondays or Tuesdays, plan to visit them on some other day of the week.

Making a detailed itinerary takes time. We spent several hours preparing this one, but it could have been expedited by not bothering to determine the exact mileage between stopping places. Except for the first day's fairly long run, it is obvious from their location on the map that the distances between all the other towns are short—short enough to require only a few hours of driving, so you don't really need an itinerary as precise as this.

The total distance for the three-week trip is 1342 kilometers (833 miles). This means driving an average of only 149 kilometers or 93 miles a day for the nine days on which you will be moving from one place to another. This is less than our suggested average day's top limit of 200 kilometers or 125 miles. Your actual mileage, of course, will be much greater because you will want to make side trips along the way.

You will note that we have allowed two evenings and a full day for Mont-Saint-Michel (not on a weekend). Then most of our stops are for three-day stays in pleasant areas where there are good hotels. From these we would explore the surrounding countryside. From Perros-Guirec we would visit the Pink Granite Coast; from Huelgoat, most of the Calvaries; from Morgat, more Calvaries and the west coast; from La Forêt-Fouesnant, the Pointe du Raz, Douarnenez, Quimper, and Pont-Aven; from Carnac, the megaliths, the Quiberon Peninsula, the Gulf of Morbihan, Auray, Sainte-Anne-d'Auray, and perhaps Guehenno. We chose Nantes because we like this city that is approximately halfway between Carnac and Chenonceaux. We picked Chenonceaux because it has several good hotels and a small, never-crowded post office.

Although this trip is planned to terminate on Sunday, July 12, in actual practice we would prefer to arrive in Paris on Monday afternoon because traffic is lighter then. In either case, you will be there in time for July 14, and Paris is by far the best city in France to be in on that day of celebration. We have stayed in smaller places and found them dull in comparison with the excitement that goes on in Paris then.

You may want to use hotels as mailing addresses when you have confirmed reservations; otherwise *Poste Restante* is better.

A simplified itinerary form

The detailed itinerary shown above is for your own use; it is unnecessarily elaborate to send to your friends. Here is a simplified form of it for distribution:

MON. JUNE 22 TO WED. JUNE 24 En route Paris to Perros-Guirec (Côtes-du-Nord). *Poste Restante*

SAT. JUNE 27 Huelgoat (Finistère). *Poste Restante*
TUES. JUNE 30 Morgat (Finistère). *Poste Restante*
FRI. JULY 3 La Forêt-Fouesnant (Finistère). *Poste Restante*
TUES. JULY 7 Carnac (Morbihan). *Poste Restante*
SAT. JULY 11 Chenonceaux (Indre-et-Loire). *Poste Restante*
SUN. JULY 12 Paris. Hotel with street address and *arrondissement.*

Long and bitter experience has taught us that people sending mail abroad can make absurd mistakes in addressing it, so put this note at the end of the itinerary:

> Allow   days for airmail letters to arrive. Please print name and address in capitals. Be sure to include the department (in parentheses) as well as the town. And don't forget to write the word FRANCE after the department name.

We have not indicated the exact number of days to be allowed for airmail to arrive because it takes different times from various parts of the world. From New York to small towns in the interior of France, allow a week.

You may, of course, change your mind about your itinerary en route. If you can go a few days later to a mailing point which you missed on the date indicated, you don't have to inform the people who have copies of your itinerary. Incidentally, you should have a list of their names and addresses so you can notify them if you do make a major change.

We try to prepare itineraries that are not too rigid because we like to be able to move around freely. For an extended trip we give mailing points a week apart, usually for Fridays. Before you even try to make an itinerary for a long trip we suggest that you read the chapters about the regions you would like to visit. And study the hotel possibilities in them too.

Travel agents

We have found that most travel agents cannot successfully plan a trip through the French countryside. With few exceptions, they don't know about out-of-the-way places, and the smaller and less expensive hotels refuse to deal with them. See Chapter 4 for an explanation. But travel agents can be helpful in making arrangements for your transatlantic crossing.

You can obtain information and free travel literature from the French Government Tourist Offices in America. Their addresses are:

610 Fifth Avenue, New York, N. Y. 10020
18 South Michigan Avenue, Chicago, Ill. 60603
323 Geary Street, San Francisco, Cal. 94102
9418 Wilshire Blvd., Beverly Hills, Cal. 90210
1170 Drummond St., Montreal, Quebec, Canada

Literature in French about the area or areas in which you are interested can be had from the local *Syndicats d'Initiative* in France. Our bibliography will give you the titles of the books and pamphlets we recommend.

Maps and guidebooks

Other publishers besides Michelin issue maps of France, but we prefer theirs, perhaps because we are used to them. The most important one is *France: No. 989, Grandes Routes* (dark blue cover; (1 cm. equals 10 km. or 1 inch equals 16 miles). You can get a good free map of France from any French Government Tourist office, but the Michelin Grandes Routes is larger and far more detailed.

Michelin also publishes nearly 50 yellow-covered sectional maps that cover France area by area. Any one of them will give you a complete list of all the others. They are constantly being revised and brought up to date.

You will probably want some of the Michelin green sectional guides that cover most of France with great thoroughness. Those on the more popular areas are available in English.

Your health

It is advisable to see your doctor and dentist for a checkup before you leave. If you have any serious food or drug allergies, their French names should be written on a card which you can show to waiters. Do this also for special diets.

In order to return to the United States, you must have an International Certificate of Vaccination, stating that you have been vaccinated against smallpox within the last three years. This has to be signed and dated by the physician who inoculated you, and then *it also must be stamped by your local or state Health Department.* This second step is important. If you forget it, you will have to be vaccinated again when you return to the United States.

Although France is a very safe country to travel in, your doctor may want you to be immunized against other diseases such as typhoid and paratyphoid. This is a matter for doctor and patient to decide.

Your passport

Hand in glove with the Vaccination Certificate is that most essential of all documents, your passport. If you have one, make sure that the three years for which it was issued do not expire while you are away. You can get a two-year renewal for $5 at one of the 10 passport issuing offices. And you don't have to wait for the renewal to come from Washington if you live near one of the offices; go there, and it will be handed to you right away. If you don't live near one, write for an application blank; fill it out, sign it, and mail it with your passport and a check or money order for $5 to the Passport Office, Department of State, Washington, D. C. 20524.

If you are applying for a passport for the first time, things are rather more complicated. If you are not a native-born United States citizen, but a naturalized one, you need only present your naturalization papers.

Aliens don't get United States passports, but they must apply (at least 30 days before leaving the country) to the nearest local office of the Alien Tax Division, Department of Internal Revenue, for a sailing permit. If they have an Alien Registration Card #1-151, they will not need a re-entry permit if they expect to return in less than 12 months. For a longer stay, they must have such a permit, which they can get from the Immigration and Naturalization Service.

What we say here applies only to United States passports. Canadians should write to the French Government Tourist Office, 1170 Drummond Street, Montreal, Quebec, for one of the free pamphlets entitled "Enjoying France as a Canadian" or "Les Canadiens en France." Either of these will give full information about getting a Canadian passport.

To return to the United States passport question: if you

are applying for a first passport, you have to do so in person; sending a secretary or an emissary won't do. If you can't get to one of the ten national passport offices, a clerk of a Federal court or a state court having naturalization jurisdiction can execute your application. Don't go on a Saturday; all these places are closed then. You may want to write beforehand to the Passport Office in Washington for printed information.

Quoting the State Department as to cost:

> The fee for a new passport is $9. The execution fee is an additional $1 unless the application is executed by Clerks of State Courts authorized to collect $2. Passport fees may be in

the form of currency or a check or money order made payable to the Passport Office.

When you have passport photographs made, order about half a dozen extra copies. You may need them later for documents sometimes required in Europe. If you are getting an International Driving Permit you will need two of them for that.

Normally, you should receive your passport by mail in a week or ten days. If you wish, it can be sent to one of the passport offices, and you can pick it up there.

When you get your passport, sign it as indicated or it will not be valid. And fill in the data requested on the inside front cover.

Guard this precious document carefully. Nothing can be more annoying than to be hampered in your movements because you don't have a passport. You will be using it as identification to get travelers checks cashed, for registering at hotels, and for a dozen other purposes. Consequently it is very easy to leave it behind somewhere. We did once and went through a day of misery until we found it at the bank where we had left it lying on the counter. Ever since then we have a firm rule that whenever we use a passport we check to make sure we have it before we depart from the building where we showed it.

Your passport is as important as your wallet. Take good care of them both at all times.

If you plan to stay in France for more than three months you must have a visa. You can get one at the Prefecture of the Police in Paris or in any department. You can apply for a visa in America, but you will have to allow about two months for it because your request has to be sent to Paris. You can avoid the visa nuisance by briefly visiting a neighboring country before the three-month period is over. Be sure to have your passport stamped at the border before going out and coming in. You may have to ask for this because in some places the frontier guards will often just merrily wave you by.

One other thing: United States consular officers in foreign countries can be very helpful, but if you are stranded abroad, the State Department says that it "will not be able to assist you to obtain passage home" or "cash or endorse your personal check or personally lend you money."

Insurance

Now comes the matter of insurance, not for your car, which we discuss in the next chapter, but for yourselves. Before you start out, check into insurance for: health; accident; baggage; cameras, tape recorders, clothing, jewelry, etc.

2. *Costs, cash—and things to arrange before you go*

We have kept careful records of what it has actually cost us in recent years to travel through France by automobile. The basic figures we give here were taken from bills or diary entries, so they are reasonably accurate. They are for two people who like to travel in comfort, but who, except on occasion, do not seek great luxury. Since we believe that one should eat well in France and at least sample its better wines, our dinner bills may seem high to the budget traveler. But they are offset by our very modest expenditures for simple picnic lunches. We admit that having breakfast in the hotel costs more than going out to a café for it, but part of the pleasure of traveling in France is having the first meal of the day brought to your room.

We show what can be saved by eliminating or reducing certain expenses, but before you cut them too deeply remember that you will be in a country where many good things are available. It may pay you—in pleasure if not in money—to spend more than you anticipated simply because France has so much to offer that it seems a shame to forego its small luxuries if you can possibly afford them.

Hotels

Generally speaking, when not in cities or expensive resorts, we stayed in one of the best hotels in each locality. And we nearly always had a room with twin beds and bathroom complete with a toilet. Including service, taxes, and some telephone calls for reservations, our average daily cost for hotels was $7.50.

Incidentally, we have figured the average rate of exchange for francs at 4.85 to the dollar (20.6 cents each), which, according to our records, was just what we got.

Food

Breakfast for two served in the room (including tip): average cost per day	$ 1.80
Picnic lunches for two at a daily average of	1.50
Dinners for two, including wine, service, and taxes, at an average daily cost of	8.70
	$12.00

Dinners for two ran from a low of $5 to a high of $15. The cost of entertaining occasional guests is not included.

Car expenses

Since we use a small European car and drive only short distances each day (say about 100 miles), we have been able, year after year, to keep our costs down to about $10 daily, including gasoline and oil. If you use a larger car and keep going all the time, you will naturally have to pay more. Remember that when you stay put in one place for a while your daily auto expense goes down.

Miscellaneous small expenses

Some of these, like the cost of passports, are unavoidable; others are optional. All we can do is estimate them. Let's say $2.50 a day for two people.

The cost per day

The basic figures on a *per diem* basis then are:

Hotels	$ 7.50	
Food	12.00	
Car	10.00	
Miscellaneous small expenses	2.50	
	$32.00	a day for two people

More about expenses

This does not cover the cost of crossing the ocean, admission fees, stationery and postage, purchases, entertaining, photographs, medical bills, drugs, cosmetics, or visits to beauty shops or barbers. We do not include these because they vary so widely. Allow what you think your minor expenditures will amount to. But don't forget that if you stayed home you would still have to pay for some of the things listed above. In estimating the cost of a trip to Europe it is only fair to deduct the expenses you would ordinarily incur during the time you are away. These would be for your car (if you drive one at home), for a summer place (if you rent or maintain one), food, beverages, entertaining, telephone calls, electricity, gas, stationery, postage, and other miscellaneous small expenses. Once you offset these, you may be surprised at how little your visit to France will cost by comparison. The longer you stay abroad, the less your trip will come to on a daily basis because you will be amortizing the transatlantic passage by a larger factor. If you go for a long time and don't have to pay rent or maintenance charges for a house or an apartment at home, you will reduce your travel costs even more.

The bills we have kept on file show that prices for hotel rooms, garages, and breakfast have increased in recent years while the cost of transportation has remained about the same. Food has undoubtedly gone up, but it is difficult to compare prices because restaurant meals vary so much in quality and expense.

Budget travel

Traveling through France on an economy budget calls for careful management. Your greatest saving would be to stay in cheaper hotel rooms and eat less expensive meals. You can go out to a café for breakfast and order fixed-price dinners with table wine, beer, or mineral water instead of vintage wine. You can also make minor savings by not bothering about garages or hotel reservations, and not going to some of the museums and other showplaces. By doing this you can reduce the daily average by a few dollars. And you can spread the cost of automobile transportation by having more than two people in the car.

To cut expenses still further means staying in camps rather than in hotels, preparing your own meals three times a day, economizing an all kinds of small items, and driving fewer miles. Yet you will still be able to see France and have a good time doing so. If you have a small surplus for occasional indulgences, that will be so much the better. And if you are young and hardy enough, you can ride a bicycle, sleep in youth hostels, and have a worthwhile visit. But don't underestimate the cost of a rock-bottom trip. Even *Europe on $5 a Day* admits that board and lodging alone will come to that much nowadays. And the ingenious KLM $5-a-day per person plan, which covers only a room in a modest hotel (double occupancy), breakfast, and sightseeing in 23 European cities, says candidly that "Not included are lunch and dinner, porters' tips, airport taxes, laundry, and all items of a personal nature such as beverages, taxi and bus fares, transfers to and from airports, theater tickets, shopping expenses, etc." Nor does this plan allow anything for transportation across the Atlantic or in Europe. A representative of the company said that one must expect to pay a total of $15 to $20 a day for each person for lunch, dinner, tips, etc., still not including transatlantic transportation. This makes our own daily average of $16 per person *including a car* seem quite reasonable.

If you go for a fairly lengthy stay in France, say two months or so, we believe that except for the cost of getting there, you can tour the country for less than you would have to spend for a comparable journey through the United States or Canada. This is because French hotels cost less than American. So do garages, parking, tolls, and many other things. Gasoline and oil are far more expensive there, but you don't ordinarily drive the long distances you do in America. Food in France is not cheap, but if quality means anything, you will realize that it is so far superior to what you get in most American roadside restaurants that it is worth the price.

Safeguarding your funds

Once you have made a fairly careful estimate of what your trip should cost, the next step is to arrange for your funds to be safe but readily available. There are several ways to do this. You can carry travelers checks which are very convenient and are easily converted into francs. When you purchase them remember that a bank or organization which you think is famous at home may be unknown in a small French town. American Express and Thomas Cook's travelers checks can be cashed anywhere in France. Cook, because of the many British tourists who have been visiting the Continent for years under its auspices, is far better known abroad than it is in America. And it charges only 75 cents for $100 worth of travelers checks instead of the customary $1.

When you buy your checks, decide beforehand how many of each denomination you want and be sure to record the numbers. The $10 and $20 checks are useful for purchases in stores, especially in those that give a discount of 10 to 20 percent. The larger ones of $50 or $100 are good when you want to have enough cash on hand to carry you over a holiday or a long stay in the country where there may be no banks. In some rural places the one bank that does exist may be open only for a few hours once a week on market day.

Country banks usually start business at 8:30 A.M., close from 12 to 2, and then close for the day at 5 or 5:30. They are not open on Saturday unless it is a market day, in which case they close Monday instead.

Hotels or restaurants will give you a poorer rate of exchange than will a bank or a bureau authorized to deal in foreign currency. If this doesn't bother you, cash your travel checks at your hotel. You will save time if not money. Even when you deal with banks, going from one to another to find the best rate may waste more time than the small difference is worth. Banks and exchange offices in large towns or resorts usually give more francs for your dollar than those in smaller places.

You will need your passport for identification when you deal with a bank. And the transaction is likely to take more time than you anticipate. Red tape is part of transacting business in French banks, especially rural ones.

Letters of credit

A letter of credit may be a nuisance on a long automobile trip because you can obtain cash with it only in a large city which has a bank that officially recognizes the one which issued it. It is simpler to carry a cashier's check—or checks—from a well-known American bank. This should be made out to you and be signed by an officer whose signature is on record in the register book kept by large European banks and travel agencies. This internationally recognized signature is essential if you want to get cash without delay. A bank draft is very similar. Ask your own local bank about these safe and very inexpensive forms of carrying money. But be sure it has an internationally recognized signature on record abroad. If it has not, request that it refer you to a bank that has.

A bank account in France

Another convenient way of getting francs for dollars while you are in France is to open a checking account with the Société Générale; it has two American branches, one at 66 Wall Street, New York, N. Y. 10005, and another at 15 West 50 Street, New York, N. Y. 10020. You can then cash checks at more than 1400 Société Générale branches throughout France. A minimum balance of $1000 is required, which means that you must keep at least that much on deposit over and above the amount of money you will need while you are abroad. You cannot draw more than $200 a week (non-cumulative), but other special services are available for larger amounts. Businessmen especially can benefit from this bank's connections with French trade and industry. And the checks, of course, can be used to pay for purchases that are to be shipped home. Stores that give discounts for payments made in travelers checks will do the same for these dollar checks.

Carrying currency

Since it now costs more to buy francs in the United States than it does in France, there is no point in acquiring any here. Even the few needed for expenses on arrival can be obtained more advantageously on your ship or at the airport when you land. As frequent visitors to France we keep a few small bills and coins for the next trip.

Some American currency will be useful for tips or minor emergencies. Small bills—coins are not wanted—may come in handy even if you don't use them until you get home and have to pay porters and taxi drivers at your port of arrival.

You may also want to carry a few bills of larger denominations as a safeguard against being stranded. They can be concealed in a money belt. The inexpensive leather ones made for men are miserable things that show obvious signs of wear in a few months. Good ones are hard to find and are high-priced. Much cheaper is a plastic belt made to be worn under the clothing. Remember, though, that thieves know all about such devices. The chief purpose of a money belt is to permit you to divide your funds so you have some cash left in case you lose your purse or wallet.

An American Express credit card can be used not only for charging bills from certain hotels, restaurants, and stores, but also for cashing personal checks for any amount up to $300, of which $50 can be had in francs while the balance must be taken in travelers checks. Your personal check, however, can be cashed only in the American Express offices in Le Havre, Paris, Nice, or Cannes.

A personal check can be used to pay for goods that are to be sent to America, because the store has ample time to clear it before making the shipment. Some hotels will accept them, especially if they know you.

If you ever run short of money while you are abroad it is nice to have someone at home to whom you can appeal for instantly cabled funds, so make such an arrangement before you depart.

Customs duty and exemptions

In recent years, United States Customs rulings have been changing so rapidly that it is hard to keep up with them. We suggest that you write to the Commissioner of Customs, Treasury Department, Washington, D. C. 20226, for copies of "Customs Hints for Returning U. S. Residents," "Tourists Trademark Information," and the mimeographed sheet entitled "Customs Duties on Typical Tourist Purchases." The first one gives information about merchandise you may want to bring back or send home. The second tells you about restrictions on bringing in certain trademarked articles, particularly perfumes, cameras, optical goods, watches, clocks, musical instruments, tape recorders, and jewelry. Most Customs duties are not as high as people think. The duty on automobiles, for instance, is only

6½ percent of the appraised value, on radios 12½ percent, and on English language books, a trivial 3 percent, while foreign language books are free of duty. But it is high on china, cigarette lighters, jewelry, and embroidery. The whole subject is so complicated that you may have trouble finding out just what the duty will be on something you want to buy while you are abroad. Retail stores there seldom know; United States embassies and consulates do, but it is an imposition to bother them unless a lot of money is involved. Anyone who expects to buy luxury goods for personal use can find out beforehand what the duty will be by asking the Custom House at home. For $5 you can purchase a copy of the book that lists all the duties charged, but don't plan on taking it with you because it is a very bulky tome.

If you have any expensive foreign-made articles like a camera, a light meter, or a fine watch, and have kept the bills which prove that you bought them here (or on a previous trip), take the bills along and avoid trouble when you return. If you don't have them, you can register each item at the Customs House—or at your port of departure—before you go. You will then be given a document covering them.

When you purchase anything of value while you are abroad, be sure to get an invoice for it and save it for the Customs examination.

Be cooperative when you deal with Customs officers, give them the information they want—and don't try to play jokes on them. We knew one well enough to ask: "What happens when some prankster says, 'I'll bet you guys can't find the $10,000 worth of diamonds I've got here.' "

He smiled and said, "Well, something like that did happen. We made the gentleman stand aside for a very thorough examination. Then we took everything apart. He didn't get out of here for quite a while. We didn't find anything, of course."

"You knew you wouldn't?"

"Sure. We were just teaching him a lesson."

Recent changes in customs laws

Travelers who have been abroad before should note that several important changes were made in United States Customs laws in the autumn of 1965. The new edition of "Customs Hints" described above will explain these rulings in detail. Basically they are:

Articles totaling $100 (based on the fair *retail* value of each item in the country where acquired (may be entered free of duty, subject to the limitations on liquors and cigars, if:

They accompany you
They are for your personal or household use
They were acquired as an incident of your trip
They are properly declared to Customs at the first port of arrival in the United States

Cigars and cigarettes: There is no limitation on the number of cigarettes for your personal use, but not more than 100 cigars may be included.

Liquor: *One quart* of alcoholic beverages may be included if you are 21 years of age or older.

Reducing the liquor allowance from one gallon to one quart was accomplished by the Kentucky bourbon producers' lobby. The New York *Herald-Tribune* told the story behind this:

> Promoting the new restriction was the domestic burbon whiskey industry (an industry scarcely in a depressed condition).
> Skillfully steering the bill through . . . Congress were two adroit Kentuckians: Democratic Rep. John Watts and Republican Sen. Thruston Morton. And behind the scenes, one of the most famed Washington operators—Thomas G. Corcoran—worked tirelessly. . . .
> Most cleverly, the one-quart whiskey limit was sold to Congress as a necessary step to hold down the outflow of dollars. . . .
> Actually, the purchase of liquor—whether one quart or one gallon—is part of the overall $100 limit on duty-free tourist purchases and consequently has nothing to do with the balance of payments.

Actually, a returning traveler can bring in more than one gallon of liquor if he pays the Customs duty and Internal Revenue tax on it. This comes to nearly $4 a quart for brandy, which, plus the original cost of a bottle purchased abroad, hardly makes it worth while. Considerable savings, however, can be made if you bring fine wines in and pay the duty on them.

The New York Times explained this on October 7, 1965:

> The Customs duty on still wines ranges from 37½ cents to $1 a gallon, while the Internal Revenue tax is 17 cents a gallon for wines with no more than 14 per cent alcohol, 67 cents a gallon for those with less than 21 per cent alcohol, and $2.25 a gallon for wines with no more than 24 per cent alcohol. The tariff for sparkling wines and champagne is $1.50 a gallon for Customs duty and $2.40 (artificially carbonated wines) and $3.40 a gallon (champagne and sparkling wine) for Internal Revenue tax.

So far, the Customs House has been fairly liberal in its determination of what is a "reasonable amount" of wine for personal use taken along as accompanied baggage. But on account of the weight involved, only those returning by ship can bring in more than a few bottles.

Anyone who plans on buying wine abroad should check beforehand as to what it sells for here and find out how the Customs rulings stand at the time. Remember also that some states don't allow any liquor to cross their borders. You may be living in one of them.

Your car

In addition to figuring costs, handling money, and informing yourself about Customs rulings, you still have to arrange for a car. Since the cost of gasoline and oil is high in France, it pays to drive a small European automobile with a manual shift while you are there. And such a car can negotiate the narrow streets and sharp turns better than a big one can. If you own a small light car you may want to take it with you, preferably as accompanied baggage on a ship. If you expect to use it abroad for 40 days or more, this will cost less than renting or leasing an automobile.

The cheapest way of sending your car across the ocean is as accompanied baggage on a ship. Since most ships have a limited amount of cargo space for automobiles, arrange this as soon as you possibly can. Steamship companies charge a rather high initial price for sending your car to Europe but average out the cost by reducing the cost of the return shipment to a fraction of the first amount. Find out all the facts and costs, because it pays to send a car abroad only if you are going to stay for a fairly long time. Include the cost of insurance for damage or loss while the car is on the ship, going and returning. You can get such insurance directly from your shipping company.

You can send your car ahead as freight and save time by flying over, but this costs more than if you go by ship and take your car as accompanied baggage.

There are, however, certain drawbacks to taking your car with you. You will be among the last passengers to leave the ship when it arrives in port because your automobile has to be hoisted from the hold and put ashore by lowering it on slings. Since the gasoline tank had to be drained, the car must now be towed to a service station. Some ports, however, now supply enough gas to enable you to drive away.

You will have to purchase a white oval plaque with your country's initials on it because French law requires that this be displayed on the back of the car. This plaque is not easy to get. We have never seen it for sale in France, and only a few big-city American stores specializing in accessories for foreign cars carry it in stock. But you can buy one for $2 from AAA World-Wide Travel, Inc., 730 Third Avenue, New York, N. Y. 10017.

Automobile insurance

Third-party liability insurance is compulsory in France. It can be arranged for at your port of entry, but it is less time-consuming and no more expensive to get it before you leave. Be sure to get an adequate amount, comparable, say to what you carry at home. In addition to Bodily Liability Insurance, you will probably want Property Damage Liability, Fire and Theft, and you may also want to be covered for possible collision damage to your own car.

Evidence of having liability insurance is the International Green Card (*Carte Verte*), which you must have with you when you drive. You will need it in case of accident and even for crossing a border. It is advisable to keep with it your policy, your company's list of European claim agents, and a blank accident report form.

Since the rules and the rates for overseas insurance keep changing all the time, we cannot even hope to state them in exact terms, but here are some of the things you should know:

Rules vary from company to company. Some make a surcharge for very young drivers or for those over 60, 65, or 70. Some refuse to insure sports cars at all. Others don't want to cover people in certain occupations. There are all kinds of variations. Consult your insurance broker about them.

You will want European insurance only for the actual number of days your car will be on the road there. You can extend this period if you decide to stay longer or cancel the policy if you cut your trip short. Don't forget to take the proper steps if this happens, and give your company enough time to make the change.

Before you go, don't forget to suspend American insurance on your car while you are away and have it restored the day you plan to get back.

Buying, leasing, or renting a car

After you have determined the cost of getting your car to Europe you can then decide whether it is worthwhile. It may very well not be unless you are going to use it for six weeks or more. If you want to buy a new European car, drive it abroad, and then ship it home, this is obviously the time to do so. You can buy one in France tax-free if you purchase it with non-franc currency and agree to remove it from the country within a year. Actually, it has to be taken out within six months and can then be brought back for one more six-month stay. You can also do this with a second-hand car if it was not manufactured in France. Cars coming under this classification carry red license numbers beginning with TT (*transit temporaire*).

Or you can buy a second-hand French car and sell it in France after you have finished with it. You can also get a new car with a purchase-repurchase agreement with the dealer who sold it to you to take it back at an agreed-upon reduced price. Since you have to buy the automobile outright, you will find that you come out very little better than if you lease.

For shorter trips, leasing or renting may be your best solution. Leasing gives you unlimited mileage, and for a trip longer than 25 days on the road will cost less than renting, although you must advance the entire charge before you start out. For shorter trips it is better to rent and pay the daily or weekly rates plus a charge for each kilometer traveled. These rates vary with the size and value of the automobile. No matter whether you lease or rent, you always pay for the gasoline.

If two or more people travel through Europe by car, their overall transportation cost is quite reasonable because they don't have to pay for porters, checkrooms, taxis, etc. When four or more people go, they get a real bargain even though they will need a larger car.

But whatever you do: ship your own car, buy, lease, or rent one, make your arrangements as long in advance as you can. This is especially important for the summer. We have often seen people disappointed because they put off trying to get a car until the last moment. Not only is everything on wheels well booked up for the summer months, but automobile factories close for vacations then, thus cutting down the supply still further.

AAA World-Wide Travel, Inc., can arrange any of these ways of getting a car for you. Hertz or Avis operate in France and you can charge their rental fees to any generally accepted credit card. With them you can pick up a car in one city and leave it in another. A travel agent can also help with this.

The New York Times Travel Section carries advertisements

(on Sundays during the early spring) of the various companies that specialize in selling, leasing, or renting automobiles in Europe. Their free literature is very helpful. If you want to buy a second-hand car, the Paris edition of the New York *Herald-Tribune* lists them in its classified advertising columns.

Caravans, camping buses, and trailers are slower, more expensive, and much harder to lease or rent than ordinary cars, but they have the great advantage of enabling you to stay in inexpensive camping sites.

Your American driver's license, proof of the right to use the car, and the Green Card which shows that you are covered by insurance are all you need for the roads of France. But before you enter another country be sure you know what is involved. Belgium, Luxembourg, Switzerland, Italy, Monaco, and Andorra ask only for the same documents needed for France, but Spain requires an International Driving Permit. You can get one for $3 from the AAA World-Wide Travel Inc., 750 Third Avenue, New York, N. Y. 10017. You will need your driver's license and two passport-type photographs when you apply. The International Permit is also useful in West Germany because the government there requires a German translation of your driver's license, and the International one has this.

In Spain, there may be still further difficulties, as any insurance company will tell you. An automobile accident there can be a very serious matter, for you may land in jail and also have your car and baggage impounded.

3. *What to take with you*

The logistics of travel can be reduced to three basic elements—the essential, the non-essential but useful, and the soon-to-be-regretted impedimenta that burden individuals as well as armies. The problem of taking too much baggage occurs in its most aggravated form when you go by ship with your own car, for there is then a great temptation to load yourself down with many more things than you really need. We know because we did it on one trip—and had to store some of them in Paris. Keep firmly in mind the fact that all visible baggage in your car should be removed each night, and the thought may enable you to resist the temptation to take too much along.

If you are going by ship you can take plenty of baggage, but you have to get it to your stateroom, to your automobile on the other side of the ocean, and then repeat the process on your return voyage.

If you are going by plane, you can take 44 pounds of luggage in tourist class and 66 pounds in first class. This is a fairly generous allowance for a short stay but not for a long one. Since you will be traveling by car after you arrive in France, you may want to take more than your air ticket permits. Excess baggage costs nearly $2 a pound, so the solution would seem to be to send an extra valise or two to France by freight or parcel post. But before you go into the export-import busiiness, note some of the drawbacks connected with it.

Air freight is very fast, but small shipments—like a valise or two—cost almost as much as excess baggage taken on the plane. Ship freight is very slow—a month or more—and is no bargain. The price for sending a 30-pound valise from New York to Paris is about $1 a pound. The cost is high because extra charges are added at every move, and some of the fees are just as much for a small shipment as they are for a big one. Parcel post is equally slow but it is economical for small shipments—about 40 cents a pound.

Before you rush into packing those parcels to be sent by mail, remember that when you ship anything from one country to another it has to pass through the red-tape curtain. You have to fill out three forms at the American post office; then, when you pick up the parcels abroad, you have to clear them through French Customs.

Trouble-free plane travel

There is a simpler way of going by plane without bothering to ship anything ahead. *Just strip your baggage down to essentials so it comes under the air allowance, and then buy abroad whatever else you need.* This will work out very well for any but an extended stay in Europe, the kind that requires both winter and summer clothing. For such a long trip you will do better to go by ship.

When you travel by air you need lightweight luggage so you don't waste any of your precious allowance. And you should carry a small spring scale marked in pounds and kilograms unless you stay in hotels that are equipped to weigh your luggage.

Take with you on the plane only such things as good clothing, shoes, an electric razor, jewelry, and other possessions you think you can't live without. A number of small objects can go with you without being weighed in. Generally speaking, whatever can be slung from the shoulder (reasonably sized camera cases, binoculars, etc.) or carried under the arm, will get by. An underarm briefcase, for instance, which is packed just as heavily as one with a handle, will ordinarily not be counted in. Coats can be carried over the arm, and what is in their pockets is nobody's business. And then there is that capacious carryall which has increased enormously in size with the growth of air travel—this is the woman's handbag that sometimes needs two strong hands and a sturdy back to lift it.

An air passenger is also allowed to take one book, an umbrella, baby's bassinet and food, and anything that can be carried in the pockets of one's clothing. It is surprising how much can. Invalids are given special exemptions for folding wheel chairs.

The strictness with which your baggage is considered to be overweight or not depends to a certain extent upon how completely the plane is booked. (In summer it will be booked full.) But the personality of the man at the scales and the attitude of the passenger handling the transaction also count. If there is a pretty girl in your party who can smile sweetly at the baggage weigher, she is likely to do better than a grumpy older person. But be prepared to pay for overweight if the creature at the scales turns out to be an ogre indifferent to feminine charms.

What to buy abroad

Plan on buying abroad all ordinary consumption goods like stationery, soap, detergents, cosmetics, non-prescription drugs and medicines (these usually cost less there). Then there are the things that France is famous for: perfume, handbags, scarves, gloves, blouses, and women's wear of all kinds. French picnic and camping gear is very good. So is everything made of plastic. And a portable reading lamp obtained in France will have the correct socket and plug for use in French hotels. If you use an electric razor you will need one that will operate on either 110- or 220-volt current since both kinds are found in different parts of the country. In Paris the current is 110-volt but 50 cycle. You must also have an adaptor plug for French outlets. You can buy one here for 50 cents or for about a quarter in France.

Ball-point pens are just as plentiful and cheap in France as they are in America. If you don't have a French-English dictionary or phrase book you can get one when you arrive and save weight. Stores that specialize in textbooks have useful conjugation guides to the very tricky French verbs that have such hard-to-remember forms.

If you are stopping first in England you can buy fine British sport jackets, topcoats, slacks, raincoats, waterproof shoes that make rubbers forever obsolete, and men's handkerchiefs. You can also have a suit made there. Many of these things can also be bought in the Paris stores that stock British goods.

Since facial tissue is expensive in France, bring as much of it as you can from America—or even from England where it can still be bought at a saving over French prices. Soft, absorbent toilet paper is hard to get outside the big-city stores that may stock it.

We have found that carrying an electric iron is unnecessary even if its weight is no problem. One of your hotel's maids will gladly do your occasional pressing jobs for a small tip.

Lightening the load for the return flight

Just before you return home by air, weigh your baggage, because the goods you have purchased abroad will have added more pounds. Discard wornout shoes or clothing and then pack a carton of non-valuable personal articles and send it home. Be sure there is nothing dutiable in it—and above all, that there are no seeds, plants, or food because the Department of Agriculture won't let such things enter the country. Mark

the package "Used personal belongings purchased in the United States and being returned home without having been altered or repaired abroad." Books or printed matter should be sent separately from your clothing parcel because the rate for them is lower.

It is much easier to send a parcel from Europe to your home than it is the other way around, because less red tape is involved, and the time element is not important. American Express, for instance, will ship trunks, valises, or parcels from France to the United States, but not from the United States to France.

If you are sure you are going to return to France in less than a year it will pay you to store some of your baggage there rather than incur the cost of shipping it twice across the ocean. American Express will take care of this for you, and will forward it to America in case you change your mind. There is another charge for this added service, of course.

Your clothes

We have found that most European laundries and dry-cleaning establishments do mediocre work, are generally slow and undependable in delivery, and are more expensive than comparable American places. Obviously there are exceptions, but you may not have time to find them. Nor is there any need to. With drip-dry clothes and miracle-fabric suits that can go for a long while without needing to be pressed, the washing and cleaning problem is not as serious as it used to be.

Because you will need a good area almost very day for washing and drying drip-dry clothes, you will quickly learn to size up a hotel room's possibility for this before you agree to take it. Finding a spot where you can stretch a line to allow water to drip without doing any damage is not always easy. A long cord often helps. You can buy a nylon one for a few cents in any French *droguerie* (which sells household goods, not drugs) and get clothespins and detergents there too. If you are traveling on a minimum budget and are staying in rooms without a private bath, you may occasionally want to take one which has that convenience so you can wash and dry clothes there.

Shoes, hats, and beachwear

Whether you travel by yacht, plane, train, or car, only your feet can take you around the places you want to see. We used a pedometer to find out how much walking we did in Europe and were surprised to find that we sometimes covered 10 or 12 miles a day. Having comfortable shoes is therefore a matter of the utmost importance.

Give new shoes a thorough tryout before you leave home, and if they aren't completely comfortable, replace them. Economize on anything you like when you travel but never on shoes, because sore feet can spoil what might otherwise be a pleasurable journey.

Take not one but at least two pairs of really comfortable walking shoes and try to change them during the day. If you can't, switch to the other pair for the next day's use.

Don't depend on buying such shoes overseas. British footwear for men is very good, but it is usually rather stiff and heavy. Even their truly waterproof shoes are no pleasure to wear. They will keep your feet dry, but you'll be glad to change into others as soon as you can. And American women just don't seem to feel happy in European shoes, perhaps because they are made on lasts that differ from the ones they are used to. Custom-made footwear is, of course, another matter.

Sandals of all kinds can be bought in France so there is no reason to bring a pair unless you have a great liking for them. Plastic or wooden beach sandals are on sale at every resort near water.

The old custom of leaving your shoes outside the door of your hotel room is dying out in France—and even in England —because of a shortage of labor. Some hotels, particularly the more expensive ones, still try to carry on the tradition, but many do not. Shoe-shining stands are rare in French cities and non-existent in the country. But you can buy all the polishing equipment you want.

You will probably find out that you don't have to dress as well on the road as you do in an environment where everyone knows you. The French themselves wear simple sports clothes when they are on vacation. They do not, however, favor the loudly checked or patterned shirts that some American men indulge in. Shorts for men or women are common in resort areas, but they are out of place in museums and are forbidden in churches.

Women are supposed to cover their arms and wear something on their heads when they enter a church, but hats for both men and women are becoming as scarce in France as they are in America. Straw hats or caps for protection against the sun can be bought anywhere. So can suntan oil or lotion.

Although women can buy—or have made—very stylish and expensive bathing suits in France, they will probably do better to get just what they want before they leave familiar home territory. Bikinis, oddly enough, are not as common on most French beaches as people from other countries would like to believe.

The men's bathing trunks sold in France are almost as scant as the lower half of a bikini, and they are seldom made of the quick-drying fabric available in America.

France is definitely interested in the new fabrics that have revolutionized American clothing, but garments made of them are still rather expensive and limited in supply. In fact, most French clothing of any kind costs more than mass-produced American apparel. And some things are just not found there. One summer when we forgot to bring a man's beachrobe, we tried to get one in France but never could find one.

Small items

Each member of your party should have a flashlight. If weight is a critical problem you can buy good ones in France. You may want to take opera or field glasses, for they will be useful for studying architectural details and for examining art or sculpture that is high above the ground.

You will get no bargains in portable radios although it is useful to have one when traveling, especially if you are interested in improving your French. The lecturers who broadcast in the morning speak slowly and clearly so you can follow what they say much more easily than you can the rapid-fire speech of the man in the street. Small, pocket-sized sets can bring in only the stations that are very near. Out in the country you need a larger radio with many transistors and a telescoping antenna. Its extra weight won't matter if you are going by ship, but it will if you are traveling by plane.

When you go by ship

So far we have dealt mostly with the problems plane travelers meet. Those who go by ship can bring plenty of baggage, but even so they may have unforeseen difficulties. If you are taking your car, you will load it at home and know just how much baggage it will hold, but if you are picking up an automobile abroad, a new factor is introduced. If the car is a very small one, it may not be able to carry all the passengers and bulky valises you want to put into it. But you can examine a similar automobile in America and find out what its capacity actually is. Don't count on putting some of the baggage on the car's roof if you can possibly help it. It will be exposed to rain and theft; it also makes the top-heavy vehicle more dangerous to drive.

You can put far more into a car if your possessions are packed in small bags that fit into corners and in-between places. A few big valises for clothing and some small ones, separately holding shoes, drugs and cosmetics, or books, maps, and guides, etc., will make loading and unloading much easier.

Each piece of luggage should have a label with your name and home address on it. Count the number of pieces every time your baggage is moved from one place to another. Otherwise you may find that you have left one or more behind. Initials or a bright spot or band of color or even a strip of tape on each bag makes it easier to find them on a pier or in an airport.

There is no stopping a serious thief, for he will steal the whole bag, cut it open, or force the lock. But the casual pilferer may be discouraged by some kind of fastening device. Most luggage, even the fairly expensive kind, has flimsy locks requiring keys that can be lost. Combination locks, which need no keys, ordinarily come only on a few brands of costly luggage, but you can have them put on bags you already own. We think they are worth the extra cost.

Camera gear

When it comes to camera cases, we long ago decided that elegant leather ones act as signals to thieves, invite overcharging, and are unnecessarily heavy. Even when you travel by car you still have to carry your camera a good many miles on foot. The camera that took the pictures in this book is kept in an old canvas case which attracts no attention. It is large enough to hold interchangeable lenses, a light meter, and a few extra rolls of film, yet small enough to be carried without undue effort. Plastic sacks and foam-rubber pads protect the equipment, while a nylon raincoat strapped outside cushions the case against shock. Yes, we have dropped it—and without doing any damage to its contents.

Another larger bag stays in the car to hold an extra camera, our stock of film, and accessories that are only occasionally needed. This second camera is identical with the first and takes the same interchangeable lenses. The one in the smaller case is loaded with color film, the other with black-and-white. This working outfit will do anything from taking color pictures of the Alps to copying black-and-white documents in a library.

France has few bargains in cameras or anything photographic, so we generally bring in what we need. This applies especially to color film which is very expensive abroad. Polaroid is too.

There are customs restrictions on the photographic material you can take to France. The very useful free booklet, "The Key for Your Trip to France," which you can obtain from any French Government Tourist Office, will give you information about this and other things you may want to bring into the country.

Special rules apply for professional photographers who should ask the French Government Tourist Office for information.

Since any size roll of film counts as one roll, it is obviously better, if you have a 35-mm camera, to take rolls of 36 exposures rather than 20.

There is no point in trying to compete with local talent by taking conventional photographs of public buildings and other well-recorded subjects. If you want such pictures, buy post-cards. Unless you are a professional photographer, the pictures you purchase will probably be better than those you take your-self. The local photographer has the advantage of being able

to study his subjects in all kinds of light and weather, whereas you will be on the scene only for a short time.

Be sure you are well acquainted with your camera before you start out. If it is newly acquired, or has not been used for a long time, try it out and have some film processed before you go abroad.

It will simplify matters if you take only one kind of film. Then you know what its speed is and just what it will do. If you must have several kinds, you can avoid confusion by putting a piece of properly labeled masking tape on the camera when you load it.

Never keep your camera in your car's glove compartment or

on the shelf below the rear window where the heat of the sun can ruin color film. Avoid also the side of the floor under which the exhaust pipe passes.

Packing

We assume that you have traveled before and know how to select the clothes you need and then pack them properly. But if you want information on this, TWA has an excellent free pamphlet entitled "Basic Travel Wardrobes," which not only has checklists for men and women but also tells you how to pack efficiently.

This pamphlet advises you to put your shoes in plastic bags when you put them into a valise, but says nothing about the dozens of other uses for these almost weightless, transparent waterproof and dustproof containers that are a boon for travelers. They can hold all sorts of small objects and are good for keeping things of a kind together. As crumpled-up packing material they protect fragile articles and fill up in-between spaces. The larger ones, of course, are ideal for soiled clothes. And a plastic bag permits you to take wet fabrics along when you don't have time to dry them where you are.

One last note about what to take. We try to get quiet hotel rooms but don't always succeed. A nearby railroad is sometimes not noticed until a train comes roaring past in the middle of the night. To guard against this or other unexpected noise, we carry ear plugs. And to shut out the early morning sun, we use eye masks. If you are a good sleeper you won't need such things. But if you sleep lightly, these devices will enable you to get a good night's rest in places where you would otherwise toss around and finally wake up in no condition to enjoy an active day of travel.

A checklist of things to remember

With everything planned and arranged for, you now have to be sure of only one thing—don't forget any essential things when you are ready to start out on your journey. We recall at least two occasions when intelligent people reached the airport and found that they had left their passports at home. Be sure you have these with you:

1. Passport
2. Vaccination certificate
3. Tickets to France
4. Driver's license and/or International Driver's Permit; registration certificate if you are taking your own car
5. Green Card and insurance policy
6. Any special medical supplies
7. A Fahrenheit fever thermometer
8. An extra pair of eyeglasses if you use them; also prescription sunglasses
9. Money in some safe form—traveler's checks, letter-of-credit, cashier's check, etc.
10. A Paris hotel reservation if you are going there

4. *Hotels and pensions*

All the hotels we list at the back of the book are—or were when we saw them—clean, quiet, and fairly modern in equipment. But a place that seemed fine when we visited it may go down in quality if it loses the skilled people who were running it so well. Fortunately, this does not often happen in the French countryside because most hotels in rural areas are family owned and operated.

We favor country hotels surrounded by gardens and prefer those with a view. We avoid large cities as much as possible, although we visit them sometimes just to vary the routine. If you stay near but not in a big city, you will pay less for your hotel and usually find it quieter.

Since this book is intended primarily for middle-income readers, the hotels we recommend have been chosen accordingly. Occasionally we suggest one that is quite expensive but we do so because we think it is outstanding. You may want to splurge occasionally. We also try to tell budget-travelers where they can find accommodations.

Hotel rates have been going up year after year in France, but this is not peculiar to that country. Prices in other nations are climbing up the same ever-mounting spiral. Surely anyone who has traveled in America should not be shocked. Nor should British people, who know what London hotels charge, have any complaint. It is all part of the general inflationary picture.

We have not given actual prices for rooms because they keep changing from year to year. Instead, we use comparative phrases like "a bargain," "low-priced," "medium-priced," "expensive," etc. We explain the meaning of these terms at the beginning of the hotel listings. This will give you an idea of costs that should bear pretty much the same relationship no matter how the value of money fluctuates.

The fact that we list a hotel means that we thought it was good. We don't mention one just to run it down, but if it has shortcomings we say so. Since we could not possibly visit every hotel in France, omission does not necessarily mean that we have checked and disapproved.

In order to be objective, we have made it a principle always to pay our own way and never to accept offers of free accommodations or favors of any kind.

Making reservations

The French Government Tourist Office in the United States or England can supply you with forms printed in French and English for asking hotels whether a room is available and at what rate. When the hotel replies, you then have to make a reservation. At this point a deposit (*arrhes*) may be required. It doesn't have to be paid in francs; a check for dollars will do. The hotel then confirms your reservation. Keep the letter so you can show it at the reception desk when you arrive.

If you are writing from a place outside France you should enclose an International Reply Coupon which you can buy at any post office for 15 cents.

In many cases—especially when asking for a reservation in an inexpensive hotel—you are more likely to get a favorable answer if you write yourself than if you have a travel agent do so. Such places operate on a close margin and can't afford to pay a commission.

The International Telegraph Hotel Code will save you words and toll charges when you want to wire for a reservation. The hotel you are staying in can usually supply you with a copy of the code. Or you can find it in the *Guide Kléber-Colombes* described later in this chapter.

If you arrive in the morning, your room may not yet have been made up, and you may have to wait hours for it to be ready. Check-out time is ordinarily noon.

When you want to make a reservation by telephone, *never call personally,* no matter how good your French is. Have your hotel make the arrangements. Hotel owners trust one another more than they do unseen clients. Don't expect an immediate answer because it sometimes takes hours to put through a long-distance call—especially in the high season.

If you change your plans or will be delayed, common courtesy demands that you notify the hotel as long in advance as you possibly can. If you have sent a deposit, ask for it to be returned to you if you are canceling out. If you cancel close to the time of your expected arrival, you probably will not get a refund.

When you arrive, ask to see the room before you agree to take it. This is customary. If the hotel is booked full you are stuck with the room you have reserved—and probably lucky to have a place to sleep. If the hotel is not crowded, you may be able to get another room more to your liking. If you don't have a reservation, you can try elsewhere. If you do have a reservation and don't like the hotel when you see it, you will have to pay for the room before going on, but you don't always have to pay the full amount. If you have already paid a deposit, you are not likely to get it back.

While you are examining the room read the notice that is supposed to be posted there, usually on the back of the entrance door. It will tell you the official price of the room and whether or not this includes service and taxes. If they are not included they can run to as much as 25 percent, although 15 percent is more customary. Breakfast is seldom included except in Paris or in resorts where many British people stay. This notice also gives the check-out time and often has a long list of the things you must not do. Among them may be an edict which says that laundry absolutely must not be done in the bathroom or in the room itself. This is a carryover from the days before drip-dry clothes. Few people pay any attention to it now. But don't hang things at the window where they deface the hotel.

Your luggage is usually carried upstairs by a woman who may be very old, very young, or very frail-looking. (For some strange reason she is seldom the husky peasant type.) She should be tipped—and also when she brings the bags down for your departure.

When tipping is included on the bill, you do not have to give gratuities to individuals. But we have found that a small tip (one franc for two people except in luxury hotels) given to the person who brings up breakfast means that we get unusually good, fast service and generous portions. Other servants who go out of their way to be unusually helpful also deserve a tip. The amount depends on how much they have done for you. Only you can judge this.

This advice about tipping does not apply to the big luxury establishments where the staff may be on hand expecting to be tipped when you leave even though you have had a large percentage added to your bill for service.

Generally speaking, we have found the service in French hotels very good. The people who work in them put in long hours and know their job.

Small hotels are usually run by a family. In them *Papa* or *Maman*—or one of the older children—can be very helpful and, of course, should not be tipped. In larger places there is usually a concierge; in big hotels, there always is. He can be of great service to you, and he expects to be remunerated accordingly.

Garages and parking

A word about your car. We don't like to let ours stand overnight on the street, but if we have to we never leave extra luggage where it can be seen. If there isn't room for it in the trunk, we have it taken into our room. Most country hotels have parking lots or interior courts, but we still don't leave luggage in view there. We are always glad to pay for garage—even though prices for them have gone up steadily—but we always ask whether we can lock the car doors. (*Peut-on fermer les portes à clef?*) If we can't, we have luggage that can't be safely stored in the trunk taken to our room. Incidentally, we had a new lock put on the trunk of our car so it can't be opened with the ignition key. If you are using a rented car, you are not likely to have this safeguard, although you can pay to have a separate lock put on. It may be worth it. We may sound supercautious, but as a result of playing it safe we have never had anything stolen from our car. Oddly enough, some French people are very careless about protecting their property. We have often seen fine portable radios or other valuables in cars with open windows.

While we are on the subject of theft, we may as well say that a good many French hotels have numbered wall boards near the reception desk where guests are supposed to put their keys when they go out. This, of course, is an open invitation to prowlers. But even in these places we have never been robbed —so far at least.

When you check in at any French hotel, you will be handed a *fiche,* which is a small card that is sent to the local police station. It has to be filled out with your passport number, its date of issue, etc. In some hotels you will be asked to leave your passport at the desk so the clerk there can fill out the *fiche* for you. The *fiche* is a nuisance, but there is no avoiding it. Don't blame the hotelkeeper or the police, because it is a nuisance to them too. In case of an accident en route, it might be useful.

Traveling without hotel reservations

Don't start out in August without a reservation. July, too, can be difficult. So are winter months in ski country. In the off season you can probably afford to take chances although you may have to accept less desirable accommodations than you would like to get.

When you travel without hotel reservations, here are some tips that may be helpful:

> Stop early while you still have a choice of rooms. Line up the possibilities in the Michelin red guide or visit the local Syndicat d'Initiative, which will give you a very complete list of hotels in the area, all classified by price. Then drive around and examine them. A great deal can be told about a hotel and its location even by a quick inspection from your car. You will at least be able to eliminate those you know you want to avoid.
>
> Go into your number one choice and see what rooms are available. We mean "see" literally. If you don't find what you want, try the others. If there is nothing satisfactory in town, drive on.
>
> You don't have to be too particular for an overnight stop, but a place to sleep in can be hard to find in a resort area during the high season. If you run into this problem, drive away from the resorts and look for a room in a small city where vacationers don't go.

Hotel and restaurant guides

France is fortunate in having the Michelin Tire people take over the task of publishing maps and guidebooks that are good to begin with and are then improved and brought up to date. Their red-covered guide to hotels and restaurants, which is issued annually at Eastertime, is impartial and truthful. Since Easter may be rather late to plan a trip for the following summer, you will probably have to do your preliminary planning with last year's edition.

The sections telling you how to use the guide are required study. The explanatory matter is printed in four columns in French, English, Italian, and German to give prices, grade hotels and restaurants, tell you when they are open, describe their facilities, supply helpful details about the more important towns (with street maps), and present much useful information about traveling in France.

Michelin is not the only good hotel and restaurant guide in France. There is also the *Guide Kléber-Colombes* which has improved enormously in recent years. Its regional summaries are especially useful (but only to those who read French.) *Kléber-Colombes* features restaurants more than it does hotels.

The Michelin hotel and restaurant guide will pay for itself many times over. It tells you to "walk into the hotel *Guide* in hand." This is sound advice. We have seen its red cover work magic. Once, while being shown a newly decorated room in a hotel in central France, we saw that the official notice posted there gave a higher price than the one quoted in Michelin. When we told the proprietress about this, she said: "Ah, yes, that is true. Shortly after Easter, when the Michelin comes out, we were granted an increase because of the improvements. But since you have the Michelin, you may have the room for the old price."

And we are sure that there have been many unnoticed occasions when the helpful red cover saved money for us. One thing you need to know about the Michelin guide is that it is very slow to recognize a new establishment. It may be years before it will list such a place. We are not so cautious. When we see a brand-new hotel we often try it out. Its proprietors are nearly always eager to please. (They have to be if they want to stay in business.) We have also seen instances where they lose some of their initial eagerness after they have built up a regular clientele.

Government hotel ratings

The French Government takes tourism very seriously, exercises much control over many of the country's better hotels, and gives them a round enamel plaque with one, two, three, or four stars on it to display out front. This official rating is a clue to the establishment's quality and price. But it is only a clue. There is a great deal of latitude, especially between establishments in different areas. Any of the French Government Tourist Offices will send you a list of "Selected International Tourist Hotels in France." A new edition comes out each year after March 1. And their pamphlet "Hotels, Relais, et Motels de Tourisme" will give you details about the government's classification system. It is available only in French.

In 1964 there were 1,000,000 hotel rooms in France, but only 340,000 of these were in *hotels du tourisme.*

Châteaux-Hotels are former castles, abbeys, or manor houses. They are very beautiful—and rather expensive. Not much less costly are the Relais de Campagne. The Logis de France are more modest in price, but they can be anything from a very ordinary little establishment to a fairly large and comfortable one. This organization, which came into being a few years after the war, did much to modernize poorly equipped country hotels. A new guide which lists *Hôtels Silencieux* (quiet hotels) has recently come out. Many of the places it recommends, however, do not come up to our standards for quietness.

Write to the following addresses for information about the organizations mentioned above:

Châteaux-Hotels, 11 rue La Boétie, Paris VIII
Relais de Campagne, Hostellerie la Cardinale, Baix, (Ardèche)
Logis de France, 22 rue d'Artois, Paris VIII
Hôtels Silencieux, 20 rue du Bouquet de Longchamp, Paris XVI.

Except in a few large vacation clubs, where large numbers of people go for low-cost holidays, the French make no effort to bring guests together in social activities. If you are interested in these inexpensive holiday resorts, write to the Club Méditerranée, 516 Fifth Avenue, New York, N.Y. 10017, or to 8, rue de la Bourse, Paris II, for information.

You can also get information about these organizations from one of the French Government Tourist Offices.

Odds and ends of information

Only the more expensive hotels ordinarily supply soap. In others you are supposed to bring your own. And you may want to provide your own soft toilet paper.

Your bed may have only a round bolster. Ask for a pillow (*un oreiller*).

Because most French hotels were built before the automobile came on the scene, their best and largest rooms were located in front so guests installed there could look out at the street—which was quiet in those horse-and-carriage days. Even when these hotels have been modernized, the best rooms are still likely to be in front looking out over a street which is no longer quiet.

Motels exist in France, but there are very few of them. And the few we have seen did not impress us much although the newer ones seem to be improving.

Special low rates are made for children under seven, but a small child is expected to sleep on a cot in the parents' room. Two or more children will usually be given a room of their own.

In France, children do not ordinarily drink milk when they are big enough to sit at the family table. The French believe that they get enough calcium in the milk served with mild *café*

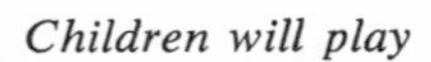

Children will play

au lait, cheese, fish, bread, certain vegetables, and ice cream. Milk, however, is always available if you insist upon it because all hotels and *pensions* use large quantities of it for cooking.

In the French countryside, milk intended for local use is seldom pasteurized. Louis Pasteur was French, but his process of heating milk to destroy bacteria that cause tuberculosis, diphtheria, typhoid, undulant fever, and several other diseases, is not looked upon with favor by people in rural France. In all fairness, however, we must say that cows are rigorously inspected, and dated posters, signed by the argicultural agent who did the work, are placed on buildings where cattle are kept.

Remember that even the most expensive hotels have some cheaper rooms. And that some of the cheaper hotels have no rooms with private baths. If you have a room without a private bath and want to bathe, notify the maid. She will prepare a tub in one of the public bathrooms for you. There will be a small charge for this.

A light strong enough and close enough to read by is seldom found even in the higher-priced hotels. You are not supposed to bring your own lamp, but if you want to read at night you will have to. Buy a portable one with a long extension cord, and get it in France so it has the correct outlet plug and bulb socket. You will need two bulbs—one for 220-volt current and one for 110. Always try the 220 one first; if it burns dimly, use the 110 one.

The same kind of test will tell you what kind of current is available for an electric razor which is made to be used with either 110- or 220-volt current. Plug in the 220 side first; if the razor runs sluggishly, the current is 110-volt. But never put the 110-volt side into an unknown outlet first because you can damage the razor if you do.

Actually, French current is likely to be higher than 110 or 220 volts, and 125 to 130 or 230 to 240-volt systems are often encountered. They don't seem to have a harmful effect on bulbs or razors with slightly lower ratings.

Hotel names

Although the name of a French hotel is not an infallible guide to what it is like, it may be a clue. Hotel du Parc is not always in a large and luxurious garden, but there is almost surely some sort of park there. Hotel du Lac means that the establishment is near a lake even though it may not have its own waterfront. The same applies to Hotel de la Plage, Beau Rivage, Flots Bleus, Mer, and other places with names which suggest that water is nearby. Grand featured in the name indicates that the hotel will be large and expensive—and probably rather old-fashioned. Terminus, Gare, Central, de la Poste, or Commerce will be in town.

Likely to be located in rural settings are hotels that have these often-used words incorporated in their names: Ferme, Moulin, Relais, Auberge, Taverne, Chalet, Beau-Site, Plein Soleil, Chaumière, Manoir, Pavillon, Residence, Hostellerie, or Prieuré. We have tried to arrange them in their probable order of cost with the most expensive ones last. Some, like Auberge, can be very cheap or very dear.

Moderne or Nouvel are not necessarily new. They were when they were built, but that may be a long time ago.

When a hotel advertises that it has *"terraces fleuries et ombragées,"* we head for it and are seldom disappointed. Oddly enough, though, many places that possess such desirable features don't bother to advertise them. Well-planned publicity for anything but big luxury hotels is almost unknown in France.

Once you get used to the way French hotels operate, you will feel very much at home in them. We have stayed in hundreds of them, and with few exceptions—very few—we remember them with pleasure. We choose them carefully and go back to the same ones again and again. French hotelkeepers have amazing memories. They are glad to see you return, and they give you a warm welcome. When you write for a reservation in a place where you have stayed before, by all means say so. It helps.

Pensions

In America and England the word pension means regular payments made to retired people. But in France *pension* (pronounced pahnseeown) means room and board. It can refer to an old-fashioned family boardinghouse, but in the sense that we use it here it means staying in a hotel at special rates for the room and all or some meals.

Except in cities and large towns, nearly every hotel in France with a restaurant is a *pension*—or would like to be, because it can make more money from food than it can from rooms. Some country hotels insist that you eat there, or they will not give you a room.

Since all French employees are required by law to be given a vacation of three or four weeks, family *pensions* are ordinarily well booked in summer. Their proprietors will welcome you for a short time if they can fit you in between the arrival and departure of other guests, but they hope you will remain for at least three days. Rates are lower for a three-day booking than for a day or two.

If you want to explore the countryside and would therefore prefer not to have lunch at your hotel you can arrange for *demipension* rates which include breakfast and one other meal. But you are likely to find that the difference between full *pension* and half *pension* is very slight, so slight in fact that you will do better to pay for three meals a day and have the hotel prepare a picnic lunch. Request this the night before, and it will then be handed to you in a neatly packed paper bag when you drive off in the morning. Our experience with such luncheons has been very good. We are usually asked what we would like to have. We have only one complaint—the hotel nearly always gives us more than we can eat.

When you are quoted a price for a room *en pension* or *demi-pension,* do not expect a deduction for a meal not taken. And note that the price is for *each* person. We saw an American couple, who were staying at an expensive resort hotel, brought up with a rude shock when they found out that their bill would be twice what they had expected to pay.

Remember that in a *pension* the food is the same for everyone, no matter what price is paid for the room. You can, however, order special delicacies if you are willing to pay extra for them.

People who have been regular guests for many years and who are booked for long stays are given preference when it comes to choice of rooms. Next in order are those who made their reservations early.

Camps and camping

Camping has become a big business in Europe, so big that hotel owners complain that it is cutting into their revenues. There are two good reasons for its enormous popularity: it costs very little, and many camp sites have better locations than hotels do. You will find camps on high plateaus with fine views, on the shores of seas and lakes, and in picturesque areas where there are no hotels at all.

Camps are very different in France from those in America. They are even divided into classes, and some luxurious ones are located in parks attached to historic buildings or on big private estates. The better camps are well-regulated and have many conveniences.

If you want to go camping, ask any French Government Tourist Office for the free pamphlet-map entitled "Camping in France." And Michelin publishes an annual green guide on the subject. If you want de luxe camps write to Castels et Camping-Caravaning, 169 Avenue Victor-Hugo, Paris XVI, for a list of them.

5. *Eating your way through France*

French cooking is justly celebrated throughout the world. It is good because the French place great emphasis on what they eat and drink, and probably spend a larger percentage of their income for food and wine than any other people. Foreigners, who often have erroneous notions of what the French are really like, think that sex is their primary interest. Sex is not ignored in France, but food is enormously important. It is produced, selected, prepared, cooked, and served with great care. Then it is eaten critically with taste that is sensitive to nuances in flavor.

There are few bargains. You pay for what you get if you want the best quality. Yet even a humble restaurant may serve an excellent meal. The French would not tolerate the miserable stuff that passes for food in many of the cheaper American and British restaurants.

The Continental breakfast

The simple Continental breakfast—coffee, tea, or chocolate with bread or rolls of some kind, butter, jam, or marmalade—is no accident. It exists because the people who cook and serve dinner in French hotels work until late at night, so kitchens are usually closed in the early morning. Breakfast is often prepared in small pantries (one on each floor in the larger places), where the supply of food is limited. You can get fruit, juice, eggs, etc., if you insist, but such extras are expensive. We buy oranges —or canned juice—in a store and thus have our own fruit on hand for breakfast. Actually, breakfast served in your hotel room is expensive if you consider what you have to pay for what you get. We suspect that the cost is high because hotel keepers, whose prices for rooms are kept under control by the government, manage to get a little extra for themselves by charging more for such a simple breakfast than it is worth.

In hotels without bedside telephones you order breakfast the night before, giving the hour at which you want it served, or else ring in the morning for the maid to take your order.

The midday meal

Breakfast in France is merely a preparation for the biggest meal of the day, which is served between 12 and 2. There are several reasons for this long luncheon period. The custom is said to have originated on the farm where horses and oxen need to rest after eating. It was then perpetuated in cities so employees could go home for lunch. It is now undergoing a change in some department stores and industry, but this may not be noticed by visitors to the French provinces.

You can avoid the heavy midday meal by eating a picnic luncheon, which hundreds of thousands—perhaps millions—of French people do when they are on the road. Official picnic groves are virtually unknown, so you may have to hunt for a good spot. Since you will have plenty of competition, it is advisable to start early. A few restaurants or bars display signs telling you that you can bring your own food and eat it at their tables (*on peut apporter son manger.*) You must, of course, buy beverages there and tip the person who brings them. Don't depend on finding such places; they are scarce and seldom attractive.

French bread

Bread is baked three times a day in France, so we usually start making arrangements for a picnic lunch about 11:30 when hot, fresh loaves can be purchased at the *boulangeries*. Nearly every community, no matter how small, has its own bread bakery.

French bread is sold according to size and weight. The loaves you are most likely to want are:

FICELLE—literally a string; enough for one person
BAGUETTE—the next larger size; enough for two

After these come larger loaves which may vary in name from place to place. They are for families—some for large families. *Bâtard, Parisien, Saucisson, Couronne, Boule, Fantaisie,* and *Gros Pain* are some of the words you may encounter. Since the bakery is required to post names, weights, and prices, you will have no trouble. You can even buy half loaves.

This bread, which is made of soft wheat, yeast, and coarse salt, is one of the things that makes a trip through France memorable.

It is baked before each meal because it does not keep well and gets stale in a few hours. You can prevent this hardening process to a certain extent by wrapping the loaf in cellophane to keep out the air.

The bread carrier

No more bread

Buying food

Cheese, vegetables, fruit, wine, beer, and mineral water can be bought even in small villages. Food stores there may have cooked meat, *pâtés,* and a few canned goods, but the selection will be limited. When you are in a city with first-rate shops you will do well to lay in a supply of the better kinds of canned foods, vintage wines, etc. Even tiny villages, however, are likely to stock tinned sardines, salmon, tuna fish, *pâté,* peas, and string beans. We usually keep a dozen or more cans of various kinds of fish and vegetables in the car at all times. We carry a can-opener, plastic dishes, napkins, knives, forks, and spoons. We also have folding stools, a board that serves as a table, and a cloth to put over it. And we keep some lemons, mustard, salt, and pepper on hand.

The fairly small, round, light-colored *Cavaillon* melons that can be bought throughout France during the summer are delicious, especially when flavored with lemon. Tomatoes, too, are very good and exceedingly cheap in season. Cucumbers, large, long, and quite different from American ones, usually cost more than tomatoes.

Since paper for wrapping food is seldom supplied in country food stores, you will need something to carry your purchases in. A plastic string bag will do nicely.

We have noticed that in some places a man is given preferred treatment in a food shop. The salespeople there apparently pity him because he seems out of place in a crowd of women customers.

Shopping should ordinarily be done by the person whose French is best. But you can buy food even without a knowledge of the language. All you have to do is point at whatever is on display. You can pick up canned or packaged goods, but you are not supposed to touch fruit, vegetables, or other unprotected items.

Unpackaged articles are sold by the gram or kilogram; 100 grams of cheese, for instance, makes a good portion for one person. The *livre* or pound is 500 grams.

Picnic lunches usually cost far less than restaurant meals, but they can be expensive if you buy delicacies in a good *charcuterie*. There you can get cooked pork, ham, cold chicken, roast beef, veal, and all kinds of attractive side dishes. The prices are high, but the food is superb, so your gourmet picnic will be worth the cost.

If you want to eat hot lunches, carry a portable stove. The stores that cater to campers have a large stock of them.

The French people go in for elaborate picnics. They put up a table, cover it with a cloth, set out napkins, knives, forks, spoons, glasses for wine, and a full array of dishes. They may even have portable cots so they can take a nap after lunch.

Water

We buy Evian or Vittel non-gaseous mineral water in food stores. In hot weather it is sometimes possible to get a bottle that has been refrigerated, but you have to ask for it. You can keep the water cold by putting some of it into a vacuum bottle; then save whatever is left over to use for washing fruit or vegetables or rinsing dishes and utensils. You pay a deposit on bottles so the empty ones should be turned in for credit at the next store.

We drink tap water in large cities and in mountain areas where it comes from glaciers, but we use mineral water when staying in villages, isolated country hotels, or farmhouses. We also brush our teeth with mineral water in such places.

Almost as difficult as finding a good spot for a picnic lunch is the problem of disposing of empty cans and refuse afterward. In many of the regularly used picnic areas you will see that your predecessors have left unpleasant souvenirs of their visit. We do not like to litter garbage on a farmer's land, so we pack it in a paper bag and try to get rid of it legitimately in waste baskets in parks or squares in the larger towns, in trash cans in a service station where we buy gas, in official garbage dumps, or, as a last resort, in the hotel where we stay for the night.

Pension food

In a family *pension,* everything centers around food. Except for a few English or Germans who may prefer to eat breakfast in the garden on fine days, most people have it brought to their rooms.

It is customary for the menu for lunch and dinner to be posted in or near the dining room or even put on your table. Some places give you a choice of two or three main dishes for lunch and may repeat the same choice for dinner. Other *pensions* give you no choice but are willing to provide something else if you request it. Only a few other dishes are ordinarily available.

Lunch is the big meal. It begins with hors d'oeuvres, *pâté,* mushrooms, or some other appetizer. Then comes a small portion of fish. This is followed by the main course which is nearly always veal, lamb, or chicken. Once in a while, particularly on Sunday, beef may be served. Vegetables like potatoes or string beans usually accompany the meat. There may be a plain lettuce salad if the hors d'oeuvres did not consist of some kind of salad. Cheese and then fruit end the midday meal. Coffee, for which you will be charged extra, is served in the living room or in the garden if weather permits.

Extra, also, are the beverages you are expected to order just as you are in any French restaurant. Your wine—or mineral water—doesn't have to be finished at each meal; what you don't drink will be on the table when you come to the dining room again. White or rosé wine will be properly chilled.

Dinner almost inevitably begins with soup, even on a hot day. This is followed by a light second course. The main course will again be meat, once in a while roast beef (*biftek*) or steak. Cheese is not ordinarily served twice a day at a *pension,* but you can get it if you want it. Dessert usually consists of ice cream or some kind of pastry. As at lunch, coffee or tea will be charged for extra and is ordinarily served outside the dining room.

When a meal is finished you do not crumple up your napkin; you fold it up neatly and put it into a cloth or paper napkin-holder provided for the purpose. Some places use napkin rings. And still seen, although not common, are the supports called *porte-couteaux,* which are used to hold your knife and fork so they won't stain the tablecloth and can be used for the next course.

We have found *pension* meals to be quite good. Perhaps one reason for this is that many country hotels have large gardens in which they grow their own fruit and vegetables so they come to the table ripe and freshly picked. And the proprietor, of course, knows where to buy the best meat, fish, eggs, and other things he doesn't raise himself.

Restaurants

In addition to the listings in the Michelin red guide, which are usually quite dependable, it is not difficult to judge an eating place in France. Appearance is important, but not all important. Here are some of the things to look for:

1. A crowded restaurant with many cars parked outside indicates, as it does everywhere, that the establishment is well patronized by people who know it. This, of course, applies only at the height of the dining hour. If you arrive very early or very late, this index of popularity has no meaning.
2. It is usually a good sign if the interior looks as if the proprietor cared about the quality of the food served in his restaurant. Yet some plainer establishments may also be excellent.
3. In tourist areas some restaurants have an employee stationed outside to persuade strangers to enter. We avoid such places because a restaurant that serves good food does not have to resort to such desperate tactics.
4. If your French is fluent enough, ask a local person to recommend a restaurant.

The all-important menu

Aside from appearance and recommendation, what counts most is the menu that is posted outside all French restaurants except a few of the most expensive ones.

Study this carefully before you go in. Note the following:

1. The price of the main dish is not necessarily a good indication of what the entire meal will cost. Remember that unless it is marked *"garni,"* no vegetables will be served with the meat. They have to be ordered—and will be charged for—separately. You will not get butter with your bread unless you ask for it—and pay extra. But it is served with radishes when you order them. You are expected to take some kind of beverage—wine, beer, mineral water, or a soft drink. The entire meal may therefore cost more than twice as much as the main dish. In January 1966 a French government decree did away with cover charges, but allowed restaurant owners to charge 10 percent more for food. It has long been said that a relatively simple meal (not including wine) would come to about 10 times the cover charge,

so we seem to be right back where we were so far as cost is concerned.

2. Note whether or not service is included. It usually is not. It will usually amount to 12 or 15 percent and may be even more in expensive places. The waiter will figure out the service charge and add it to your bill. It is customary to leave the small change for him. For example: if the bill comes to 18.80 francs, he will appreciate it if you will let the 1.20 francs in change remain on the table. If the restaurant has a wine steward (*sommelier*) he should be tipped about a franc for each bottle served and more for very expensive wines.
3. *Le Menu Touristique*. This is a fixed-price meal that is the best buy in most restaurants. Service is nearly always included. Table wine (*vin ordinaire*) may be. If you take this meal, you will be well fed, but you will not get the finest dishes the restaurant has to offer. The specialties for which it is best known are seldom on the price-fixed menu. Some restaurants offer more than one fixed-price meal, sometimes as many as three or more. There is a least expensive one, a medium-priced one, a higher-priced one, and then perhaps a *menu gastronomique,* which can be an elaborate feast that costs quite a lot of money. On this you may get some of the restaurant's specialties.
4. S.G. means *selon grosseur,* according to size. Ask what the price will be before you place your order.

French restaurants are rated by the government's star system in which the ranking is similar to what it is for hotels.

Along the road you will find the *Restaurants Routiers,* which cater to truck drivers. The food there is plain, but it can be surprisingly good. Portions are large; prices are fairly low. Restaurants in railroad stations can be excellent; some are superb. In the larger cities you will find *Self-Service* eating places that are like American cafeterias.

What a French meal consists of

Lunch ordinarily begins with hors d'oeuvres; dinner with soup. The words hors d'oeuvres cover a lot of ground in France. They can be anything from the elaborate selection of dozens of tempting "tasty" dishes brought to your table on a wheeled cart in a fine restaurant to a few sardines with lettuce in a *pension.*

At lunch, melon, grapefruit, or an egg dish may follow the

hors d'oeuvres, although fish or shellfish is more likely to be served. The choice varies according to locality. Near the Atlantic it is very great; less so near the Mediterranean; in the interior, a few freshwater species, notably trout or pike, are available. The trout are often kept in a tank from which they are taken out alive. Actually you can get almost any kind of fish anywhere in France because it is shipped as soon as it is caught.

In the interior and in places near the Mediterranean, the fish are usually much smaller than the big ones taken from the ocean. Sometimes they are very small indeed. *Friture du lac* (or of rivers, streams, etc.) may be no larger than minnows. They are fried whole and are eaten that way.

The main course follows the fish. Veal is served everywhere; so is lamb, pork, chicken, and beef. Veal is prepared in dozens of different ways, all of them delicious. Lamb, however, is almost sure to be undercooked to the point of being pink. Pork is a staple dish that can nearly always be depended on. Chicken, especially the ones that come from Bresse, are of such fine quality that they make our much cheaper mass-produced poultry seem tasteless by comparison. Sometimes Bresse chickens come to the table with little metal tags that show their place of origin. *Coq au vin* is made with white wine, as well as red.

Beef is expensive; it costs as much or more than it does in America, as a visit to a market will prove. Yet steaks are ordinarily less expensive in most French restaurants than they are in America. Depending on the price charged for it, beef can be anything from a thin slice of *entrecote grillé* to some of the world's finest steaks. They rank as follows: *steack grillé, tournedos,* and *filet mignon.* In a good restaurant, where you pay a good price for steaks, they will be thick, tender, and fine-grained. They are cooked to your order as *bien cuit* (well-done); *à point* (medium); *saignant* (rare); or *bleu* (very rare). A piece of parsley-butter will almost always be put on top of the steak.

Turkey is rarely served in France; guinea hen is more often on the menu. Game and the various kinds of wild birds that are used as food are treated in the sections where they are found.

Dinner is a shortened version of lunch with one or two minor courses omitted. It usually—and in some places always—begins with soup, which is brought to the table in a tureen.

We have never had soup in France that was anything less than magnificent. Even modest restaurants and *pensions* excel in the art of making it.

Why French cooking is so good

Now, to get back to French cooking:

The preparation of a meal begins in the market where the raw material is purchased. Anyone who has ever watched a French food buyer at work can see that he—or she—is an expert. Nothing but the best will do, and each article is carefully examined for freshness, plumpness, ripeness, color, or whatever seems important.

Then the long and often arduous task of preparation begins. Many French dishes take a day or more to complete. Marination, slow simmering, and other time-consuming processes may be required.

When a dish is ready, it comes to the table beautifully decorated and served. The French are artists in handling food, and they believe that it should not only taste good but look attractive.

Plain eaters sometimes complain that the sauces made by French cooks are too rich for their stomachs. The solution is simple: you can have the sauce served on the side or omit it altogether. Your waiter will be helpful, especially if you say that it is a matter of medical diet—*régime médical.*

After the main course, a *galantine* or *pâté de foie gras* may be served if the meal is a very sumptuous one. Then come vegetables. They are picked while they are still small and tender and are cooked only for a short time, so they arrive on the table as delectable morsels fresh from the garden. Asparagus is blanched and not green. *Petit pois* are truly small peas, sweet and soft. Mushrooms of many kinds are served. Some, like *cèpes,* are expensive because they grow wild in the forest and have to be searched for. So do even more costly truffles which can be found only by trained sows or dogs whose sensitive nostrils enable them to locate the underground delicacies that grow on the roots of oak trees. The animal is never allowed to touch the valuable truffle; as soon as he finds it, his owner does the digging. Even the potato is elevated to new heights of delicacy in France; small, very white ones are served.

In the North, cooking is done with butter; in the South, with olive oil. Périgord provides walnut oil, which is especially good for salads. Garlic is used in Provence and in other southern areas. Nice has given its name to the famous *salade niçoise* which is almost a meal in itself. Ordinarily, salad follows the vegetable course, but a *salade niçoise* may be served instead of hors d'oeuvres.

After the salad comes one of the great glories of France—the cheese. French wines and cheeses are incomparably the finest in the world. And they are both so numerous in variety that very few people, even French gourmets, have sampled more than some of them. Many delicate wines and cheeses do not travel well or are produced in such small quantities that you cannot obtain them outside the area where they are made, so it is advisable to try them where you can get them.

More than 300 kinds of cheese are made in France. Only about two dozen varieties are ordinarily shipped abroad. They are well-known ones like Roquefort, Camembert, Gruyère, Brie, Pont l'Évêque, Port-du-Salut, and Munster. In New York you may even find Cantal or Reblochon. If you want to sample others, you must do so in France. Restaurants will be glad to tell you which are the local specialties; so will storekeepers. Some that we have found to be especially delicious are: Bleu d'Auvergne, Cantal, and Saint-Nectaire from the Massif Central; Livarot, Briquebec, and Neufchâtel from Normandy; Bleu de Gex and Comté from the Jura; and Sassenage, Bresse Blue, and Reblochon from various parts of France.

Remember that some cheeses are available only at certain times of the year and that they are at their best when they are in season. You cannot hope to taste them all, but even to experience the delight of eating a few of these superb delicacies is something to look forward to when you are planning a trip to France.

After cheese comes dessert which may consist of pastry, a *soufflé, marrons,* a *mousse,* or any one of dozens of other sweets. Then fruit may be served and after that coffee, perhaps with *petits fours.*

During an elaborate meal a separate wine may accompany each major course—white with the fish, red with red or dark meat, and white for light-colored meat or dessert. On special occasions an exceptionally fine vintage, usually of a red wine, may accompany the cheese. Except at a wedding feast or a ceremonial dinner, champagne is not served at a meal intended for sophisticated gourmets.

For more on wine see the next chapter.

A meal as complicated as the one just described is seldom encountered nowadays except on state occasions. But you can order all or any part of it. The restaurant is yours to command, and the chef will put himself out to please a customer who cares about fine food. If you really want him to do his best, consult with him and give him a full day to get anything he may need.

French table manners

This brings us to French table manners. They differ somewhat from the formal British or the more informal American ones. Like the British, the French tend to keep the fork in the left hand, but they do not make a fetish of it. They take soup from the point of the spoon and not from the side. This seems sensible—and the French are a very sensible people.

Service tends to be more formal than it is in an American restaurant. Even in a simple place, your plate is always put on the table with the restaurant or hotel name facing you properly. If you drop a knife or fork on the floor, a fresh one will be brought to you on a plate on which a napkin has been put to keep the utensil from rattling around. Incidentally, don't judge French service by what you may have seen in most French restaurants in America. Trained waiters brought from France deteriorate rapidly.

France has developed some special tools for eating. Snails are picked up by a spring clamp and are removed from the shell with a narrow two-pronged fork. Small shellfish are sometimes served with a pin to enable you to pick them out of their shells.

The polite French ordinarily remove all the meat from lobsters and *langoustes* as well as the smaller *langoustines* and pile it up on the plate so it can be mixed with mayonnaise. But they are very tolerant, so if you want to eat your shellfish bit by bit no one will object. A fingerbowl should be brought to the table after this course; if it is not, ask for it (*un rince-doigts*).

In a good restaurant, the waiter will prepare the fish for you by skilfully deboning it.

The meat course is served and eaten very much the same as it is in other civilized parts of the world. A few vegetables, however, are handled differently in France. Asparagus is supposed to be eaten only with a fork, but we have seen it picked up by hand in some very fine restaurants.

When it comes to handling peas, the French refuse to go along with the British who mash them so they can be picked up on the underside of the fork turned upwards. In England the use of the upper side of a fork is apparently thought to be sinful. Sinful, too, would it be for a Briton to hold a fork in his right hand. The French—unless they have been educated in England—are more forthright. They eat whole peas with a fork held in the right hand just as Americans do.

One thing the French are very particular about is the proper treatment of drinking glasses. Before taking any beverage, the mouth should be cleared, and the lips are then wiped with a napkin *before and after* drinking. The glass must always be kept clean. Women should note that a lipstick-stained glass is regarded as an offense against good manners.

Pears, apples, peaches, and apricots are held by a fork in the left hand and peeled by a knife in the right hand. The neatly peeled fruit is then cut up and eaten with the fork. It should never be touched by the fingers. Grapes are washed in a bowl of water which the waiter will bring to the table.

Cheese may or may not have the rind cut off, depending upon the variety and your feeling about it. A small piece, cut off by knife, is picked up by the fork, placed on a bit of bread, and is then conveyed to the mouth by the left hand. Very soft cheese may be spread on a morsel of bread.

Melons are usually eaten by cutting them with the silver knife (not the steel one) and taking up the cut piece with a fork. But the style *à l'américaine,* which calls for a spoon, is coming in.

As in England, it is considered bad manners to taste coffee or tea with a spoon. Spoons are used only for stirring the liquid. And salad should never be cut with a knife. The British permit this, but the French and the Americans stand united in opposing the use of a knife on lettuce.

In the dining room, French children are well behaved and

are never noisy (babies excepted). As to adults, they too are quiet there except at parties—wedding parties especially—when much imbibing releases inhibitions.

One thing you can be sure of: you will enjoy eating in France. We always have, and we have had many hundreds of meals there. Of all these, we can recall only two that were poor. The others varied from good to magnificent.

6. *The wines of France*

Wines of the various regions are treated in detail in the chapters dealing with those regions. See, for instance, the Atlantic Coast, Burgundy, Champagne, etc.

Americans, to whom wine is a sometime thing, may find it hard to believe that it is an integral part of everyday French life. But it is. Producing and selling it is one of the nation's major industries, and it is consumed seven days a week by nearly everyone who is old enough to hold a glass.

You can, of course, order beer or mineral water. Many people—even French people—do. But if you ignore wine when you are in France you will be missing something that should not be missed. Those who disapprove of all alcoholic beverages —or who cannot touch them for medical reasons—may not be interested in this chapter. But those who want to learn more about wine will have a great opportunity in France because it is the world's foremost wine nation.

We don't want to pose as experts. We enjoy drinking good wine and like to visit the places where it is produced. What we have to say is for those who want to learn—just as we did—from background reading and experience. We list some books in the bibliography that may help your education. A few are paperbacks which you may want to take along for reading on the way.

Table wines

If you don't want to pay the high prices that better wines cost and expect to use only the kind that has no hint of origin or age, you need to know very little. And you will be drinking what 95 percent of the French people do except on ceremonial occasions.

When you ask for such wines you have only to specify whether you want white or red—or, when it is available—rosé. Red wine is most often used; white, less so; rosé, still less. Red wine is served at room temperature. White and rosé should be cooled, for they are likely to be more acid than red wine. Table wines are perfectly good beverages to accompany a meal. They require no ceremony and no comment. You drink them, and that's that.

These inexpensive wines are all rather dry (*sec*). Dry simply means that the wine is not sweet; very few French wines are—and no ordinary ones ever are. We will talk about sweet wines later when we get to the more expensive vintages.

We have seen people make a wry mouth when they tasted a dry wine for the first time. Then they called it "sour"—which is the wrong word, because a wine is sour only when it is turning into vinegar and is no longer fit to drink. Dry is the normal taste of nearly all wines.

French children, who are brought up on wine, know what to expect when they drink a dry wine. Adults who encounter it for the first time apparently must acquire a taste for it. They will have to take our word—which can be substantiated by what millions of experienced wine drinkers would say—that it is a taste worth acquiring.

Wine and food

The decisive factor in asking for red or white wine—or rosé for that matter—is the kind of food you are planning to eat with it. This is usually but not always a clear-cut choice. Basically the rules are:

RED WINE goes best with red meat, game, lamb, veal, turkey, duck, goose, kidneys, and stronger cheeses.

WHITE WINE goes best with fish, seafood, chicken, eggs, brains, sweetbreads, and soft mild cheeses; sweet white wine with dessert or fruit.

Either RED or WHITE WINE, depending largely on how the dishes are cooked, may be served with veal, *pâté de foie gras,* lamb, ham, chicken, and duck.

ROSÉ WINE is a nearly universal beverage especially useful with a meal in which several people are having different kinds of meats.

EXCEPTIONS: pork, except for thinly sliced ham, is not considered a suitable meat to be accompanied by wine. This is also true for strongly flavored fish like herring, mackerel, or shad. And hors d'oeuvres prepared in vinegar should not be eaten with wine.

These are the rules, but they don't have to be strictly adhered to except for formal dining when a different wine will be served for each main course.

Vintage wines

So far, living with wine has been relatively simple, and if you are content with it at that level, you will have no problems. The need for more than a superficial knowledge starts after you get past the ordinary table varieties. When a wine comes in a bottle with a label on it, you either have to know what to order or meekly take what is recommended.

Let's say that you know the difference between red and white wine, dryness and sweetness, and can tell which wines go with various kinds of food. You are now ready to proceed to the better wines. But first you must learn how to read those hard-to-understand but informative labels.

The French government jealously protects the rights of its wine-drinking citizens and has laws that define what the bottler of a wine may say about its contents. When you buy a bottle of cheap wine it may have no label at all, or, if it does, the label may say nothing more than *Vin Rouge, Vin Blanc,* or *Vin Rosé,* and perhaps give the alcoholic content. The next best label also identifies the region from which the wine came, such as Bordeaux, and may even state the vintage year. This does not mean much because the wine produced in the Bordeaux region might have had a poorer grade from some other place added to it.

Bordeaux wines

If all the wine in the bottle did come from Bordeaux and is of good quality it may rate having the phrase *Appellation d'origine Contrôlée* on its label. In this case it will read *Appellation Bordeaux Contrôlée.*

From here the next move is from Bordeaux as a region into one of its five communes, namely Graves, Medoc, Pomerol, Saint-Émilion, or Sauternes. The label may carry the name of a château (Château Latour, Château Margaux, etc.) and say *"Mis en bouteilles au Château"* or *"Mise du Château,"* which means "bottled at the Château." You are now getting into the highest quality of Bordeaux wines.

But there is still a step beyond this, for there is obviously a difference in quality among the wines produced by the various châteaux. This is indicated by dividing them into classified growths (*crus*), of which there may be many, starting with the regal *Premiers Grands Crus* and working down to *Cinquièmes Grands Crus* (fifth growths). Below these are the *crus* not called grand; then come *Superior, Bourgeois, Artisan,* and Peasant growths.

Once you leave the Bordeaux district the classification system has new complications. Burgundy does not designate its best wines with château names, and Champagne, which is the third great wine-producing district of France, does not use the *Appelation Contrôlée* system at all, haughtily believing that the word "champagne" is in itself a sufficient guarantee of quality. And then, in some other districts, which are not so distinguished as Bordeaux, Burgundy, or Champagne, both the *Appellation Contrôlée* system and a more modest one called *Vins Delimités de Qualité Supérieure* (Wines of Superior but Limited Quality) may be in use.

Nor is this all. There is still the matter of the vintage year, the name of the shipper, and, most difficult, the thousands of vineyards and subsections of vineyards that only an expert can hope to remember and be able to grade in the order of the probable quality of the wine they produce. It is all very well to look at a label and say knowingly, "Ah, yes, a 1959 red Burgundy, a fine year, a Pommard which is also good, *'Grand Clos des Épenots'*—m-m-m, yes, ah yes indeed . . ." Well, where are you? Do you know that *Grand Clos des Épenots* is a *Premier Grand Cru* and that *Épenots,* although it is one of the largest vineyards (26 acres) in the Pommard area, is also one of the best? If you do, you are wasting your time reading any further because you are obviously a highly qualified expert with a phenomenal memory. But what are less well qualified people to do?

That is a hard question. They can either spend a lifetime trying to acquire the enormous body of knowledge that a wine expert must possess or they can carry their education to the point where they have a good overall command of the subject and don't even attempt to go into its minute details. If you, for instance, know that the bottle of wine just described was good because it was a Pommard, good because 1959 was an excellent year for it, and that the listing of a vineyard (*Épenots*) was a further probable guaranty of quality, you know as much as most well-informed wine-drinkers do.

Burgundy wines

Although there is more to the wine-growing region of Burgundy than the famous Côte d'Or, this small area produces some of the world's most prized—and most highly priced—wines. They are not necessarily better than the best Bordeaux wines; they cost more because the most sought-after ones are made in extremely small quantities. Some of the most noted vineyards are only two or three acres in extent.

The precious bit of land that comprises the Côte d'Or stretches south for about 50 kilometers from a little below Dijon. It is only a few hundred yards wide, and nearly all of it is on the west side of Route N74, for the gentle slopes facing southeast have just the right soil, drainage, and sunlight—all of which are needed to produce the very finest wine grapes. The best sections of the vineyards are halfway up the 200- or 300-foot hills. If too high, a cold wind may blow over them; if too low, they don't get enough drainage.

The wines of Burgundy are far more difficult to understand than those coming from any other part of France. The northern part of the Côte d'Or is called the Côte de Nuits, while the southern section is the Côte de Beaune. Below this is Maconnais; still farther south is the huge Beaujolais district; and, entirely separate, is Chablis, which lies some distance away to the northwest.

Both red and white wines are made in all these districts, but the Côte de Nuits is best known for its great red wines; so is the Côte de Beaune, except that the finest white Burgundy, Montrachet, comes from there. Chablis is celebrated for its white wines; Maconnais is better known for white, and Beaujolais for red.

Now things become even more difficult because some of the famous vineyards in the Côte d'Or have been broken up into small holdings. As a result, great names like Chambertin, Romanée, Clos Vougeot, and Pommard require further specification if you want to know precisely what you are getting.

Burgundy does not have châteaux bottling as Bordeaux has, but it does have equivalent phrases: *"Mis en Bouteilles au Domaine," "Mise au Domaine,"* or *"Mis en bouteilles à la Propriété."* There are still other variations, but the label must carry the name of the *domaine* or *propriété*. There are hundreds of these. No one but an expert can hope to know more than a few of them.

Champagne

What you have learned about the châteaux bottling of Bordeaux or the *mise au domaine* of Burgundy will not help you when it comes to judging a bottle of champagne. Incidentally, there are good still champagnes (*champagne nature*) as well as the more famous sparkling ones. Pink champagne, which was once thought to be very special, is losing its popularity. Sparkling Burgundy, which has nothing to do with champagne, is poorly thought of by knowledgeable wine-lovers.

Sparkling champagne is a difficult and time-consuming wine to make, which explains why it is so expensive. The process is described in the chapter on that region. What you need to know at this point is how to order it, how to interpret the label, and what to expect when you taste it.

It is a blended wine made from the grapes of more than one vineyard in the Champagne district, which centers around Reims and Épernay. If the wines used are all of the same year, the blend will be a vintage champagne and have a date on its label. If it has to be mixed with wines from other years, it will be a non-vintage champagne, which costs less.

Not the name of a vineyard but the name of the blender-producer is what counts with champagne. There are nearly two hundred of them, but you can narrow down the best-known ones to about a dozen of the largest houses. This does not damn the others; it just makes a group small enough to cope with. Listed, not in order of quality, but alphabetically, they are:

Avala-Montebello-Duminy
Bollinger
Charles Heidsieck
Heidsieck Monopole
Krug
Lanson

- Mercier
- Moët et Chandon
- Mumm
- Perrier-Jouet
- Piper-Heidsieck
- Pol Roger
- Pommery et Greno
- Taittinger
- Veuve Cliquot

Perhaps the most important thing you need to know about champagne is the difference between *Brut, Extra Sec, Sec, Demi-Doux,* and *Doux. Brut* (the t is pronounced) is the dryest, usually the most expensive, and the one preferred by those who know wines. *Extra Sec* is not as dry as its name indicates; it is a bit on the sweet side. The others are sweet, sweeter, and very sweet. Sweetness masks the true taste of the wine.

One last note about champagne. During your travels, the bottle you order will surely be opened by someone who is skilled in handling it. Watch him and learn. When a bottle of champagne is opened properly, the cork does not jump out with a loud pop followed by a rush of foaming wine. To allow that to happen is wasteful. A well-removed cork comes out quietly, and the wine can be poured gently. The bubbles are then all in the glasses and not on a napkin, the floor, or someone's clothing.

Côtes du Rhône

This district is really a southern extension of Burgundy. The long summer with its hot sun produces full-bodied, sturdy wines that travel well and keep for a long time.

France's most famous rosé, Tavel, comes from the Rhône. So do several excellent but not great red wines: Côtes Rotie, Hermitage, and Châteauneuf-du-Pape. The latter is produced in a large area, which means that there is a plentiful supply of it. This keeps the price down and makes it a good buy.

The *Appellation Contrôlée* system applies to the Rhône wines, and the better ones are estate-bottled. The warm sun gives them a rather high alcoholic content.

Alsatian wines

Although a few red wines are made in Alsace, white wines are the great specialty there. They are put into tall, narrow, greenish bottles like the ones used for German Moselle. Alsatian wines are similar to those produced on the eastern side of the Rhine. Both sections are located far to the north, and the Alsatian district is really a southern extension of the German wine regions.

Alsatian wines are named after the grapes from which they are made—Riesling, Traminer, Muscat, etc. Sometimes this is combined with the name of a district; Riquewihr-Riesling is an example. Since grape varieties rather than geographical areas distinguish them, the *Appelation Contrôlée* system does not apply to Alsatian wines. Instead, they are upgraded as quality and alcoholic content increase.

They are often blended, in which case *Zwicker* is added to the name. Fine blends are worthy of being called *Edelzwicker*.

They are nearly all very dry, light, delicate, and even slightly perfumed. One variety, Tokay, which has no connection with Hungarian Tokay, is very sweet and noticeably scented.

Wines of the Loire Valley

The best of these are white; some are rather sweet. No great wines are made here, but the *Appellation Contrôlée* system applies. Best known are Pouilly-Fumé, a good dry wine; Rosé d'Anjou, and the Vouvray and Saumur wines, some of which are sparkling, *mousseux,* or *pétillant*. These sparkling wines are less expensive than champagne, tend to be sweeter, and are seldom shipped to the United States where our customs laws work against them by charging duty as high as is put on champagne. Muscadet, from the area around Nantes, belongs with the Loire Valley wines.

Other regions

The vast quantity of wines produced in the south of France along the shores of the Mediterranean from the Riviera to Roussillon (including Corsica) and for miles inland are the ones that most French people drink because they are inexpensive. Lots of sunshine makes them plentiful; huge volume makes them cheap.

The more northerly wines from Périgord, central France,

the Alps, and the Jura are of somewhat higher grade, but they do not rank with the best. We point out some of the more interesting local varieties in the chapters on these sections.

Fortified wines like Port and Sherry, to which extra alcohol has been added, come from Portugal and Spain and do not concern us here.

Learning about wines

Books will give you the terminology of the subject, but only actual experience in tasting wine can tell what words like dry, sweet, full-bodied, velvety, etc., really mean. You can learn more about wines in Paris than in any other place. In its fine stores and restaurants you can get wines from all over France. Only some of the lesser-known local ones will be missing.

One way to begin your education is to order half-bottles. Wine purchased in smaller sizes will add to a slightly higher cost than the full bottles, but you gain in experience what you lose in money. The use of half-bottles also enables you to order a white wine for the fish and a red one for the meat course. And they give you a chance to sample more wines while you are in France.

This book does not deal with Paris, but certain restaurants there specialize in furthering their customers' knowledge of wine. Our favorite is L'Oenothèque (the Greek word for wine is *oinos*). It is located at 37 Rue de Lille, which runs behind the Quai Voltaire near the Rue de Bac in the 7th *arrondissement*. All French restaurants serve wine, but L'Oenothèque is devoted to it. Its exterior is rather plain and unrevealing, but inside you will find hundreds of bottles standing in illuminated racks around the walls. You can learn a great deal by ordering half-bottles of excellent wines to go with the food available there. The cellars of the restaurants that Michelin rates with three stars are larger and better stocked than L'Oenothèque, but only a millionaire can afford to get his education in wine in them.

Also in Paris is the Rôtisserie de la Reine Pédauque, 6 Rue Pépinière, in the 8th arrondissement, near the Gare Saint-Lazare. It owns vineyards in Burgundy and has an establishment in

Beaune where you can taste the wines it handles. The restaurant in Paris has a wine shop attached to it.

Tips about wine

Except in the heart of the regions where great wines are produced, only big, expensive provincial restaurants have fine wines. A modest restaurant in the Bordeaux or Burgundy districts will probably stock a good selection of excellent vintages, but a similar place in an area that is not known for its wine will almost surely have a poor cellar. Keep this in mind as you travel around the country. Concentrate on the better wines while you are in the area where they are produced. When you are not, drink the lesser-known *vins du pays.* Local wines are often very good, but they are seldom shipped, so you should try them while you have the chance.

You can get a great deal of information about serving wine by watching a *sommelier* or an expert waiter at work. He shows you the label and then cuts the foil away from the bottle with a knife, wipes the top with a napkin, extracts the cork with one sure, easy motion, smells it, wipes the bottletop again —carefully this time—and then pours out a little wine in the glass of the person who ordered it. That person then savors and tastes the wine and nods approval if it is satisfactory.

When the *sommelier* pours the wine he always serves from the right, whereas food is served from the left. And he never—but never—fills the glass to the top because there must be some space above the wine to let its emanations, called aroma and bouquet, be savored. To release them you need room to swirl the wine around in the glass.

What we have just said concerns only fine vintages. Such ceremony will be omitted if you are being served an ordinary table wine. At a *pension,* the bottle may be placed on your table with its cork already removed.

One thing you need to know is how much wine to order. A half-bottle is enough for two people, yet a wine-loving couple can consume a full bottle without being unduly affected. But a full bottle can be stretched to serve as many as eight people if they are all content to have only one glass each.

Vintage years

It is very easy but a bit naïve to carry a little card with what are supposed to be the best vintage years printed on it. The trouble with this is that the wine from one part of a district may be superb in the same year that it is mediocre in another part. And in a so-called bad year, the wine from some regions may be quite good. Therefore, anything said about vintage years must be taken with a certain amount of caution.

Since no wines last forever, and very few last more than a decade, an out-of-date vintage chart is useless. Older wines, even if exceedingly good, are scarce and very expensive. The wines that are likely to have a long life are the great red ones; in fact, they need six to ten years to reach full maturity. Sweet white wines last for many years, dry ones from three to eight.

A very rough rule of thumb, which has numerous exceptions, is that by coincidence most recent odd years since 1955 (except 1963 and 1965) were good ones. But so were a few even years, notably 1962 and 1964.

When we collected an impressive-looking lot of vintage charts with star or numerical ratings we found some amazing discrepancies. One, for instance, maintained that every wine produced in France from 1953 to 1963 was "good" or better. This is obviously absurd, for 1956 was a poor year for most vintages, while 1960 and 1963 had many that were poor or fair, especially for the Châteaux of the Médoc. So were other years in certain regions. We decided not to use either kind of arbitrary rating system. Instead we have condensed about ten experts' opinions. Naturally, these men are not infallible. And wines change with time. Some mature in the bottle; others do not; some may get worse. Note that dry white, rosé, and Beaujolais red wines have limited lives and should be used while still fairly young.

Here, with many reservations, are summaries of what the experts say. This list has been checked by several qualified people in America and France.

1955 A very fine year; in some regions, nearly great. Exceedingly good for red Bordeaux and champagne, with red Burgundy almost as good, though showing signs of old age. Dry white wines and rosés are now too old.

1956 A poor to only fair year for red wines except Rhône. Dry white and rosé are now too old.

1957 Generally a good year except for champagne. Dry white and rosé are too old.

1958 A poor year for red wines except Rhône and some Bordeaux. Dry white and rosé are too old to drink now and should be avoided if they are still found on the market.

1959 This was the memorable year of sunshine which produced many wines that ran from very good to truly great. The one exception is the wine from the Rhône valley which was too hot that summer. Dry white wines, rosés, and Beaujolais are scarce and most have passed their prime.

1960 A mixed year, with few good wines (mostly white Burgundies and Châteaux of the Médoc) and many poor ones. Even the experts disagree about this year. One, for instance, gives a top rating to Rhône wines while another calls them only average.

1961 Another great year, even better for Bordeaux and Burgundy than 1959. Beaujolais was at its best, but time has run out for it. Most of this year's red wine was superb; white only slightly less so.

1962 A fine year almost everywhere; not great but exceedingly good.

1963 Spotty: poor for Bordeaux, especially Sauternes; poor, too, for red Burgundy and Beaujolais; fair for white Burgundy and the Loire; and quite good for Alsace. The experts disagree about the Rhône wines of this year and rate them from mediocre to fairly good.

1964 A good to fine year almost everywhere except for Sauternes. Tops for red Burgundy and Bordeaux, champagne, and Beaujolais.

1965 A very poor year with a few rare exceptions. Good Rhône wines, very good Chablis, fair wines of the Loire.

1966 This year is likely to be a good one.

If you are interested in learning how to taste wines the way an expert does, write to Le Comité National des Vins de France, Suite 310, 610 Fifth Avenue, New York, N. Y. 10020, for a copy of Fernande Garvin's informative booklet "French Wines."

Visiting the wine regions

France has so many vineyards that after a while they become part of the scenery and go almost unnoticed. But the more famous ones are worth visiting and so are the great wine centers in Bordeaux, Burgundy, and Champagne. Cognac, where brandy by that name is distilled from the wine of the region, is also an interesting stop.

The city of Bordeaux has a *Maison du Vin* where you can get information about the vineyards in the area. In Burgundy, the town of Beaune has a wine museum, an information center, many *caves,* and numerous stores that sell specialized agricultural implements for viniculture. Champagne has extensive underground establishments where you can see how that famous bubbly wine is made.

Hotel reservations are needed in the wine districts when the grapes are gathered. This takes place from mid-September to mid-October. The *vendange* begins early in the warm south and is put off as long as possible in the colder north. After a rainy summer, grapes are allowed to stay much longer on the wines in the hope of getting longer exposure to sunshine.

In most French wine-growing regions, you will be welcome to visit the vineyards, the cellars, and the bottling places. The sign *dégustation* means that you can taste the wines—and also buy some if you wish. To explore the dark, cool cellars and sample the wines taken from the casks by means of a long glass pipette is an experience no tourist should miss.

Generally speaking, the best-known establishments, which are connected with the production of great or at least fine wines, are the most interesting to visit. We have found that those you

inspect personally remain in your mind, and long afterward, when you taste a wine that comes from a place you recall fondly, it will summon up pleasant memories of grapes ripening in the sun, of green vineyards stretching along gentle slopes, and of cool, dark, richly redolent *caves* or *chais* where thousands of casks bring the liquid pressed from the grapes to maturity. Every taste is a reminder of your stay in France. What better souvenir could anyone want?

7. *Driving on French roads*

We have many happy memories of driving through the French countryside, and they are not all of sun-dappled, tree-lined roads, quaint villages, or vineyards laden with ripening grapes. Some are of a more practical nature. We recall with pleasure the expertness of rural automobile mechanics, the helpfulness of local people along the way, and the pleasant surprise of encountering police who were good-humored and courteous. This, of course, does not apply to all French police, but it does to a number of them. The fact that we drive a French car with an American license sometimes puzzles them, but they usually decide that we deserve special consideration for bringing a Peugeot back to its native land for an Antaeus-like renewal of strength from contact with Gallic earth.

We feel relaxed and at ease on the roads of France. There are few superhighways, but excellent paved roads cover the entire country. And they are well-marked with signs that give the information you need. The indicators that point to roads leading to towns may be a bit confusing until you get used to them, because they are at right angles to the designated route rather than parallel to it.

There is no nonsense to the way the French mark their roads. If the pavement is bad, a sign reading *"Chaussée Deformée"* or *"Route Mauvaise"* candidly says so. And it usually goes beyond that to tell you how many kilometers you will have to drive on a defective surface.

France uses the International Road Signs on which symbols that anyone can understand replace written language. Triangular ones indicate danger; circular ones give instructions; rectangular ones offer information. Pictures of these signs can be found in the French Government Tourist Office's free pamphlet, "The Key for Your Trip to France."

Words on signs

Sometimes the French also use words on their road signs, so the driver must learn that *virages* means curves and that *sortie de camions* means watch out for trucks turning on or off the road at a factory or quarry entrance. More puzzling is *betteraves* placed under the symbol of a skidding car. The word means sugar-beets, but it can also apply to other things. It warns you that the road ahead is temporarily slippery because something has been spilled on it—not necessarily sugar-beets.

Some expressions may be even odder than this. *Nids de poule,* for instance, is not about hens brooding on their nests; it advises you to drive slowly because the road ahead is pitted with round holes that look like chicken nests.

Still other words or phrases that we have encountered on French road signs are:

serrez à droite—squeeze right
tenez votre droite—keep to the right
voie ferrée—railroad
un train peut en cacher un autre—the train you see can hide another train approaching behind it
passage à niveau—level crossing
gravillons—gravel
gravillons roulants—loose stones on the road
goudron—tar
piétons—pedestrians
voie rétrécie or *route étroite*—narrow road. This may be followed by *Priorité en Face,* which means that the first car to enter the passage has the right of way.
route barrée—road barricaded
fin d'interdiction de dépasser—end of no-passing zone
stationnement autorisé jours pairs (or *impairs*)—You may park on this side on even (or uneven) days of the month.
chute de pierres—watch out for fallen stones
défense de doubler—no passing other vehicles
piste cyclable—bicycle path
poids lourds—heavy trucks
ralentir (or ralentissez)—go slowly
sens interdit—do not enter
sens obligatoire—you must go this way
sens unique—one-way traffic
double sens—two-way traffic
voie sans issue—dead-end street

impasse—dead-end street
feu—traffic light
déviation—detour
signaux sonores interdit—use of horns forbidden
défense de klaxonner—use of horns forbidden
fin de chantier—end of construction zone
pont coupé—bridge out of commission
interdiction de parquer—no parking
interdiction de stationner—no parking
secours routier—first-aid station
travaux—men at work
cassis—bump ahead (sometimes a dip for draining the road)
tournons brusques—hairpin turns

The most important words you are likely to see on a French road sign are *stop,* which is obvious, *priorité à droite* (vehicles on the right have priority), and *passage protégé* (entrance to this road is protected by a stop sign).

The driver on the right has the right of way

This brings us to the key to driving safely in France. The idea that a driver on the right has precedence over a driver on the left has been so firmly impressed upon the mind of every French person that you must keep yourself constantly aware of it. It is so universal a principle that if your car is hit on the right side in an accident that fact will be held against you.

At a crossroad, *priorité à droite* means that traffic coming from your right can go ahead. You may have to wait for a line of cars to pass.

Passage protégé is intended to cancel this right-hand priority, but you have to keep alert because French drivers are so used to taking advantage of coming from the right that one of them may ignore the sign and dash onto the highway. This can happen —and when it does, the oncoming vehicle is often a heavy truck that is practically invulnerable in an accident.

Watching out for trouble on the right is exceedingly important in France. When you get used to it you will see that if this right-hand priority is always obeyed by everyone, it brings order out of what would otherwise be chaos. It makes driving possible in large public squares where hundreds of cars converge in what seems to be a hopeless tangle. Allow the man on your right to proceed and remember that the driver on your left then expects you to go ahead. In that way everything straightens itself out. Breaking this rule infuriates the French. If you do so, you are likely to hear automobile horns sounded in angry protest. You may also hear some uncomplimentary epithets.

In cities, right-hand priority is even more important than in the country because urban drivers take it for granted that if you are on their left, you will keep out of their way when they come hurrying down a cross street. That is why city driving at night is actually safer than it is in the daytime. You can flash your headlights on when you approach a dubious-looking corner. But the driver on your right will go ahead anyway; you merely slowed him up for a moment by telling him that you were there. If the situation was reversed, he would expect you to do the same thing. Right-hand priority makes good sense—once you get used to it.

The next thing you need to know about safe driving in France is something that has never been written up before. French automobilists are aware of it, but on what is almost a subconscious level. We call it:

The hierarchy of the road

There is no speed limit in France on the open road, and the driver of a fast car seems to feel obligated to pass a slower one. If you look in your rear-view mirror and see an automobile approaching, you can usually tell what its driver will do if you know his rank in the hierarchy of makes. We would classify European motorcars as follows:

1. Sports cars: Ferrari, Maserati, Alfa-Romeo, Lancia, Aston Martin, Austin-Healy, Triumph, MG, Jaguar, Jensen, Porsche, and any low, flat automobile obviously intended for speed. They will inevitably roar past and quickly disappear down the road.
2. Powerful cars: Mercedes-Benz, Citroen DS-19 or ID-19, Peugeot, the larger Fiats, Rover, Taunus, Cortina, Zephyr, Vauxhall, Opel Rekord or Kapitan, and the bigger versions of smaller makes.
3. All the small cars down to the Citroen 2 CV. But remember that the more recent 2 CV's have been given more power and may surprise you. A Volkswagen can cruise along at 70 mph, but the Volkswagen bus is slow.

You don't have to recognize all the different kinds of cars you will see because a general idea of their shape, size, and silhouette is enough to indicate what their drivers are likely to do.

We have purposely not included the Rolls-Royce or its near twin, the Bentley. They can move along at a good clip, but they are usually owned or driven by sedate people who prefer a slower pace. Nor have we listed any American cars, because it is hard to predict what their drivers will do.

Knowing the hierarchy of the road is helpful, but it does not solve everything. What happens, for instance, when one car comes up behind another of the same make? That depends on the drivers.

And there are ranks within the categories. A big Citroen will almost surely pass a Peugeot. And a Peugeot 404 will probably overtake a Peugeot 403 because it has a more powerful engine. A Ferrari or a Maserati, which are really racing cars, will pass everything in sight.

The French attitude toward speed

But don't get the idea that French roads are used as racecourses. You may occasionally see a fast driver whizzing by, but except on the main highways, traffic on the rural roads of France is usually well-behaved. When you are far from cities or resorts you will see fewer cars than you would on comparable American thoroughfares. That's why driving in France is still a pleasure.

The French government's attitude toward speed on the highway should be known to drivers from other countries. The semi-official expression *"rester maître de sa vitesse"* really means "be master of your car under all circumstances." Speed is to be judged under the conditions that exist at the moment. According to the French, a car is safer at 75 miles (120 kilometers) an hour on the open road than it is at 19 miles (30 kilometers) an hour when it has to go through a town on market day.

In the summer of 1966, in an effort to reduce accidents caused by reckless driving, the French government set up roadside courts at which offenders could be fined on the spot. This drastic measure has made drivers slow down and proceed more cautiously.

Average daily mileage

We assume that you are not interested in proving how fast your car can go, but want to see the country and enjoy your trip. To do so, allow plenty of time for stops along the way. We have said that our daily average is about 125 miles (200 kilometers) when we are going from place to place. Our overall daily average is much less. This may not seem like much to travelers who come from countries where drivers cover many hundreds of miles a day. But such countries, with long, open stretches of straight modern highways, are very different from France, where a centuries-old road system has merely been improved and macadamized. Nor is such a fast passage necessary or even desirable, for there is something worth stopping to see every few miles along most of the routes. The countryside, the architecture, and the people and their customs change from one small area to another. If you want to savor what France has to offer, you should take it leisurely just as you would a fine meal prepared by one of its chefs.

Note that we have said a daily *average* of about 125 miles. Obviously, we do more than that when we are eager to get somewhere. Our records, however, show that 200 miles (320 kilometers) is about as much ground as we want to cover even when in a hurry. You can, of course, do a lot more. We know about grim motorists who dash from a Channel port to the Riviera in one long day of continuous driving. (It is 1100 kilometers or about 700 miles from Calais to Nice.) The very thought of making such a grueling run in a single day is depressing.

Three types of French roads

We avoid major highways like N7, the overburdened artery that goes from Paris to Lyon, Avignon, Aix-en-Provence, and the Riviera. Circulation on it is often blocked by slow-moving trucks behind which long lines of cars creep along until their impatient drivers can swing out and dash by.

Actually there is no need to travel on the more popular Routes Nationales. Except around Paris and a few other big cities, they are not multilaned highways; one side road after another leads into them; and they run through many communities, large and small. Despite the fact that they are more thoroughly patrolled by police than any other type of road, their safety record is poor. In 1960, 55 percent of the automobile accidents in rural and small-town areas occurred on them. Approaches to built-up sections have the highest collision rate, probably because cars suddenly have to slow down there, and the *passages protégés* cease at the point where traffic enters an urban region.

Instead of using the heavily traveled national routes, we seek parallel road systems which are far pleasanter and not much slower. You can apply this principle all through France, for the secondary roads there are almost as good as the so-called primary ones. Except in wilderness areas, it is hard to find a public thoroughfare that is not paved.

The key to the designation of the various kinds of French roads is:

N plus number—Route Nationale, main highway. The more important ones usually have low numbers.
D plus number—Route Départementale, good secondary road.
VO plus number—Voie Ordinaire, minor road that may or may not be good.

Distances are stated precisely. The more important roads have white stone markers with rounded red tops placed at the end of every kilometer along the way. In between, there may be nine smaller square white stones to indicate the 100-meter distances. The red-topped markers give the number of kilometers to the next large town.

Michelin has marked many *voies ordinaires* with a square white cement block placed on top of a pedestal. This gives the VO number and the distance to the nearest village.

Only small back roads in the remote countryside are unmarked. If you venture there, you will have to ask your way.

The fact that there is no speed limit in France does not mean that you can cover a lot of territory rapidly. Even the main highways seldom by-pass towns or villages, so you have to slow down frequently as you drive through them. You can average about 37 meters (60 kilometers) an hour if you keep moving steadily—and that is about all. To make better time means pushing hard, seeing little, and tiring yourself out.

Shipping your car by train

If you are in a hurry you can put your car on one of the overnight trains that carry cars accompanied by their passengers. There are several of these; most of them run from the Channel ports or from Paris to Lyon, Avignon, or the Riviera. Your automobile is carried on a freight car attached to the train while you sleep in a *couchette* or a *wagon-lit* and rejoin your vehicle in the morning. You thus save time, gasoline, wear and tear, and can consider the rather high cost as the equivalent of paying for an expensive hotel room overnight. SNCF, French National Railroads, will give you information about such a trip and tell you what it costs.

The Touring Club de France can be of great help to you, not only as an automobilist but as a skier, a small-boat sailor, a horseman, an amateur aviator, a hunter, a fisherman, a skin-diver, a photographer, or a camper. Membership costs $10 a year for an American, with an extra charge of $5 a year for adult members of his family who drive or want to participate in its many activities. Since the membership year is a calendar one, it is better to join early, say in January, than later. The New York office, at 26 Broadway, New York, N. Y. 10004, will send you literature. The Touring Club de France is not affiliated with any American automobile association, so there is no reciprocity of membership favors. The AAA has an office in Paris at 9 Rue de la Paix.

No matter how long your stay in France is to be, your car must have the white oval national plaque we described in Chapter 2. The Michelin hotel guide has a list of the abbreviations used on these plaques to indicate the country of origin. It also identifies the department numbers on French cars: 75 - Seine; 06 - Alpes-Maritimes; 69 - Rhône, etc.

Local speed limits

As you drive along the roads of France you will note that every community, no matter how small, is identified by a name sign. And each town has a round symbol that tells you just how fast a private car or a truck may go while passing through its streets. French drivers tend to exceed the allowable speed, but if you want to avoid trouble you will do well to obey the local law.

In built-up areas not posted, the top speed permitted is 60 kilometers per hour (37 miles).

If you arrive in a town at 12 or 2 o'clock when workers are going to or returning from lunch, you will have to crawl along in low gear, for pedestrians and cyclists take it for granted that motorists will look out for them. And you may not, except in a case of genuine emergency, sound your horn in a built-up section. One trick to get through a seemingly immovable mass of solidly packed people is to rev up your motor to let the indifferent crowd know you are there. They may then allow you to pass.

You may also be delayed by farm animals on a country road. Their owners take them from one field to another—perhaps with the help of a dog—and will ordinarily signal to let you know when you can proceed. Unattended cows, sheep, or goats, however, are sometimes encountered in thinly settled areas.

The bicycle problem is not as bad in France as it is in Holland, Denmark, and other countries where most of the people use two-wheel, foot-powered transport. Nor are there anywhere near as many motor-scooters as there are in Italy. But bicycle riders often insist on going two or more abreast, which makes them hard to pass. There is nothing you can do about it except be patient and careful.

Since the French prefer to keep their existing roads in good condition rather than build new ones, they are constantly repairing them. You are required by law to slow down when you pass road workers, and you should, for what they are doing is for your benefit. You will see them all over France, patching the paving, sometimes widening the road, cutting away plants and shrubbery along the sides, and marking the surface with dividing lines to indicate where you may or may not pass another car. The police are very particular about these painted lines. It is an offense not only to cross a solid line but even to run on or straddle it. In fact, this is considered worse than speeding, so keep well over on your own side.

French police

The matter of speed regulation has baffled France for years. Efforts have been made to reduce speeds on the open roads to 100 kilometers per hour on weekends, but they have not been successful. Never forget that there are always more police on the roads on Saturdays and Sundays than on weekdays. They often hide behind a building and dash out to nab an offender entering a town. And they have the right to fine you on the spot. Actually, you can go to court, but you are almost sure to lose, so it is better to pay up with good grace.

You will see several kinds of police on the French roads and in the towns and cities. They all have the power to give you a ticket or arrest you. You will note that they travel in pairs. In small towns there may be only one officer, but he can instantly summon others. France is very well policed. Sometimes these men can be helpful, but you can always count on their being tough.

What we have just said about the French police may sound rather forbidding. But we have never had any trouble with them. Unless your French is flawless, don't get involved in an argument with an officer of the law. You are not likely to win even if you can talk faster than he can. Tourist gossip has it that you should forget all your French when you are stopped by a policeman. Then he may get disgusted by your lack of ability to communicate and let you go.

Accidents

But if you have an accident, especially a serious one, the police will be very much involved. The French government is greatly concerned about automobile accidents, and the police have strict instructions to study each one carefully and turn in a complete report about it. Summaries are published annually in book form with charts, maps, tables, and long columns of figures which are presented in such detail that you can calculate the risk you run at any given place at any given time. These statistics do not prevent accidents, but France has a better record of safety on the road than West Germany, Great Britain, Italy, or Belgium.

When the police take over after an accident, they face a formidable task. Not only do they have to make a diagram of the position of each car involved, with exact measurements between them, but they also have to have photographs made and write detailed replies to scores of questions on a printed form. All this takes time, and traffic can back up for miles until the road is opened again.

The filled-out form is sent to Paris to supply statistical data for the annual report. Some of the information is interesting, such as the fact that Tuesdays, Wednesdays, and Thursdays have the fewest accidents, while Sundays have the most. The first weekend in August has the highest rate of accidents because vacationists start out then. The hour of greatest danger is between 6 and 7 P.M. which is almost twice as bad as the seemingly comparable hour of 12 noon to 1 P.M. But darkness is coming on during the evening period, and people are tired then.

Road accidents are what make automobile insurance compulsory in France. You will not be allowed to enter the country unless you can show a *carte verte,* which is not a green card but a green document. (Refer to Chapter 2 for more information on insurance.)

Although the French try to be fair in their judicial procedures, the odds are always against a foreigner—as they are everywhere, especially if he doesn't speak the language well. If you have an accident involving bodily injury ask a police officer to *"dresser un constat,"* i.e., make a report. If police are not available, get a *Huissier* to draw up the report for you. He is a legal official somewhat like a British bailiff. He has no exact counterpart in America, but he should be dealt with as if he were acting as your attorney—in other words he has to be paid for his services. Either he or you must notify your insurance company immediately.

The number of automobiles on French roads increased from 4,000,000 in 1955 to 6,500,000 in 1960, and then to 10,000,000 in 1965. This means that millions of people with relatively little experience are now driving. Since the newcomers have yet to acquire the unconscious skills that come only from spending a lot of time behind the wheel, they are still in the apprenticeship stage. But France, unlike England, does not insist that these tyros display a big red L (for learner).

In addition to the Green Card, which you must have, you will find a parking disk useful. You need one in cities with a *Zone Bleue* where the parking areas are marked *Disque Obligatoire.* You set it at the time you park, and place it under the windshield where it can be seen. If you don't move your car by the end of the time limit indicated, you are likely to get a ticket.

Police, however, tend to be lenient with drivers of cars with foreign or TT licenses. But if you have a rented car they won't know you are a visitor to France.

Parking disks, plain or fancy, can be bought at automobile supply stores and most service stations. In Monaco the public parking attendants will give you one free as a good-will gesture. So will some of the French gasoline companies.

Driving at night

Under ordinary circumstances you will be bedded down at night and are not likely to have to drive long distances in the dark. But if you do, make sure your gas tank is full, because most service stations are closed then. Since they are usually located in or near towns there is practically no chance of finding one on the open road.

Gasoline

Although we advise you to have a full tank of gasoline when you travel at night, we suggest that you not ask a service-station attendant to fill it up for daytime driving. Automatic shut-off delivery lines are scarce in France, so you may get a spill-over. And you may want to make another stop for gas in order to use the service station's toilet.

French gasoline prices are the highest in Europe. They are so much lower in Switzerland that people passing near the Swiss border sometimes visit that country just to fill up the fuel tank.

Government coupons, which formerly enabled tourists to purchase gasoline for about 20 percent less than the regular price, are no longer available. They went out of existence late in 1963.

Two grades of gasoline are available, ordinary and super. We always use the latter because it helps cars go faster uphill and prevents knocking. It costs only a few centimes more per liter than the ordinary grade, which is rather poor stuff. You don't have to purchase gasoline by the liter; you can ask for 10 francs worth, 20 francs worth, etc. Remember that gasoline is called *essence*. The signs you will see at service stations for Gas-Oil (gaz-whal) are for the mixture of gasoline and oil used in the two-cycle motors on scooters, some farm machinery, and a few automobiles.

You are supposed to carry one of the red triangles (with reflectors on it) that are placed on the road to warn other drivers when you have a breakdown.

You should watch your gas supply even in the daytime whenever you are going to make a long run through sparsely settled country. This is especially true in mountain areas. We have been on roads through the Alps where there were no service stations for 60 kilometers or more.

All French cars are required by law to have yellow headlights. You can easily make yours that color by painting the glass with a quick-drying amber fluid sold for this purpose. It can be washed off later with lacquer remover.

Europeans generally are opposed to using bright lights except on the open road when no traffic is in sight. In France you are obliged by law to lower your headlight beams when another car approaches. In cities, where horns are forbidden, especially at night, headlights are flashed on and off as signals to warn pedestrians, to inform a driver ahead that you are about to pass, or to make your presence known to the driver of a car that may be coming down a street to your right, etc. Except as warning signals, *headlights are not used in cities.* On a well-illuminated street you must use only your parking lights. On a dark street you may use your dim lights. During the war, the French realized how very little illumination was needed for a careful driver to make his way through a city and have ever since frowned on using bright headlights in town.

Except for what has been explained here, the rules of the road for safe driving are very much the same in France as they are elsewhere. Motorists from other countries should take special care, however, for they will not do well in court—or even in a police station—if the charge is a serious one.

8. *The country and the people*

We are, we admit, so much in love with France that it is hard for us to be impartial about a country where the word "glorious" does not seem out of place. Some of the happiest hours in our lives have been spent there, and no matter how often we go back we are never disappointed.

Americans have long been enchanted with France. From Franklin and Jefferson to Gertrude Stein, Hemingway, and now Mrs. Jacqueline Kennedy, they have found it a pleasant land. Nearly a century ago, one of our writers who is better known for caustic wit than for praise, said:

> We have come . . . through the heart of France. What a bewitching land it is! What a garden! Surely the leagues of bright green lawns are swept and brushed and watered every day, and their grasses trimmed by the barber. Surely the hedges are shaped and measured, and their symmetry preserved, by the most architectural of gardeners. Surely the long straight rows of stately poplars that divide the beautiful landscape like the squares of a checkerboard are set with line and plummet, and their uniform height determined with a spirit level. Surely the straight, smooth, pure white turnpikes are jack-planed and sandpapered every day. How else are these marvels of symmetry, cleanliness, and order attained? . . . We had such glimpses of the Rhône gliding along between its grassy banks; of cosy cottages buried in flowers and shrubbery; of quaint old red-tiled villages with mossy medieval cathedrals looming out of their midst; of wooded hills with ivy-grown towers and turrets of feudal castles projecting above the foliage; such

> glimpses of Paradise, it seemed to us, such visions of fabled fairyland! . . . And it *is* a pleasant land. No word describes it so felicitously as that one.

That was Mark Twain, writing about his first trip through France, a railroad journey from Marseille to Paris, for *Innocents Abroad,* a book that is usually thought of as being exceedingly critical of the Old World.

2000 years of battle

There are many good reasons for France to be such a pleasant place. It was richly endowed by nature, and man has worked on it for several thousand years with genuine love for the soil and the landscape. Seacoasts and mountains, vast plateaus and fertile plains, long, navigable rivers, safe harbors, and numerous good sites for towns and cities all helped to make France one of the most desirable land areas in Europe. And the fact that the best trade routes from the Mediterranean and the central part of the Continent led through it to Atlantic and Channel ports made this geographically favored nation a coveted prize for people who lived in less fortunate places. As a result, France has always been a battleground. Like neighboring Belgium, it has been invaded since earliest times by armies that sought to subjugate its people and plunder its wealth. Sometimes they succeeded. Julius Caesar conquered Gaul and made it part of the Roman Empire. It remained in Roman hands until Western Europe was overrun by barbarian hordes. England, too, ruled large areas of France for centuries. And nations around the rim held bits and pieces for as long as they could maintain their claims to them.

But all that happened long ago and might have been forgotten if three successive German invasions from 1870 to 1940 had not crippled and humiliated this proud country. The scars of the First and Second World Wars are still visible. Fields torn up by shells in 1914–1918 mar parts of Northern France; empty Nazi blockhouses stand at every possible landing place along the coasts; even small villages have war memorials, and military cemeteries dot the land. In some areas the shattered bones of the war dead are so close to the surface that the rain washes them out.

During the Second World War, Nazi armies occupied most of Northern and Western France while Vichy for a time was the seat of what was left of the French Government. When the Allies landed in North Africa early in November 1942, the Nazis took over the entire country. What happened under their monstrous rule is a seldom-told story. They executed nearly 30,000 hostages while another 40,000 met their deaths in prisons inside France. At the eastern end of the Ile de la Cité in Paris is a memorial crypt to 200,000 French people who were deported to German labor camps from which they never returned. Evidences of the Nazis' five years of occupation can be seen everywhere. But all their swastikas and military posters, which once defaced walls and sidings throughout France, were obliterated the moment the invaders were driven out.

André Malraux gives this dramatic instance of the steadfast unity of the French country people during those terrible years:

> In a village of the Corrèze district [in south-central France] the Germans had killed a number of our underground fighters and sent an order . . . to have them buried secretly at dawn. It is the custom in this region for all the women to be present at the interment of any member of their village, each one standing by the graves of her own family. No one in the village knew the men who had been killed; they were natives of Alsace. When their bodies arrived at the cemetery, carried by our own peasants between menacing ranks of German submachine guns, the night, withdrawing slowly like the sea, disclosed the black-clad women of Corrèze, motionless, from top to bottom of the rocky hill, spaced out in silence, each by her own family grave, waiting to attend the burial of these French dead.

In the wake of these wars came a disastrous inflation that nearly wiped out everyone who was dependent upon fixed incomes paid in francs that decreased alarmingly in value.

Practically every home in France has been affected by war. It lies heavily upon the land, and everyone old enough to remember the years of battle and enemy occupation knows how terrible they were. Visitors should realize that they are in a country which has suffered much and endured much, but which has always fought bravely and has again and again risen above its enormous losses to take a leading place among the nations of the world.

The land

This fair and much fought-over land is the largest country in Western Europe with an area of 212,822 square miles, which means that it is bigger than all the New England and Middle Atlantic states put together, much bigger than California, and almost as big as Texas.

The 47th parallel, which is north of Duluth and Quebec, runs a little below Nantes, Bourges, and Besançon to divide France into north and south, while a line drawn from Dunkirk to the western shore of the Mediterranean would partition it into east and west. The four resultant sections are approximately equal in size.

Because the winds blowing across the Atlantic hit western France, that part of the country is air-conditioned by the sea, so that the weather there is never very hot or very cold. Rains do come in from the ocean, though.

The same Atlantic weather prevails along the shores of the English Channel, where it is likely to be cooler and even wetter. Inland, from Paris to Strasbourg, and from there almost to the southern limit of the Alps, is also cool and well-watered. But the south, the golden crescent that stretches along the Mediterranean from Italy to Spain, has more warm sunshine and less rain than any other part of France. Corsica is part of this area.

The Vosges, the Jura Mountains, and the Alps serve as a wall against the east while the Pyrenees rise from coast to coast along the Spanish border. The volcanically formed Massif Central almost bridges the broad gap between the two mountainous groups. Rivers emerge from these highlands to flow to the Atlantic or the Mediterranean. But everywhere, in the mountains, the valleys, the fertile plains, and the seacoasts, the French people have made the land their own, and have often cut it into small parcels as a result of the inheritance law passed at the time of the Revolution, which gives each child an equal share of the family's land. Farms have been prevented from becoming hopelessly miniscule because one heir sometimes buys out the others' interests.

But this system of dividing the land has reduced the size of farms so much that in some parts of the country it does not pay to use agricultural machinery. When you travel through the French countryside you will note that in hilly sections horses and oxen are still very much in evidence. In Auvergne you may even see a pair of cows patiently hauling a farmer's cart.

Brittany, Périgord, Corsica, and some parts of the Alps have farm buildings, equipment, and methods that have gone almost unchanged for centuries. Such farms are picturesque and photogenic, but they are not profitable or comfortable for their owners.

All this is slowly changing. Small holdings are being put together to be worked as a unit. The walls and fences that required so much labor to build are coming down. Tractors are replacing draft animals, and electric lines are bringing in light and power.

But efforts to keep young people on the farm are not always successful. Many of them are leaving to go to urban communities where life is easier. The older peasants still cling to the land, but when they die their heirs may have no use for what their families held on to for generations. In some villages, roofs are falling in. Around them are once-cultivated fields that are now being allowed to go wild. This, of course, is not peculiar to France, but to see it happen in that previously well-tended country is sad.

The boundaries of France have varied considerably over the ages. Not until 1947 did the nation reach its present extent. A plebiscite in 1860 had made Nice and Savoy part of the nation, but two small bits of territory in the Alps near the Italian frontier were not to become French territory until 87 years later. These are Tende and Brigue, which are about 60 kilometers (37 miles) north of Menton. Another frontier curiosity is Llivia, a tiny Spanish enclave a few miles above Bourg-Madame and the border of Spain. It is a Spanish town entirely surrounded by France.

Nearly all of Alsace and much of Lorraine were lost to Germany in 1871 at the end of the Franco-Prussian War but were regained after the First World War.

Faults and failings

It is too much to suppose that France, which has been magnificent in adversity and ever ready to fight to maintain its preeminence in world affairs, should be without faults. Its 50 million inhabitants are very much like other people, and both they and their government are less than perfect.

The government's shortcomings could be more easily corrected than the people's. The postal system, except for its quick Paris deliveries, is cumbersome and inefficient. So are the telephones it operates. One has to experience the French telephone system at first hand to realize how very bad it is in handling most long-distance calls. It sometimes takes hours to put through a call, especially in summer when the trunk lines are hopelessly overloaded. Stories are told about impatient people, who, disgusted at the long wait after placing a call, went by airplane to see the person they wanted to reach and were then present when the operator rang up to say that they were on the phone.

The post offices are run by civil servants, who evidently are a privileged class in France. They seem to take delight in watching the hand of a sensitive letter scale move past the five-gram mark that is the point where the already exorbitant overseas airmail-letter rate again goes up. And five grams will just permit a note written on thin paper and put into an airmail envelope to get by.

It is not true, however, that all postal clerks are intent upon making life difficult for anyone who is on the wrong side of the *guichet*. It is not even true that they are all surly, unobliging, or downright rude. We have met some rather pleasant ones, particularly in small towns. We recall a certain village postmaster fondly because he trusted us for the fee when we were short of change for a much-wanted *Poste Restante* letter from home.

Civil servants play an important role in France because they are in daily contact with the public—and not just with the tourist public but with the French public. Improvement of their attitude and of the communications they control would be a tremendous boon to France and make it not merely a better place to visit but also to live in.

The French postal service comes out very badly when it is compared with England's, for the British post office is not only one of the world's best—it also happens to be manned by unfailingly courteous and helpful clerks.

Another thing in which the British are more civic-minded than the French is in admission fees to museums, art galleries, and other public institutions. The prices to enter such places in England are generally quite reasonable and in many cases, like the British Museum, the National Gallery, and the Tate Gallery, no charge at all is made. This means that you can revisit them again and again without having to pay for the privilege. In fact, you can drop in, spend a few moments looking at something you are especially interested in, and then go on to some other place.

In France there is nearly always an admission charge, except on a limited number of free days, and the price keeps going steadily up. In addition to that, there may be an extra charge for a special exhibit inside the museum.

As a result, you have to pay far more for visiting public institutions in France than you do in England. In the Château Country, especially, each day may cost you an appreciable sum of money for admissions and tips to the guides.

England wants to educate its people; so does France, and in all fairness it must be said that students, teachers, and groups of people are given lower rates there for admission to museums and other places of educational interest. But England puts its museums in the category of free education for the public, whereas France apparently feels that the public should pay something for being allowed to look at the national treasures.

Dead hands reaching

Much of what is wrong with France is a carryover from the past. "That is how it was always done, and therefore that is how it must always be done—forever, and forever, and forever." Thus speaks the traditionalist who tries desperately to cling to his grandfather's bootstraps even though the old gentleman is in his grave, and his bootstraps were buried with him.

The inevitable 12-to-2 closing period is a good example of the way the dead hand of the past still rules France. In order to have the customary big meal, which must be eaten in the middle of the day, nearly the whole nation locks its doors and disappears from sight at noon. It is not bad enough that banks, business offices, and stores are shut during these two hours—museums, libraries, palaces, châteaux, and public attractions of all kinds are also closed. This affects the tourist more than it does the native who is so used to the two-hour luncheon period that he takes it for granted. But the visitor, who arrives at a place he has traveled far to see, will find the gates being closed in his face if he gets there shortly before twelve o'clock. He usually goes on and misses what he came to see, so the museum, château, etc., loses attendance and revenue.

Surely at least some part of these places could be kept open from 12 to 2. A skeleton staff of guards could be on hand to watch over a limited area so visitors could have something to do until the magic hour of 2 o'clock arrives.

We recently had an unpleasant reminder of the way the 12-to-2 closing period can affect a traveler's life. On a hot summer day we arrived in Dijon to go to Paris by train. We hardly ever use French railroads because we know what their local trains are like, but this time we had no choice in the matter. We got to the station shortly after noon and were informed that all the porters would be out to lunch until 2 o'clock, 16 minutes after the train left. We had to drag our heavy bags down the stairs to the farthest *quai,* No. 5, then up the stairs and along the platform to heave them into the train. We sagged into our seats, puffing, panting, perspiring, and cursing. Needless to say, at that moment we had—and still have—a very dim view of French railroads and the absurd idea of having no porters on hand during the tradition-bound 12-to-2 closing period.

The 12-to-2 closing period annoys tourists, but it has a worse effect on France than most of its citizens realize. When streets and roads are jammed with pedestrians and bicyclists rushing from or to work, statistics show that the number of serious automobile accidents rises sharply. And a heavy meal with wine induces drowsiness for hours afterward. Production suffers, mistakes are made, and factory accidents increase. The leisurely two-hour midday meal may be a pleasant tradition, but it is hampering France in its effort to keep up with the modern world. The nations it is in competition with do not break their working days in half but keep going all day long with only brief intervals for a light lunch.

Inconvenient equally for the tourist and the native is the insistence of nearly all French employees on taking their annual vacations in August as if that were the only month in the year that France is worth traveling in. This concentrated demand for accommodations results in overcrowded resorts and causes many people to go to some other country. Efforts are being made to persuade vacationers to select another time for their annual flight from the cities, but so far such efforts have not been noticeably effective.

Other nuisances

Not only annoying but actually dangerous to health are the dirty, smelly public toilets and sewage lines that empty into water where people go swimming. It is odd that such offensive things should be tolerated in an otherwise clean and orderly nation that shows great concern for its citizens' well-being.

Another nuisance that only the national government can correct is the extraordinarily high price of gasoline. The cost is high not because French oil refiners are greedy or inefficient, but because taxes amount to about 57 cents per American gallon. It is true that enormous sums of money need to be spent to modernize French roads, but is seems unfair for the motorist to have to pay the entire bill. Others also benefit from better roads and should pay at least part of the cost of improving them.

All these things bear more heavily on the French people than on the tourist. There is nothing anti-foreign or anti-tourist about them; they affect everyone, the tourist temporarily, the citizen all the time.

And that brings us to the interesting question: why do the French put up with such drawbacks, nuisances, and menaces to health? They certainly do not go unnoticed. Protest, loud and vehement, appears regularly in the press. The man in the street grumbles and complains about the high price of gasoline, the insolence of office, and the inefficiency of the post office and its telephones. But he is so used to the 12-to-2 closing that he assumes it is a universal custom. Since he probably takes his own vacation in August, he can only curse out others who crowd the resorts then. And as for dirty public toilets and badly planned sewage lines, his own town may be among the worst offenders. "That's how things are, that's how they always have been, and that's how they always must be," he says piously and makes no attempt to improve the situation.

The old order changeth

But the world is changing around him, and tradition is losing its hold on French life and customs. In recent years many French people have broken out of their long, self-satisfied isolation to visit other countries. Unfortunately, the most favored nations have been Spain and Italy where conditions are no better. But at some future time they will go to other nations that have good plumbing, sensible working hours, spread-out vacation times, excellent post-office and telephone service, modern highways, and reasonable gasoline prices. Then, after much soul-searching and loud argument, France may come into its own and take its true place among the most advanced nations of the world. Conceivably, this could happen fairly soon, for the French move quickly once they decide to move at all. Signs of progress are beginning to appear, especially in the larger cities. Someday France will be an unalloyed delight not only for tourists but for its own people as well.

Not faults but misunderstandings

Most of the faults we have mentioned require government action to change them. But many of the things that tourists think are wrong with France or the French people are not really faults at all.

One of them is the popular notion that the French are cold, unapproachable, and hostile to foreigners. A truer way to put this would be to say that they are reserved, that they place a high premium on their friendship, and that they have suffered so much at the hands of outsiders—armed invaders actually—that they are cautious in greeting strangers.

It is especially difficult for hearty, outgoing Middle-Western or Western Americans to understand a people who are so unlike themselves. No, the French do not casually invite newly-met visitors from abroad to have dinner in their homes. When they do invite a guest, dinner will be as formal as they can possibly make it with elaborately cooked dishes and carefully selected wines, all of which takes time to get ready.

The Frenchman's home is not just his castle; it is a veritable fortress where his wife and children and his most cherished possessions are kept in a well-guarded, high-walled inner donjon tower which strangers are seldom allowed to enter. Some French hosts prefer to take their guests to a good restaurant where it will be easier—and perhaps even less costly—to entertain them. The family is sacred in France. Its solidarity and well-being come before everything else.

Another reason why the French may seem to be a bit standoffish is that most of them—even the educated ones—do not speak any language well but their own. They may have studied English in school, but that does not mean that they are at home with it. They are therefore hesitant to expose themselves to ridicule. Visiting Americans who cannot speak French—or who speak it badly—should sympathize with them.

The best place to meet the French people is in the country when they are on vacation. At a *pension*, the guests are necessarily brought into close contact. If language is not too great a barrier, you have a chance to become acquainted with the other boarders. (They always like to hear about America.) You are not likely to make lifelong friendships from these casual encounters, but they will give you some insight into the way French people think and act.

Tourism

Since tourism is a major industry in France, exceeded only by steel and automobiles, the government naturally considers it important. It also seems to feel that visitors have not been well treated in recent years because the record shows that many of them stay briefly in Paris and then hurry on to Spain or Italy where prices are lower and the natives are supposedly more cordial.

To improve the French image with travelers, the government has given presents of perfume and flowers to women arriving from other countries. It has also offered rewards to employees who go out of their way to be kind to tourists. More practical is the large fund of national credits being made available for building or modernizing hotels.

Unfortunately, the government seems to be concentrating its efforts on a very small segment of the traveling public, a segment that has been vociferous in its complaints but not always justified in making them. These are the people who think that money paves their way, who can't be bothered to learn even a few French phrases, and who expect everything to be exactly as it is at home. Perhaps such travelers can be attracted to France by the promise of free flowers and perfumes; perhaps they are taken in by the put-on smiles of employees who hope to get prize money. But we don't think that bribery can purchase genuine good-will.

If the French government wants to spend money to encourage tourism it will do better to try to bring in visitors who will appreciate the really fine things the country has to offer—its art, its history, and its natural beauty. France has little to gain by building up the tenderloin trade, but it can gain a great deal if it persuades professional people, students, artists, and molders of public opinion to visit various parts of the country. Such people's allegiance cannot be bought with perfume, flowers, or paid-for smiles, but it can be won. And once it is won, it remains pledged for life. France needs permanent friends, not transient tourists who flit through Paris and the Riviera and never return.

Wedding march

9. *Some tips about traveling in France*

We are convinced that the best way to see France is to travel by car. Even if you can't drive it is worth trying to team up with someone who can. And those who say that they can't afford to go by automobile probably haven't investigated the relative costs thoroughly. For a single person, traveling by car is admittedly more expensive than going by bus or train; for two people the costs run close; for three or more the car is cheaper.

In figuring comparable costs, include expenses for porters and taxis if you have been thinking of going by train. And if you want to reserve seats in the often overcrowded second-class cars, include that too.

And don't forget that when you use public transportation in France, you may have to wait hours for connections. You may also find that in some places the last bus or train departs at such an early hour that your visit will be cut short. Instead of being a slave to timetables, you are gloriously free when you go by car.

This is especially true if your knowledge of spoken French is not good, for you have to ask many questions—and be able to interpret the rapid replies—when you buy railroad or bus tickets, ask about destinations, or make inquiries of any kind. On the road, signs tell you what to do and maps guide you. You seldom have to ask questions, and if your French is poor, gestures and pointing at the names of places on a map will help you get to where you want to go.

When you plan your trip, be sure to allow time for fairly long stays in pleasant areas where you can rest for a while. Remember that travel is not all just sightseeing; you need time to digest what you experience. You are supposed to be going on a pleasure trip, not a cross-country race.

Read about what you are going to see

If a place is worth visiting, it is surely worth reading about beforehand. Too many tourists wander around looking slightly baffled because they are so poorly informed about what they are seeing that it means very little to them. Since it does not mean much, it will not make much of an impression and will therefore soon be forgotten. You will be surprised how easily you can forget what you traveled so far to see.

Traveling is not all just fun; you have to work at it. Work should begin at home before you start out. And the best place to begin your journey is in a library where you can find out about the country you want to visit and then decide just which part of it you want to concentrate on.

Two kinds of reading are required: one for general background; the other for specific information about places and the people associated with them. We suggest that you make notes to refer to while you are abroad.

When we are on the road we read each night about what we expect to see the next day. Even if we have read it before, we go over the text again to impress details upon the mind.

If you don't know what lies ahead, you may miss seeing something you really want to see. That has happened to us. We drove through Châtillon-sur-Seine one year without knowing that the celebrated Trésor de Vix is on view there. We read about it—quite accidentally—during the following winter and then went out of our way the next year to see it. It was worth the special trip, but we were annoyed at our own oversight for having missed it the first time.

Few travelers have the opportunity to revisit France as often as we have had, but they should not let themselves think they have to see everything that is to be seen because they are not likely to be there again. Travel is increasing and becoming easier to do. Count on coming back. If you enjoy your trip as much as we hope you will, you will surely want to return. And you probably will, so save something for the next visit.

We think it is far better to cover a relatively limited area thoroughly rather than dash around burning up gasoline and energy. But we find that it is hard to convince people of this. Only after they have exhausted themselves on an over-ambitious journey are they willing to settle down and savor the pleasure of staying longer in fewer places.

Memory aids

We urge you to keep a daily record of your travels, even if only a sketchy one. If you don't, everything will run together afterward and become confused. You won't remember all the places you saw, and your recollections will grow dimmer as time obscures them. You may not even be able to recall the name of a hotel or restaurant you want to recommend or return to.

Instead of keeping a travel diary, some people prefer to write long descriptive letters home, which they can reclaim and keep together as a record of their journey. There is no reason, of course, why you can't make a daily record and write such letters too. The very act of writing about what you have seen will help you to remember it.

To appreciate a new place, one has to approach it as an artist would. It can be described on paper, recorded on canvas, or expressed in music. Since few people can be artists, they have to preserve their impressions in other ways. Certainly photographs—especially in color—can do a great deal to make your journey come to life again. Their only disadvantage is that they are so quickly and easily taken that the camera rather than the mind usually does most of the work. Even better than photographs as pictorial reminders are rough sketches that can be made without any training or artistic ability. This is not as absurd as it may seem. Try it, and you will find that you have to look with an analytical eye that breaks the subject into its elements and compels you to study, rather than merely glance at, what is in front of you.

In all probability your untutored drawing will be very crude, so bad that you may not want to keep it. You don't have to. The picture has been etched upon your mind, which is where you want it to be. The clumsy sketch doesn't matter.

Eventually you will learn to look at things as an artist does. Your photography will also improve. So will your visual memory. After a while, the mind you have trained to retain pictorial images will enable you to own some of the world's greatest works of art. For the few brief moments you stand in front of one in a museum, it is yours. When you have learned how to impress its outlines and colors upon your memory, it is yours forever. And no one can charge you with theft, for what you have taken has not deprived the museum of anything. The art object is still there. The museum has lost nothing, but you have gained a great deal.

Indirect reminders

In addition to being direct reminders, photographs may also prompt the memory to recall other things by association. When you look at a photograph long after you took it you may say: "Oh, yes, down that street to the right is that good restaurant where we first tasted *ombre chevalier*. And later that evening, I remember, we walked along the ramparts and watched the stars come out." The restaurant and the ramparts, of course, do not appear in the photograph, but the picture stirred your memory to action and much came back which you thought you had forgotten.

Being reminded by association happens every time we return to a place we have visited before. A general impression and a few details are all that ordinarily remain in the forefront of memory. When we revisit a place, however, the mind runs ahead to anticipate what lies around the next corner and even what is beyond that.

This ability to recall by association can probably be improved if you work at it. After you have been to a place you want to remember, try to revisit it mentally, going step by step over the route you took. People too often wander around in a fog, not really looking at anything. If little or nothing comes through that fog, the mind obviously cannot be expected to retain what it never received.

We said that you have to work at traveling if you want to get the most out of it. You do. It is perfectly possible to take a pleasant trip somewhere and simply enjoy each day, but if you want to remember more than vague impressions, you have to make an effort to do so. It is a nuisance to take time out to make records, especially when your days are filled with activity and you want only to rest when you return to your hotel. But even a brief record is better than no record at all.

Maps and photographs

One thing we do to straighten out each year's journey is to use a marking crayon on the map to indicate the roads we took. (This should be done daily; otherwise you may soon forget which road you actually did take.) Then, on a master map, we mark each year's route in a different color. Only in this way—or by referring to the annual travel diaries—can we recall what year we visited any given place.

Outdoor market

Another memory aid is to shoot hundreds of inexpensive 35-mm. black-and-white photographs and make only contact prints of the whole lot, unless, of course, some of them do turn out to be so good that you want to enlarge them.

Incidentally, it is essential to label and date photographs as soon as possible, otherwise you may forget what they represent. We say this from bitter experience because we did not always do so and now can't tell where some of the unlabeled ones were taken. This is not important if they are of easily recognized monuments like the Pont-du-Gard or Chenonceaux, but minor places are hard to identify.

A happy phrase

One French aphorism we have found useful is *"c'est la chance de la route."* If something goes wrong, it is the luck of the road. If there is a pleasant surprise, that too is *"la chance de la route."* This is the philosophy a traveler needs in order to take whatever happens, good or bad, without becoming unduly wrought up about it. This attitude will help you to endure much, never be annoyed, and accept gratefully whatever good fortune you encounter along the way.

Too many tourists are more interested in meeting people from their own country than they are in becoming acquainted with the French. And too many of them seem to take pleasure in finding fault and making unfavorable comparisons than in noting what is good.

One mistake tourists often make is to take it for granted that no one within hearing distance can understand what they are saying when they talk to each other in their own language. This is not necessarily so. More French people understand other languages than you think. Your critical remarks may be overheard—and will not be well received.

French architecture and how to appreciate it

Since you will see many ancient buildings in France—or in any European country for that matter—you ought to know something about the evolution of architecture to appreciate them fully.

Except for rock tombs and a few Gallic forts, very little is left of anything built before the Romans invaded France. Some trace of the Roman occupation exists almost everywhere, but the most impressive Roman ruins are found in the south, particularly in Provence and the Rhône valley.

After the Romans were driven out by the barbarian hordes, most buildings were constructed of wood or other perishable materials, so hardly anything of that early period exists. Medieval stone castles and churches preserve the history of early French architecture better than private dwellings do. This is because they were solidly built and were intended to last. They have—magnificently.

We talk about castles in the chapter on the Château Country. But old churches exist everywhere in France. The subject of ecclesiastical architecture, however, is so vast that we can only outline it here.

The long-neglected Romanesque churches built before the Gothic style became predominant in the second half of the twelfth century have at last come into their own and are now greatly admired and much visited. Good examples of these Romanesque buildings can be found throughout France, but some of the finest of them are in the southwest, especially in Périgord where Moissac and Conques are world-famous. The Pyrénées, Burgundy, and most of western France have many others.

Incidentally, don't become confused about the use of the word *roman* in French. It refers to the period from the end of the Roman Empire to the twelfth century and is translated in English by the word Romanesque, while *romain* refers to ancient Rome or its civilization.

Outstanding Romanesque buildings are described in the regional chapters that follow. The churches are noted for their massive construction, heavy columns, vaulted ceilings, round arches, and primitive sculpture and frescoes.

Gothic architecture evolved from Romanesque and is much lighter with slim, high columns, pointed arches, flying buttresses to support side-thrust, more sophisticated sculpture, and fine stained-glass windows with delicate carved stone tracery. The transition was gradual, so gradual that there are churches which have elements that are partly Romanesque and partly

Gothic. Even more important is the fact that churches were constantly being altered to fit changing needs. As a result, a building that was once all Romanesque may now have early sections that were left unchanged and were incorporated into later Gothic additions.

In general, both Romanesque and Gothic churches follow a basic floor plan, which is in the shape of a cross. The long central section, where the congregation is ordinarily seated during ceremonies, is called the nave; the side-arms are the transepts; the upper part of the cross is the choir; chapels beyond this, usually clustered around it, make up the chevet, a word that is the same—and is pronounced the same way (chevay) in both French and English. Ordinarily, a French church is oriented so that the congregation sits facing the altar, the choir, and the east because the holy city of Jerusalem lies in that direction. The setting sun therefore strikes what we think of as the front of the church and illuminates—in later Gothic structures—the great rose window there. The western doorway—and some of the others as well—may have over it a sculptured group of figures usually centering around Christ and the twelve apostles. A vivid depiction of the gate of hell is often part of the decorative scheme.

In Périgord, particularly at Périgueux, you can see Romanesque churches which have a strong oriental influence that was brought to France by the Crusaders when they returned from the Near East. These buildings have domes, and their chevets may consist of a rising cluster of small domed chapels.

You will also see churches that served as fortresses into which all the people of the community could retire to an upper loft, pull up the entrance ladders after them, and fight off the invaders by shooting down at them and pouring hot oil on their heads. Even some of the larger cathedrals—Albi, for instance—were built so they were practically impregnable.

Many churches seem to be larger than the community's needs, but they were built that way to serve as places of pilgrimage. Between pilgrimages, they were centers for people who lived near enough to go to them for the rites of passage—birth, first communion, marriage, and death.

The buildings associated with the churches—cloisters, abbeys, baptisteries, and ossuaries—were usually built in similar styles. In some cases, however, the style of the subsidiary buildings may be different because they were constructed centuries later. It is difficult for modern people, who are used to seeing huge edifices planned and completed in a year or two, to understand that the ancient churches were not constructed with such speed. They went up slowly, and as the years passed, many alterations were made. Sometimes whole parts were pulled down and rebuilt. Men were born in the shadow of the uncompleted cathedral, worked on it as adults, and were buried in its graveyard. Their sons carried on, and their sons after them, sometimes through many generations. A few of the big cathedrals, however, were built more quickly. Chartres took only 46 years to complete, Sens 50, Amiens 68, and Notre-Dame in Paris 74.

The year 1200 marks the apogee of Gothic cathedral building in France, but work on some of them (Rouen, Bourges, and Beauvais) went on until the 1500's. Cathedral building came to a halt because the wars of the late Middle Ages required defensive structures, so that stonemasons and builders were compelled to work on castles and forts. War became more important than religion, and the quest for power replaced the search for salvation.

Then came the Renaissance churches that seem very unchurchlike in appearance.

The early buildings were usually the strongest and most carefully put together. Henry Adams says: "The great cathedrals after 1200 show economy, and sometimes worse. The world grew cheap, as worlds must."

The word cathedral does not just mean a large church; it must be the seat of a bishop and therefore the head church of a diocese. Some churches that once were cathedrals no longer are, and in some cases, others have been made into cathedrals. At present, 89 do have bishops, while 30 do not—perhaps temporarily.

Certainly no one should miss seeing the great French cathedrals of Notre-Dame, Chartres, Bourges, Amiens, Reims, and Strasbourg. But others are also well worth visiting. The huge, unfinished cathedral of Beauvais, which was to be the biggest of them all, is only a part of a church because work on it stopped before the vast nave could be built. Albi, which is an enormous red-brick structure, looks more like a fort than a cathedral. Clermont-Ferrand's dark and somber cathedral was built of black lava. Autun is noted for its superb tympanum and for the other fine sculptures made for it by Giselbert. Since France has 119 cathedrals, you can spend a lifetime studying them.

But the smaller churches should not be neglected. Some of them are of extraordinary interest. And each one is a repository of local history, a center of genealogical information, and an example of architectural evolution.

The urge for church building during the period around the year 1200 was a remarkable manifestation of the human spirit. There are many stories about men and women of the nobility offering not only their wealth but their services to further the building of the great cathedrals. They even hauled stones and helped to put them in place. But these were only gestures that would not have completed a single chapel. The huge cathedrals that loom high over the French landscape are memorials to the laborers and skilled workmen who spent their entire lives creating these structures that reach toward Heaven.

When you visit a French church, large or small, remember that it is no longer the way it was when it was first built. The bright colors painted on the sculptures are gone, although faint traces of them can sometimes still be seen if you look carefully.

And the violent attacks made on the Church by the Protestants in the sixteenth century and by the Revolutionists at the end of the eighteenth century destroyed much ecclesiastical art. Headless statutes, empty niches, plundered tombs, and shattered stones remain as testimony to the violence of those times.

Guides

There are English-speaking guides in France, but you will seldom find one—especially in the provinces. Most professional guides are government employees who speak nothing but French, and some of them speak it so rapidly or with such a pronounced local accent that it is hard for anyone who has not grown up with the French language to understand what they are saying. That is why we suggest that you read up beforehand on what you are going to see. You can have your guidebook in hand and review the text while the guide rattles on with the set piece he has memorized. Some guides are better than others, of course. And a few are very good; they even speak so clearly and distinctly that foreigners can follow them.

In some commercial establishments such as the champagne wine cellars, the caves where Roquefort cheese is made, and the perfume factories of Grasse, you will be taken through by a company guide. It is customary to leave a tip just the same.

One franc per person is about right unless the guide has gone out of his way to do extra favors for you, in which case he should be given more. We have, on occasion, been so very well treated by guides at places in which we had a special interest that we did not just tip them—we rewarded them.

On occasion, you may want to employ a local person who knows the area to take you around to explain things. One can usually be found by inquiring at the *Syndicat d'Initiative*. Make your financial arrangements before you start on your tour.

The new franc

The new franc is no longer so new; it came into being in 1960 and has completely superseded the so-called "old" franc except that many coins and bills marked with the old franc are still around. One new franc (NF) is equivalent to 100 old ones, so 100 *nouveaux francs* (NF) are worth 10,000 *anciens francs* (AF).

The new franc is now supreme, and everything would be easy if the old currency were retired—which it is not—and if many people who are used to dealing with the old franc would forget it and say 500 new francs instead of 50,000 francs with "old" implied but not spoken.

Perpetuating the confusion is the way sensational newspapers often try to make large amounts of money seem even larger by referring to them in old francs instead of new. A headline may read "Robbers seize 2,000,000 francs!" and then qualify this by stating somewhere that the francs are AF (old ones).

Paper currency wears out, so AF bills, especially in the smaller denominations, are becoming scarce. But coins last for a long while, so long in fact that countless sad souvenirs of the German occupation of France are still in circulation. These are the small aluminum one- or two-franc (AF) coins marked *Etat Français* instead of *République Français* on one side and—significantly—*Travail . Famille . Patrie* instead of *Liberté. Égalité. Fraternité* on the other. The Nazi invaders could not tolerate Liberty, Equality, and Fraternity, so they made their puppet Vichy government to impose the Teutonic ideas of Work, Family, and Fatherland upon their helpless French victims. There are other unpleasant symbols on these coins. A double axe replaces the head of Marianne, the symbolic representation of the French Republic, while oak leaves are substituted for the original horns of plenty. As a study in national psychology, these coins are worth a careful examination. You may want to keep a few as curiosities.

Part Two ⚜ *Places to Go*

A note for forgetful readers and for those who skip

We know we have said all this before, but we are repeating it here so you can keep it in mind before reading these regional chapters.

1. We do not attempt to give an over-all coverage of France or of any part of it. We tell you from personal experience what we think is worth seeing and advise you how to get there. Then we give a brief, impressionistic sketch of the place. For further details we recommend books and pamphlets at the end of the book.
2. We hope you can travel with leisure and savor the country as you go. For those who are pressed for time we give shortcuts—and even indicate what can be missed.
3. If you are starting out in the late winter or early spring, try to begin your journey in the south and work north. For late summer or autumn, do the opposite, You can pick up our trail anywhere along the way.
4. Consult the hotel and restaurant section in the back of the book so you can establish bases in the areas you expect to visit.
5. Review the chapter on driving in France before you start out on the road. *This is important.*

10. *Normandy*

We are starting with the southern part of Normandy only because it is a convenient area to put first. From Paris you can just as well commence your tour by going through the Château Country or head straight for Brittany. Normandy is popular with people on vacation from England and Paris because its beaches are easily reached by air, rail, or automobile. As a result, hotel and restaurant prices tend to be higher there than they are farther west or south. Yet even the most expensive resorts also have lower-priced accommodations.

We are treating the northwestern section of France in two separate parts. The North Channel Coast from Le Havre to the Belgian border is covered in Chapter 24, while the area from Rouen to Mont-Saint-Michel and the countryside south of it are dealt with here.

The long stretch of beaches from Honfleur to Cabourg (the Côte Fleurie) has many well-known seaside resorts; but the shore area from Cabourg to Mont-Saint-Michel is thinly settled.

Although this is your first opportunity to try the central-base technique we described in the Introduction (p. 13), Normandy is not the ideal place for it. For one thing, it has too high a concentration of hotels on the Côte Fleurie, and too few anywhere else except in cities like Rouen, Caen, and Lisieux. You will find that the system works better in Brittany, the Château Country, and other regions where hotel locations are more evenly distributed.

Assuming that you want to make your first base of operation on the Côte Fleurie, the hotel you will stay in should be chosen carefully. We suggest that you read about the hotels listed in the back of the book, choose one, and then make a reservation.

If you don't insist on being right on the sea, there are some excellent places in the country back of Honfleur. Cabourg, which is on the ocean, is more centrally located for making day trips to Caen, Bayeux, the invasion coast, and the interior.

You will need another base to cover the area farther west. There we suggest staying in Carteret on the Cotentin peninsula. It has a fine sandy beach, enormous sand dunes, and some fairly good hotels. From it you can go on to Coutances, Mont-Saint-Michel, and Brittany.

The interior of Normandy is farm country, fertile and rich, with gnarled old trees and ancient half-timbered buildings. There are even some small mountains in the so-called Suisse Normande west of Falaise.

Not only the coast of Normandy but much of the interior was fought over when the Nazis had to be driven out in 1944. Battles, accompanied by intensive air bombings and heavy artillery fire, went on for nearly three months. Many fine old buildings were damaged or destroyed, but most of them have been replaced or amazingly well restored.

Weather

Since Normandy is dominated by the winds that have come from southern England, its weather is likely to be—well, very much like the weather in Southampton or Brighton—cool, cloudy, and with what the British call "bright intervals." This means that clouds may suddenly mask the sun and that rain may fall. The resorts around Deauville have casinos, movie houses, and other indoor entertainment to keep their guests amused in bad weather. But there are plenty of things to do outdoors too. One of them is just to drive around and explore the Norman countryside, which is beautiful even in the rain.

England has long been closely associated with Normandy, and both were settled by fierce invaders who came from Scandinavia more than a thousand years ago. Normandy gets its name from these Northmen. Like Brittany, it remained isolated from the rest of France until fairly recent times, so its people are somewhat provincial and set in their ways, especially in the interior.

Driving from Paris to the coast

You can easily go from Paris to the coast of Normandy in one day by taking the direct route along the Seine and then heading for Pont-Audemer and the shore.

If you will allow two days for the journey, you can visit Les Andelys and Rouen. N14 runs northwest from Paris for 79 kilometers (49 miles) to a fork where D125 goes off to the left to Les Andelys, 16 kilometers (10 miles) away. You will arrive in Grand-Andely first; its twin, Petit-Andely, is on the Seine; high up above it are the white walls of the ruined Château Gaillard, which was built in 1196-1197 by Richard the Lion-Hearted to prevent the French from coming down the Seine to seize Normandy. After his death, Philippe-Auguste besieged it late in 1203. It withstood a long attack until one of the French soldiers got the ingenious idea of climbing up the latrine drains.

The Château was used for 400 years after its capture. Then

The Château Gaillard

Henry IV ordered it to be destroyed in order to break the power of the Norman barons. It served as a free stone quarry for generations.

But a good part of the building remains, especially the section around the massive donjon. There are earlier fortresses in France (Langeais is 200 years older), but the Château Gaillard is a fine example of the first French feudal castles. It is especially interesting because of the clever way its architect fitted its walls to the irregular, strategically located site.

To visit the Château, drive to the parking place on the Allée du Roi de Rome; leave your car there and go on foot up the path leading to the entrance where a guide will take over. The huge donjon faces the river; the ruined châtelet, at the other end of the plateau, marks the southern boundary of the fortified area. Some of the hollowed-out chambers in the soft rock were used as cells. In them, two queens charged with adultery were imprisoned. One of them, Marguerite de Bourgogne, was strangled here in 1314 with her own long hair.

On a sunny day, the terraces around the Château are so peaceful that one can forget the many personal tragedies that took place on these historic heights. If the ghosts of the slaughtered do return to haunt these lofty ruins, they at least have the courtesy not to appear when tourists are there.

Rouen

From these heights you can see long stretches of the Seine as it winds its way toward the sea. If you don't care to stay overnight in Les Andelys, where there is a pleasant and inexpensive hotel with an outdoor dining terrace (the Chaîne d'Or), you can drive direct to Rouen by taking N313, D126, and N14 for 39 kilometers (24 miles). Or, if you want to see more of the Seine, you can follow its right bank for miles by continuing on N313, D19, N321, and N13*Bis*. This route will bring you into Rouen along the *quais* from which you can make a right turn to reach any part of the city you wish.

Unless you are headed for a hotel, we suggest that you park your car at or near the Place du Vieux-Marché, and explore the center of the old city on foot.

It was here that Joan of Arc was tried, condemned, and

The market place where Joan of Arc was burned to death

burned at the stake on May 30, 1431. The site in the market place is marked by a monument with a low railing around it. Behind it is a statue of the nineteen-year-old martyr. And in the timbered building, against which the statue stands, is a panel bearing her plaintive words:

Saint Michel,
Sainte Catherine,
Rouen, Rouen, are you to be
my tomb; is it here
that I must die?

She was afraid of fire and begged to be beheaded instead—seven times over, she said ingenuously. But she was led to the market place and burned to death.

You will see many places associated with this young girl in the narrow strip of land that runs from Domrémy, where she was born, to Rouen, where she died. She was never outside this small section of France, but she left an indelible impression on the entire world. Her story is not legend; it is well documented and has been retold by some of our greatest writers, Mark Twain and George Bernard Shaw among them.

From the Vieux Marché walk east along the Rue du Gros Horloge, passing under the famous early sixteenth-century clock tower to visit the cathedral. It was damaged during the war but has been restored. Its crypt dates from the eleventh century, but construction of the building went on until well into the sixteenth century. Beyond it are the attractive churches of Saint-Maclou and Saint-Ouen.

Rouen was the birthplace of Pierre Corneille, Gustave Flaubert, and Jean Louis Géricault. The houses in which the first two men were born are now museums, while the Musée des Beaux-Arts has a room devoted to Géricault's paintings. Flaubert lived across the river at Canteleu-Croisset in a house which was then in the country but which is now in a heavily industrialized area.

Rouen is a big manufacturing city and the fourth largest port of France. The banks of the Seine are lined with cranes and factories, truck traffic is heavy, and unless you are interested in modern industy, you will do well to go on to the Norman beaches. Except for the expensive toll bridge at Tancarville, the

Rouen

FRENCH GOVERNMENT TOURIST OFFICE

Half-timbered construction in old Rouen

Seine can be crossed only by ferry between Rouen and the sea. We suggest that you take N840 south and then N180 west to Pont-Audemer (50 kilometers or 31 miles) along the southern shore of the Seine to Honfleur (24 kilometers or 15 miles), which is one of the most delightful small ports of France.

Honfleur

Honfleur was founded in the eleventh century. From it came some of the early explorers of Canada, Cartier and Champlain among them. It has centuries-old stone basins to provide safe mooring for barges and fishing boats. Masts, nets, all kinds of maritime gear, and colorful narrow buildings make the harbor a photographer's dream.

Some of the buildings are only one window wide; a few are seven stories high; all have slate roofs with dormers, while overhanging upper stories are common. The whole ensemble, with fishing boats and drying nets adding depth to the three-dimensional façades, shows how ancient ports grew up slowly, piece by piece, until they acquired a beauty that is lacking in our more efficient modern harbors.

Honfleur is a living maritime museum, but it is still an active port. By great good fortune it came through the Second World War unharmed.

Many nineteenth-century painters, including Corot, Courbet, Daubigny, Boudin, and Jongkind have left their impressions of the town on canvas. Some of their work can be seen in the Municipal Museum.

The streets around the harbor are lined with half-timbered and slate-shingled houses. Sainte-Catherine, which was built of oak at the end of the fifteenth century, is the largest wooden church in France. Its slate-encased bell tower is a separate building. As French churches go, Sainte-Catherine is unique. It was made of wood because it was built at a time when stonemasons were in such great demand in other parts of France that only ships' carpenters were available to construct a church for Honfleur.

On the hill west of the town is the early seventeenth-century Chapel of Notre-Dame de Grâce. Ship models hang from the ceilings there, and the walls bear votive plaques from sailors who give thanks for safe returns from perilous seas and ship-

Honfleur

wrecks encountered in voyages long ago.

The sixteenth-century stone Lieutenance, where the king's governor used to live, still stands near the ship basins. Its round corner turrets and tiled roofs add a romantic touch to a part of the town that is an almost unchanged heritage from the past.

Deauville and Trouville

The best-known resorts on the Côte Fleurie are Deauville and Trouville, which are separated by the Touques River—and by a far wider social division.

Bathing costumes—and customs—of the past were far more colorful on these famous beaches than is generally thought. Wheeled dressing-cabins were pulled out into the sea so the bather could go down a couple of steps to enter the water. What people wore then was much more imaginative than it is now. An account written in 1869 describes the bathers at

Trouville who were dressed in "the suits of motley, the harlequins, the Mephistopheles, the spiders, the grasshoppers green, and the other eccentric *costumes de bain*—culminating in a lady's dress trimmed with death's heads, and a gentleman's, of an indescribable colour, after the pattern of a trail of seaweed." Perhaps we are missing something now when large areas of bare skin, unadorned, all look pretty much alike.

Deauville. This world-renowned resort has a permanent population of only about 5000. But the season is at its height during the few weeks in July and August when the fashionable crowd arrives to attend the horse races. The big and very expensive luxury hotels, the Casino, and the theater are located behind wide lawns, gardens, and tennis courts that separate them from the beach. A broad cement walk runs along the edge of the sand with bath houses and other low wooden structures built along it. The beach is public, so you can see whatever there is to see. Girl watchers interested in comparing styles in bikinis will do well here.

Trouville. Deauville is for the international set, but its sister resort next door is middle-class French. Deauville was built in the early 1860's as a planned resort, while Trouville just grew up. It was a small fishing village when a group of artists and writers from Paris discovered it in the 1830's. Deauville owes its existence to the elegant Duc de Morny, who wanted an exclusive watering place for himself and his friends. He chose the flats at the mouth of the river so horses could be raced on level ground.

The Norman beach resorts became popular as a result of railroad-building in the 1840's and 50's, which made it possible to get there from Paris in hours instead of days.

Trouville, which is strung along the base of the hills behind its beach, is larger (population about 7000) than Deauville and is far livelier during most of the year. It has a huge outdoor swimming pool in front of the seaside Casino where its top-rated hotels are located. As usual, the less expensive ones are farther away from the water. Although one can stay in Trouville for relatively little money, its better restaurants are not cheap. Good French eating places—especially in resorts—seldom are.

Both Deauville and Trouville were literally the last refuges of French royalty. Louis-Philippe stayed in a private house in

Trouville before fleeing to England after the Revolution of 1848. And in September 1870, a few days after Napoleon III surrendered to the Germans at Sedan, his wife Eugénie escaped from Deauville with the help of an American dentist, Dr. Thomas W. Evans, who persuaded the owner of a British yacht to take her across the Channel. The weather along the Atlantic coast that night was so bad that the great new turreted battleship, H.M.S. *Captain,* which was on a trial run, turned over and sank with a loss of 473 men. By an odd coincidence, the big warship was under the command of Captain Hugh Burgoyne, a cousin of Sir John Burgoyne, the owner of the yacht that carried the Empress safely to England.

Cabourg and Dives

Nineteen kilometers (12 miles) farther west on N813 is another popular resort area that is a miniature replica of Deauville and Trouville. These smaller places, Cabourg and Dives-sur-Mer,

The beach in Cabourg

FRENCH GOVERNMENT TOURIST OFFICE

are similarly related to each other. Both sets of resorts are twin towns separated by small rivers. And Cabourg and Deauville are haughty sisters to their Cinderella twins.

Since Cabourg and Dives are located near the middle of the strip of seacoast that runs west from Honfleur to the invasion beaches of the Second World War, they are convenient places from which to explore most of Normandy. Cabourg and Dives are quieter than Deauville and Trouville and are somewhat less expensive.

Dives is old—it developed without plan or reason, as most naturally settled communities do—but Cabourg was deliberately created in the 1860's to be a fashionable beach resort. Dives-sur-Mer is no longer on the sea, for its harbor is silted up, and open water is now far away. It was from here that William the Conqueror launched his invasion of England in 1066.

Dives has a big electro-metallurgical plant far out in the marshes. Except for the Église Notre-Dame (which has a list of the men who helped William the Conqueror invade England) and an ancient wooden market building, Dives has little to attract tourists.

Cabourg is a typical French seaside resort, complete with Casino, esplanade, and numerous villas built to look like old Norman half-timbered country houses. The town is laid out in an ingenious plan. The Casino and the Grand Hotel face the water at the center of a wide half circle. From the central gardens, residential streets radiate out like the spokes of a fan.

Marcel Proust came to Cabourg in the years before the First World War to stay at the Grand Hotel. Here the young writer went through the experiences he recounts in the second part of *Remembrance of Things Past*. In the volumes entitled *Within a a Budding Grove* (*À l'Ombre des Jeunes Filles en Fleurs*), the Cabourg of that day (which Proust called Balbec) is brought to life again. It was here that Proust first met his fascinating but elusive young heroine Albertine, who was one of the band of pretty girls that bicycled through the town and roamed the beach.

Except for the omnipresent automobiles that have replaced the carriages of Proust's time, little has changed in Cabourg. The Grand Hotel is still a fashionable center, and attractive young girls still use bicycles, stroll along the esplanade, or lie in the sun.

The invasion beaches

Cabourg is the westernmost of the famous Norman pleasure beaches; beyond it is the coast where the Allied invasion of Normandy took place. The fighting began at the Orne when gliders towed by airplanes dropped British troops on the night of June 5–6, 1944 (D-Day). Their objective was to capture "Pegasus" Bridge, the key to the waterways leading to Caen.

While the huge invasion fleet was crossing the Channel, more British and Canadian paratroopers and infantrymen were dropped behind the three beaches known in code as Sword, Juno, and Gold. These stretch from the Orne River to Port-en-Bessin. The American sector begins at a point west of there and runs part of the way up the Cotentin Peninsula. Omaha Beach goes from Port-en-Bessin to the Baie des Veys, while Utah Beach is beyond that.

N814 crosses the Orne River, turns north to Riva-Bella, and then runs west for miles along the shore. Much damage was done here, but most of the buildings have now been repaired or replaced. Some of these innocent-looking summer cottages were placed on top of concrete forts to disguise them. Except for occasional war memorials or wrecked German blockhouses (a few with guns still in them), there is little evidence that thousands of men fought to the death here.

The flat shores rise gradually until they become bluffs at Arromanches, where they are high above the sea. It was here that one of the two enormous temporary harbors was built in record time just after D-Day. A storm that lasted from June 16 to 19 nearly demolished the artificial ports, but they were repaired well enough to bring in the vast numbers of men, motorized vehicles, and the tons of supplies needed to follow up the landings on the beaches. A museum in Arromanches commemorates the landings. It has models of the ingeniously designed caissons, floating docks, piers, and roadways that were towed over from England. Dioramas, photographs, and motion pictures clarify what happened on that eventful day.

Little remains now of what was for a short while the world's most active port. In clear weather, the tops of some of the caissons can be seen, and along the shore are a few that have been washed in by storms. None of the sunken ships show

Remains of the artificial Second World War port

above high tide. Rough seas and salvage crews have removed the superstructures and everything else that could be torn loose.

More permanent than these battered relics are the miltary cemeteries. The largest and most impressive is the American one at Saint-Laurent overlooking heavily fought-over Omaha Beach. Here 9385 white marble markers indicate the burial places of some of the 25,000 American soldiers who died in Normandy. Near the cemetery is a monument to the men of the 5th Engineer Special Brigade who landed here to clear a way for the troops.

This area has a high concentration of battles. Only two miles south of Saint-Laurent is Formigny, a history-making affair in which cannon enabled 4000 French soldiers to rout 7000 English in 1450. The casualties with the new weapon were startling: 5600 English to just 12 French.

Beyond Saint-Laurent, N814 runs along the edge of the sea to Vierville. This stretch of beach saw some of the worst of the fighting on D-Day. A marker shows where the first temporary American military burial place on the Normandy beaches was located.

And here is the Pointe de Hoc where the Nazis were supposed to have had a battery of six big guns that could pour down a heavy fire at the troops landing on both Omaha and Utah Beach. This battery had to be taken, and it was, against almost impossible odds, by American Rangers who climbed the cliffs with ropes and scaling ladders. When the Germans were finally killed or driven out of the blockhouses, no cannon were found in them. Pointe de Hoc still shows the effect of concentrated naval gunfire; hundreds of big shells were lobbed up there before the little band of Rangers went in to do their deadly work. The French have left this battleground untouched for future generations to see. The remains of the reinforced concrete blockhouses, blasted apart by high explosives, are almost hidden by the weeds that have grown up around them.

Utah Beach and Sainte-Mère-Église

Beyond the Pointe de Hoc and Grandcamp, N814 turns south to join N13 which goes around the Baie des Veys. N13D branches off to Utah Beach. The land here is low and swampy

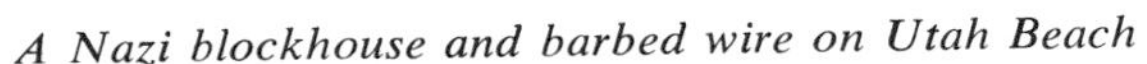

A Nazi blockhouse and barbed wire on Utah Beach

Sainte-Mère-Église

with a series of causeways leading to D421, a road that runs along the shore behind the sand dunes.

Utah Beach is flat and wide and deserted. Only the partly destroyed Nazi blockhouses half hidden in the dunes are reminders of what took place there. In some places you can see where American rifle bullets hit. Rusted strands of German barbed wire can be found, but the soft sand has swallowed up most of the many tons of metal that landed here.

There is a small museum at Sainte-Marie-du-Mont with tanks and landing barges standing outside it. Below it is a brightly colored marker which is the first of many that indicate the route the American Army took to reach the German border.

Several narrow paved roads run back from the beach to rejoin N13, on which Sainte-Mère-Église is located. This now famous church was the center of the first American air drop in this sector. The placid-looking building, surrounded by a wide stretch of open ground, was the scene of great drama durin the night of June 5—6. One man's parachute got caught on the steeple, and he hung there while the battle raged around him. Nearby is a museum built by the French to commemorate the American landing. Its parachute-shaped roof shelters one of the gliders and many relics of that memorable night.

The Cotentin peninsula

From here D15 runs through a green wilderness that was a battleground in 1944. It goes on to Carteret on the west coast of the Cotentin peninsula. This little-visited resort has some of the finest sand beaches in northern France. Enormous dunes line the shore, but there are paved roads behind them. An excursion boat goes to the island of Jersey when the tide is right.

From Carteret you can explore the entire peninsula. The northern tip, west of Cherbourg, is wild, barren, and treeless. Cherbourg itself is a war-wrecked, newly rebuilt commercial port like Le Havre and of little interest to tourists.

Coutances, 51 kilometers (32 miles) south of Carteret on N503, N800, and D2, has an extraordinarily large and beautiful cathedral with its façade pock-marked by aerial bombs. This is no ordinary church. Vauban, Louis XIV's noted military engineer, spent hours examining it. Viollet-le-Duc and Ruskin paid high tribute to it, and Henry Adams in *Mont-Saint-Michel and Chartres,* after praising its massive central tower, said: "No other cathedral in France or in Europe has an interior more refined . . . more tender—or more carefully studied." Another authority has called it "one of the most graceful churches of the First Pointed Age in France." Work on it began before the Norman invasion of England in 1066.

Only a few people come to see this impressive building, probably because it is in such a remote area. It stands neglected in a small town where it dominates the landscape and the sea for miles around.

Farther south on N171 (29 kilometers or 18 miles) are Granville and Donville-les-Bains. The latter is a typical beach resort, but Granville is an interesting old town situated on a jagged peninsula, which made it easy to defend against a land attack.

As you drive from Granville to Avranches (26 kilometers or 16 miles) you will occasionally get glimpses of a tall spire apparently rising from the sea. This is Mont-Saint-Michel.

From the Jardin des Plantes, on the west side of Avranches, you can get a good view of it.

Avranches is noted for two things far separated in time. It was here in 1172 that Henry II of England did penance for his responsibility for the murder of Thomas à Becket. The church in which his punishment took place was destroyed during the Revolution, but the site, called La Plate-Forme, is marked. And it was from Avranches in 1944 that General George Patton launched his lightning attack on the Nazis. The soil on which his monument stands—and the trees around it—were brought from America.

The interior of the cathedral of Coutances
FRENCH GOVERNMENT TOURIST OFFICE

Mont-Saint-Michel

South of Avranches the road runs along the marshy coast with Mont-Saint-Michel clearly in sight. This world-famous shrine is built on a conical upthrust of rock that stands high above the water and the low-lying land. It is best seen at a distance and it a truly thrilling sight. A long causeway leads out to it, and cars are parked on the hard sand near the entrance. There is a charge for parking, as there is for nearly everything else in this overpublicized, sadly commercialized, once-wonderful place. The magic of the distant view vanishes when you enter the gates because the narrow, winding, uphill streets are lined with souvenir shops and eating places. Even Mère Poulard's restaurant, which was famous for its hospitality as well as for its omelettes, now hurriedly turns out quantity-produced egg dishes for a stiff price.

During the summer the street is so jammed with people that it is like a subway in rush hour. (Sundays are impossible.) After you have struggled your way up to the entrance of the Abbey, you may have to wait for a long while to be admitted to the big anteroom where you buy a ticket and then may have to wait again for a guide to take a large group of tourists through. If you must have an English-speaking guide, you will probably wait even longer.

Each guide moves his party along rapidly in order to make room for the next group. Unless you stand close to yours, you will not be able to hear what he is saying. The tour of Mont-Saint-Michel is one of the things they do not do well in France.

This is a shame, for the Mount deserves all the praise that generations of writers, art critics, and commentators have lavished on it. It is unfortunate that population pressure, increased travel, and the desire to make money by selling tourist trinkets have made it rather unpleasant to visit under ordinary circumstances.

There is only one way to see Mont-Saint-Michel properly and that is to stay overnight. The hotels are not particularly good, but you will be able to examine everything at your leisure and watch the tides rush over the enormous stretches of sand. If you want to see the tides at their best, plan your visit to co-

FRENCH GOVERNMENT TOURIST OFFICE

Mont-Saint-Michel

incide with the full or new moon. And at any time be sure to be among the first visitors to the Abbey, which opens at 9 A.M.

Before you go there, read up on this historic group of buildings perched high on a rock, for you will have little time to appreciate them when a harassed guide takes you through. Henry Adams' two essays, "Saint Michiel de la Mer del Peril" and "The Merveille" explain much but not enough. Mont-Saint-Michel is exceedingly complicated—and not only as architecture. So you must prepare yourself in advance for this remarkable relic of the Middle Ages. Then, when you know what to expect, the complexities of the superimposed structures, which are intricately fitted together in a glorious three-dimensional puzzle that took centuries to put together, may make some kind of sense.

Richard I, Duke of Normandy, founded a Benedictine Abbey here in 966, so Mont-Saint-Michel has just celebrated its 1000th anniversary. Its enormous popularity as a tourist attraction will undoubtedly increase. With 600,000 visitors coming there each year it already ranks third in France as a place that must not be missed, with only the much more easily reached Eiffel Tower and Versailles surpassing it. Perhaps the incongruous souvenir shops will someday be banished to the mainland so the ancient buildings on Mont-Saint-Michel can be restored to the quiet dignity they once had—and should have again.

The interior

You can visit the interior of Normandy by taking day trips from the coast, by making a circular tour of it, or by stopping off along the way if you drive direct from Paris to Brittany.

Characteristic of certain parts of it are the heavily wooded, densely undergrown areas called *bocage*. Those who have driven in England may have some idea of what *bocage* implies, but there is nothing like it in America. The country is too new for that, and it takes centuries of work to establish the elaborate barriers typical of such areas. The word itself merely means a small wood that is not a natural forest but part of a farm. But in Normandy *bocage* is almost inevitably accompanied by impenetrable hedges built on top of low stone walls that have been covered by soil and vegetation. These are very useful as fences, and they provide shade for cattle, but driving along them is like going down a road hung with green curtains on both sides. Soldiers who were in the battle for Normandy will remember that these hedges acted as effective tank barriers until a clever mechanic invented a simple cutting device to let the trapped vehicles get through.

Intensive aerial bombardment and heavy shelling were a sadly necessary part of the grim campaign that followed the battle for the Normandy beaches. More than 200,000 buildings were destroyed, whole villages disappeared, and entire sections of cities were reduced to rubble. During this relentless holocaust, which went on all through the summer of 1944, some 80,000 Norman civilians were casualties.

Sturdily constructed old churches and castles stood up amazingly well under the devastating rain of high explosives. Their thick stone walls, built to defy time and the elements, were pierced, breeched, and sometimes shattered, but they were seldom knocked down. As a result, most of the more important historic monuments in Normandy still remain and have been so skilfully repaired that it is hard to believe that they went through a modern war. Even the cathedral at Saint-Lô, which was so terribly battered that it was thought that it could never be restored, is now being rebuilt.

Evreux and Lisieux

If you are driving west from Paris you can visit Evreux and Lisieux on the way. N13 passes through them and then goes on to Caen and Bayeux.

Evreux, which has been largely rebuilt since the war, is now a better place to live in than it was in the 1930's when the little river Iton was used as a sewer. Today the river's clear waters flow past public flower gardens and new houses. The cathedral survived the bombing and is well preserved. We visited it during a storm and watched its gargoyles dutifully spit rain-water away from the building to prevent its stone carvings from being eroded.

The church of Saint-Taurin, which is nearer to the middle of town, has a thirteenth-century silver-gilt reliquary that is a masterpiece of the goldsmith's art as it was practised during the Middle Ages.

Lisieux lost practically all its old houses during the war, but its cathedral and its modern (1937) Sainte-Thérèse Basilica escaped serious damage. Lisieux, like Lourdes, is a place of pilgrimage devoted to the memory of a young nine-teenth-century girl. Thérèse Martin was born in 1873 at Alençon only six years before the death of Bernadette of Lourdes. Thérèse grew up in Lisieux. Devoutly religious and well able to express herself in writing, she died at the age of 24 and was canonized in 1925. She is one of the two Carmelite saints in Victoria Sackville-West's novel *The Eagle and the Dove* (1943).

The cathedral (Saint-Pierre) has a Lady Chapel built by Pierre Cauchon, the former Bishop of Beauvais, who pro-nounced the death sentence upon Joan of Arc. The people of Beauvais refused to let him return to their city, so he became the Bishop of Lisieux. It is said that he built the Lady Chapel as an act of penance for what he had done. The men of his time, however, were apparently not satisfied that he had ab-solved himself, for he was excommunicated after his death, and his remains were thrown into a sewer. Joan's ashes had been cast into the Seine, so no physical trace of the Maid or her relentless persecutor exists.

FRENCH GOVERNMENT TOURIST OFFICE

Caen: the Abbaye aux Dames

Caen

Caen is closely associated with William the Conqueror. He and his wife built its major churches, two important abbeys, and the huge Château.

The city had to be attacked when the Nazis holed up there after being driven out of their defenses along the coast. During the summer of 1944, thousands of planes bombed the area, utterly destroying many of the old half-timbered houses. But as usual, the more solidly built structures, such as the bigger churches, the two abbeys, and the massive Château withstood the rain of fire. Caen has been intelligently restored with many well-designed modern buildings, fountains, and public squares. It has several good restaurants where you can get the world-renowned dish, *tripes à la mode de Caen.*

The men's abbey was built by William the Conqueror, while his wife, Matilda, was responsible for the women's abbey. Since construction began on both of them before 1066, they are 900 years old—a great age for buildings that have been in constant use. They are big and impressive and have stood up amazingly well through centuries of revolution, religious and political wars, and inclement weather.

The Conqueror was buried in his abbey. A plaque marks the spot, but his bones were scattered during the Revolution, so that no tangible remains exist.

Saint-Pierre is later than the two abbeys (fourteenth-century); its richly decorated exterior makes it a notable sight even though it was damaged by aerial bombs. The Château dominates the center of the city and stands between the men's and women's abbeys.

Bayeux

Bayeux is known throughout the world for its famous tapestry, which depicts 58 scenes in the Norman conquest of England in 1066. Actually it is not a tapestry at all, but a long narrow strip of white linen on which are sewed cut-out pieces of colored cloth to form spirited figures of men and horses, ships, and incidents of battle. It runs for 230 feet around a large room in the Musée de la Tapisserie near the cathedral. It is worth careful study, for it is a contemporary pictorial record that tells more about the invasion of England than most written accounts do. Its great length made it possible to drape the memorial cloth around the nave of the cathedral on ceremonial occasions. It is also very beautiful, and is a valid document that can be admired for its colorful design and fine needlework as well as for its historical importance.

This remarkable chronicle of war came near to being destroyed during the Revolution when it was about to be used as a cover for a military wagon. It was saved only because a townsman offered to supply a heavier piece of fabric in exchange for it. Napoleon was more appreciative; he had it displayed in the Louvre—not for its beauty but as a propaganda device at the time he was planning to invade England.

Across the way from the museum is the Bayeux cathedral, which was built during William the Conqueror's lifetime. Over the centuries it has withstood a number of fires, several attempts to destroy it, and the natural ravages of time. As a result it is not all of one piece—few old churches are—but its soaring arches and spires still reflect the aspirations of the Middle Ages. The tympanum over the south porch describes the career of Thomas à Becket, who had close ties with both England and France.

Since Bayeux came through the war almost undamaged, it still has many half-timbered old houses. Some of the best of them are on the Rue Bourbesneur.

Falaise

Deeper in the interior and 34 kilometers (21 miles) south of Caen is the little town of Falaise where William the Conqueror was born in 1027 as the illegitimate son of a tanner's daughter named Arlette.

Falaise, although badly damaged in 1944, has the castle in which the Conqueror was born and the fountain at which his father, the Duke of Normandy, cast lustful eyes at the beautiful Arlette while she was washing her family's clothes there. An equestrian statue of the man who made the date 1066 memorable stands unscathed by the intense fire of the battle for the town that became the last pocket of Nazi resistance in Normandy.

South of Falaise is Argentan with two fine old churches, both of which were damaged in the war. The whole area around it was a battleground during the struggle for the Mortain-Falaise pocket. This quiet town's previous encounter with history took place in 1170, when Henry II uttered the fatal words: "Who will avenge me of this turbulent priest?" His thoughtless remark sent four eager murderers to Canterbury to slay Thomas à Becket.

Horse country

Thirteen kilometers (8 miles) east of Argentan is the Haras du Pin, one of the French government's 22 national stud farms for improving the breed of horses.

The enormous Percherons and other huge stallions that live in luxury in the Haras du Pin's beautifully kept 250-year-old stables may seem as strange—and almost as big—as elephants to the average city-dweller.

This *haras* was founded in Louis XIV's time and was designed by his noted architect, J. H. Mansart. There is no charge for admission, but you are expected to tip the attendant who shows you around. People who are old enough to have grown up with horses will have a holiday here. Even the odor of the stables brings back remembered yesterdays.

A few miles to the southeast of the Haras du Pin is Mortagne and the Perche country that gave the giant horses their name. France has many spas where numerous hotels of all grades are clustered around the thermal establishment. Some of them are a bit too clinical to suit healthy travelers. But a few are just quiet country places where you can have a restful vacation for almost any price you want to pay.

Bagnoles-de l'Orne is a good example of such a spa. It is 39 kilometers (24 miles) west of Argentan and is located in forest country. Some of the little hotels located outside the town are great bargains.

Food in Normandy

Mont-Saint-Michel marks the western end of Normany; beyond it is Brittany. The two have some things in common, but Normandy is fertile and green whereas much of Brittany is rocky and bare. Brittany's best food comes from the sea. Normandy has good seafood too, but it depends largely on the soil for sustenance.

The salt marshes along the edge of the sea are used as grazing grounds for flocks of sheep that produce the justly famous *pré-salé* lamb with its natural salty flavor. But the great specialties of Normandy are its dairy products. Its lush meadows feed the cows that give the milk and cream from which butter and the famous Camembert, Pont-l'Évêque, Livarot, and Neufchâtel cheeses are made.

Fat hogs supply meat for the *charcuteries* of France, which specialize in all kinds of pork products—sausages, *pâtés,* hams, and other delicacies. From the Norman beef herds come steaks and the tripe which is cooked *à la mode de Caen* or *à la mode de la Ferté-Macé.*

The ocean waters around Normandy supply all kinds of fish, lobsters, shrimps, and the delicious dark purple crabs locally called *poupards* (or *pouparts*). This section is the home of *moules à la marinière* which are now served everywhere, but Norman cooks seem to know best how to prepare the mussels from their own waters. Scallops, too, are a specialty of the region. Not only *coquilles Saint-Jacques* but *coquilles à la Normande* are made from these tasty little shellfish.

Since Normandy does not have the long hours of sunlight needed for growing grapes, it produces no wine. But its climate is ideal for apples. Cider, both soft and hard, is the local drink, and from it is distilled smooth-tasting but powerful Calvados (applejack). A hearty Norman eater will take a glass of this halfway through his meal to fill up *le trou Normand* and restore his appetite which may have been dulled by too much good food.

Since you can eat so well in Normandy, you will need exercise to keep your weight down, but you can get that too. The swimming is good, and you can play tennis or golf, go riding, or try your hand at karting on a course with bales of straw to keep the sputtering little gasoline-powered cars from going off the pavement. There are plenty of things to do besides eating, although a superb Norman dinner can make your stay in this bountiful province a gastronomic treat.

11. *Brittany*

Brittany is a huge peninsula jutting far out into the Atlantic. Its ancient mountains have been worn down to stumps, so its highest point has an altitude of only about 1300 feet. Its shores are indented with numerous little bays and narrow inlets, while curiously shaped rock formations are to be found almost everywhere. Since roads crisscross the land in all directions, it is not hard to get around.

To see Brittany properly you will need at least three bases, one in the north, where we recommend the beach resort of Perros-Guirec; one in the west, where you can stay in Huelgoat, which is inland, or Morgat or Sainte-Anne-la-Palud, both on the coast; and, in the south, Carnac, which is also on the shore. All the coastal places have fine sandy beaches. Naturally, there are plenty of other possible bases. Near the south coast, but not on it, is La Forêt-Fouesnant with one of the most beautiful and luxurious hotels in Brittany. If you want a big, fairly plush beach resort with lots of hotels, La Baule, on the eastern part of the south coast, is the place for you. Incidentally, the tides in Brittany, like those in Normandy, run high.

Aside from its beaches, Brittany's greatest attractions are its justly celebrated outdoor religious statue groups, the Calvaries, which are mostly in the west; its remarkable megaliths, which are almost everywhere but which are concentrated around Carnac; and its huge, sea-sculptured pink rocks near Perros-Guirec. Associated with the Calvaries are fine old churches, sacred fountains, and the annual *pardons* at which you can see the traditional Breton costumes.

We have been in Brittany many times and have discovered new and exciting things on every visit. It is supposed to be rainy there, but we have had lots of sunny weather in the summer months. The south coast, incidentally, has the best weather.

If you can spend only a short time in Brittany, we suggest that you stay in Carnac and make day trips from there.

A land of traditions

Only 80 years ago a writer could say of Brittany:

> The peasantry are almost as wild as their country, excessively quaint in their costume, wearing broad-brimmed hats and flowing hair, and in some districts trunk hose . . . of the 16th century; in others wrapped up in goatskins in winter . . . a costume which was handed down from their ancestors. They are usually spare and wiry in their persons but strong, active, and hardy; coarse-featured, squalid in their habitations, rude and unskilful in their agriculture. They are almost unchanged in their manners, customs, and habits; modern innovation has not entirely rubbed off the rust of long-continued habit; old legends and superstitions still retain their hold on the popular mind. They present a curious picture of a primitive state of society; and if a century behind their neighbours in what is called improvements, they are at least not corrupted by revolutions and commotions. In no part of France are the people, both of upper and lower orders, more observant of their religious duties, of festivals, fasts, &c.; nowhere are the churches so thronged. . . . The indescribable forms of many of the caps worn by the Bretonnes are worth remarking. Both Norman and Breton caps are pleasing auxiliaries to the scenery, which they enliven by their snowy whiteness. Old point lace is not infrequently discerned on peasant heads, and these curious and costly "coiffures" sometimes adorn the brows of more than one generation in turn.

A generation later in 1910 the *Encyclopædia Britannica* (eleventh edition) told its readers that in Brittany "witchcraft and the influence of fairies are still often believed in."

This long-backward province has become part of the modern world since then (France's experimental space-age telecommunications station is located there), yet many of the old customs linger on. In fact, there is an active movement to preserve the Breton language, folk songs, and colorful costumes. You can still see women wearing lace caps while they do housework, and you can watch traditionally dressed teenagers dance in the streets to the tune of bagpipes (*binious*) if you are lucky enough to be on hand at the right time. Nowhere else in France are you likely to see the ways of the past continue into the present as you are here.

In some of the more remote areas life is still quite primitive. A narrow dead-end road leads into a tiny village where thatched-roof stone houses, all of the same pattern, cluster closely together. In places where the winter winds are strong, there are no windows on the side from which the cold blasts come. On some farms, cattle and people live under the same roof, although seldom in the same room as they used to.

Wooden shoes are fairly common, for Brittany usually has rapidly changing climate with sun one moment and rain the next. The clouds, piled up in great masses, add to the beauty of an already photogenic landscape.

The eastern half of the peninsula is called High Brittany (*Haute Bretagne*), the western is low Brittany (*Basse Bretagne*). The east is more modern, more industrialized, and more urbanized.

A Breton farmhouse

The west is more primitive, nearer to the soil and the sea, and more like what we think of when we vizualize Brittany as a land of colorful costumes, thatched roofs, and fishing villages. It, too, is changing, but at a slower rate.

Brittany has many prehistoric remains and tangible reminders of the Roman occupation, but most of the ancestors of its present-day inhabitants arrived in the fifth century A.D. when the Celts fled from the British Isles to escape the Anglo-Saxons who were invading their country. The Breton language, as it is spoken today, is so much like Welsh that the two people can understand each other—with some difficulty—when they speak their native tongues.

Breton place names

The roots of some of the Breton place names show their Celtic origins:

guic, gui = town; as in Guimiliau
goat = wood (also *goët, hoët,* or *coat*); as in Huelgoat (high wood) and Penhoët (end of the woods)
ker = house or village; one of the commonest prefixes in Brittany
lan = church, enclosure, or consecrated land (also *lann, lam*); as in Langoat (church in the woods)
loc = hermitage or holy place; as in Locmariaquer (holy place of Mary)
palud = marsh; as in Sainte-Anne-la-Palud
pen = head or point; as in Penmarc'h
plou = parish, village, or tribe (also *plu, ploe, pleu, plo, pley, or plu*); as in Plounévez (the new parish), Pleumeur (the big parish), Ploudiry (parish in the oaks)
tre = place, homestead, subdivision of a parish, or a tiny village (also *tré, tref*); as in Trégastel, Trévezel
trou = valley (also *tro, traou*)

Before the Celts arrived, the coastal sections were called Armor, "the land near the sea," while the interior was named Argoat. The root given above shows that this means "the land of the woods." Armorica is the ancient name for all the country between the Seine and the Loire, which includes part of Normandy.

This great stretch of land on the southern side of the English Channel has close ties to the British Isles. Since it is equally popular with the French, who can get there easily from Paris and the big cities of the North, Brittany tends to be crowded in summer. And it does not have as many accommodations as its natural beauty and fine beaches deserve. The more attractive hotels have all their rooms booked up long in advance for the entire month of August. Some of the reservations are made a year ahead by guests who return every summer.

Mont-Dol

When you leave Mont-Saint-Michel and head west, you have a chance to see the celebrated Mount's little-known twin, Mont-Dol. This is another granitic upthrust, but it is inland and not so high as its more famous brother. Yet it was once an island like Mont-Saint-Michel.

To reach Mont-Dol's summit you drive up a narrow, winding, steep, but very short road, which looks more difficult than it actually is. On top are a few small farms, a windmill, a small chapel, and a grove of huge chestnut trees. We had lunch under these trees and fed our surplus bread to the ducks in the tiny pond nearby.

The bones of many extinct animals have been found here, and the numerous half-buried stone walls and foundations show that the place has been inhabited since earliest times. Legend says that Saint Michael was engaged in a terrible battle with the Devil on Mont-Dol. A hollow in one of the rocks is supposed to be the Saint's footstep.

There is a good view over the wide marshes, which are much less extensive than they were centuries ago because an unceasing effort is made to reclaim land from the sea.

Saint-Malo, Dinard, and Dinan

Going west from Mont-Dol you can take the longer route by way of N176 and then, at Dinan, turn north on N166 to Dinard for a total of 48 kilometers (30 miles), or you can drive directly on D4 for 24 kilometers (15 miles) to Saint-Malo. From Saint-Malo you will have to cross the Rance on one of the frequent little car ferries that go to Dinard.

Saint-Malo is a walled town which for many centuries was the headquarters of daring corsairs who were sometimes licensed by the king to operate as privateers against the ships of countries with which France was at war. But it outgrew its piratical origins and became a respectable seaport.

The Rance is a long, narrow estuary lying in a drowned valley with steep sides. The range of the tides here is so great that enormous quanties of sea water rush in and out twice a day. Docks and landing stages have been ingeniously adapted to permit boats and ships to take on or discharge passengers, automobiles, and cargo at any phase of the extreme tides. This rapid change in the height of water is to be used to supply power from a big tidal basin called a *marémotrice* where giant turbines will turn electric generators.

Saint-Malo was heavily bombarded by American guns and planes in August 1944 in order to drive out the Nazi troops that were holding the fortified port. A marvelous job of reconstruction has been done, and the old town now looks as if the broken pieces had been picked up, made whole, and then put back together again. The narrow streets, which always seem crowded, should be visited on foot rather than by car.

There is much to see in Saint-Malo: the castle and its historical museums, the ancient ramparts, and the cathedral, which is still under restoration from extensive war damage. The romantic poet Chateaubriand was born at Saint-Malo in 1768 and was buried there in 1848. A causeway, which is covered by water at high tide, leads to his tomb on the Île du Grand Bé.

Dinard, on the western side of the Rance, is a favorite beach resort for British tourists who concentrate there so thickly that accommodations—even high-priced ones—may be difficult to get. Dinan, to the south, is another town that is popular with English people, even though it doesn't have a beach. But it has good places to walk, for the promenades along the ramparts lead around the entire city. The Jardin Anglais behind Saint-Sauveur is where such walks usually begin or end. There is a fine view over the Rance from the broad terrace.

The Saint-Malo-Dinard-Dinan triangle is likely to be crowded and is always rather expensive. If you will drive 143 kilometers (89 miles) west from Dinard on N168 and N786, you can stay in Perros-Guirec which has two sandy beaches, spectacular scenery along the shores near it, and many good hotels, some of them overlooking the sea.

On the way along the so-called Emerald Coast it is worth making a short detour on D16 and D16A at Saint-Aide (west of Matignon) to see Fort la Latte, which is an almost untouched medieval walled stronghold built on a small promontory (actually two small islands linked by drawbridges). It has been used as a setting for motion pictures, and some of the wooden catapults and other hand-operated wooden machines of war that were built as props are still in place. And there is a genuine old and very well-preserved brick oven for heating cannon balls red hot so they could be hurled at attacking ships to set them on fire.

At the end of the peninsula from which this fort projects is Cap Fréhel where high purplish cliffs rise abruptly from the sea. Gigantic rock masses that have split off from the mainland are densely populated by seabirds that nest here.

A few miles farther along the coast is Sables-d'Or-les-Pins, a small but attractive beach resort.

The Pink Granite Coast

At Saint-Brieuc (the "c" is silent) N786 leads to the Pink Granite Coast through Paimpol, Lézardrieux, and Tréguier and then to a junction with D6 which goes to Perros-Guirec. Paimpol was the setting for Pierre Loti's novel *Pêcheur d'Islande* (1886) about the fishing fleets that went to Iceland. Tréguier was the birthplace of Ernest Renan. Its Cathédrale Saint-Tugdual, with two square towers and unusually wide Gothic windows, has a fifteenth-century cloister.

Perros-Guirec is a lively resort with a Casino, a sailing school, and various kinds of indoor and outdoor entertainment. It is a good center from which you can make short expeditions to the interesting areas described below. And there are boat trips to the nearby islands. If you look carefully you will see that the pleasant beaches are dominated by massive Nazi blockhouses built to repel a possible invasion from England.

Route 786D follows the coast from Perros-Guirec to Lannion, which has a wide stone staircase that serves as a street. This part of Brittany is noted for some of the most strangely formed rocks to be seen anywhere in the world. Huge reddish-colored boulders, many of them the size of a house, have been tossed around and carved by the sea into all sorts of grotesque shapes, some of which resemble animals, fish, or human beings. Often one gigantic rock is perched precariously on top of another. This is a fascinating area to explore and photograph.

At Ploumanac'h, tremendous piles of pink rocks that look like castles rise from the sea. Children play among the massive stones along the shore and paddle in shallow water on the numerous beaches. One of the children's favorites is the Plage de Saint-Guirec. There the spot where the Saint landed in the sixth century is marked by a small stone oratory that is partly inundated when a very high tide comes in. A stone statue has replaced an earlier wooden one in which the girls from the neighborhood used to stick pins in order to induce the marriage-blessing Saint to find husbands for them.

The Trégastel peninsula is a fairyland of strange sea-shaped rocks and prehistoric menhirs and dolmens. It also has a great pile of enormous boulders with natural caves under them that have been inhabited since earliest times. The Nazis drove out the fishermen living in them and used the shelters for storing ammunition. They now house a small museum with all sorts of odds and ends from the neighborhood. On top of the rock pile is a crudely fashioned modern cement figure of God.

The calf's head

The old man

Perros-Guirec

The Christianized menhir near Saint-Duzec-en-Ploumeur

The old and the new at the telecommunications center, Pleumeur-Bodou

Along the back roads are many prehistoric megaliths in unexpected places. We remember seeing a dolmen used as a cattle shed. Standing alone on D21 near Saint-Duzec-en-Pleumeur is a large menhir that was Christianized in the seventeenth century by having a stone cross put on top and a number of mystic symbols cut into one side. (See page 191 for definition of megaliths.)

Farther east on the same road, at Pleumeur-Bodou, is an enormous white plastic sphere that houses the equipment of the French government's Telecommunications Center. It is an exact duplicate of the American station at Andover, Maine. These two ultramodern installations handled the first transatlantic transmission of television images when they were relayed by Telstar on July 11, 1962.

Morlaix and beyond

West of here the shore is lined with one small beach resort after another. If you turn northwest at Lanmeur on D78 to explore the rocky coast north of it, at Primel-Trégastel you can see a very white, very small seamen's chapel perched on top of a stony mound. Inside is a large ship model hanging from the ceiling. And down below, carefully hidden, is a Nazi coastal fort. Its builders evidently chose the site because they thought that invaders would not fire on a church.

Seafood abounds in this area. You can visit lobster pounds (*viviers*) and other places where shellfish is kept before being shipped.

If you continue toward the west, you must eventually come to Morlaix, because it is only there that you can get past the long estuary that runs in for miles from the sea. A railroad bridge on high arches takes trains across. Down below it is the town, with many exceedingly old houses on its narrow streets.

Here you can drive south to the interior town of Huelgoat (Hwelgat), go on to the western coast of Brittany, or turn north along the estuary to visit Saint-Pol-de-Léon and Roscoff (28 kilometers or 17 miles) on the shore.

Saint-Pol-de-Léon is noted for its two big churches, the Kreisker Chapel with its elaborate belfry, and the former cathedral. In the latter building are four shelves containing nearly 50 small wooden boxes shaped like chapels. Each one, neatly labeled and dated from 1552 to 1864, has a peephole so you can look in to see the skull of a local notable. These people were not beheaded. They died and were properly buried; then, after some years, their skeletons were dug up to make room in the graveyard and were stored for a while in an ossuary, while their skulls were given permanent places of honor in the cathedral.

One of these ossuaries—no longer used as such—can be seen in front of the church in nearby Roscoff. The façade, incidentally, has several bas-reliefs of sixteenth-century ships.

Roscoff also has an important oceanographic center, where the Charles Pérez Aquarium is open to the public. The seashore here is studded with rocks, and the flat beaches are covered with water that comes in from a great distance when the tide rises.

This part of Brittany is almost unknown to tourists from abroad, yet it is exceedingly beautiful in its own way. If you like to roam around little-visited territory, try this area. You will find plenty of reasonably good hotels in Roscoff, but there are no luxury establishments along the northern coast once you leave Dinard. Perros-Guirec's best hotels cost about half of what

Dinard's top hotel charges. West of Perros-Guirec, prices are even lower. Huelgoat, in the interior, is another inexpensive place in which to stay. And Huelgoat is a centrally located town from which you can visit the justly celebrated Breton Calvaries.

If you are coming south on D9, D42, and D14 from Morlaix you can see Plougonven on the way. This is fairly small and compact as Calvaries go, but it has some good sculptured figures.

Starting out from Huelgoat you can make exploratory trips to a score or more of places where old churches, ossuaries, sacred fountains, archways, and Calvaries express the essence of the Breton spirit in carved granite. And along the roads are literally thousands of stone crosses with figures carved on them. There

The Plougonven calvary

were more than 5000 of these at one time, but imperishable as they seem to be, some were destroyed during the French Revolution when so much religious art was smashed, while more was bombed during the Second World War.

The Calvaries

The Calvaries date from about 1450 to 1650. Weather and time have given them a mottled surface that is overlaid with lichens in subtle shades of green. Although Webster defines a Calvary as "a representation in the open air . . . of the Crucifixion, consisting of three crosses with the figures of Christ and the Thieves, often life-sized, and sometimes surrounded by figures of others present at the Crucifixion," some of the Calvaries also depict other scenes from the Saviour's life. They do so because one of their primary purposes was to serve as illustrations when

AFTER QUEFFÉLEC

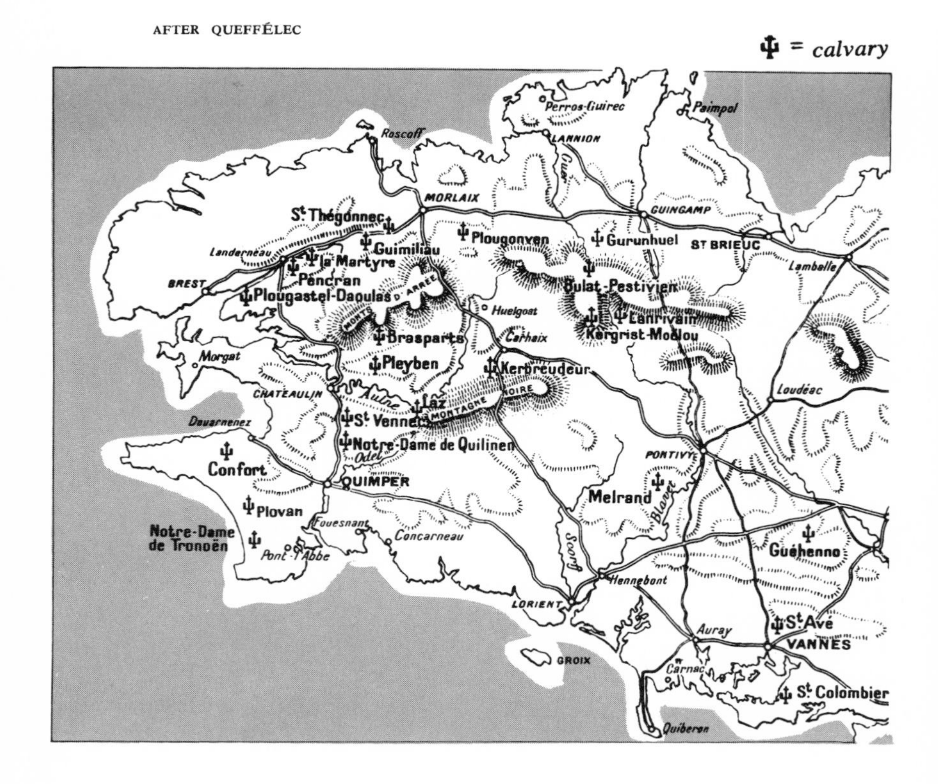

the local priest wanted to instruct peasants who could neither read nor write.

These touching and vividly imaginative figures were painted with bright colors when they were first made. Most ancient sculpture was. Traces of pigment can still be found on the representations of Egyptian and Greek gods and even on the incredibly old prehistoric animal reliefs of Périgord. But we, who have inherited only the washed-out, faded, and weather-worn remains of these once brilliantly painted statues, tend to think that they always were as colorless as they now are.

The outstanding Calvaries, with three or four exceptions, are in western Brittany. The map shows how you can go from one to another in a relatively short time. You can make a high-spot tour in a day or so, or you can give these remarkable groups of figures the attention they deserve.

Most of the sculptors who made them were untutored, untraveled stonemasons who undoubtedly learned a great deal from studying each other's work. In this way a fairly uniform style evolved although no two Calvaries are exactly alike. Rivalry between towns helped to encourage this religious art, for when village A did something fine, village B wanted to outdo it. Then village C, of course, had to outdo them both.

As a result, Brittany is rich not only in Calvaries but in beautifully decorated churches with finely carved altarpieces and pulpits. Figures of all kinds, some of them amusingly grotesque, peer out of nooks and crannies, while grinning gargoyles serve the practical purpose of draining the roofs.

We suggest that people who have time to see only the most impressive Calvaries concentrate on Plougonven, Saint-Thégonnec, Guimiliau, Plougastel-Daoulas, and Pleyben. You can visit others along the way. La Martyre and Pencran are easily reached. And La Martyre has a notable caryatid in its ossuary. The Calvary at Brasparts is worth a special trip to see the *Pieta* that Gauguin used as a subject in his painting entitled *"Calvaire-*1899," now in the Musée Royal des Beaux-Arts in Brussels.

Also on this route is the Roc'h Trévézel (near the junction of N164 and N785), where a splintered upthrust of tilted slate runs along a ridge that is only the remains of what was a great mountain before millions of years of erosion wore it down to its present size. There is a fine view from this isolated rock.

Details of various calvaries

Other religious art

Associated with the churches and their Calvaries are arches of triumph and ossuaries. There are also sacred fountains which may or may not be near a church.

Saint-Thégonnec has a very large and elaborately decorated arch of triumph, while Guimiliau (with 200 figures on its Calvary), Pleyben, and Sizun have simpler ones.

Some of the ossuaries, which are no longer used for storing bones, have been transformed into shops where postcards and booklets are sold. In the crypt of the ossuary of Saint-Thégonnec is a late seventeenth-century life-sized statuary group of Christ being entombed. The startlingly lifelike figures are brightly polychromed and in fine condition.

The sacred fountains are widely scattered across Brittany. They are usually sunk down into the ground with stone retaining walls around them. Many are now put to practical use for washing clothes. Good examples may be seen at Berven, Clohars-Fouesnant, Saint-Avé, and Saint-Gilles-Pligeaux.

Sacred fountains are known throughout the world and are held in high esteem in the Near East where water is scarce. There is no shortage of water in Brittany, but such fountains are plentiful there. They are needed when *pardons* are held, for large numbers of people concentrated around a church require something to quench their thirst. Bottled wine helps, but the water from the fountains is believed to have a special virtue.

All the churches and the religious objects associated with them are made of stone taken from the hard, long-lasting granite core of the Breton peninsula. Stone, carved or uncarved, is important everywhere in France but nowhere so much as it is here. Long association over countless centuries with this intractable material made the men of Brittany into expert masons, stonecarvers, and sculptors. Much of the skill developed during past generations, however, has been lost. There are still some trained stoneworkers left, but they are becoming scarce. In fact there are hardly enough of them to keep the ancient monuments in repair.

The west coast

There are, of course, more ways of seeing western Brittany than stopping at Huelgoat and radiating out from there. You can go west from Roscoff or Morlaix and explore the little-visited northern coast, which is cut into by several long, narrow estuaries called *abers*. The most interesting part of this trip is the area at the far western end where the Pointe de Saint-Mathieu is located. There a lighthouse stands near the ruins of a sixth-century monastery. And from the top of the cliffs is a good view over the ocean and the long line of small islands that stretch out to the northwest. At the end of them is Ushant (L'Ouessant) which can be reached by boat from Le Conquet. This island is the westernmost part of France. Still rather primitive and with few accommodations (simple and inexpensive), it may have a future as a resort because it is out in the Gulf Stream where the temperature is usually higher than on the mainland. Fog, however, is common there.

The whole area for miles north of the Pointe de Sainte-Mathieu

Detail of the Saint-Thégonnec calvary

is sparsely settled, and hotels are few and far-between. Some small ones exist near the shore, but you may have trouble finding one you like—or that isn't booked up. They are not expensive; they also are not very modern in plumbing or equipment. You may have to go on to Brest, where there are plenty of places suitable for an overnight stop.

Brest was so heavily bombed during the Second World War that its central section is all new. It is not very interesting for tourists because only French citizens are allowed to visit the naval installations or even the Château.

The shoreline south and east of Brest is so much indented that you will need a map to locate the various places mentioned below. The yellow Michelin Carte 58 shows it in detail.

Unless you have a great desire to see the lonely seacoast north of the Pointe de Saint-Mathieu you will probably do better to head south from Roscoff or Morlaix and go to Huelgoat so you can use that pleasant little town for a base.

But if you are passing through Brest, the famous Calvary Plougastel-Daoulas is just across the Elorn River. It, too, was somewhat damaged in the war. From here you can make a wide swing to get around several inlets by taking D33 and N170 south to N787 which then leads west along the narrow peninsula on which Morgat is located. Near the town are sheltered sand beaches and a number of sea caves that can be visited by boat. Morgat has a number of hotels, some of which are fairly expensive as prices in Brittany go.

The central one of the three peninsulas that project from the long extension of land is the most interesting. At one end of it (Pointe de Pen-Hir) on D8 you can see the rocky islets called the Tas de Pois. North of this is Lagatjar where more than 100 menhirs were erected in rows by prehistoric men.

At the tip of the southernmost little peninsula is Cap de la Chèvre, an isolated high point of land. This was a strongly held Nazi fortified position which still shows the effects of the heavy naval bombardment needed to smash the big guns that commanded this part of the coast. D255 leads to it.

South of Morgat is tiny Sainte-Anne-la-Palud with a fine old church where a *pardon* takes place on the third Sunday of August. At other times this whole area is very quiet. A good but not inexpensive hotel on the beach makes this a most desirable stopping place if you can afford it. From here you can drive a few miles east on D61 to visit Calvaries at Saint-Vennec and Quilinen.

Huelgoat

Morgat and Sainte-Anne are good places to stay in if you have plenty of time and are looking for quiet beaches. But Huelgoat is better located for exploring western Brittany; it is also an attractive old town with a lake and extensive woods in which there are pleasant, well-marked paths. Along the water courses are great piles of enormous boulders that have been tossed up by freshets long ago. Some of these rounded rocks resemble walruses or completely fanciful beasts. One group is called the Virgin's Kitchen because its oddly shaped stones are supposed to look like enormous utensils suitable only for a heavenly cook. Near it is a long, exceedingly heavy monster named *La Roche Tremblante*. This massive bit of granite doesn't exactly tremble of its own accord, but a husky young man can lift it up a few inches if he knows just where to heave.

There are all sorts of interesting stopping places along the paths. Grottoes are common; so are tree-shaded pools. More sensational is Le Gouffre, where the fast-moving Argent River suddenly plunges down into a rocky hole to run underneath the surface for a while. A sign posted above the crashing waters recounts the legend of a local princess who had her discarded lovers thrown into the abyss. No mortality figures are given.

At the edge of the town is Le Chaos de Moulin where a stream rushes through tumbled rocks of all sizes and shapes. The word *"chaos"* (pronounced kah-ohss) is not ordinarily defined in a French dictionary to describe a wilderness of strangely-shaped stones, but French people know what the word means in this sense. The stark, disordered beauty of a good *chaos* seems to appeal strongly to them, and they will go out of their way to see one. You will find others in France, usually in remote places.

North of Huelgoat and west of D14 is a giant menhir which stands alone in a barnyard.

If you have stayed in Morgat instead of Huelgoat you can go on N787 and D63 to Douarnenez (47 kilometers or 29 miles). At

Plonvénez-Porzay you pass D61 which leads west to Sainte-Anne-la-Palud (already mentioned). From here you can proceed to Douarnenez on D107 and D7, but by staying on D63 for 4 kilometers more you can visit Locronan, a village with unusually handsome Breton stone houses. Don't miss it. It has an interesting fifteenth-century church, a small museum, weavers whose colorful Breton fabrics are on sale, a remarkable wood carver, and a pleasantly decorated restaurant that Michelin stars.

Douarnenez

Douarnenez is a fishing port where all kinds of catches from the Atlantic are brought in. It specializes in sardines. Except for watching the fish being unloaded from the boats, the town has not much to offer, but the area around it is rich in legend. The small offshore island is called Ile Tristan, and King Mark is supposed to have had his castle at Douarnenez. This, of course, is according to Breton—not British or German—versions of the immortal tale of Tristan and Isolde. Whether or not the island actually played a part in the story of the star-crossed lovers, it did have a bloody history in the late sixteenth century when it was occupied by Guy Eder de la Fontanelle, who delighted in torture and was himself broken on the wheel by the king's orders. Since he devastated Douarnenez in 1595 in order to obtain building stone to fortify his island, houses earlier than that date are rare on the mainland.

Somewhere in the wide bay north of Douarnenez is supposed to be the site of the sunken city of Ys (Ker-is). Here King Gradlon's dissolute daughter had a torrid affair with the Devil. One night her demon lover persuaded her to steal the key to the gates that shut out the sea. When he maliciously opened them, the city was engulfed, and the wicked princess was turned into a siren whose voice, they say, can still be heard when the sunken bells of Ys are rung by storms.

Since Douarnenez is an important fishing port it naturally has first-rate seafood. And *crêpes,* which are a Breton specialty, are especially good there.

Crêpes are made from wheat or buckwheat flour. They are large, very thin pancakes cooked quickly on a griddle, and are then spread with butter, sugar, cheese, ham, eggs, jelly, jam, liqueur, or whatever else seems appropriate. (*Crêpes suzette* are a sophisticated and very expensive big-city version prepared at the table with orange-butter, liqueurs, and brandy.) Since anyone can set up a *crêperie* with a tiny investment for the griddle and a few utensils and dishes, there are many of these simplest of all eating places throughout Brittany. Cider or coffee can be ordered with the *crêpes*.

Tréboul, just west of Douarnenez, has a beach and a number of inexpensive resort hotels, some of which have a good view of the sea.

The Pointe du Raz

The 37-kilometer (23-mile) trip from Douarnenez to the Pointe du Raz goes through treeless countryside that is wild and bare with occasional glimpses of the ocean. You pass Confort which has a small Calvary worth stopping to see. Beyond Pont-Croix you can take D43 through the center of the peninsula or N784 which goes along the south shore.

At the Pointe du Raz the granite cliffs are several hundred feet high. When the full Atlantic swell crashes against them it lashes the water into white foam as it surges around the scattered rocks and islets. This is a dangerous part of the sea where many ships have been wrecked, as the statue erected to Notre-Dame-des-Naufragés testifies. To the north is the Baie des Trépassés (Bay of the Dead) which was given that name because it is said that corpses from the wrecks used to drift ashore there.

Nor is this all that is sinister about the place. If you explore the level fields above the Pointe, you will come across trenches and gun emplacements left by the omnipresent Nazis. But the sea and the rocky paths leading down to it seem innocent enough nowadays. There is salt spray in the air, and the incessant sound of thunder as waves break over the rocks.

Far out is the Ile de Sein, a small barren island which can be visited by boat when the ocean is not too rough. This tiny spot of land is inhabited by fishermen who earn their living from the sea while their womenfolk do the work at home. The little community, with its hardy breed of men, played a heroic role in the last war. All its able-bodied adult males crossed over to England to enlist in the Free French forces there. In 1946 General de Gaulle came to the island to award it the Liberation Cross.

If you have time and want to see more rocks and sea, drive around the Baie des Trépassés to the Pointe du Van from which there is a fine view of the coast. Then you can return on V091 and D7 along the northern shore of the peninsula.

From Douarnenez to Quimper is only 22 kilometers (14 miles) on N165. Or you can drive due south to the Penmarc'h peninsula. This requires doubling back on some obscure little roads that lead west to the coast, but the trip is worth the trouble. And if you get lost occasionally you will be wandering around an interesting part of Brittany.

The Calvary at Plovan is near the water, but its chief interest is that it shows how a simple roadside cross evolved into what eventually became an exceedingly complicated form of religious art. East of Plovan are the ruins of the thirteenth-century chapel of Languidou where the stone frame of a delicate rose window stands gaunt and empty against the sky.

A few miles farther south is the often-photographed Calvary of Tronoën which is the oldest of them all (1450–60). It is beautifully located near the sea and has a background that varies with the moods of the ocean and the wide expanse of sky above it.

Still farther south is the Penmarc'h peninsula where a powerful modern lighthouse has replaced an older one. Roads wind around this interesting bit of land and make it possible to drive close to the shore. You can find some small and inexpensive hotels at Saint-Guénolé north of the point and at Lesconil farther east along the coast.

Northeast of Saint-Guénolé is a museum of prehistory with exhibits that cover the centuries betwen the Stone Age and the Roman occupation of Gaul.

This area has a sad history. It was far more fortunate and more densely populated until the end of the sixteenth century when the ruthless Fontenelle, who was mentioned in connection with his murderous deeds at Douarnenez, killed the people living here, destroyed their houses, and ran off with their fishing boats.

Quimper

From Penmarc'h you can drive north on N785 to Quimper, passing through Pont l'Abbé where the Musée Bigouden has examples of local peasant art.

Quimper is a venerable-looking city and wears its age proudly. It is noted for the decorative pottery to which it gives its name, for its lacy-steepled cathedral, and for its many shops in which you can buy all sorts of Breton handmade products, including lace and embroidery.

The great cathedral, which was begun in the thirteenth century, was not completed until 1856 when the two towers were finished. The interior, with its many tombs, chapels, and works of art, is a living history of the community. In front of the steeples is a statue of legendary King Gradlon whose daughter's affair with the Devil caused the city of Ys to sink beneath the waves.

Quimper has two museums, the Musée Breton, which has folk art and local history, and the Musée des Beaux-Arts, with many paintings, including some of the school of Pont-Aven, which Gauguin made famous.

There are some excellent country hotels around Quimper. One of them, inland near La Forêt-Fouesnant, is expensive but worth the cost. An even more expensive one is on the shore at nearby Cabellou, but it lacks the charm of the one in the interior which is surrounded by acres of truly magnificent gardens. There are many less costly hotels near the water in this area, but most of them are rather seedy and offer poor value. Beg-Meil has a fine beach, but its best hotels are overpriced. So are those in Bénodet. You will do far better on the Penmarc'h peninsula.

Concarneau and Pont-Aven

Going east from Quimper, the next important stop is the fishing port, Concarneau, where the Ville Close, a small walled-in island in the harbor, is connected to the shore by a passage that could quickly be closed to invaders. There life goes on much as it did long ago, while the more modern part of the city is busy with commercial activities.

Only 15 kilometers (9 miles) east of Concarneau is Pont-

Aven, a small town that few people would bother to visit if it had not been made famous by Gauguin's paintings. He did not discover it. The area was so picturesque and living there was so cheap that other artists had found the place before he did. In 1886, when Gauguin first went there, John Murray's conventionally proper British guidebook was already saying that this "very primitive village, situated on a beautiful wooded creek," was even then "overrun by American and English artists."

The Pont-Aven School, however, of which Gauguin is by far the best-known member, consisted mostly of French painters, Emile Bernard and Charles Laval among them. The year 1886 was important in Gauguin's life, for he was then evolving the style he was to make his own. In 1887 he went with Laval to Martinique and returned to Pont-Aven early in 1888. Van Gogh then persuaded him to come to Arles, which he did in October.

Pont-Aven had great attractions for Gauguin. "I love Brittany," he wrote in a letter to a friend. "When my wooden shoes ring on its granite stones, I hear the dull, muffled, but powerful tone that I try to put in my painting." Some, but not many, of the things that appear in his pictures of Brittany can still be seen. One of them is in Pont-Aven's Chapelle de Tremalo, where there is the large fifteenth-century wooden crucifix that was the inspiration for "Le Christ Jaune." This figure made such a great impression on Gauguin that he also painted a self-portrait with part of it in the background.

Pont-Aven today is a far cry from what it was in Gauguin's time. The "beautiful creek," which was never a creek but an arm of the sea, smells bad at low tide. The village itself is prouder now of its illustrious visitor than it was when he was there. The countryside around it has not changed much, but only at festival time can you see the colorful peasant costumes which were then worn every day.

Pont-Aven has a restaurant which Michelin rates with two stars.

This part of Brittany is haunted by Gauguin's presence, for in 1889 and 1890 he lived at Le Pouldu, a tiny hamlet on the shore where the estuary on which Quimperlé is located reaches the sea. This was after his visit to Van Gogh at Arles. At this time Gauguin was working with tremendous activity, not only at painting but at sculpture, decorated pottery, ornamented furniture, and polychrome bas-reliefs. With the help of his friends, he painted pictures on the walls of the inn where he was staying. Since he was still unrecognized, no one thought his work had any value, so this casually-created art was allowed to perish.

Quimperlé and Port-Louis

Quimperlé is built on both shores of the Laïta which begins here where two small rivers meet. The names Quimper and Quimperlé both mean a junction of two streams (*Kemper*).

Quimperlé has two parts—an upper town on the hilly west bank and a lower one on the east side. Each has its own church. Towns flanking a navigable estuary are common in southern Brittany. And they have been there for a long while, as the ancient buildings along the quais indicate.

From Pont-Aven to Quimperlé is 17 kilometers (10 miles); from Quimperlé to Lorient is 20 kilometers (12 miles). Lorient is a city risen from the ashes, for it was almost entirely destroyed during the last war. The target of the intensive bombing was a row of submarine pens that the Nazis had built with astounding speed. They were so well constructed that direct hits by huge bombs made little impression on the thick cement roofs, and the pens remained in such good condition that they are now used by the French navy. Foreign tourists are not allowed to visit them, but they can be seen at a distance from Port-Louis on the other side of the wide estuary.

The rebuilt city of Lorient is not very interesting, but its waterfront is. The fishing port of Keroman handles an enormous amount of cargo, and at various places along the shores of the harbor you can see yards where the stubby, steel powerboats that bring in the catches are being constructed or repaired.

Port-Louis is a good example of a strongly fortified harbor. You can reach it by ferry from Lorient; if you go by car you have to drive up to the Pont du Bonhomme or to Hennebont to cross the long estuary. If you are pressed for time you may prefer to miss Lorient and Port-Louis and drive directly from Quimperlé to Hennebont on D62 and D26 (23 kilometers or 14 miles). At Hennebont you can go on to Auray on N165 (28 kilometers or 17 miles), which you will surely want to see, but we strongly recommend that you visit it later and take D9 to N781 which runs near the shore to the base of the Quiberon peninsula and the village of Carnac. This is our favorite part of Brittany, a section that has everything you can want, including the probability of good weather. Since a few thousand other people also know this, desirable accommodations, which are not plentiful to begin with, are scarce in summer. Campers and caravan drivers are in luck here, because there are many more good spots for them than there are for people who have to stay in hotels.

Carnac

When you have found a satisfactory base, you can spend days exploring the country for miles around. We have, and we never tire of it. Carnac and La Trinité-sur-Mer seem to us to be the most conveniently located places. There are two parts to Carnac, the inland village, which is more interesting to see than to stay in, and Carnac-Plage where the hotels are on or near the beach.

Swimming is very good in this area, but only when the tide is high. At other times the water recedes so far that it is almost out of sight.

Carnac is world-famous for its megalithic monuments which are more numerous here than anywhere else. Alignments of them run for miles, and almost every type of prehistoric stonework can be found in the neighborhood.

Megaliths

The word "megalith" comes from Greek roots meaning "big stone." The various megalithic forms are:

1. The menhir (Breton for "long stone"). This can be a single, upright rock which stands in lonely splendor to mark something that is hopelessly lost in the mists of time. It is believed that menhirs had a religious purpose, but they may also have been put up to commemorate a person or an event. The tall, smoothly shaped ones probably have some phallic significance. Until very recently—and perhaps even now—a peasant wife who wanted to bear a child would rub herself against one that was supposed to have magic powers. Not all menhirs, however, are so symbolically formed. Some are merely big shapeless rocks that have been stood on end.
2. Alignments. These consist of numerous menhirs ranged in fairly straight rows. The individual stones are often care-

Alignments of menhirs near Carnac

Passage grave

fully graduated in size, with the largest ones placed nearest to the culminating point of the alignment. Because the menhirs are drawn up in serried ranks, legend has it that they represent soldiers turned to stone. There are several alignments in Brittany. The four almost continuous groups at Carnac contain nearly 3000 menhirs. Originally, there were even more, but some have been moved away or destroyed. Church opposition to these idolatrous symbols caused many of them to be pulled down and smashed. Farmers and road builders broke up others.

3. Cromlechs. Upright stones arranged in circles, ovals, or other regular geometric patterns are called cromlechs in Brittany. (In Wales ancient rock tombs are given that name). At Carnac the alignments lead to them, and the graduated menhirs reach their greatest height there. Religious ceremonies of some kind were surely staged in these stony glades. We have no idea of what the rituals were, but they certainly had nothing to do with the Druids, who appeared on the scene long after the megaliths were put in place.
4. Dolmens. These are burial chambers walled with large rocks on which big flat stones serve as roofs. After the burial, the rocks were covered with earth. In most cases, the mound has been removed by man or weather—or a combination of both. The French Government is now replacing the protective soil, especially on dolmens where the interior has been decorated with carvings on the rock walls. When the burial chamber is covered with many smaller stones and soil to make a very large mound it is called a tumulus. There are relatively few of these. Carnac has one of the most impressive (Saint-Michel), and there is another (Gavrinis) on an island in the nearby Gulf of Morbihan.
5. Passage Graves and Gallery Graves. The passage grave (*dolmen à galerie*) consists of a double row of flat rocks placed on their sides to lead to a larger chamber. Both the long entranceway and the chamber were roofed with flat rocks. The gallery grave (*allée couverte*) is a passage without a chamber at the end of it. Both types were probably used as family burial places and served that purpose for many generations.

Burial chambers like these are common in western Europe. France alone has more than 6000 of them. They were built by men who came from places farther east along the Mediterranean about 5000 years ago and settled in coastal areas where the earliest examples of their work are to be found. They brought with them the concept of the mysterious Mother Goddess who had been worshiped since earliest times in the Near East. As her cult spread westward through the Mediterranean world, her images were cut into imperishable rock. In Brittany her feminine attributes were usually depicted in abstract terms.

The period of these Neolithic monuments is a landmark in mankind's evolution, for it commemorates the transition from a nomadic type of existence to a more settled one. It was then that a steady supply of food produced by agriculture replaced dependence upon the chance finding of wild animals, fish, insects, nuts, fruit, and berries as means of sustenance.

This was also the time that metals began to be used, that cloth became a substitute for skins and furs, that sails made longer voyages possible, that wheeled transport came into being, that architecture was developed, that urbanization started, and that the way for written records was prepared. All these were evidences of the dawn of civilization, and the megaliths are the solid and enduring monuments to mankind's emergence from savagery.

Except for earth burials, the megaliths are the first deliberate bid for permanence that European men had ever made, for their earlier efforts, like cave paintings and sculpture, were undertaken as part of magic ceremonies to obtain meat for immediate use and not to influence the far-distant future. Even the occasional human images depicted on cave walls seem to have no planned connection with what was to come.

But the megaliths do. These crude stone monuments still cry aloud the feelings of men who had learned what death means. They are tangible expressions of the poignant reminder: "When this you see, please think of me." As such they are the ancestors of all the objects that men have created in order to make themselves remembered.

And surely the megaliths, which mark an advance in humanity's long struggle upward, are far worthier of honor than the war memorials, victory arches, and trophies of military conquest that celebrate nothing but man's regressions into barbarism during his endless wars.

While you are in or near Carnac be sure to see its church because it is of more than ordinary interest. Over the entrance is a stone baldaquin which is said to have been carved out of a menhir. This unusual ornament was called ugly a century ago, but it seems graceful to modern eyes.

The interior of the church has wooden ceilings with figures painted by an unknown artist. Outside, there is a brightly colored statue of Saint Cornély (Cornelius) placed between two oxen because he is their patron saint. And nearby is a good example of one of Brittany's sacred fountains.

The Carnac alignments

Before going to see the megaliths near Carnac we suggest that you visit the museum there. It is small, but it has thousands of prehistoric objects found in this area. It also has plaster casts of large stones with interesting symbolic decorations carved on their surfaces. These are better examined here in comfort and in a good light than they are *in situ* in dark underground places. The museum in the Château Gaillard in nearby Vannes also has much prehistoric material, although it is badly displayed.

Your second stop should be the Tumulus Saint-Michel, which rises above the ground northeast of the village. From this there is a wide view over the surrounding countryside, and an orientation table mounted on a lec'h will help you locate things. (A lec'h is later than the megaliths. It is usually smaller and has been carved by iron tools into a geometrical shape.)

The enormous tumulus, which is nearly 400 feet long by 200 feet wide, is made of stones and earth piled up high. It is so big that it dwarfs the chapel built on its eastern end. The unlighted rock tombs inside the mound can be visited with a guard who will use an electric torch to illuminate the interior. (You will do well to bring your own flashlight.) When this tumulus was excavated, a number of ceremonial ax-heads, necklaces, and charred bones were found in it. These are now in the museums at Carnac and Vannes.

The next visit should be to the alignments that begin north of the town and run eastward toward the Crach River. The long parallel rows of stones, mute witnesses to a long-vanished and little-known civilization, are very impressive whether they are seen in bright sunlight, fog, mist, or under the greenish rays of the full moon. They are as remarkable as Stonehenge, and, of course, are for more extensive, because the English monument is a rather compact group of stones standing almost alone on a treeless plain. The Carnac alignments run for nearly four miles past farms, woods, ponds, villages, and medieval ruins. And all around them are other megalithic monuments of various kinds.

The alignments are not as old as the earliest rock tombs, and it is obvious that more planning and labor were required to put all the stones into parallel rows which are usually graduated in size from one end to the other. A rock tomb could be built in a fairly short time by using a few big flat stones, but the alignments required an enormous supply of material of various sizes.

This raises a question that has never been satisfactorily answered. How did the men who constructed the alignments solve the problem of supply for this complicated job? To arrange stones in graduated rows is far more difficult than to put them up in random order, because you need the right-sized one to put in place next. This requires having a great many stones of various sizes on hand to choose from.

And it must be remembered that the alignment builders had to move these heavy rocks—perhaps on wooden rollers—by muscle power. Then each one had to be dropped into a previously prepared hole in the ground and held upright while soil was tamped down around its base. An enormous amount of manual labor was required to build these elaborate alignments. But Brittany cannot have had a large population in these early times. Where did all the people come from to provide so many man-hours of work? Unlike Egypt, Brittany did not have numerous slaves to command. Nor did it have Egypt's year-round good weather.

Planning something to be made of stones that are graduated in size is especially difficult when you have no metal tools to cut them. It is true that the alignments are not perfect so far as gradation is concerned, and that some of the stones are not neatly in position, but the passage of time may account for much of the irregularity. Over a period of many centuries, some stones have fallen and perhaps have been replaced; others have been broken or chipped away, or, most important of all, have sunk down into the ground to different depths depending on the nature of the soil beneath them.

There can be no doubt, though, that the intention of the builders was to have rows of graduated stones. What we see now are the mutilated remains of something that was originally in better order, but enough is left to show clearly what the builders intended.

There is still another large alignment farther west near the village of Erdeven. This is the Kerzerho group with 1129 menhirs. Part of it can be seen from Route N781. And there are several smaller alignments in the neighborhood.

Locmariaquer

At Locmariaquer, which is only 13 kilometers (8 miles) east of Carnac on route N781, are some of the most remarkable megolithic monuments in Brittany. Here is the largest menhir known, now fallen and broken into four huge pieces. When it stood upright centuries ago it was nearly 70 feet high. To erect so big and heavy a stone called for engineering skill of no mean order.

Only a few feet away from it is the Table des Marchands, which is an enormous flat stone serving as a roof over a passage grave. Until recently, this rock tomb had been stripped bare of its earth covering, but the French Government has put the soil back in place in order to protect the important monument. It is worth protecting, for the ceiling and end-stones are richly carved.

Also in or near Locmariaquer are other rock tombs, one of which is alongside a farmer's barn and was used in recent times as a cattle shed. There is also a tumulus that once was as big as Saint-Michel's in Carnac, but it has been pillaged for stone for so long that it is now only a remnant of its former self. A narrow path leads down to the low-ceilinged burial chamber which can be visited, although there is little to see there.

On the way from Locmariaquer to the sea is still another ancient tumulus called Mané-Er-Hroeck where a rich trove of ax-heads and ancient jewelry was found when the interior was excavated more than a century ago. And near the beach is a long passage grave known as Les Pierres Plates which has carved stones inside it.

You can take a boat trip from Locmariaquer around the Gulf of Morbihan. But before starting out on the water, let's go back for a while to explore the long Quiberon peninsula which has scenic grandeur and historic associations as well as megaliths.

Quiberon and the Côte Sauvage

The Quiberon peninsula is a long, very narrow strip that projects 14 kilometers (9 miles) to sea. This strange bit of land, which has been built up by sand deposits on what was originally a string of islands, has two very different coasts. The eastern one, which is well protected from winds and waves, is a pleasant shore lined with towns and scattered houses. But the west side faces the Atlantic Ocean, and the full force of the waves cutting into the rocky cliffs there makes its name, La Côte Sauvage, the wild coast, very appropriate.

The Quiberon peninsula, which is mostly sand and rock, has had a remarkable history. The megalith builders came to it in ancient times and left evidences of their work, one of which is a heart-shaped menhir standing near the water.

In 1759, during a gale at night, a naval battle took place off the coast of Quiberon that put an end to Louis XV's plans to invade England. A British and French fleet fought here in the classic tradition of eighteenth-century sea warfare with ships being dashed on rocks or burned to the water's edge.

Then, in 1795, during the French Revolution, about 10,000 Royalists were landed at Carnac from British ships in an effort to seize power from the Revolutionists. It was a disastrous attempt. Within a few days the would-be invaders were rounded up and forced to fall back to the peninsula which proved to be a trap from which they could not escape. Wholesale executions began on Quiberon and at places inland where some of the prisoners were taken.

Quiberon Bay, which the long strip of land shelters from Atlantic blasts, was the scene of a brief episode late in the American Civil War, for it was here that the Confederate ironclad *Stonewall* took on coal before starting to cross the ocean to attack Northern ports. She never reached the American mainland, however, because the war was over by the time she got to Havana.

Then in the Second World War, the Quiberon peninsula again made history when the Nazis, driven out of other coastal areas, concentrated their forces there. The narrow land was a death trap for them as it had been for the Royalists. When what was left of the German troops surrendered, it was found that they had shot fifty French captives in the fort they had used as their headquarters.

Visiting the Côte Sauvage

As you drive out on the Quiberon peninsula you will pass Fort Penthièvre and a monument to the prisoners the Nazis shot there. A short distance beyond this is an obscure road that leads west to the most spectacular part of the Côte Sauvage. But it is not a real road, and it soon becomes nothing but tracks

The Côte Sauvage

wandering across the fields. Then a military reservation with barbed-wire fences squeezes the right of way into a narrow strip along the top of the cliffs. Here the "road" gets even worse with soft sandy spots, ruts, and tight places where only one car at a time can get through. But it is passable, and you will see other automobiles out there. If you don't want to drive, leave your car in the fields and walk along the shore.

No matter how you get there, be sure to go, for this is a glorious stretch of coast with superb views of the ocean and of great arches carved out of the rocky cliffs by the ever-pounding surf. There are many small sandy beaches, and you may see people venturing into the water, but swimming is said to be dangerous here.

The Côte Sauvage is strange territory where almost anything might happen. Along this stretch of it we once saw the carcass of a giant deep-sea squid washed ashore. It was so big—and odoriferous—that a crew of men had to be sent down to the beach to bury it in the sand.

If you don't want to venture into the wilder parts of the Côte Sauvage, you can see a tamer section of it farther out on the peninsula where an excellent modern road runs along the western side. Eventually you will come to Quiberon, a land's-end resort like Provincetown or Penzance. On a fine summer day the little town may be so jammed that finding a place to park is difficult. It has a good sandy beach, but that too may be crowded. Fortunately, there are plenty of equally good beaches in this part of Brittany.

You can take a boat trip from Quiberon to Belle-Ile and return the same day. You may want to stay there for a while, for this good-sized island has a number of inexpensive hotels. The best way to arrange such a vacation is to take a day trip, explore the terrain by bus, and make a reservation in the hotel of your choice after inspecting it. Don't expect luxury accommodations, because Belle-Ile is a very simple place. But it is quiet, and the bathing is good.

When you return to Quiberon, drive back along the more thickly settled eastern coast. An alignment of menhirs cuts through part of the tiny resort, Saint-Pierre. Here you will find a little port for sailboats, a sandy beach, and one of our favorite *crêperies* (Ty-Koz), which has a terrace looking out over the bay.

Exploring the Carnac countryside

The area around Carnac has so many megalithic monuments that we cannot even attempt to list them all. A few are: the Kercado circular barrow; the Kerlescant rock-chambered tomb, which has a porthole cut through it, perhaps to enable the souls of the departed to escape; and the giant menhir of Manio, which stands alone in a glade in the pine woods. On the road from Carnac to Ploemel is a group of oddly assorted religious objects that span thousands of years. Two modern polychrome statues of the Virgin are part of a conglomeration of menhirs, lec'hs, and other ancient monuments.

There are many little roads to explore. They lead to picturesque Breton villages, run past unnamed menhirs and dolmens, and sometimes end on the shores of long, narrow inlets where oysters are raised.

The cultivation of these shellfish is an important local industry because it is only here that the Amoricaine *Ostrea edulis* variety is found. Called *les plates* by their growers, these oysters are also listed by restaurant owners as *belons*. Under any name they are small but superbly good, far better than the more widely known Portuguese oysters that are grown all along the coast of France.

Producing *les plates* in the Gulf of Morbihan is a complicated process that requires three or four years for the final result to be ready for market. Curved tiles are placed in the water for newly hatched oysters to fasten themselves on and remain there until they can be transplanted to wooden crates that are neatly stacked up on the bottom of the inlet. At low tide the greenish-colored boxes filled with growing oysters stand high above the water. The mixture of salt and brackish water in the estuaries fattens the captive mollusks for the market. You can taste them wherever you see the sign *dégustation d'huîtres*—and you will encounter this sign often in Brittany and along the Atlantic Coast.

The Gulf of Morbihan

This inland sea, with its many islands, is one of the most beautiful bodies of water in Brittany. It is of recent origin and was inundated in historic times, perhaps only 3000 years ago. You will have proof of this when you see the two circles of menhirs on Er-Lannic, for some of them are partly covered by the rising tide although they must have been put in place on what was then dry land. Splendid megalith monuments as yet unknown to modern man may be under the water here.

The best way to visit the gulf is to take one of the motorboat trips from Locmariaquer, Port-Navalo, or Vannes. Try to get a launch that is roofed over to protect its passengers from the hot sun or a sudden squall of rain.

These boats stop at the Ile aux Moines to let you visit the northern end of this enchanting island with its many prehistoric remains. To make a longer stay you can go there from the mainland on one of the frequent ferries that leave from nearby Port-Blanc. There are several quiet hotels on the island.

The excursion boat passes the drowned menhirs of Er-Lannic and goes close enough to the Ile de Gavrinis for you to see the huge tumulus there. But if you want to visit the interior to examine its famous carved rock walls you have to go by ferry from Larmor-Baden. The trip down the eastern shore of the Auray River to Larmor-Baden is worth taking. Along the way, if you want to hunt for them, are many small burial mounds still ringed with stone circles.

You can go around the gulf by car, passing through Vannes, then down N165 and N780 to Sarzeau and Port-Navalo at the entrance to the gulf. If you turn off the main road at Saint-Colombier and drive south for 4 kilometers on V04 you can see the ruins of the once-great thirteenth-century Château de Suscinio.

From Sarzeau, D198 leads to Saint-Gildas-de-Rhuys, which is close to the sea. Abélard, who had been born near Nantes in 1079, spent ten years here as head of the monastery after his affair with Héloïse was so brutally terminated. He hated the place, which was remote and primitive in those days, and finally fled from it because he thought the monks were trying to murder him.

Near Arzon is a small peninsula with a remarkable carved-rock passage grave near its tip. It is a casualty of the last war, for the Nazis built a concrete fort on top of it.

Auray

Another excursion from Carnac is one to the interior. Your first stop is Auray (13 kilometers or 8 miles) at the head of an estuary of the same name. Below the town itself is the ancient harbor, which was far more important in the days of sailing ships than it is now. A stone bridge connects the Saint-Goustan quarter to Auray. Down here are some of the oldest houses you are likely to see in France. They lean at crazy angles over the narrow streets where overhanging upper stories shut out the light which is also dimmed by gray slate-shingled side walls.

Benjamin Franklin landed here—without intending to—on December 3, 1776, because his ship, the 16-gun sloop-of-war *Reprisal,* was prevented by unfavorable winds from sailing up the Loire to Nantes. He was on an important mission to negotiate a treaty with Louis XVI, but travel was uncertain in those days. After a difficult voyage, which made the 70-year-old man so weak that he could hardly stand when he came ashore at Auray, he had to go overland in a "miserable" post-chaise to Nantes. But en route he noted that he encountered "the fairest woman I ever beheld." Unfortunately, she was not going in the same direction and therefore disappears from history forever unidentified.

If you drive north from Auray on N168 you will find the Chartreuse d'Auray. Just inside the gate is a chapel in which the remains of several hundred of the Royalists who had landed at Carnac were placed in an underground vault in 1823. Visitors can peer through a hole in the floor to see the dimly lighted skulls and heaped-up bones. A short distance to the east, on D120, is the Champs des Martyrs where the prisoners were executed. A monument that looks like a Greek temple overlooks the field.

Route D120 goes on from here to the Basilica of Sainte-Anne-d'Auray where some of the best attended *pardons* in Brittany take place. A good example of a sacred fountain stands in the open space in front of the church.

North of this, D133 leads to Grandchamps and then to N778 which goes still farther north to Guehenno where the easternmost important Calvary in Brittany is located. It is an especially fine one with unusual groupings of figures. Behind it is an ossuary of the simplest, plainest kind.

Northeast of Guehenno is Josselin with a round-towered château which is still occupied by descendants of the family that built it. It is a formidable castle even though it was constructed in the fifteenth century when such buildings were becoming decorative rather than defensive.

If you go east on N24 you will come to Ploermel with some fine old houses. Beyond that is the Forest of Paimpont where the sorcerer Merlin is supposed to have dwelt with Viviane, who held him there by a magic spell. This is the legendary Forest of Brocéliande, which played an important part in the Arthurian legend. Somewhere in it, concealed by a hawthorn tree, is the tower in which the immortal lovers live on, oblivious of the external world and the passing of time.

La Baule

From Auray to Vannes on N165 is 18 kilometers (11 miles). Vannes has the Cathédrale Saint-Pierre, which was under construction from the thirteenth to the nineteenth century, some interesting old residences, and ancient half-timbered washhouses along the river's edge.

N165 then goes 41 kilometers (25 miles) to La Roche-Bernard where a modern suspension bridge carries traffic above the Vilaine. On the other side of the river you have a choice of continuing on N165 for 109 kilometers (68 miles) to Nantes or of going south on N774 for 25 kilometers or 16 miles to the wonderfully well-preserved walled town Guérande where you can see how people lived in southern Brittany during the fifteenth century when these fortifications were built. This is a delightful place which has changed very little in appearance since the days when people had to put walls around a town to protect it from attack.

It is only 6 kilometers or 4 miles from here to the noted beach resort La Baule. This, like Deauville and Trouville, is twinned with the somewhat less fashionable Pornichet. Like its Norman counterparts, La Baule and Pornichet are recent creations. They are known for their good climate, for you are more likely to see the sun shine here than in any other part of Brittany. And sunshine and warmth are important assets for seaside resorts along the Atlantic coast of France.

If you stay in this area by all means drive west to nearby

Le Croisic and D45 which runs along the top of the sea cliffs beyond it. The man-made hill near the railroad station is called Mont-Esprit and was put there during the difficult winter of 1816 to give employment to local workers. There is a good view from the top of it of the marshland to the north. This swampy area was an open bay in historic times. Now the flat meadows are covered with square little basins for making salt from sea water evaporated by the sun. This formerly important industry is dying out, and many of the *salants* have been abandoned or converted into ponds for storing live shellfish.

When you drive east from La Baule you pass the port of Saint-Nazaire, a former Nazi submarine base. It was the scene of a British commando raid in 1942 and was later almost blasted out of existence by a series of air attacks. The new town is a good example of truly intelligent postwar planning. Its ingenious method of providing space for off-street curbside parking deserves to be emulated elsewhere. Certainly it is simple enough; lengthy recessed areas one-car wide run parallel with the street to make room for a row of parked automobiles which are thus kept out of the traffic stream.

From Saint-Nazaire follow N771 to Savenay (28 kilometers or 17 miles) and then, just beyond it, take N165 for 33 kilometers (20 miles) to Nantes. This is the beginning of the Loire River valley. The Muscadet vineyards are east of Nantes, and most of them are on the other side of the river. While you are in this area be sure to sample this unpretentious white wine that goes especially well with seafood. Muscadet is popular and inexpensive in northern France, but is little known—and far more costly—in England and America.

Nantes

When you drive west, Nantes is the gateway to Brittany; when you go east, it is the entrance to the Château Country of the Loire. As a result it combines the cultural features of both provinces. The part of the city we like best lies between the Ducal Château and the Erdre Basin. This includes the cathedral and the wide promenade north of it. The commercial area around the docks was heavily bombed during the war, but this older section came through very well.

The Ducal Château is closely connected with Anne of Brittany (1477–1514), the woman who impressed her memory not only upon her native province but upon the entire nation, for she married two French kings, Charles VIII and Louis XII, and thus united Brittany to France. Her father began the building of the Château, and Anne continued it after his death.

The wide moat surrounding the massive structure no longer contains water but is carpeted with grass. A drawbridge gives entry to the inner court where a community of noblemen and their servants could live completely cut off from the rest of the city. The big wellhead near the entrance shows how they could get water if they were besieged.

The buildings have remained unchanged, and visitors can see how grand an existence the nobility led in those days. It is notable that Nantes, which has preserved this setting for things as they were while the nobility ruled unchallenged, was the scene of some of the most terrible mass killings of the Revolution. When Jean-Baptiste Carrier was sent there to suppress Royalist reaction, his followers loaded hundreds of suspects on barges, tied men and women together in a "Republican marriage," and then pushed them overboard to drown. In some cases, whole barges jammed with the condemned were sunk, but this was regarded as wasteful. Carrier's *noyades* became famous, but not for long, because he went to the guillotine in 1794.

The Revolution put an end to the Nantes slave trade with Africa and the West Indies which had made the profits that built some of the city's finest homes. Shipping declined then but increased again in the mid-nineteenth century when Saint-Nazaire was connected to Nantes by a canal. Now the river has been deepened by modern dredging methods so large ships can once more tie up to the city's wharves.

The cathedral is a vast building that took more than four hundred years to construct. The vaulted ceiling of the nave is extraordinarily high, so the soaring effect of the supporting columns is accentuated. The elaborate white marble tomb carved by Michel Colomb for the parents of Anne of Brittany is in the south transept. One of the four figures at the corners (Justice) is Anne herself.

North of the cathedral a tree-lined promenade leads to the Erdre canal basin where the stone-lined banks look like those along the Seine in Paris.

Food and wine

Brittany has relatively few good restaurants because it is largely a rural area where the local people seldom dine out. Most of the better restaurants are in hotels, and there are some that are quite good. See our section on hotels and restaurants for recommendations.

Many of the best eating places are in the larger communities. Nantes has several where you can not only get seafood for which the province is famous, but also excellent local artichokes, cauliflower, and strawberries, as well as fresh vegetables and fruits from the fertile Loire Valley. Ducks, chickens, and other poultry from there serve as an introduction to the many culinary delights that lie ahead. You may want to try *cotriade,* a Breton version of *bouillabaisse.*

Brittany, of course, is noted for its lobsters. Both the *langouste* (clawless) and the *homard* (with claws) are found here. There is a curious misconception about them: The original term, *homard à l'américaine,* is correct because it refers to lobsters with big claws like those that come from the northeast coast of North America. *Homard à l'armoricaine,* as it is now often called, is a good example of what Fowler calls true and false etymology. As a result, it is just plain wrong.

Good wine can be grown only in places where there is neither too little nor too much sunlight during the course of a summer. Nantes is at the western end of a limiting northern border that runs east to Champagne, Alsace, and Germany. The wines in these districts have one thing in common—the best of them are white and dry.

The French vineyards begin here, but when you reach Bordeaux, Burgundy, and Champagne you will see the art of making wine at its best.

A note on Provinces vs. Departments

The idea of dividing France into provinces developed over the centuries as the country emerged from a Roman colony to an unorganized group of local kingdoms, duchies, and dependencies. Some provinces were big geographical units like Normandy, Brittany, Auvergne, Provence, Burgundy, and Lorraine. Others were smaller political subdivisions like Saintonge, Angoumois, and Venaissin. The latter, being purely artificial, were soon forgotten. The former, which made sense in geographic, ethnic, and linguistic terms, have endured even though the nation was sliced up into departments by an act of the National Assembly on January 15, 1790. The new Revolutionary government wanted to obliterate the national organization of the old regime with its favoritism, unjust and unequal taxes, and unfair distribution of power. The departments were small in area, roughly equal in size, and named after their rivers, mountains, or other natural features.

The departmental system, with some evolutionary changes, still exists. It is in daily use for post office addreses, administrative affairs, automobile licenses, and other governmental or legal purposes. But except in a few instances, such as Jura, Vosges, Ardennes, Landes, Dordogne, and Tarn, the departmental name is seldom mentioned when people refer to a part of France. The First World War made some departmental names prominent, i.e. the Marne and the Somme; it also revived the old provincial names of Picardy and Flanders.

In addition to provincial and departmental names, a few new sectional names have appeared in recent times and gained acceptance, i. e., the Riviera, Périgord (which covers the Dordogne, Lot, Corrèze, and parts of neighboring departments), and the Alps. The Alps, of course, have always been there, but the ground they occupy was once called Savoy and Dauphiné, and now is part of half a dozen departments, only some of which have "Alpes" in their names.

The Loire River valley, where the great châteaux are located, is often referred to as Touraine. Actually, the royal province of that name was a relatively small one encompassing the city of Tours, while the châteaux stretched out in a long line through the provinces of Anjou, Orléanais, and Berri. There seems to be no point in calling this section Touraine. Nor does the name Loire make sense because the Loire is a river and not part of the land of France.

We shall therefore refer to the area as the Château Country, which is what most visitors call it anyway. Châteaux are certainly its most outstanding features. Other parts of France have high concentrations of castles, but nowhere else are there so many impressive ones as here.

By any name the Château Country would be delightful, for it is green, richly productive, and quietly beautiful. The kings and noblemen of France, before they became enamored with Versailles, knew what they were doing when they chose this section for their palaces, hunting lodges, and country retreats. The memories they left behind in some of their sumptuous buildings are, unfortunately, not all pleasant, but that is because some kings, noblemen, and ordinary human beings behave badly when they allow the lust for power to dominate their actions.

The countryside itself, however, is a smiling and happy one. And it has memories of Joan of Arc, Rabelais, Balzac, and of many brave lords and fair ladies.

12. *The Château Country*

The Loire Valley has no spectacular scenery, no mountain crags, no waterfalls, no natural wonders to bring out oohs and ahs from tourists, but it is one of the most beautiful parts of France, and one of the most visited. People go there to see man-made things, the châteaux that were built for the kings and noblemen of France.

Most of them are on or near the Loire River, but some are on its tributaries. The area is so small (only 286 kilometers or 178 miles from Angers to Gien) that you can cover it in a series of day trips from three bases. We suggest one near Saumur, another near Amboise or Chenonceaux, and a third anywhere from Chambord to Orléans.

The Château Country has more than castles. It has many small roads to explore, and along them are more picnic sites than one usually finds in France. As you drive along, you will see houses built into the limestone cliffs, you will pass châteaux which are so little known that the guidebooks don't list them, and you will encounter something worth seeing at almost every turn. Food and wine are especially good here. In fact, this part of France deserves a longer stay than most people allow for it. We have been here again and again and keep coming back. It takes time, patient exploring, and more than one visit to see the Château Country properly.

In the days of the kings great forests covered much of the land, and game was plentiful. Some of the châteaux began as hunting lodges; even the most elaborate ones were often used as bases from which a royal party could ride out for a day's sport.

The châteaux in time

People who have seen the Louvre, Versailles, and the many imposing châteaux around Paris may wonder why the kings of

France kept building castles in the Loire Valley for nearly two hundred years. They came here when Paris was in the hands of the English from 1421 to 1446. Charles VII was in Chinon at the time the British invaders were besieging nearby Orléans in 1429. He and his successors stayed in the Loire Valley even when the English were finally driven out of France and had to abandon their last foothold, Calais, in 1558.

The story of French royalty's association with this area begins with Charles VII, although he was no builder. Châteaux had been constructed here for a long while, for Langeais and Beaugency have donjon towers dating back to the tenth and eleventh centuries. The spur of land above Chinon had been used for strongholds since Roman times, and some parts of the Château occupied by Charles VII had been built as early as the tenth century. Loches has a history as old as Chinon's; Angers is more recent, but it is a fine example of a feudal stronghold that is still in good condition even though the tops of its towers have been chopped off. If you are interested in tracing the evolution of châteaux from massive stone forts to pleasant country mansions, Angers is a good place to begin. Since the Loire Valley has examples of every type of castle from the earliest to the latest you can find practically everything you want to see.

The purely defensive ones continued to be built so long as the only weapons used against them were crude, hand-operated wooden machines of war. In the fourteenth century, when gunpowder began to be used to fire heavy missiles that could smash stone walls, the *château fort* lost its effectiveness, and the *château de plaisance* slowly replaced it.

Actually, the disappearance of the castle as a dwelling place was no loss, because life in its cold interior was cramped, uncomfortable, and monotonous. Even the lords and their ladies could not live well in these almost windowless structures where keeping people from being slaughtered was more important than making them comfortable. By the sixteenth century feudal strongholds had become obsolete. But some remain standing to this day because it is easier to let such substantial buildings stand than it is to go to the trouble of razing them. A few were modified or rebuilt, others were maintained by owners who lived elsewhere, while many were just quietly allowed to fall into ruins.

For once, a new weapon—gunpowder—had a good effect

upon society, and walls that no longer had to be almost solid could have windows in them to let in the light.

The early châteaux in the Loire Valley belonged to local noblemen; royalty began to build there when Charles VII's successor, Louis XI, ascended the throne in 1461.

Charles VIII enlarged Amboise where his life began in 1470 and ended in 1498. Louis XII (1462–1515), who succeeded him, lived in Blois and added a wing to it. So did Francis I, who was a great builder. He began the construction of Chambord in 1519, but it was still unfinished when he died in 1547.

Chambord is the largest château in the Loire Valley and the last one of any importance that was built in this region by the French kings. With Henry IV their attention shifted to Paris, although some of the châteaux of the Loire served as royal residences until Louis XIV created the vast complex of palaces at Versailles in the seventeenth century.

Most of the other châteaux of the Loire are late, even though some of them replaced earlier ones on the same sites. There was a rash of building in the first third of the sixteenth century when Chaumont, Chenonceaux, Azay-le-Rideau, and Villandry were constructed. Cheverny, as we know it now, was finished in 1634.

The châteaux in space

The royal splendor is gone, and some of the palaces are bare and unfurnished, but they serve as an intimate record of a way of life that once prevailed in this part of France. A few are still privately owned and lived in.

There are more châteaux in the Loire Valley than you can hope—or probably want—to visit. For your convenience we have placed them in several groups. The first lot of nine consists of what we consider a representative selection: Angers; Chinon; Langeais; Loches; Chenonceaux; Amboise; Blois; Cheverny; Chambord.

This list of nine includes the châteaux that were truly royal residences—Chinon, Loches, Amboise, Blois, and Chambord. Louis XI built Plessis-lès-Tours and spent his last years there, but only a part of it remains. Langeais was the scene of a royal wedding, and kings undoubtedly visited many of the other châteaux, but only the five named above were really lived in for any length of time by French royalty.

If you are in a hurry, or are not much interested in châteaux, you can reduce this list to three: Chenonceaux, Chambord, and Cheverny. This will permit you to see: the most beautiful, Chenonceaux; the biggest and most impressive, Chambord; the most intimate, still-lived-in one, Cheverny.

You may be tempted to visit others when you drive past their entrances. But don't try to see too many in one day. Since they are closed for the long luncheon period, it is difficult to do more than one in the morning and two in the afternoon. Even this is probably too much unless you are including some of the minor ones not yet mentioned. Remember also that two interesting cities, Tours and Orléans, are along the way, and that you will be near many other fascinating places. Going through the châteaux can turn out to be a chore because you have to be part of a group that moves along with a guide who usually has too much to say in rapidly spoken French. And after a while, these magnificent buildings all begin to look alike. It is better to concentrate on a few and give them your attention. Save the rest for future visits to France.

Chambord stands empty; so does Blois for the most part. Others, like Chinon and Vendôme, are in ruins. But history was acted out in these palaces, and an aura of what went on still clings to the ancient walls and lingers in the wide stairways, private chapels, and rooms that once resounded with laughter, gay conversation—and angry words. They also witnessed bitter feuds and murder most foul.

These are not ordinary buildings. They are saturated with human emotion. The centuries lie heavily on stones that have been stained with blood and tears, while ivy curls around windows that once framed faces you now see in portrait galleries. The châteaux are more than architecture; they are part of the history of France.

Their history is told vividly on summer nights when *Son et Lumière* spectacles are staged at more than a dozen of them. Sound, recorded on tape, and light, used dramatically to illuminate the buildings (or parts of them), re-create the memorable events that once took place in these châteaux. Even if you do not understand the French spoken by well-trained actors, you will find these carefully planned presentations worth attending.

A list of châteaux and places to visit

We have combined the châteaux mentioned above with some of the more interesting places in the Loire Valley. Here they are, arranged in geographical order from west to east. Each one is described in some detail so you can decide which you want to see.

Angers. This enormous château with seventeen towers and thick connecting walls was built in 1228 to 1238. It makes no pretense of being intended for anything except defense and was considered impregnable in its day. Henry III ordered it demolished during the Wars of Religion, and the tops of most of its towers were removed until they were level with the curtain walls. Work progressed so slowly that the king was assassinated before destruction could go any farther, so the castle remains as it was at the end of the sixteenth century. Enough of it still exists to show what a major feudal stronghold was like. The moats are filled in with gardens now, and the truncated towers rise above the modern city of Angers, but the very size of the building is impressive. A statue of King René stands here because he was born in the castle in 1409. You will encounter him again in Aix-en-Provence, where he died in 1480. In the courtyard is a gallery where one of the oldest and largest French tapestries, the Apocalypse, is on display. Across the river is the Ancien Hôpital Saint-Jean, which is primarily an archeological museum, but much of the very early hospital has been preserved as it was. Those interested in old pharmacies may want to go to Baugé to see a very fine example of one in the Hôpital Saint-Joseph. Baugé is 38 kilometers (24 miles) east of Angers on Routes N23 and N766. Its Château and sixteenth-century church are also worth visiting.

Plessis-Bourré. The word *plessis* occurs often in this part of France, for it means a country residence. But Plessis-Bourré is no ordinary dwelling place. It was built in 1468 to 1473 by Jean Bourré, Minister of Finance to three kings. Since he had just completed the construction of Langeais, the two châteaux have much in common. They are both sturdily built castles with round towers, thick walls, and gates defended by drawbridges. But Plessis-Bourré has a wide moat around it, and it is this placid body of water that gives the otherwise grim building a certain charm. It is about 15 kilometers north of Angers on Route D107, then east for a short distance on D108. Since Plessis-Bourré is rather isolated you are not likely to find it crowded.

Saumur is not just a château but is also a town of some importance where a famous military training school has been located for two centuries. The needs of modern warfare have changed its cavalry into tanks and armored cars.

The Château stands on a hill above the city and is now used as a museum of decorative art. It also has the celebrated museum of the horse where practically everything associated with that faithful animal is displayed.

Fontevrault. The best way to reach this ancient abbey is to follow Route N147 along the left bank of the Loire from Saumur to Montsoreau where it turns south to the village of Fontevrault. (Montsoreau has a rather late château that can be visited.) But instead of going south at this point we suggest that you stay on the river road for a very short distance in order to see the Église Saint-Martin at Candes. This extraordinary church is built on the site where the saint of that name died in 397. It was constructed in the twelfth century and fortified three hundred years later. But it is a decorated fort, for its handsome porch is a work of art with statues, grotesque animals, and twisted vines carved in stone.

Candes is located at the confluence of the Vienne and the Loire, a site which made it important when those rivers were navigable. Near the church is a fine view of the place where the two streams meet.

Return to Montsoreau to get to Fontevrault. The Abbey is in the eastern part of the town on Route V04. Some of the buildings have long been used by the French government as a prison, but guides take visitors through the big Abbey church. It is the northernmost example of the kind of domed Romanesque architecture that is seen at Périgueux and Cahors. The church has many associations with England, for a small chapel in the right transept has the tombs of King Henry II, his wife, Eleanor of Aquitaine, his son, Richard the Lion-Hearted, and Isabel of Angoulême, who was married to another of his sons, King John of Magna Carta fame. And Henry II was, of course, the king whose feud with Thomas à Becket brought about that devout churchman's death at Canterbury in 1170. These remarkable Plantagenets were buried at Fontevrault at a time when it was a great abbey with a church that was regarded as a fitting place for the tombs of royalty.

That the Abbey of Fontevrault was well populated then can be seen from its strange-looking Romanesque kitchen which has 20 chimneys clustered around a pointed central tower. Food was prepared here for the 4000 nuns, monks, lepers, and visitors housed in the abbey buildings. A somewhat similar but smaller and later abbatial kitchen exists in Glastonbury, England.

Chinon. You can continue east on VO4 and D117 to reach Chinon. On the way you will pass La Devinière, the country house where François Rabelais is believed to have been born

Fontevrault; the Abbey kitchen

about 1494. The building is now used as a museum of objects associated with the author of *Gargantua.* A statue of him stands on the shore of the Vienne at Chinon near the Rue de la Lamproie where his parents lived at Number 15.

The ruins of the great Château of Chinon rise above the town and can best be seen in their entirety from the river bridge. The Château has three parts, the latest and easternmost of which, the British-built Fort Saint-Georges, is in almost complete ruins. The central section, called the Château de Milieu, is also largely dismantled, but the Château de Coudray, on the west, is in fair condition.

Chinon, which is one of the most historic spots in France, is in ruins because Richelieu, during the wars against the Protestants in the first half of the seventeenth century, ordered all the ancient feudal strongholds not needed for protection against invasion to be pulled down. Not only Chinon, but Les Baux, La Rochelle, and other fortified places, were deliberately wrecked. In some cases, as at Chinon, the stone structures were so extensive that they could not be demolished except by years of effort. Enough immediate damage was done to make the defenses useless; then the public was allowed to cart away stones. This went on for decades until Chinon was only the ghost of its former self. Not time or weather or even earthquake has destroyed historic monuments so effectively as crowbars and pickaxes wielded by unthinking vandals in search of free building material.

When you reach the plateau on which Chinon was built, you will pass the scattered stones that were part of King Henry II's Fort Saint-Georges, go under what is left of a tall clock tower, and enter the long expanse of ground where the palace in which Joan of Arc first met Charles VII once stood. All that remains of the big hall, where one of the most moving scenes in French history was enacted, is a wall with a large fireplace high up on it. The floor of that room is gone, so the place where Joan walked toward the king and his courtiers hangs in midair. A bronze plaque on the wall informs the visitor about what happened there on March 9, 1429, when logs burned in the now-suspended fireplace, and the huge hall was filled with men in brightly colored medieval costumes.

Beyond this sad ruin, and separated from it by a deep moat, is the Château de Coudray where Joan lived for a short time in

Chinon: houses that haven't changed since Joan of Arc saw them 500 years ago

Remains of the room where Joan of Arc first met Charles VII

a round tower that still exists. Near it are the ruins of the little Chapelle Saint-Martin where she prayed for the Dauphin to grant her daring wish to free France from the British invaders.

History reaches a high concentration at Chinon. Here Henry II of England died in 1189 and was found stripped of his clothing. Here, in 1308, more than a hundred Knight Templars were imprisoned, tortured, and put to death. And here, in the winter of 1498–99, Louis XII received Caesar Borgia who had come from Rome with the Pope's bull of divorce that permitted the King to put aside his unwanted wife to marry Charles VIII's widow, Anne of Brittany, and thus be sure that that region remained a part of France. Borgia traveled in great style with 80 mules to carry his baggage and with drummers and trumpeters to announce his arrival. This was the last great scene of pageantry at Chinon; after it the kings of France turned their attention elsewhere, and the big castle on the hill slowly declined.

Its buildings were so massive and strongly built that the Grande Salle where Joan first met the Dauphin was still intact in 1758. It was between that time and 1855, when Prosper Mérimée persuaded the Departmental government to save Chinon, that the worst damage was done. Since then parts of it have been restored.

The town of Chinon has been far better treated than the Château that was the reason for its existence. Things have changed very little there, and some of the oldest residential buildings in France are still in active use. Some of them are undoubtedly the same as they were when Joan of Arc came to Chinon in 1429. The very stone she is supposed to have used as an aid for dismounting is pointed out. But five hundred years is a long time, and there is no reason to believe that anyone would have noticed where or how an unknown girl got off her horse when she first arrived. The modern statue that portrays her riding into battle is full of movement so far as the horse is concerned, but the figure mounted on it is stiff and awkward. Artists have not done well with Joan. The combination of utter simplicity and world fame seems to be too much for them.

Richelieu is a bit out of the way, but it is worth making the trip south on Route N749 to see it because it is a well-preserved example of seventeenth-century town planning. Its walls, gates, church, and large covered market are all intact. The residence of the château-destroying Cardinal who built the town was pulled down early in the nineteenth century, but its fine large park is open to the public.

Ussé. This fairy-book Château on D7 north of Chinon is said to have been the inspiration for Charles Perrault's "Sleeping Beauty." It stands on the south shore of the Indre, and has had one of its four wings removed in order to improve the view of the river.

Langeais is in the town of that name on Route N152. It looks like a feudal stronghold when you approach it from the main street, but it has a rear court and gardens that soften its severity. Built in 1465–69 by Jean Bourré, who then went on to construct Plessis-Bourré, it was the scene of the wedding of Anne of Brittany to Charles VIII in 1491. It was restored and furnished with period pieces by a wealthy French owner who left it to the state. As a result, the ancient Château now looks very much as it must have when it was first built. A tenth-century donjon stands in the garden. Across the street is a Renaissance house in which Rabelais is believed to have lived. It is known that he was closely associated with life in the Château.

Cinq-Mars-la-Pile. Five kilometers from Langeais on Route N152 is a 100-foot-high tower which is so old that no one is quite sure when it was built. It may be of Roman origin.

Villandry is on the southern shore of the Cher on Route D7. Most of the châteaux in this region have beautiful gardens, but Villandry's are outstanding. The donjon of an earlier fortress has been incorporated in the present Château. It was constructed by Jean le Breton, who was in charge of building Chambord, so Villandry is almost as late as Francis I's great castle. It was restored and the gardens were replanted in modern times, but the Renaissance style has been carefully preserved.

Azay-le-Rideau is south of Villandry on the northern shore of the Indre. This enchantingly beautiful Château, which is now a government-owned museum of the French Renaissance, has an unhappy early history. The building that preceded it was occupied by a garrison of Burgundian troops when Charles VII passed by in 1418. He was insulted by some of the soldiers, and in retaliation ordered the entire lot of them, some 350 men, to be executed and the town burned. A century later, when an ambitious financier undertook the construction of the present Château, he became so involved in compromising deals that he had to flee the region and died soon afterward in the north of France. The building was then taken over by Francis I, who occasionally stayed in it while Chambord was being built.

The L-shaped Château is surrounded by moats filled with water from the Indre. Since it was never intended to be a defensive structure, its walls are pierced by large windows and its corner towers, although machicolated, were made that way only as a half-jesting reminder of the battlements of earlier strongholds. Its rich furnishings and its delightful location give Azay-le-Rideau a high rank among the smaller châteaux of the Loire Valley.

Saché. Across the river from Azay-le-Rideau and 6 kilometers to the east of it, is the Château de Saché, which was owned by the Margonne family in the first half of the nineteenth century. Balzac, who was born in Tours in 1799, often used to come here for lengthy visits. His room has been kept as it was, and there is a small museum of memorabilia associated with him.

Tours. The city of Tours is located on a long, narrow strip of land between the Loire and the Cher rivers, so it has two waterfronts, the northern one of which (on the Loire) has always been the more important. It is a very old city and had a great amphitheater in Roman times. Tours owes much of its long-continued fame to Saint Martin, a Roman soldier who became converted to Christianity and died in Candes in 397. His tomb in Tours became a place of pilgrimage during the Middle Ages. The huge church that covered the tomb was damaged by the Protestants in 1562. Shortly after the Revolution, it was pulled down so a street could be driven through what was formerly the nave. The modern Basilique Saint-Martin is built on a corner of the original site and has the saint's tomb in its crypt. The old clock tower, the Tour Charlemagne, and part of the original cloisters are all that remain of the vanished church.

Tours has been subjected to many attacks during the centuries, the most serious of which took place in our own time. In June 1940 the Germans bombarded the city and started a fire that consumed 30 acres of buildings in the central section along the Rue Nationale. Then in 1944 there was more fighting when the Germans were driven out. Some 9000 people perished in Tours in the Second World War. The bombed-out area has since been rebuilt, but the modern structures there are all in the International Indistinguishable style that makes so much of postwar Europe look alike.

Fortunately, a good part of the old city east and west of the center was not damaged in the war. The part northwest of the Tour Charlemagne still has many old houses. Most of them are on the streets around the Place Plumereau.

On the east side of the city, the Cathédrale Saint-Gatien came through the war unhurt. Even its fine old glass remains intact. This cathedral took more than three centuries to build and was not completed until 1547, so it combines several late Gothic features. The tomb of the young sons of Charles VIII and Anne of Brittany, which was originally in the destroyed church of Saint-Martin, now stands in a chapel here. The portrait statues of the tiny children show how royal infants were dressed in the 1490's.

Behind the cathedral are some of the stone walls of the Roman city. South of it is a garden where an enormous cedar tree has been growing for centuries. Here, too, is the Musée des Beaux-Arts which has a Rembrandt and a Mantegna among its many paintings.

In a suburb in the southwest of Tours is what remains of the Château of Plessis-lès-Tours, which Louis XI built for himself and in which he died in 1483. By the end of the nineteenth century it had become a storage place for the carts of cesspool cleaners; then it was owned by a doctor who maintained a museum of vaccination in it. It was purchased by Tours in 1932. On the upper floor is the room—and what is left of the bed—in which the king died. The building has been made into a museum of objects associated with its builder. It also has early paintings of Tours, things connected with the silk industry, and other local memorabilia.

On the other side of the Loire are the ruins of the great abbey church of Marmoutier where Pope Urban II launched the First

Crusade in 1095. In the bluff behind it are rock tombs and caves used as retreats by the early saints.

Le Mans, which is famous for the annual 24-hour auto race that takes place there on a June weekend, has one of France's more important cathedrals. It is 82 kilometers (51 miles) north of Tours on Route N158.

Loches is 39 kilometers (24 miles) south of Tours on Routes N10 and N143. Like Chinon, Loches stands on a rocky plateau that has been encircled by stone walls to make it a vast fortified enclosure that could be entered only through well-defended gates. But Chinon, even though it is in ruins, seems like a fair and sunlit place compared to Loches, which has a sinister reputation and a forbidding appearance. Even its well-preserved church, Saint-Ours, has something strange about it. Between tall steeples at either end are two hollow pyramids that roof the nave. They look like the peaked hats of Inquisitors. An English writer has said that they "give an indefinable feeling of terror."

Among the kings who have resided at Loches is Charles VII, whose mistress, Agnes Sorel, is remembered for her good influence on that monarch. Joan of Arc and Agnes Sorel both did their best to put some iron into his flabby soul. Perhaps it was their urging that made him continue to try to drive out the English and mold France into a united nation.

Agnes Sorel's tomb is in Loches and so is Anne of Brittany's beautifully decorated little oratory. Many other people are associated with this grim Château, but Louis XI's fearsome presence dominates it. The donjon tower and the prison at the western end of the plateau were his province, for it was in them that he acted out his cat-and-mouse role.

In the fifteenth century, a French king had absolute authority and could do as he wished. If he was a warped and distorted monster like Louis XI, he could give his sadistic impulses full rein. The kings of France of this period were a sorry lot, but this one was notorious even in that cruel age for the way he mistreated human beings. He and his like were building up a gigantic resentment that was to drown the nation in blood during the French Revolution. The donjon is now only a shell without floors or a roof, but the round tower next to it still has its prison cells intact. Worse than these, though, are the underground cells in the Martelet. It was in this part of Loches that Louis XI kept his enemies confined. Some remained shut up for years in cramped cages; others were tortured in the Question Chamber which still exists.

Amboise is another château with dire memories of wholesale slaughter. Even from the other side of the Loire you can see the iron balconies that were used as gallows during the terrible massacre of the Protestants in 1560 when so many hundreds of them were killed that the palace became uninhabitable because of the smell of death that lingered there for days.

Fortunately, the earlier history of Amboise is less bloody than this. The Château is a remarkable building situated so that the front part of it faces the river while the rear opens on gardens on the level plateau behind it. It has two towers with wide spiral ramps up which horses could carry their riders to the upper floors of the Château.

The history of Amboise is closely associated with Charles VIII, who was born there in 1470. After a stay in Italy he brought Italian workmen back with him to decorate the building. He died there in 1498 after having hit his forehead against the too-low stone lintel of a doorway that is shown to visitors.

Francis I is also associated with Amboise. It was he who brought Leonardo da Vinci there from Italy. The aging artist stayed on until he died in 1519 at the nearby Clos Lucé where there are models of the many ingenious machines he designed. His remains are in the little Chapel of Saint-Hubert on the terrace behind Amboise.

The Pagoda of Chanteloup is a pleasing example of the eighteenth century's interest in Chinese art and architecture. It was built in 1775 to 1778 by the Duc de Choiseul after he was exiled from the court in 1770. His elaborate château no longer exists, but this 140-foot-high tower, which he built to show his gratitude to the local families, is still in excellent condition. Use the approach from D31 a few miles south of Amboise. Otherwise you may find yourself stranded on small country roads that seem to go toward the Pagoda but then turn tantalizingly away.

Chenonceaux. You can continue south on D31 and then drive east on N76 to get to this most attractive of all the châteaux of the Loire Valley. Chenonceaux is a water palace built on a bridge that spans the Cher River. A long approach through a forest, extensive and beautifully kept formal gardens, and a guardian tower mark the way that leads to the Château itself. We suggest that you see its exterior from the waterfront gardens before entering the building. It is at its photogenic best late in the afternoon when the sun stains its walls with a rich golden hue that is reflected in the water below the arches on which Chenonceaux stands.

The Château has a relatively uneventful and peaceful history. The earlier part of it was built in 1515 to 1522 by Thomas Bohier and after his death was given to the crown in 1535. Francis I used it occasionally; then Henry II presented it to

Amboise

Chanteloup

Chenonceaux

Diane of Poitiers who had the bridge extended across the river. When Catherine de Medici came into power after Henry II's death in 1559, she made Diane exchange Chenonceaux for Chaumont. Catherine had the long galleries of the present Château built over the arches of the bridge. The interior is beautifully furnished and has many royal portraits of the period.

Chaumont, which Diane occupied after Catherine de Medici forced her to give up Chenonceaux, stands on a high bank on the southern shore of the Loire on Route N751. It formerly had four sections enclosing a square courtyard, but, as was done at Ussé, one of them was pulled down in order to have a view of the river. The present building replaces an earlier château that was destroyed in 1466; construction of this one went on from 1466 to 1511. Catherine de Medici occupied it from 1530 to 1559. After Diane de Poitiers took it over in a reluctant exchange for Chenonceaux, she continued to have work done on it. The French government purchased the building in 1938.

Chaumont's entrance, which is defended by two massive round towers and a drawbridge, shows that it was designed to be a feudal fortress. After the section facing the river was demolished in the eighteenth century, the Château became the pleasant terraced-garden building it is now. The interior is furnished and has many fine tapestries and objects of art.

Blois is on the north side of the Loire on Route N152. This historic château, which is closely connected with French royalty, was built from the thirteenth to the seventeenth century. It is remembered for its handsome outdoor stairway and for the dramatic murder of the Duc de Guise. It came near to being destroyed by a great fire in June 1940 when a Germany army attacked the town. It was saved only by the desperate expedient of blowing up the buildings near it to block off the advancing flames.

This big, rambling palace was built over so long a period of time and to suit so many different tastes that it is a jumble of styles, yet the entire structure is better integrated than one would expect under such circumstances. Its best part is the wing built by Francis I, which has the famous exterior staircase; its worst is the late pavilion of Gaston of Orléans who wanted to rebuild the entire Château but who died in 1660 before he could

Blois: the great stairway of Francis I

tear down the old one. The Louis XII wing on the east has a handsome equestrian statue of that king in a deep embrasure over the entranceway.

Blois is haunted by two monstrous figures, Catherine de Medici and her son, Henry III. Catherine stirred up enough trouble between Catholics and Protestants to bring on the massacres at Amboise in 1572 and in Paris on Saint Bartholomew's Day in 1588. Together, these two creatures caused the deaths of thousands of French people. Henry III was assassinated at Saint-Cloud in 1589. His mother predeceased him by a few months.

Catherine's apartment, now without furniture, as is most of the Château, has a large built-in cupboard with several hundred small compartments. Four of them are disguised to look like immovable parts of the cupboard. It was in these that she is supposed to have kept the poisons she used to get rid of people who stood in her way.

Henry III dealt more openly with his enemies. This effeminate fop, who liked to dress up in women's clothes, had 45 followers to carry out his orders no matter what they were. A group of these *"mignons"* murdered the Duc de Guise early in the morning of December 23, 1588. The guide who takes you through Blois will give you a blow-by-blow account of the killing.

With Blois, you have now seen the worst side of the power-mad rulers who had exploited France for at least two centuries. When Henry IV became king in 1589 that long-suffering nation at last had a normal, non-psychotic man on the throne.

Beauregard, which you can stop off to see while on your way to Cheverny, is a small château notable for its long gallery with 363 portraits of famous seventeenth-century figures, for the splendidly decorated ceiling of that gallery, and for its floor, which is paved with old Delft tiles.

Cheverny, after the gloomy horrors of Loches, Amboise, and Blois, is a delight to visit. Here beauty reigns, and all is serene. Most of the other châteaux are formal palaces, some of them haunted by unpleasant memories, but Cheverny is a beautiful home which is still lived in by descendants of the family that has owned this property for centuries. The present Château was built in 1634, but the family was here even before that time.

Cheverny stands in a large park with many long vistas. The Château itself has a rather formal exterior, but its interior has room after room furnished with seventeeenth-century pieces. The most elaborate is the King's Chamber, which is rich with color and decorated with large tapestries.

Even more interesting than this grand mansion are the outbuildings that show how luxurious life has been there. The walls of the trophy room are covered with two thousand antlers taken from deer that have been hunted in its great park during the last century. And the kennels, with a pack of about 60 dogs, is an animated place where the animals live in caged-in canine splendor.

Valençay is far to the south of the cluster of châteaux concentrated along the Loire and its tributaries. It is 55 kilometers (34 miles) from Blois on Route N156. Valençay is another late Renaissance building (*c.* 1540), with two huge domed towers that set it apart from most of the architecture of the region. It belonged to Talleyrand from 1805 until his death in 1838. A museum of objects associated with this shrewd diplomat gives some idea of the various phases of his long career from the time he spent two and a half years in exile in America during the Revolution to his last quiet days at Valençay.

Chambord is in the heart of the Château Country, only 18 kilometers (11 miles) east of Blois. This huge palace is a foretaste of Versailles. Francis I kept 1800 men working on its construction from 1523 to the end of his life in 1547. His successors then carried it to completion.

The great Château, with a forest of decorative chimneys rising from its roof, stands in the midst of a park that is more than 13,000 acres in extent. In the days when royal hunting parties started out from the palace, the ladies of the court used to go up to the flat roofs to watch for the king's return.

The Château was still in use as a royal residence for a century after the death of Francis I, for Louis XIV occasionally spent time there before Versailles was completed. Molière's *Monsieur de Pourceaugnac* and *Le Bourgeois Gentilhomme* were presented in Chambord before the king in 1669 and 1670.

The enormous multistoried building now has hardly any furniture in it. Its most unusual feature—aside from its fanciful chimneys—is a double spiral staircase on which people going up one do not meet those who are going down on the other. The building is so large that it has 440 rooms, 365 of them with fireplaces.

Despite its size and architectural importance, Chambord plays a secondary role in history. In comparison with the dramas for which Chinon, Loches, Amboise, and Blois are remembered, relatively little happened here. When Arthur Young, the British agriculturist, visited Chambord in 1787, while Louis XVI was still on the throne, he said: "I could not help thinking that if the King of France ever formed the idea of establishing one complete and perfect farm under the turnip culture of England, here is the place for it."

But Louis XVI, unheeding this good advice, went on his way to the guillotine, and Chambord never became a turnip farm.

During the closing days of the Second World War, the Germans, who were pulling out of the district, threatened to set the Château on fire. They were dissuaded by the local priest, and the four-hundred-year-old building was thus saved. The Germans did not know that it was acting as a storage place for some of the greatest treasures of French art that had been brought there from Paris.

Beaugency has one of the earliest military structures in the Valley of the Loire. This is the so-called Tour de César, a rectangular eleventh-century donjon that stands in the midst of a group of ancient buildings that are clustered around the Abbey and church of Notre-Dame. Beaugency also has a charming Renaissance Hôtel de Ville. Near it is a square clock tower that was used as a prison during the sixteenth century.

Meung-sur-Loire. On Route N152 between Beaugency and Orléans is the little town of Meung, which is one of the landmarks of French literature, for it was here that François Villon planned his masterpiece, "The Great Testament." According to the 30-year-old poet's own words, the Bishop of Meung kept him in a pit all summer and gave him nothing but bread and water. This was in 1461, the year in which Louis XI became king. When he passed through Meung on October 2, the town's prisoners were set free, and Villon, now near the end of his short life, was able to put his long poem down on paper. Woven into it are a dozen shorter ones, the famous "Ballade des Dames du Temps Jadis" among them. With "The Great Testament," French literature breaks away from medieval formalism and becomes personal, concerned with reality, and aware of the hard lot of the common man.

Orléans. Every year, on the eighth of May, a feast is celebrated in this ancient city to commemorate the day in 1428 when Joan of Arc drove away the English army that had been besieging Orléans for seven months. It was her first and perhaps greatest military victory.

The city was then surrounded by high walls and had many old buildings; but few of the ancient monuments survived the damage done in the Second World War. The Cathédrale Sainte-Croix still stands, an oddity of ecclesiastical construction, for its Gothic style dates from the seventeenth century. It replaces three earlier buildings—one of them Gothic—which stood on the same site. The most recent of the three was destroyed by the Protestants in 1567 when they exploded a mine inside it. Few buildings have suffered as much as this one has. It was damaged again in the Second World War, but it has been so well restored that it is now in good condition. A statue of Joan of Arc stands in one of the chapels, and there is another in the Place du Martroi; but nothing else exists to remind the visitor that she was here.

While you are in this part of France you may want to visit the superb cathedral in Chartres, which is only 72 kilometers (45 miles) away. Ordinarily one goes there from Paris, but the trip is shorter and easier—with fewer traffic problems—if you drive from Orléans.

Saint-Benoît-sur-Loire. A few miles east of Châteauneuf on Route N152, D148 turns south to Saint-Benoît. Few people bother to go out of their way to see this now little-known but once celebrated place, but it is well worth the slight detour, for Saint-Benoît is one of the most impressive examples of Romanesque architecture in France. Originally it was the abbey church of a great monastery that was attacked by the Protestants in 1562. The monastery buildings were destroyed during the French Revolution. As its name indicates, the remains of Saint Benedict were enshrined there after being brought from Italy in the seventh century. At one time the Abbey and the town that grew up around it had a population of 15,000. In recent years Benedictine monks have returned to Saint-Benoît and are reconstructing some of the vanished buildings. Masses in the huge church are celebrated for their Gregorian chants. The public is admitted to them on Sundays and religious holidays.

Sully-sur-Loire. Route D60 runs along the northern shore of the river to a bridge that leads to the Château de Sully. This fortress-like building with machicolated round towers is surrounded by a moat that is fed by water from the Loire. It has associations with people so disparate as Joan of Arc and Voltaire. During the Second World War the Château was partly damaged and is now being restored.

Gien also felt the effects of bombing in that war. Two of its churches were almost completely destroyed, but one of them, the Église de Sainte-Jeanne d'Arc, has been rebuilt in modern style. Bricks were used throughout, even to the round supporting pillars and vaulted roof. Only the fifteenth-century belfry tower is original. The very early Château, built in 1484, was also damaged, but it has now been made into a Museum of the Hunt. It has a large collection of weapons of all kinds, some of which belonged to famous men. Tapestries, paintings, and engravings depict hunting scenes of long ago.

Bourges. Although this city is not in the Loire Valley it is only 74 kilometers (46 miles) from Gien and should be visited for its Gothic cathedral which ranks high among the great religious buildings of the world. Its stained glass is only one of its many glories. Bourges also has the beautiful Renaissance house of the wealthy merchant, Jacques Coeur.

Food and wine

As you travel around France you will note that the regions which have fine wines also have fine food. Since the Loire Valley produces some excellent wine—white especially—one expects to find delicious food to go with it. You will not be disappointed. The food available here is some of the best in France. There are very few great luxury restaurants, but Michelin awards a star to about a dozen places that vary from very good to excellent.

Since high-quality fish, game, poultry, and vegetables are all indigenous to this country, they come to the table fresh and well cooked. And what is not native is shipped in from nearby Brittany, Normandy, the Ile de France, and Burgundy, so there is never any shortage of first-rate foodstuffs. There are some cheeses, a few made of goat's milk, but they are not well-known. Any good restaurant, however, will serve cheese from all over France. Land is too valuable along the Loire to be used as pastures for cows.

Perhaps it was because kings and noblemen brought their cooks from Paris when they came to the Loire Valley that that region has excellent eating but relatively few truly regional dishes. The practice gave the section high standards but apparently discouraged invention. However, some native specialties

Sully

do exist although you will almost surely find them served elsewhere as well as here. Some of them are: *jambons de volaille* which are not hams but boned chicken legs cooked in wine and served cold; all kinds of genuine ham and pork sausages; chicken cooked in blood; and *andouillettes* or tripe sausages which have become popular in other parts of France. Eels, too, are cooked to perfection here; so is carp. And there are all sorts of delicious little cakes, cookies, and pralines. The local fruit is especially good.

In our chapter on wine we mentioned Pouilly-Fumé (not to be confused with Pouilly-Fuissé which comes from Burgundy), Vouvray, and Saumur wines, some of them sparkling. And Muscadet, which is produced near Nantes but is a Loire Valley wine. Try also some of the lesser-known local varieties like Sancerre, Chinon, Quincy, and Jasnières.

13. *The Atlantic Coast*

If you are coming from Bourges when you leave the Château Country, take Route N151 west to Châteauroux and Poitiers. On the way you will pass through Saint-Savin-sur-Gartempe, 41 kilometers (25 miles) east of Poitiers. Don't miss the abbey church, for it is to Romanesque architecture what Chartres is to Gothic. This remarkable building, which is worth visiting for its architectural interest alone, has what are probably the finest murals of this period anywhere in France. Frescoes as early as these are scarce, for most of the very old ones have faded, been removed, or covered over. These are in good condition and would be far better known if they were located in a less remote place.

At Châteauroux you have a choice of continuing west to Poitiers and Les Sables-d'Olonne or of going south on N20 to Limoges and then on N21 to Périgueux and Périgord. We suggest that you read the chapters about the Atlantic Coast, Périgord, the Pyrenees, and Roussillon before you decide on the order in which you plan to visit these regions. Since they are large, time will be a factor.

The Atlantic Coast from Nantes to the Spanish border is 561 kilometers (nearly 350 miles) long. Its chief attractions are its beaches, the area where cognac is made, the wine country around Bordeaux, and the little group of resorts near Biarritz. There are no mountains, much sand (some of it piled up in high dunes), many fishing ports, pine forests, and relatively little agriculture except for the growing of wine grapes.

Since this area is a long, thin strip that borders the sea, it is difficult to recommend more than a few places worth using as bases to explore the surrounding countryside. Most of the interior is of little interest.

Here are a few suggestions:

For beaches alone: Les Sables-d'Olonne, Royan (see our comment later in the chapter on the water here), Arcachon, and Hossegor. Of these we like Hossegor best.

For the wine country we would recommend staying in Bordeaux. We ordinarily avoid cities; when they are very big and heavily industrialized we don't even want to go near them. But Bordeaux is not much larger than Nantes and is smaller than Nice. (It has a population of 254,000.) Its main advantages are that it is centrally located, it has many excellent restaurants of all grades, and it offers unusually good value in them and in its hotels.

We describe some of the smaller possible bases throughout the chapter.

Poitiers and the Vendée

If you like seaside resorts, go to Les Sables-d'Olonne. The road to it from Bourges leads through Poitiers, which is not an easy city to get through by car, so you may want to avoid its traffic. But Poitiers has much to offer to anyone interested in ecclesiastical architecture. Here is what is perhaps the earliest Christian monument in France, the so-called Church of Saint Jean, which was built as a baptistery in the first half of the fourth century, and which is now a museum of Merovingian artifacts. Near it is Notre-Dame-la-Grande with an elaborately sculptured façade in which many statues form a part of the decorative scheme. The Cathedral of Saint-Pierre and the Church of Sainte-Radegonde are also good examples of the architecture of this part of France.

Two great battles were fought at Poitiers. The first, in which Charles Martel drove out the Saracens in 732, prevented this part of Western Europe from becoming a Moslem colony. The second, in 1356, was disastrous for France, for it was then that Edward, the Black Prince of England, captured French King Jean II after slaying most of his knights and soldiers. This bloody encounter was one of the most important in the Hundred Year's War (which actually lasted for 115 years—1337 to 1453). During this overlong century France kept fighting the English invaders to drive them off the continent.

The coastal area around Les Sables-d'Olonne is the once-famous Vendée where the counterrevolutionary attempts of the local peasants and priests, who backed the Royalist cause in 1793, turned into open warfare. Troops sent in to repress the insurrection devastated the land and conducted mass executions. Balzac's novel, *Les Chouans,* deals with the spread of this fighting to southern Brittany.

Les Sables-d'Olonne

This modern looking resort with its long, flat, sandy beach is crowded in summer when thousands of families go there for their annual vacation. The town is far older than it looks. It is said that the Phoenicians made it a regular stopping place when European sea-trade routes first began. It is still an important fishing port, but is so laid out that the commercial shipping area is far away from the bathing beach. The boats go up a canal that leads to inland docks.

Since Les Sables-d'Olonne is a family resort, prices there are lower than they are in more fashionable places like Deauville or Biarritz. It will be jammed in August, but you should have no trouble finding accommodations at other times.

The stretch of the Atlantic coast from expensive La Baule to even more expensive Biarritz has many less costly seaside resorts.

From Les Sables to La Rochelle is 95 kilometers or 59 miles. N149 leads east to Luçon where Cardinal Richelieu began his career. Henry IV made him bishop of Luçon in 1606 at the age of 21. He was so young that he had to go to Rome for a special dispensation and did not take up his duties in Luçon until he was 23. He worked there for six years and then went on to Paris and fame. The buildings associated with his stay, the Cathédrale Notre-Dame and the adjacent episcopal palace remain very much the same as they were then.

At Luçon you can continue east for 5 kilometers to Les Quatre Chemins and then go south to La Rochelle on N137 and N22. Or you can be more venturesome and head directly south on D50, then east on D25, and south again on D10A to the swing bridge that crosses the elaborate network of canals running through the low-lying country here. After that, D105 and D106 lead along the coast to La Palice, a shipbuilding town that would be of no interest to tourists except for the fact that the ferry to the Ile de Ré departs from it. Both this island and the larger Ile d'Oléron, south of La Rochelle, are interesting places to visit and have simple, inexpensive hotels.

La Rochelle is an ancient but very lively seaport that went through two long sieges in 1573 and 1627. Grim towers and walls that were here long before the sieges still line the inner port. And its arcaded streets make it look different from other French cities.

N137 runs south along the shore for 30 kilometers or 19 miles to Rochefort. It passes a number of fish-catching devices called *carrelets.* These are platforms built along the shore from which huge nets spread out on metal frames are dipped into the water and are then raised up by hand-turned winches.

Rochefort-sur-Mer was a great shipbuilding center in the days when men-of-war carried sails. The naval museum has models of them, and the old Arsenal at one time was a well-stocked storehouse of everything needed to outfit one of His Majesty's wooden warships. In the nineteenth century some of the first steam-powered French naval vessels were built here.

N733 connects Rochefort with Royan which is only 40 kilometers or 25 miles away. But if you want to go to the Ile d'Oléron you will have to turn right at Saint-Agnant and take D123 to Marennes and Le Chapus to get the ferry that carries cars to the island.

Royan

Royan was destroyed during the Second World War so everything there is very new. Most remarkable of all the recent structures is the Église Notre-Dame, a modern church built of concrete with soaring lines and an exterior resembling a ship. The interior is a novelty in ecclesiastical architecture. It is light, very large, without any supporting pillars, and has modern stained glass.

Royan, however, is best known as a family beach resort. It is a fine place to see French children at play. One drawback about this otherwise excellent resort is the fact that the current from the nearby mouth of the Gironde is unpleasantly muddy. If you want to stay here, try to find a hotel north of the town where there is clean ocean water.

When you leave Royan you have several choices. You can

cross the Gironde by ferry and run down the long peninsula to Bordeaux which is only 103 kilometers or 64 miles away by this traffic-free route. Along the way you can visit the Medoc vineyards north of Bordeaux.

The ferry will put you ashore at the Pointe de Grave. This strategic area, which is the key to shipping on the Gironde, was held by the Nazis throughout the Second World War. You will see a monument to the American troops who landed here in 1917; it is a replacement for the original one that the Nazis destroyed in 1942. Before they were driven out in 1945, they

Royan: the postwar church of Notre-Dame

blew up all the useful maritime installations here.

If you don't want to bother with the ferry, you can drive to Bordeaux on the roads that parallel the eastern shore of the river, in which case the trip is 129 kilometers or 80 miles long. The third choice is to go east to Saintes and Cognac, after which you can head south to Bordeaux or go on to Périgord, returning to Bordeaux and its famous wine district later.

Saintes is more interesting than it may seem, but you have to go exploring to find its best features. It has the ruins of a Roman arena and the Arch of Germanicus which was moved to its present location more than a century ago. Near it is an Archeological Museum with Gallo-Roman artifacts.

The old part of the city on the west side of the river has many ancient houses and public buildings. Here, too, is the former cathedral, Saint-Pierre. And Saint-Eutrope, which is only a fragment of a church above ground, has beneath it an enormous Romanesque crypt that can be visited.

Cognac

This town and the area around it has been made world famous by the brandy that is distilled from the grapes grown here. The district is divided into seven parts, of which the one immediately south of the town, centering around Ségonzac, produces the very finest cognac, Grande Champagne. Surrounding this, and still south of the Charente, is Petite Champagne, which makes the next best. (The word "Champagne," as used here, has nothing to do with the bubbly wine produced in the north of France.) To the northwest is the tiny section known as the Borderies. Beyond these, and stretching in every direction to include places as far away as La Rochelle, Royan, Angoulême, and Chalais, are the three large areas or Communs, Fins Bois, Bon Bois, and Bois Ordinaires. Only brandy distilled from the wine made from grapes grown in these seven districts can be called cognac, and the right to use this name is jealously guarded by the people who distill the celebrated brandy.

The wine made here is regarded as a somewhat less than mediocre beverage and is somewhat hard and acid wth a rather low alcoholic content. During the winter it is distilled in primitive pot-stills (*alambics*), which are very much like the small alembics that were used in the laboratories of the ancient alchemists. Some of it is distilled in small, portable apparatus that is moved from village to village.

Everything about cognac (except its marketing) is done in time-honored, traditional ways. The twice-distilled brandy has to be stored for a while to mature. The wooden casks used for this purpose are almost as important as their precious contents, for no material is good enough for them but selected oak staves from the forests of Limousin and Français. Cognac makers are so particular about the wood used in their casks that they favor that which comes from the center of the forest where lack of sunlight causes the trees to grow slowly, producing a dense, solid wood.

There is good reason for them to be concerned about this, because one of the greatest losses in the process of making cognac comes from evaporation through the pores of the wood. It takes 10 bottles of the original wine to produce one bottle of cognac.

The original distillate has to be tasted by experts, judiciously appraised for skillful blending with other distillates from other areas of Cognac, and is then stored in casks again until it reaches maturity. The finished product is about 80 proof or 40 percent alcohol.

When you buy cognac you get what you pay for. The least expensive varieties come from the less-favored districts and are not as old as the more expensive kinds. Incidentally, cognac should be kept in full, tightly corked bottles rather than in half-empty ones. A connoisseur will put what remains into a smaller bottle so it can be sealed without having an airspace above it.

The following marks indicate the relative age (and cost) of the various cognacs:

***	three to 15 years old
V.O.	very old (10 to 20 years)
V.O.P.	very old pale (15 to 30 years old)
V.S.O.P.	very superior old pale (30 years old or more)

Since there is some overlapping and a considerable spread of years, these markings are only relative.

Sometimes these variations are used:

V.V.O.	very, very old
X.O.	extra old
V.V.S.O.	very, very superior (reserve)
V.V.S.O.P.	very, very superior old pale (vintage)

Equally important are the sources from which the cognac came. When you buy a Fine Champagne cognac that has been matured in casks for many years, you are getting a superb product that is the result of much skill and time. Part of the high cost goes to cover the portion that was lost by evaporation. That is the inevitable tribute you must pay to the air and the sun. And the long investment of the producer's capital while the brandy was maturing also adds to the price.

Nevertheless, we think that good cognac is one of the greatest bargains you can get in France. Except for the very, very select and exceedingly expensive very special old superior, very pale, etc., variety, excellent Fine Champagne cognac can be bought for less than the price of a bottle of ordinary whisky in France, England, or America. Perhaps cognac's only drawback is that excessive indulgence in it will result in a hangover that makes one from other liquors seem like only a slight headache.

You will see many more brands of cognac offered for sale in France than at home. A brand you never heard of may be excellent—or it may not. Price is the best indication of its probable quality. Cheap brandy is raw and harsh; good brandy is delicately flavored and smooth. Oddly enough, the difference in price between a bottle of inferior stuff and a superior one is not very great. It is only in the upper reaches that cognac becomes truly expensive.

Any brandy is best served in a thin tulip-shaped glass that curves in at the top to concentrate the bouquet. The bowl of the glass should be held in the hand—never by the stem—because heat brings out the bouquet.

In a café or restaurant, you do not ask for cognac unless you want to specify brand and age. Ordinarily, you simply say *"une Fine."*

Other French brandies

Although cognac is a great brandy, it is not the only one made in France. Armagnac, which comes from three districts in the department of Gers, is stored in barrels made of black oak, which gives it a darker color than most cognac has. It is also richer in tannin. Armagnac tends to be somewhat cheaper than cognac although much depends on the relative quality of each. There are three grades: Grand-Armagnac, Fin-Armagnac, and

Petit-Armagnac.

Armagnac has devotees who swear by it. The British connoisseur, P. Morton Shand, said of it: "Not undeservedly its flavor has been likened to the scent of wood-violets softly exhaling through the mingling aromas of ripe quinces, greengages, and burnt hazel-nuts . . . . It has, if a slightly fuller and less refined bouquet, far greater softness, perfume, and range of flavour than nine cognacs out of ten, while it has the advantage of being naturally quite fit to drink after maturing for only five or six years in the wood."

Both cognac and armagnac are made from wine. The residue of skins, pips, etc. (known as *marc*), left over from the pressing of the wine grapes, is mixed with water, and then distilled to make a brandy called *eau-de-vie-de-marc*. This is made wherever grapes are pressed in France. That which comes from Burgundy is said to be the best. Although little known to tourists, *marc* is a great favorite with French people.

Visiting Cognac

The town of Cognac's chief claim to fame, aside from that which it has acquired from its brandies, is the fact that Francis I was born there in 1494. Some parts of the château in which his birth took place still exist. Its cellars have long been used to store casks of Otard cognac. These *chais* can be visited, as can the establishments of Hennessey and Martell. In the latter place we saw casks of cognac taken up to the top of a multistory building where the bung was knocked out so the liquor could pour into a shallow stainless steel trough which feeds into glass pipes that carry the brandy down to huge wooden storage tanks on a lower floor. From these it is distributed through other glass pipes to bottling machines. There women paste on labels and neatly package the finished product. We were given several free samples when we left.

Beyond Cognac

From Cognac you can go east to Angoulême, with its ancient ramparts and its associations with Balzac, proceed from there to Limoges, famous for its porcelain, and then go on to Aubusson. Aubusson is very picturesque, although its narrow main street, where signal lights permit traffic to go in one direction while temporarily holding up cars bound the other way, is something that has to be experienced to be believed. But Aubusson is noted for its modern tapestries, the making of which was inspired by the late Jean Lurçat, the modern artist who broke with tradition by reducing the number of colored strands to a manageable few. Here you can see the slow and painstaking hand process by which these tapestries are made.

Or, if you wish, from Cognac you can go southeast to Périguex, the gate of Périgord, or drive southwest to the wine country around Bordeaux.

Bordeaux and its wines

The city of Bordeaux covers a lot of ground. And broad open areas, such as the Esplanade des Quinconces with its bordering Allées, the Jardin Public, and the promenades along the river give the town a feeling of spaciousness. It has an eighteenth-century theater, the beautifully decorated Cathédrale Saint-André, several interesting museums, the remains of a Roman amphitheater, and for those who enjoyed visiting the Catacombs in Paris, the Tour Saint-Michel, where the crypt contains 70 corpses exhumed several hundred years ago and so well preserved by the soil in which they buried that they are still in excellent condition.

Bordeaux is famous, however, not for its parks or monuments, but because it is the center of one of the most important wine-growing areas in France. No matter from which direction you approach the city you will pass vineyard after vineyard. We have already discussed the wines in our chapter on that subject; now, while you are in the Bordeaux area, you can visit some of its better-known wine-producing châteaux and taste some of their justly-famous wines. Not all are open to the public. Inquire at the Maison du Vin in Bordeaux or at a Syndicat d'Initiative in any of the towns for the names of those that are.

The Medoc wine-growing district is north of Bordeaux, Graves is southwest, Sauternes due south, Entre-Deux-Mers on the east side of the Gironde River, while Saint-Émilion is east of the Dordogne.

The Michelin map Number 71, incidentally, covers this area more completely than Number 75 does.

FRENCH GOVERNMENT TOURIST OFFICE

Bordeaux

Visiting the vineyards

If you didn't take the ferry from Royan to the Pointe de Grave and drive down the peninsula west of the Gironde where the celebrated Medoc vineyards are located, you can easily reach them from Bordeaux by going north from there on D2. This road takes you to the Château Margaux, the Château Beychevelle, and the Château Latour. It then goes on to Pauillac, where the equally famous Château Lafite-Rothschild and Château Mouton-Rothschild are north of the town.

Route N113, which leads south from Bordeaux, goes through many vineyards in Graves and Sauternes. Turn right on D108 to the Château de Labrède, which is noted not for its wine but for its beauty and the fact that it was the home of Charles de Montesquieu (1689–1755). Although this noted writer has been dead for more than two centuries, his living quarters are kept just as they were when he occupied them. The Château de Labrède like Chenonceaux, makes clever use of the water surrounding it. Even a small and separate garden-island is attached to the main house by a connecting causeway. The Château can be visited. Its library of 7000 volumes is one of its main attractions.

Route N113 goes farther south to Barsac where the rather sweet wine of that name is grown. On the other side of the Gironde River is Cadillac which has a château by that name. It is noted for its fine wines and also for its double whispering gallery where people can talk to each other across a wide space without being overheard.

Still farther south on Route N113 is Preignac, where you turn right on D8E and then right again at the intersection where D8E becomes D8 to reach a minor road that leads to the Château d'Yquem. Here one of the world's most highly prized dessert wines is produced. It is golden in color and quite sweet. It is also very expensive, but connoisseurs say that it is worth the price. The Château itself is not particularly impressive, but anyone seriously interested in vintage wines will surely want to see it.

On the eastern side of the Dordogne River is the town of Saint-Émilion after which this wine district is named. While you are here be sure to see the extraordinary subterranean church that was carved out of solid rock centuries ago. There is another old monolithic church at Aubeterre-sur-Drone about 75 kilometers (47 miles) northeast of here. Both are in good shape, for the fact that they are underground has protected them from weathering and decay.

From Bordeaux it is 60 kilometers (37 miles) on N650 to the beach resort of Arcachon. On this road, only a few miles out of Bordeaux, is L'Alouette, where there is a good restaurant with an attractive garden. South of Arcachon is a long ocean beach. At the end of it is the Dune de Pyla, the highest sand dune in Europe, more than 300 feet above sea level. There are several good hotels on this beach.

Arcachon is noted for its oysters. A road 68 kilometers (42 miles) long circles the wide bay to Cap Ferret on the other side of the narrow inlet between the cape and Arcachon.

The Landes

When you head south from Arcachon, you drive for miles through a tremendous stretch of land forested with pine trees.

The Château d'Yquem

FRENCH GOVERNMENT TOURIST OFFICE

You can go through this quickly by taking N10, which is straight and fast. Or you can go along the coast on D83 and then take D146 east to reach N652, which goes south. It is slower but more interesting than N10, for it passes a number of lakes and ponds and at some points is very close to the sea.

No matter how you cross the Landes you will be going through country that has long been a problem to France. Efforts to hold back the wandering sands were made as early as the eighteenth century. The pines you see were planted here and are a valuable crop of useful trees. Vast tracts of them were burned in the 1940's. Now the replanted forests are watched over by fire wardens, and regulations about camping and picnicking are very strict.

In the early days, before the pine trees were planted, this tremendous tract of land was an unhealthy swamp where the peasants walked on stilts. Drainage and the carefully tended pine forests have reclaimed this once unproductive area. Incidentally, the unpretentious hotels in the little beach resorts along the coast are some of the greatest bargains in France.

Once you leave Vieux-Boucau, you are out of the low-cost area. Soustons, a lake resort with several good hotels and restaurants, is somewhat more expensive, and prices go up until they reach a peak at fashionable Biarritz. You can drive directly from Vieux-Boucau to Hossegor by going south along the shore on D79.

Hossegor

Hossegor is located on a salt-water lagoon connected by a canal to the sea. On the shores are a number of fine private residences and some excellent hotels. The ocean beach is only a short distance away, and there are hotels there too.

Hossegor itself is a garden spot where the roads wander through pine forests past villas occupied by well-to-do French families. This charming resort, quiet, gay with flowers and handsome shrubs, is to our mind one of the best places to stay on the lower part of France's Atlantic coast, although nearby Cap-Breton also has much to offer. South of here is the conglomeration of Bayonne, Saint-Jean-de-Luz, and Hendaye, all celebrated, all worth seeing, but so far as we are concerned, all easily visited from Hossegor, where we prefer to stay. It is

The Atlantic Coast near Saint-Jean-de-Luz

possible to find relatively inexpensive accommodations in the big resorts, but you will get far less there for your money. Rated in order of cost—a reflection of their standing in fashionable circles—they are: Biarritz (most), Saint-Jean-de-Luz (less), and Hendaye (least). Bayonne is not a resort, but a small industrial city on the Adour River. It has an impressive-looking cathedral (Sainte-Marie) and a Basque Museum that serves as a good introduction to the Basque country you are now entering.

Biarritz

Just as Deauville was the brain-child of the Duc de Morny, Biarritz came into being as a stylish watering-place because the mother of Eugénie de Montijo used to bring her daughter here. When Eugénie married Napoleon III, she persuaded her husband to visit the place she remembered so fondly from her girlhood. Started as a royal resort, Biarritz has maintained its social standing ever since. It has several top-luxury hotels, the most expensive of which was formerly Eugénie's seaside villa.

Biarritz has more than one beach. La Grande Plage is open

to the full Atlantic surf, but its southwestern end, where rock formations protect the inner waters from rough seas, is quieter and more beautiful. The town itself has all the usual attractions for wealthy tourists who want to gamble in the two Casinos, watch the races, or play golf or tennis.

Farther south is the little resort of Guéthary and beyond that is Saint-Jean-de-Luz, where Louis XIV was married to Marie-Thérèse of Austria in 1660. This was a great occasion celebrated in truly regal style. The church in which the wedding took place, Saint-Jean-Baptiste, is richly decorated in the Basque manner.

Saint-Jean, like Biarritz, has a fine beach that is crowded with bathing cabins, tents, and—when the weather, the tide, and the hour are right—with people.

At Hendaye you are on the border and can look across the Bidassoa River and the bay to the mountains of Spain. If you

Biarritz

FRENCH GOVERNMENT TOURIST OFFICE

have any idea of entering that country, remember that you must have an International Driving License.

Hendaye has two separate parts, the beach and the town. The climate here is so mild that palm trees and other semitropical plants flourish. In fact, this whole stretch of beaches, including Biarritz, which is famous for its hydrangeas, is a continuous garden where great quantities of flowers are grown.

Wines and food

The fine vintages of Bordeaux and the great brandies of Cognac give this part of France a special distinction. Few wines are made in the Landes except for some little-known local varieties. One of them, *vin de sable,* is worth trying. It is produced from vines grown in sandy soil, as its name indicates.

The Bordeaux region, like most of France's leading wine districts, is noted for its food. Bordeaux itself is the best place to become acquainted with the many good local dishes. Since nearly all the nearby countryside is covered with vines, few farm animals are raised here, so no cheeses are made. The coastal waters provide oysters, mussels, and all kinds of fish. Here you can get the lampreys that achieved fame in 1135 when England's Henry I died in Normandy from overindulgence in them. In Bordeaux they are cooked in red wine and are regarded as a great delicacy. Eels, too, are favored in the Bordeaux area. And so is shad, which comes in season in the spring.

Small wild birds, especially ortolans, which are trapped and then fattened for market, are one of the specialties of the region. They are very small indeed and make a full meal only when eaten in quantity.

In Bordeaux you can get the large fleshy mushrooms called *cèpes,* which grow wild throughout much of France. Cooked *à la Bordelaise,* they are a special treat.

The Landes has plenty of seafood and small wild birds, one of which is called a *bec-fin.* Cooked *à la landaise* they are a true delicacy, although you may have trouble finding such a dish because good restaurants are scarce here.

This part of France is proud of its potatoes, and you may be lucky enough to get *pommes de terre à la landaise.* Calorie-watchers, however, should avoid them because they are cooked with ham, goose fat, and other delicious but weight-inducing ingredients.

Since most of the local food specialties served in Biarritz and points south really belong to the Basque school of cooking, they will be treated in the chapter on the Pyrenees.

The Biarritz area is the gateway to the Pyrenees, but it is also easy to drive north to Périgord from there. Study your map and decide how you want to go. It is even possible to visit the western Pyrenees as far as Lourdes and then turn north to Tarbes and Périgord. There is no simple solution for this problem. You must decide for yourself the order in which you want to visit these regions. We are putting our chapter on Périgord next because we think it makes better sense that way, even though it may seem more logical to proceed from Biarritz to the Pyrenees.

14. *Périgord*

Although most of the regions described in this book are geographical units that have come down through the centuries more or less intact, what we refer to here as Périgord includes more than Périgord itself. Périgord, strictly defined, is the area around and east of the city of Périgueux. For the sake of convenience we have added more territory. Perhaps the best way to describe the section we deal with here is to say that it is the country drained by the Dordogne, Lot, and Tarn rivers. The ancient province of Guienne covered most but not all of it. People living in Toulouse (which is south of the Tarn) or Albi would deny that their cities are part of Périgord, but we have had to set boundaries somewhere, because no real ones exist. In Departmental terms, what we call Périgord consists of Dordogne, Lot, Tarn-et-Garonne, Tarn, with portions of Haute-Garonne and Aveyron.

Few tourists other than French and English know this part of France. It was beginning to be opened up to the world when crowds flocked to its northwest corner to see the prehistoric paintings in the Lascaux Cave, but this underground gallery had to be closed in April 1963 when microorganisms were found growing on the pictured walls. As a result, fewer people now come to the area. Yet even without Lascaux, Périgord has many other prehistoric caves worth visiting. And it has more than prehistory, for this is a land where nearly every hilltop is crowned with an ancient village or a castle, where smiling river valleys wind through the mountains, and where the regional food is as delicious as it is reputed to be. Here Romanesque churches are at their best, and here some of their sculptured decorations are true masterpieces of art. We have been to Périgord many times, and people we have sent there to visit it return with praises for its hospitality and its wonders.

Périgord has had a hard past. That is why so many castles stand on its hills and why so many of its churches had to be fortified. No family living in an ordinary house was safe during the long centuries when zealous armies slaughtered in the name of religion and ruthless marauders infested the countryside. Périgord suffered again during the Second World War when the Nazis, terrified by the Allied landings in Normandy and southern France, retaliated by a campaign of brutality that matched those of the past in ferocity and fiendish ingenuity. Not only Resistance fighters, but women and children were put to death in villages that were burned to the ground, sometimes with the inhabitants locked up inside their churches.

The Château de Fayrac

In the heart of the region are the great limestone plateaus of Périgord and Quercy called *"causses."* Rainwater filters down through them to hollow out caves, while rivers cut gorges and valleys in the soft rock. Much of the area's charm comes from carved stones, waterworn cliffs, and strange underground formations.

Since this is a rather large territory to visit, we suggest that you stay somewhere near the Dordogne River to explore the northern part and in or near Cahors for the southern section. There are many more good hotels north of Cahors than there are south of it. And most of the prehistoric caves are in the north.

For the north we suggest that you use a hotel in or near Les Eyzies-de-Tayac as a base; for the south, one of several good places in the country near Cahors; and then, as an added convenience for exploring the eastern section, a base located anywhere from Rocamadour to Saint-Ceré. There are plenty of excellent hotels, and most of them are quite inexpensive—some are real bargains.

Moissac, Montauban, Toulouse, Cordes, and Albi are best visited when you are leaving this area to go farther south or east.

When you approach Périgord from the west or north—say from Royan, Bordeaux, Angoulême, or Limoges—you will be entering that part of France which is called Languedoc. This is the whole area south of a wide arc drawn from a point above Bordeaux through Lussac (south of Poitiers) and Montluçon to a point just below Grenoble. Its name comes from an old form of the word "yes" (*"oc"*), while Northern France is called Languedoïl, derived from that region's pronounciation of "yes" (*"oïl"*).

In Périgord you will come across dozens of towns with names ending in "ac"—a short form of the Latin genitive plural "acum." Bergerac, Moissac, Alvignac, Beynac, Figeac, and Quessac are a few examples.

The French language sounds much harsher in the *langue d'oc* than it does in Paris and the North where the *langue d'oïl* tradition shaped current pronunciation. In Périgord you will hear the clicking *ac* and *oc* when country people speak.

Perigueux

If you enter Périgord from the northwest, which is perhaps the best way to be introduced to it, you will have a chance to visit Brantôme with its old abbey buildings converted into a town hall and a school. In the caves behind them the monks carved life-sized groups of religious figures out of the rock. And Bourdeilles, which requires a slight detour to reach, has an odd double castle.

Périgueux was once two towns separated by a wall. The lower part in the river bend had its own church; so did the town on the hill. Now it is all one city. The lower section dates back to Roman times, as the ruins of an arena and a huge circular tower attest.

Both of Périgueux's churches are interesting. The one on the hill, the Cathédrale Saint-Front, was built in the twelfth century when the Byzantine influence responsible for San Marco in Venice was strong. Saint-Front is not the only domed church in Périgord (others are in Souillac and Cahors), but it is certainly the largest and most impressive. Its cupola-topped domes and its tall tower with a colonnade-supported, tile-covered cone make the building look unlike any other great French cathedral. Despite some clumsy nineteenth-century restoration, Saint-Front is notable for its design and its huge scale. The best view of it is from the river bridges; seen from them it looms up white and enormous above the town. But it should also be examined close up, because its dome-topped interior is impressive. The other and smaller church, the Église Saint-Étienne de la Cité, which is near the Roman arena, is also domed.

Périgueux has a good museum with much prehistoric material from the area you are about to enter.

The prehistoric caves

When you leave Périgueux you can visit a prehistoric cave by going along Route N89 to N710 and then taking D6 at Les Versannes. This leads through typical farm country to Rouffignac (one of the towns burned by the Nazis) where you can go through a very big cave on a narrow-gauge electric train that carries visitors for nearly a mile along the winding course of a dried-up underground stream which had cut its way through the limestone rock ages before man appeared on the scene. Incidentally, cave bears inhabited Rouffignac long before men did. You can see the scratches their claws made on the walls.

This cave has been known since the sixteenth century, and casual visitors have gone through it since then, as is shown by the inscriptions they left on the walls and ceilings. Not until 1956 was attention drawn to the fact that the cave had many drawings and engravings presumably done by prehistoric men.

Water-shaped cliffs along the Dordogne River

We say "presumably" because it was immediately charged that they were not old. Several professional archaeologists examined them, and a majority declared that they were authentic. There the matter rests, but it is not settled. The distinguished British archaeologist, Glyn Daniel, who knows a great deal about the controversy, says that he is not convinced of the authenticity *in toto* and that he is still puzzled by Rouffignac. He suggests that this cave be visited after you have seen others so you can make comparisons.

From the Rouffignac cave (which is outside the town) Route D32 leads to D47, which takes you to Les Eyzies-de-Tayac, a center for prehistorians from all over the world.

Les Eyzies-de-Tayac

If you are at all interested in early man and what he did, this is the place to stay, for there is a heavy concentration of caves, shelters, and excavations in the area around the small town. Les Eyzies is on the Vézère River, and several wide valleys stretch away from it in different directions. These valleys all have one thing in common: they are bordered by limestone cliffs carved millions of years ago by the runoff from the huge glaciers of the Ice Ages. The cliffs are honeycombed with great numbers of hollowed-out places that range from shelters under overhanging rocks to long, twisting passages penetrating deep into the *causses*. These were made by underground streams that no longer exist. With so many convenient shelters available in an area where game was plentiful, it is no wonder that prehistoric men settled here and remained for such a long time. Babylon, Egypt, Greece, and Rome were short-lived compared with the static, relatively peaceful occupation of Périgord where millennia rather than centuries measured the duration of the inhabitants' stay.

These early men lived before writing was invented, so they left no history other than what is recorded in their tools and weapons, and, above all, in the sculptures, engravings, and paintings they made on the walls of sanctuaries hidden far below ground. In western Europe, only the caves in northern Spain come near to rivaling the artistic wealth of this part of France. No one can explain why art came to flower so early here, but it did.

In Les Eyzies, the National Museum of Prehistory is located in a restored fortress-castle halfway up a cliff where primitive people inhabited the rock shelter. The monstrous-looking, grotesquely long-armed modern statue near the Museum misrepresents the early men who lived here. The few portraits they made of themselves show that they were far less brutish in appearance.

In 1868, excavations in Les Eyzies revealed skeletons that were among the first found of *homo sapiens,* who replaced the Neanderthals in France about 35,000 years ago. Since the excavations were made in a rock shelter called Cro-Magnon, that name was given to this type of man. The shelter no longer exists; the garage of the Cro-Magnon Hotel now covers the site.

Much of what we now know about early man was first learned near Les Eyzies. And the finds were named after the obscure villages and hamlets where the evidence was uncovered. Not only Cro-Magnon, but Mousterian, Magdalenian, and other anthropological terms that are now world-famous come from sites in this area.

When you plan a day for exploring the caves remember that they are closed from 12 until 2 o'clock while their caretakers eat lunch. La Mouthe and Font-de-Gaume may be seen all year, but most of the others are open only during the tourist season between Easter and All Saints' Day (November 1). Some of the smaller caves, where a local resident is in charge, may be visited any time you can persuade the guardian-guide to show you through. Almost without exception, the guides in the caves speak only French. Even though admission is charged, they expect to be tipped.

Since the temperature in the caves is quite cool even in summer (45 to 55 degrees Fahrenheit), you should dress accordingly and wear old clothes or a raincoat. A waterproof hat is also advisable, for some of the caves are not only dripping with moisture but may have low ceilings where a hat will protect your head against a nasty scrape. The Abbé Breuil used to wear a beret stuffed with newspapers when he explored the caves. Rubbers or waterproof—and slip-proof—footwear are useful.

One thing every visitor should take is a flashlight. In narrow passages, the guide may be far ahead, pointing out hard-to-see engravings on the walls. You will need your own light when you reach them.

Prehistoric sites near Les Eyzies

La Mouthe. If you stopped to see Rouffignac, the easiest of all the caves to visit, you may now be willing to try a more difficult one, La Mouthe, which is on a dirt road about a mile south of Les Eyzies. You have to stop at a farmhouse (identified by a sign) to summon the guide who uses an acetylene torch to illuminate the tour. Be prepared for some wet spots underfoot. You will soon see that La Mouthe is an unspoiled cave, for it remained unknown until 1895 when the entrance was cleared of rubble that had been lying there undisturbed for thousands of years, and the winding tunnel behind it was then discovered. There can be no doubt about the great age of the art in La Mouthe; in some parts of the long passage, stalactites, which had formed since prehistoric man had last been there, had to be cut away to gain access.

On the walls are figures of bisons, reindeer, woolly rhinoceroses, and mammoths. Most interesting of all, however, is a painted engraving of what is believed to be a hut. This may be the world's oldest representation of a human dwelling, the remote ancestor of all the countless pictures of people's houses that have been made since then.

Font-de-Gaume. (1 mile or 2 kilometers east of Les Eyzies on Route D47.) This electrically lighted cave, reached by a 1300-foot path mostly uphill, has been known for several centuries. It is regrettable that it was discovered so soon, for generations of curiosity seekers have defaced some of the figures on its walls. Among the 200 paintings and engravings are those of mammoths, reindeer, and bison, a woolly rhinoceros, and a lion. There are also many geometric symbols which some scientists think may represent houses; others believe they depict animal traps or are simply tribal marks. No one actually knows. Cave art has not yet been subjected to enough comparative study to make the interpretation of its meaning anything more than guesswork.

Les Combarelles. (2 miles or 4 kilometers east on Route D47.) Easy to reach because you can drive right up to the entrance, Les Combarelles is uncomfortable to explore. It consists of two very long twisting tunnels hollowed out of the limestone. It is wet in places, always narrow, and sometimes has low ceilings. Although it is wired for electricity, the only light is that provided by the guide's single electric bulb plugged into outlets along the way. Unless you are near this light you will see little, so it is imperative to have your own flashlight here.

Despite the discomfort, Les Combarelles is a remarkable cave, for it has hundreds of engravings cut into the sides of its winding passages. Most of them are difficult to make out because a new one was often drawn over an existing one. The act of making a picture seems to have been the primary idea; what it looked like did not matter so much. Only by placing a light so that it shines across the rock surface to throw shadows across the incised lines can you see the engravings that were made by sharp-pointed pieces of flint.

Les Combarelles, with its wide easy entrance which leads to both passages, has been known for many years and was long used as a stable. The pictures on its walls were discovered in 1901 when trained observers began to search for engravings. The other, more recently opened gallery, has still more pictures, but only a specialist in Paleolithic culture is likely to want to see them after stumbling through nearly eight hundred feet in the first one.

Cap Blanc. (4 miles or 7 kilometers on Route D48.) This is not a cave but an overhanging rock. Excavations made in 1909 reveal an impressive frieze of six horses modeled in high relief on the rear wall. Originally there were other animals (bison, wild cattle, and perhaps reindeer) on this wall; now all but fragments of them have flaked away. Traces of pigment indicate that the entire frieze was once resplendent with color.

Many other places around Les Eyzies are worth seeing, for instance: the extensive ruins of a very large prehistoric rock shelter at Laugerie-Haute which collapsed and preserved everything just as it was until the debris began to be excavated about a century ago; the charming old village of Le Moustier, where a scale shows the thickness of the layers of prehistoric deposits laid down there; and the Pas du Miroir that not only has prehistoric remains but the foundations of a medieval fortress.

You can spend days roaming around the country near Les Eyzies. You will find that men and beasts still use the natural shelters, for many serve as cattle sheds, while some of the houses which people occupy cling to the cliffs or are backed up into cave entrances.

As we have said, Lascaux has been closed since April 1963. This magnificently painted cave was discovered on September 12, 1940, when four boys exploring a wooded hillside near Montignac saw their dog fall into a hole where a tree had been uprooted by a storm. They went down to rescue the animal and made one of the most important finds in the history of art. It was an unfortunate time for such a discovery, because the Germans had overrun northern France in June and were soon to take over the rest of the country. News of the find was not kept secret, but the cave was not opened to the public until it had been air-conditioned and massive bronze doors had been installed to seal the entrance. This was in 1948. During the years that followed, only a small group of people could visit the cave, and they were supposed to leave before the next group came in. But the paintings were so truly remarkable that crowds arrived from all over the world and were willing to wait for hours to see them. By 1960, destructive green mold had made its appearance. Three years later it was spreading so rapidly that the cave had to be closed.

A great deal of scientific work has been done to find a way to preserve the paintings and also to permit the public to see them. Inventive ingenuity will doubtless solve the problem, but until it does you will have to be satisfied with color photographs of these murals. They show curved walls and ceilings in the Hall of Bulls decorated with pictures of huge wild cattle, all kinds of horses, some splendidly antlered stags, and a strange mythical beast with two long horns. Then come two narrow corridors with still more paintings and engravings. There are more than 600 figures in the cave, some of them difficult to see because one picture is often painted on top of an earlier one, creating a confusing palimpsest on which generation after generation of artists left their marks.

Lascaux, however, has fewer of these superimpositions than most Paleolithic caves—a fact which has led some experts to believe that it was used for a relatively short time, perhaps only for about a thousand years. Then its pictured beasts were sealed away for hundreds of centuries.

As a result of its comparatively brief period of use, Lascaux has greater unity of decoration than most painted caves. It also has relatively few species of animals depicted on its walls. There are no mammoths, for instance, and their absence probably indicates that they had disappeared by the time of the Lascaux artists.

The dating of the pictures has been a matter of dispute. An outstanding expert on Paleolithic culture, the late Abbé Henri Breuil, who based his estimate on the techniques used by the artists, believed that Lascaux was decorated about 20,000 years ago. Radiocarbon dating, however, indicates that 15,515 ± 900 years was the probable date of human frequentation.

Lascaux has been called the Sistine Chapel of painted caves, for, like Michelangelo's famous ceiling, it is noted for its color. Actually, the pigments in Lascaux are limited to ochre for yellow, red, and light brown, and oxide of manganese for dark brown or black. In one place, mauve and purplish-red appear, but these colors are exceedingly rare in prehistoric art.

The cave has one painting with a human figure in a scene showing a wounded bison facing the rigid corpse of a man he has presumably just killed. Alongside the corpse is a throwing stick and a stylized bird mounted on a short pole stuck into the ground. A two-horned rhinoceros is shown unconcernedly wandering away, but the different style in which it was painted indicates that it may not have been part of the same scene.

This narrative picture, unusual in Paleolithic art because it involves a human drama, is located at the bottom of a narrow 16-foot shaft. Engravings and the worn condition of the rocks around the top of the shaft testify to the fact that this area was the holy of holies of the underground sanctuary. But difficulty of access made it impossible for visitors to see this remarkable illustration of a prehistoric hunt even when the cave was open to the public.

All kinds of protective devices have been suggested to make it possible to allow the public to visit Lascaux again without damaging the paintings. Breathing masks, glass or plastic passageways, and other methods of preventing tourists from bringing in more contamination have been proposed, and it is reasonable to believe that science will someday solve the problem.

Two caves besides Lascaux that have fine prehistoric paintings (Cougnac and Pech-Merle) are described later in this chapter.

While you are in Les Eyzies, be sure to visit the little twelfth-century church of Tayac which is within a short walk from the town. Its two massive, very wide and well-protected towers in the front and rear make it different from most of the other fortified churches in France.

As you drive around watch for some of the things that are typical of Périgord. On farms you will occasionally see ancient *pigeonniers,* which are larger and more solidly constructed than modern pigeon houses. And you may encounter oxen with their eyes covered by a bit of cloth so they won't be distracted by anything outside their routine chores. When you approach, give their driver time to put a reassuring hand on their heads; then pass slowly. Oxen apparently have never gotten used to cars, especially those that whiz by too quickly.

Bastides

Many towns in Périgord have the word *"bastide"* (from *bâtir,* to build) incorporated in their names—La Bastide-Murat, La Bastide-du-Haut-Mont, La Bastide-du-Vert-Bouyssounade, etc. Other *bastides* do not have that word in their name; instead, they are called "new" (Villeneuve d'Aveyron, Villeneuve-sur-Lot) because they were created as complete units from the eleventh to the fourteenth century, whereas most towns just grew up with their origins long forgotten. The *bastides* were founded as part of an effort to establish strong, well-defended settlements in thinly populated areas. Special inducements were offered to attract people to these new communities. They were granted liberal charters that, among other things, permitted serfs to gain freedom and prisoners of war to escape execution.

The *bastides* were laid out with protective walls enclosing a rectangular area with streets running in a grid pattern. In or near the center, a public square was set aside as a marketplace. The town's church abutted on this, and arcades around the square were common. Not only the French but the English invaders encouraged the building of *bastides.* Many good examples of them still exist. Villefranche-de-Rouergue and Monpazier preserve their original form almost unchanged.

The *bastides* are of great interest, not only as early specimens of town planning, but as landmarks on mankind's long, hard road to freedom. When they were built, common people had little more status than beasts of the field. Every *bastide* is a memorial to liberty and, as such, deserves respect.

You can drive from Les-Eyzies-de-Tayac to Sarlat for 21 kilometers (13 miles) on D47 or take the much longer but far more interesting route that swings around in a semi-circle through Saint-Cyprien, Les Milandes, Beynac-et-Cazenac, and Domme to arrive finally in Sarlat. This involves wandering around on little back roads, but the area is worth exploring.

Les Milandes is on an obscure road that leads through lush green country on the south side of the Dordogne River. It is not easy to find (although the way is marked), but this is the

The Dordogne Valley

medieval village (complete with castle) that was beautifully rebuilt at great expense by the American singer Josephine Baker. She undertook the enormous task in order to provide a home for a dozen orphans she had adopted from countries all over the world.

Les Milandes welcomes visitors. It has several grades of hotels, a night club, a big swimming pool, a children's playground, and all kinds of sports and games for adults. The resort has had its ups and downs. We have seen it at its best when it was in full swing, and we have seen it when it was not doing as well as it should. It is an idealistic venture that deserves to succeed. Its substantial stone buildings are nearly 500 years old; they have been carefully restored and should last for a long time to come.

Sarlat: medieval streets

FRENCH GOVERNMENT TOURIST OFFICE

Sarlat: rehearsing for Cyrano

Across the river is Beynac, where a thirteenth-century castle, perched on the heights above the Dordogne Valley, can be visited. It is interesting in itself, and it has a superb view.

On the south side of the river and east of Beynac is Domme, a strongly fortified *bastide* standing on high ground that terminates abruptly in a steep cliff overlooking the valley. The little park there is a fine tree-shaded place for a picnic lunch.

Underneath Domme are caves in which prehistoric men and long-extinct animals lived and left their marks behind. They are visited nowadays for their remarkable stalactites, stalagmites, and other strange shapes that calcite sometimes takes when water deposits it in caves.

Sarlat

Sarlat is an active cultural center in summer when theatrical performances are given there. Don't judge the town from its main street, which is lined with modern stores and commercial establishments. The old section east of this has two churches. On a hill above one of them—Saint-Sacerdos—is the Lanterne des Morts, a tall, conically-shaped twelfth-century tower that is believed to have served as an overnight resting place for corpses before they were buried in the cemetery.

Across the way from the church is one of Sarlat's handsomest Renaissance dwellings, the Maison La Boëtie, where Montaigne's friend of that name was born in 1530. There are so many historic buildings in Sarlat that the old section has been made a classified monument.

The town suffered terribly during the years between 1521 and 1523 when an army of mercenaries infected it with a plague that killed half of the inhabitants. Then it was inundated by a huge waterspout that destroyed some of the encircling walls. A monument listing the names of Nazi victims in the Second World War shows that Sarlat has had more than a normal share of trouble in modern times. Nor was Sarlat the only local target of the Nazi scourge. At Saint-Julien-de-Lampon, a few miles east on the south shore of the Dordogne, they drove men, women, and children into the church and set it on fire. They did this at Paluel and also farther north at Oradour-sur-Glane (near Limoges), where they slaughtered hundreds of citizens and burned the town.

Souillac

This small town, like Sarlat, once had an important abbey to which the massively domed twelfth-century church belonged. The church was badly damaged during the Wars of Religion. When it was repaired, some of its fine Romanesque sculptures were built into the walls again, but not necessarily where they had been before. One of them, the dancing Isaiah, is truly a masterpiece. Most Romanesque figures are rather static, but this one is filled with life and movement. If you want to photograph it you will need flashbulbs or a tripod for a time exposure because the light falling on it is not bright enough for ordinary film.

When you get to Moissac you will see a superb sculptured figure of Jeremiah. Similarity of style indicates that it may have been created by the same unknown master who was responsible for Souillac's Isaiah.

The interior of the church at Souillac deserves careful examination even though it is somewhat disfigured by wooden scaffolding that braces up the over-heavy domes. Elaborate pillars with grotesque figures of men, women, and beasts support stone arches, while sculptures in high-relief decorate the walls.

Cougnac

South of Souillac is Gourdon, where the recently opened Cougnac cave is just outside the town. Cougnac is well-lighted and easy to explore. In addition to its prehistoric paintings, it has an impressive display of stalactites, stalagmites, and other concretions. When the cave was discovered in 1952, it was found that time had deposited a thin layer of clear calcite over

Souillac: the dancing Isaiah

the pigments that prehistoric men had put on the walls. This transparent coating, which guarantees the great age of the paintings, also sealed them safely away from the air and moisture that has taken such a heavy toll of cave art elsewhere.

In addition to fine paintings of mammoths, ibex, and the giant elk, Cougnac has several pictures of human beings which were seldom used as subjects by Paleolithic artists. And, as was usually the case when people were depicted, the ones seen here are crudely sketched. The artists who could draw realistic-looking beasts evidently hesitated to give lifelike shapes to men.

East of Souillac is the extraordinary *causse* country. This arid land, where the inhabitants seem to have spent most of their lives building stone walls, is nearly worthless for farming, but it has many attractions for travelers. One of them is Rocamadour, where pilgrims have been going for 800 years to a religious city built on the side of a 400-foot cliff.

Two roads lead from Souillac to Rocamadour. Route D15 is the easier one, but D43 is more interesting. About halfway, Belcastel, a picture-book stronghold, stands on a projecting spur of rock that commands the Dordogne valley. Near this is the electrically lighted Lacave cavern which is noted for its enormous size and splendid calcite formations. At one place an underground lake reflects the numerous stalactites hanging over it. You go through part of the cave on an electric train.

At Lacave you can play it safe and go south on D23 past Cales to the intersection where you turn left on N673 to Rocamadour. Or you can take the much shorter but not very good VO that passes the tiny village of Cantaloube on the way. The Michelin Carte 75 does not bother to give this road a number, but it is passable and not really difficult.

Rocamadour

One advantage in coming to Rocamadour on this back road is that you arrive at a plateau above the town. This means that you walk down instead of up. From the lower street an elevator (for which you pay) will carry you part of the way up, but you then have to walk from its exit to the top. It is also worth driving over to the parking lot on the high ground at the eastern end of the valley (L'Hospitalet) to get a good view of the town from afar. Binoculars will be useful there. If you want to take photographs on a bright day, you will need morning light because the sun is behind the buildings in the afternoon.

Rocamadour has three levels. On top is a stronghold built to defend the town from an attack from the plateau. Halfway down is the religious city where a cluster of churches, chapels, and shrines center around a primitive wooden statue of the Virgin. One of them is a subterranean chapel; others use the cliffside as a wall. Here too is an exceedingly old bell that for centuries has allegedly rung of its own accord when a miracle occurred. Leading up to the religious city is a long flight of stone steps for devout pilgrims to use when they go on their knees to the shrine. Down on the floor of the valley is the business section where shops selling souvenirs and religious articles, restaurants, bars, and other commercial establishments are crowded closely together. Hotels located on the cliff take their guests' baggage up on wooden platforms hauled by ropes.

Although Rocamadour is a very active place, it is only a

Rocamadour

shadow now of what it was during the Middle Ages when tens of thousands of pilgrims came from all over Europe to camp in the meadow below the city while they awaited their turn to worship at the renowned shrine. Kings and queens were among the penitents who undertook the long, hard journey to this remote part of France.

The most celebrated of the royal visits was that made in 1170 by Henry II, the English king whose clash with Thomas à Becket had brought the Archbishop of Canterbury to his death. The British king's rebellious son, Henry Court-Mantel, robbed Rocamadour's sanctuary. He soon repented, put on a hair shirt, and died on a bed of ashes in nearby Martel.

Rocamadour's origins as a holy place are rather obscure, but tradition has it that Zacchaeus, who had been a devoted follower of Christ in Palestine, came here to live in a cave. Some versions speak of a Saint Amadour who found the perfectly preserved body of Zacchaeus many centuries later. Others say that the name Rocamadour is derived from a cave-dwelling hermit who loved the rocks—*roc-amator*.

Rocamadour has been sacked and pillaged many times. After the French Revolution it was neglected and had to be partly rebuilt in the nineteenth century. As you walk around you will see empty foundations and ruined walls. Restoration, however, has been done so well that most of the buildings now seem to be in excellent condition. Like Mont-Saint-Michel, Rocamadour is spoiled by overemphasis on the tourist trade. On a busy day the lower section is solidly parked up, and you may have trouble finding a place for your car along the one narrow street that crosses the town. Nevertheless, this ancient cliffside shrine is a place to see. Don't let inconvenience or heavy traffic stop you from visiting it. There is plenty of parking space on the top level. Then, as we have suggested, you can walk down the sloping paths with their stations of the cross until you reach the religious city.

The Causse Country

When you go east from Rocamadour you are in *causse* country proper, where stone walls crisscross the land in every direction. It is not all desolate; in some spots, such as nearby Alvignac, trees and green fields abound. The little country village of Alvignac is one of our favorite places in which to stay. (This book began there.) The miniature spa Miers (pronounced (Mee-erce) is within a walk, and the charming town by that name is just beyond it. The Gouffre de Padirac is only a few minutes away by car.

In this huge cavern you can see how water reacts on limestone over the course of millions of years, hollowing out the rock to let underground streams flow through it. The Gouffre de Padirac differs from caves you may have visited because it has no entrance except for the huge open shaft—an enormous hole in the ground—that gave it its name, *gouffre,* which means gulf or chasm. At one place a subterranean river swirled around for enough eons to dig out a conical-shaped hollow space in the roof of the cavern. The distance between the top of this and the surface of the ground finally became so small that the earth collapsed and left a big round opening. This one is more than 300 feet in circumference and nearly that deep. When you look down into the vast pit you will see a hill in the middle of it. This consists of some of the rocks and earth that fell down when the ceiling caved in.

Elevators take you to the bottom where you walk to a landing from which boats are rowed along the underground river. After you go ashore, you make your way up to the interior of another huge conical dome with its ceiling still intact. In the center of this is a great mound with a little pond of clear water on top of it. Calcite formations cover the ceilings, walls, and floors. The cave is lighted by electricity to display its most dramatic features.

Some of the small towns in this area are decidedly worth seeing. You can visit them by making a semicircular tour from Padirac to Cahors. Especially interesting are:

Martel. This village came into being in the eighth century after Charles Martel had won a victory over the Arab invaders. In gratitude he built a church around which a walled town grew up. As we have said, the rebellious Henry Court-Mantel, son of Henry II, came here nearly five centuries later to repent and die after having pillaged the sacred shrine of Rocamadour.

Carennac. Some ancient towns in France are slowly falling into ruins because no one cares about them, but this one, which is built on the heights above the Dordogne, is such a gem that a group of people who call themselves the Friends of Carennac are trying to preserve it. It is noted for its twelfth-century Romanesque church which has a fine tympanum and a small cloister with a vaulted ceiling. In the interior is an unusually good Deposition in the Tomb. Fénelon, the author of *Télémaque,* lived in Carennac from 1681 to 1696 as the Abbey's prior.

Castelnau. The interior of this fortress near Bretenoux was set on fire in 1851 by an unscrupulous owner who wanted to collect insurance. It was then restored by an opera singer who left it to the state.

Autoire. At the head of a great valley a waterfall plunges down from the high rocks. Below it is the handsome little village of Autoire with storybook houses and a building the French call a *gentilhommière* (a little country château). This one has a tiny round tower clinging to one side.

The Château de Montal. Like Castelnau, this small but attractive building was almost destroyed in the nineteenth century when a heartless buyer began to sell it off piecemeal. Again a more sympathetic purchaser appeared on the scene, reacquired as many of the plundered pieces as he could, and put them together again until the Château now seems as good as new. He, too, left the restored building to the state. Montal has a sad history. It was built early in the sixteenth century by a mother as a gift for her son. But he was killed in battle and never saw it.

Saint-Céré. France has many towns with very old streets and houses. They seem to be older and more picturesque than usual here. High above the town is the rugged-looking Tours de Saint-Laurent which was owned by the famous tapestry designer, the late Jean Lurçat.

From Saint-Céré, or from any point not too far south of it, you can make an interesting side trip through the country to the east to see Figeac, Conques, Rodez, and Villefranche-de-Rouergue.

Figeac has some old houses with open attics. Its Hôtel de la Monnaie is an unusual thirteenth-century mint of a design seldom seen in France. (It looks as if it might have served as the inspiration for some of the older public buildings in Southern California.)

Conques. This tiny hill village possesses one of the greatest treasures of religious art, the bejeweled reliquary of Sainte Foy. And its church, with its fine tympanum, is another treasure of early Romanesque art.

Rodez is a good-sized town with a tall-towered reddish-colored Gothic cathedral that is truly impressive inside and out. Two fine old houses have been made into the Musée Fenaille which has rare carved menhir statues and examples of local art.

Villefranche-de-Rouergue. Although the town's walls have been torn down, the center of this thirteenth-century community shows very clearly what a *bastide* was like. As was typical, a church occupies one side of a public square lined by arcades. Across the river is the fifteenth-century Chartreuse which was purchased by the town during the Revolution to be made into a hospital that is still used.

If you don't want to make the trip just described and prefer to return from Saint-Céré to a hotel base west of there, we suggest you take D19 and then D43 along the southern shore of the Dordogne, where the country is unusually beautiful. On the way you will pass a popular bathing place at Pauliac.

If you are driving south from Saint-Céré, take N681 from Gramat in order to see the primitive village of Rudelle with its fortified church. It is a dramatic example of the dire need that even the smallest community had for protection in medieval times.

Then, at Marcilhac, are the very impressive ruins of a great Benedictine abbey that was destroyed in the Wars of Religion. Impressive also are the carvings in high relief on the walls and capitals.

Marcilhac is on Route D41, a pleasant road that runs along the northern shore of the Celé River. Medieval strongholds were built into crevices in the steep limestone banks. These were used by the bands of robbers called *routiers* who pillaged the country in those lawless times. Some of these fortified dens can be seen farther upstream near Brengues and Corn. You may hear these referred to as Châteaux des Anglais because some of the marauders were deserters or demobilized soldiers from the English armies that were then occupying much of ancient Guyenne.

A few miles southwest of Marcilhac is Cabrerets where the Château du Diable was one of the *routiers'* dens. The town has an excellent museum of prehistory installed in the Château de Gontaut-Biron. And nearby is a cave which is the most interesting one in this part of France now that Lascaux is closed. It is called Pech-Merle and can be reached by a well-paved road that runs uphill from Cabrerets to a small entrance park with a place for picnic lunches and plenty of room for cars.

The cave is lighted by electricity; it is easy to walk around in, and is fairly dry underfoot. Pech-Merle is large, a veritable cathedral among the caves of the region, and is handsomely decorated by nature as well as by man. Numerous stalactites hang from the ceilings, and stalagmites reach up toward them from the floors, sometimes to join in a solid column. There are also rare disc-shaped concretions. Nature has staged an odd stunt here that demonstrates how desperately living things struggle to keep alive. You will see a long probing root from an oak tree coming down in search of water. It stretches in a thin, perfectly straight, hairy column from the high ceiling of one of the caverns to moisture on the floor below.

Long-extinct cave bears once inhabited Pech-Merle. Some of their skulls and bones are still there, and the limestone walls are marked by their scratches and rubbings. Inbedded in the calcite deposits on the floor are fossilized remains of their droppings.

Also preserved in the clay floor are footprints of people who entered this cave long before the civilizations of Mesopotamia and Egypt began. To see these prints is to bring the remote past back with a rush. Oddly enough, these people's feet were longest from the heel to the tip of the second toe instead of to the end of the big toe as most of ours are. Yet these men were very much like us; one of them was carrying a stick, and the imprints it made as it bounced along on the soft clay can still be seen. The smaller footprints of a child about twelve years old are among the other marks. They were probably left by a young initiate who was about to be introduced to the secret ceremonies that rule the lives of primitive people.

The painted caves were dedicated to the ritual magic of the hunt. Since the artists usually placed their work far from the entrance, the sculptures, engravings, and paintings that tell us so much about their makers remained almost unknown for thousands of years. When a few examples were found in the nineteenth century, they were scoffed at, for no one would believe that they could be so incredibly old. Scientists and scholars, as well as the ignorant, all refused to believe that men could have their racial origins so far back in time and that tangible relics of them still existed.

On the walls and ceilings of this sanctuary cavern are mysterious symbols that scientists cannot interpret. Among them are round blobs of pigment called punctuation marks; they occur in seemingly significant patterns in Pech-Merle as well as in other caves. They were placed in groups by themselves, in company with hand tracings, and in and around the paintings of animals.

Other unexplained man-made marks are finger doodles that were traced in soft clay which has since hardened. Those that seem to have been scrawled at random are called macaronis or meanders. Others make complicated designs in which attempts at pictorialization seem to appear. On the ceiling of the main chamber (the Hall of the Hieroglyphs), are three crude drawings of women with long, pendant breasts. It is difficult to find these figures in a tangle of interlaced finger drawings, but they are worth the trouble of trying to do so because pictures of people are rare in Paleolithic art. Pech-Merle has another example of the pictorialization of human beings. This is a small figure painted in red on the ceiling of a recess off the Main Hall. It represents a man (perhaps masked) with a number of straight lines pointed at him which are thought to be spears.

But the glory of Pech-Merle is its pictures of animals. Here the mammoths march again; with them are wild cattle and horses, the European bison, the Giant Irish Elk, and reindeer—all species that have long since disappeared from France, and, except for the reindeer, from the entire world.

Cave paintings tell us something about the way our primitive ancestors hunted large and powerful beasts. In Pech-Merle, a cow is shown falling from a height. We know from other sites in France, notably one at Solutré (near Macon in Burgundy), that prehistoric men drove animals over cliffs in order to obtain meat from those killed by the plunge. A falling figure in Lascaux—in this case a horse—verifies the fact that this kind of hunting was widespread.

Pech-Merle's outstanding masterpiece is the painting of the chequered horses. It shows two life-sized animals spotted with round blobs of paint identical to the so-called punctuation marks. In fact, a curved line of these marks runs around the head of the upper horse. An odd accident of nature gives this creature two heads, a small one painted by the cave artist, and a larger and far more realistic one of rock shaped like the head of a horse. Both animals have numerous human handprints outlined around them.

To visit this long-sealed subterranean sanctuary where men practiced ritual magic in prehistoric times is an experience that should interest everyone who cares anything about art, history, or anthropology. And, overwhelming as the immediate impact of the pictures is, they seem to become even more impressive in recollection. Long afterward, the magic of this spellbound place will return, and the beasts that stand forever in a cavern where they were imprisoned so long ago will be seen again by the mind's eye as it reviews this memorable scene from the far-distant past.

Yes, we recommend going to Pech-Merle. It is easier to visit than overcrowded Lascaux was, and it has some features that the more celebrated cavern did not have.

There are so many picturesque old towns in this part of France that some travelers, after having seen dozens of them, may get bored with the thought of visiting more. But Saint-Cirq-Lapopie, which is on the Lot River south of Cabrerets, is an unusually good one. It stands on a rocky spur above the valley, and its streets are steep and narrow. High above the town is a fifteenth-century church that was probably designed to serve as a fort as well as a place of worship, although it has no machicolations or other defensive works. All the houses are so old that the French government has made the tiny village a classified monument.

Cahors

The road to the west winds along the Lot until it reaches Cahors, 33 kilometers (20 miles) away from Cabrerets. There is a good hotel at Laroque-des-Arcs on the northern shore of the river only 5 kilometers east of Cahors.

Cahors itself lies in a bend of the Lot in a location that could be defended from attack. It had three fine very old bridges, but two of them were stupidly demolished during the past century and replaced by ordinary modern ones. Fortunately, the one that was allowed to remain is a masterpiece of medieval design and construction. Work on the Pont Valentré was started in 1308 and went on for two generations.

It is a fortified bridge with three tall stone towers rising from it while crenelated gates defend the approaches. This massive structure has defied floods, storms, and time so successfully that it still carries traffic across the river. The Devil is said to have helped to build it, a job he performed for his usual fee—the

Cahors: the thirteenth-century Pont Valentré

FRENCH GOVERNMENT TOURIST OFFICE

architect's soul. But he was tricked out of his reward by being told to bring up water in a sieve—an impossible task at which he naturally failed. A small modern statue of His Satanic Majesty high up on the central tower commemorates the legend.

The Pont Valentré and the domed Romanesque Cathédrale Saint-Étienne are Cahors' chief attractions, but it has many others. A protective wall that once ran completely across the base of the peninsula on which the city stands, ended in a massive barbican and a rectangular structure with one side left open so the populace could see condemned prisoners hanged when they were strung up in the Tour des Pendus. On the west side of the Lot is the rapid-flowing spring that the Romans called Divona when they built a small community around it.

The Cathédrale Saint-Étienne is surrounded by typical narrow ancient streets, but there is enough open space to get a good view of the much admired tympanum over the north doorway. Built about the same time as the Pont Valentré, the church was equally well qualified to serve as a defensive fortress for the citizens of the town. The cloister was added two centuries later.

Cahors has long been celebrated for its good red wine. Arthur Young, the British traveler who was there in 1787, said that it was an "excellent, full-bodied, great spirit without being fiery, and to my palate much better than our ports."

Montauban and Moissac

Route N20 leads south for 60 kilometers (37 miles) to Montauban which is more than twice the size of Cahors. Arthur Young went there too and praised the promenade for its view of the Pyrenees nearly a hundred miles away.

Much of Montauban is built of red bricks. Even the fourteenth-century bridge over the Tarn River is made of them. It is still in use, although it no longer has its original towers as Cahors' Pont Valentré does. Near it is the Musée Ingres, for that distinguished draftsman and portrait painter was born in Montauban in 1780. The museum has an extensive collection of his work, including nearly 4000 drawings. And his violin, which he claimed meant more to him than his ability to paint, is on display there.

The sculptor, Antoine Bourdelle (1861–1929) was also born in Montauban. The museum has many examples of his work,

Moissac: Jeremiah

Moissac: entrance to the Abbey church of Saint-Pierre

drawings as well as pieces in the round.

Only 19 miles to the west (31 kilometers) is Moissac, which is an essential stop for anyone interested in Romanesque art. Its Église Saint-Pierre, built in the twelfth century as part of the Abbey, has sculptured decorations that rank among the finest of the period. As we have said, the unknown artist who created the superb dancing figure of Isaiah in the church at Souillac may be the same one who wrought the miracles at Moissac.

The finely conceived and beautifully carved figures in the tympanum over Saint-Pierre's doorway represent the tremendous scene portrayed in the fourth chapter of the Revelation of Saint John. There is "the *one* who sat on the throne"; around Him are the strange beasts and the four and twenty elders "clothed in white raiment" while "on their heads are crowns of gold." This sculptured scene is magnificent now; it must have been glorious when it was first completed, for it was then rich with color and gold.

Below it is the doorway with its curiously shaped supporting pillars. The middle one is a masterpiece that any museum would be proud to have. Elongated, grotesque lions and lionesses twist upwards on it with their gaping mouths expressing their demonic ferocity. On the left side of the pillar is the figure of Saint Paul with his right hand raised while his left hand holds a closed book. On the right is Jeremiah. The face of the prophet is so sad, so filled with melancholy and deep thoughtfulness that it ranks with the greatest sculptured images of the world.

And then, around the doorway and inside are more masterpieces of Romanesque art, although none can match those at the entrance.

Behind the church is a cloister with sculptured capitals that are worth studying for their imaginative treatment. A stone with a chiseled inscription says that the cloister was built in the year 1100, a date which predates the superb doorway by a generation. The church, like most very old religious buildings, is a mixture of periods with the work of one century intricately woven into the structure of earlier ones.

Toulouse and Albi

You can go direct to Albi by returning to Montauban on N127 and then taking Route N99 for 72 kilometers (45 miles). Or, if you want to visit Toulouse, drive south from Moissac on N113 and N20 for 66 kilometers (41 miles).

Toulouse, the fourth largest city of France, has too many cars and not enough parking space. Like Montauban, much of it is built of red brick. Even the huge Basilisque Saint-Sernin is made of brick and stones. Curiously enough, the bricks seem to have withstood centuries of weathering better than the stone has. It is an extraordinary building with a massive five-story tower that supports a pointed steeple. The crypt is a storage place for bits and pieces of saints and apostles—a sort of holy charnel house.

Toulouse has a number of beautiful old churches and buildings as well as several museums. The Musée des Augustins (sculpture and painting) is installed in a former convent building to which a cloister is attached. The Natural History Museum has a fine collection of prehistoric material, but it is badly arranged.

FRENCH GOVERNMENT TOURIST OFFICE

Albi: the cathedral

The best way to see this bustling industrial city is to find a central parking place for your car—if you can—and then go around on foot.

Toulouse has 330,000 people; Albi only 42,000, but the smaller town is far more interesting. Its tremendous cathedral, Sainte-Cécile, is built of red bricks that have lasted for nearly seven centuries. Only one section is made of other material—the ornate sixteenth-century carved stone porch on the south side which stands out white against the red of the bricks.

The great building has very few openings near the ground level because it was intended to be a fort as well as a church. But unlike most fortified churches, this one was not designed to protect the people of the town but to give refuge to the clergy at a time when the Inquisition was making the Church unpopular. Red is an appropriate color for the building; enough blood was shed over religion in this part of France to stain the thousands of bricks that make up its walls.

Despite the church's unhappy origin and rather forbidding exterior, the interior is exceedingly beautiful. An intricately carved rood-screen surrounds the choir while a Gothic-arched roof rises high above it. Paintings and decorations make the walls glow with color.

Near its eastern end is the Palais de la Berbie which is now an art museum devoted largely to the work of Henri de Toulouse-Lautrec, the late nineteenth-century painter whose pictures portrayed the seamier side of life in Paris. This vitriolic, stumpy-legged, and very unhappy little man was born in Albi in 1864. His family gave the museum 160 of his paintings and 380 of his drawings, lithographs, and posters. Works of a few other modern artists are displayed on the third floor.

The cathedral at Albi is the scene of a *Son et Lumière* spectacle on summer nights. So are several other places in Périgord, notably Toulouse, Cahors, and Rocamadour.

Food and wine

Périgord food ranks high in France, but there is nothing fancy about it. Perhaps this is because the area is still a relatively simple one without big cities or top-rank luxury hotels. Michelin rates about a dozen restaurants in Périgord with one star. None of them is truly elegant, but along with many others they all serve good food.

Truffles and *paté de foie gras* have given the region its gastronomic fame, and many of its best dishes contain truffles. Not butter but goose fat or walnut oil is ordinarily used for cooking. Garlic begins to make its appearance here, for you are on your way to southern France where it is almost universal.

Since most of Périgord is harsh mountainous country with few lush pastures for cattle, the milk from which cheese is made is more likely to come from sheep or goats than cows.

While you are in or near Sarlat, try to get one of its local specialties, *pommes sautées à la Sarladaise,* which is made with sliced potatoes and truffles cooked in a covered pan with sweet white Monbazillac wine.

Monbazillac is said to be in the same class with Château d'Yquem as a fine white wine. And local experts say that Queyssac is even better. You may have to go to that little hilltop town northeast of Carennac to get it, for so little is made that it is not shipped out.

We have already mentioned the excellent red wine of Cahors. Other good wines of the region are likely to be produced in the west, where Périgord joins the Bordeaux districts along the lower reaches of the Dordogne River.

15. *The Pyrenees*

The great Pyrenees chain of mountains, which serves as a natural border between France and Spain, can be conveniently divided into two sections: west, from the Atlantic to Luchon; and east, from Luchon to the Mediterranean. Although there might be some dispute about naming Luchon so arbitrarily as the dividing point, there is no doubt that the two regions are distinctly separate from each other in many ways. The western part has Atlantic weather; the eastern, Mediterranean, which means that the skies are clearer there. The west is more densely populated, and its resorts are far more fashionable. But the greatest difference between the two sections—aside from weather—is that the people living in them have completely separate languages, traditions, architecture, and costumes. The east is Catalan country; the west, Basque.

As for bases, we suggest that you drive from the Atlantic coast, inspect Saint-Jean-Pied-de-Port on the way, and then use Argelès-Gazost as a center. This requires a long trip through the mountains, so an early start and hotel reservations are advised. From Argelès you can visit Lourdes, Cauterets, and Gavarnie.

If you want still more mountain scenery you might stay for a while at Luchon or its even more fashionable and expensive dependency, Superbagnères, which is higher in altitude and harder to reach. Otherwise we suggest that you keep going and find an interesting base farther on in the eastern Pyrenees. This is not easy. Foix is centrally located, but we hesitate to recommend any of its hotels. The same applies to Tarascon-sur-Ariège which is otherwise a convenient base from which to visit some of the best prehistoric caves. Ax-les-Thermes is a fine place to stay in, but it does not make a good base of operations because it is on a mountain road where there is very little to explore by car. You can make a day trip to Andorra from there, but there is no reason why you shouldn't spend more time in that tiny highland republic, which is one of the bargain paradises of the world.

If you do stay in Ax-les-Thermes don't be deceived into thinking that nearby Prades (northeast on N613) is the place where the famous music festivals are held. It is just a small, obscure village. The town you have heard so much about is farther east on N116.

Few tourists stay in this part of the eastern Pyrenees, which is why hotel resources are so underdeveloped there. Farther east, Font-Romeu and Molitg-les-Bains are rather expensive and not very exciting resorts. We know people who rave about Collioure and other towns along the Mediterranean coast, including Canet-Plage, but we were not impressed. Perhaps we have been spoiled—spoiled by beautiful seaside resorts in Brittany and on the Riviera where the coast of France is at its best.

The Basques

Just as Brittany is the home of a proud and sturdy people who cling to their traditions and language, so are the western Pyrenees the home of a somewhat similar people—the Basques. Their language has long puzzled etymologists who are naturally interested in speech that seems to have hardly any connection with words used elsewhere.

The Basques call their strange language "Eskuara" and themselves "Eskualdunak." While you are in their country you will see signs that will be absolutely unintelligible even if you are an expert linguist.

The Basques live in territory that stretches from Bilbao, Spain, to Bayonne and Tardets in France. They are a fiercely independent people who are noted for their expert seamanship, their fighting ability, and their many animated dances that have been carried down, almost unchanged, from primitive times. Their game of *pelota,* which is similar to *jai alai,* is played on a big court with a high cement wall for the ball to bounce against. You will see these courts everywhere in the Basque country.

The game is a fast and exciting one. The rather heavy, solid goatskin-covered ball is caught in and thrown from a curved wicker basket known as a *chistera,* which serves as an extension of the player's arm. When the ball is hurled with great force at the concrete wall, it hits with a resounding crack, bounces back with incredible speed, has to be caught in one of the player's *chisteras,* and is then thrown back at the wall again and again until someone misses or strikes the wall below a meter-high line.

The Basques are—and for centuries have been—expert shepherds. That may be one of the reasons why so many of them have emigrated to other countries where their skill in taking care of sheep is in great demand. Several hundred thousand have gone to South America and thousands of others are working in our Western states.

When you leave the coast and head east along the Pyrenees it is only a short run of 40 miles or so to Saint-Jean-Pied-de-Port. There are several ways to reach Cambo; from there N618 goes southeast through valleys where motoring is relatively easy. The main highway for those who want to make speed is N117 which passes through Pau, Tarbes, Saint-Girons, Foix, and Quilan to Perpignan. From it you will get occasional good but distant views of the Pyrenees. Far more interesting is the parallel road, N618, because it is much nearer to the mountains. This runs past attractive small towns, wanders through green valleys, and sometimes goes up to high passes. From it you will see herds of sheep pouring like streams over the slopes. They block the road, and you will then have to wait for their shepherd to clear the way. His heavy cloak shows that he is prepared for any kind of weather. Rain, sleet, and bright sunshine follow one another in rapid succession in the mountains. But the road is always passable, even in winter, for the snow is plowed then.

Although N618 winds around the foothills of the Pyrenees, there is no reason to follow it all the way. We will indicate some alternate routes. Because of the slopes running down from the mountains, roads paralleling the Pyrenees are scarce.

Saint-Jean-Pied-de-Port

This town owes its existence to the fact that it is located at the northern end of a long, narrow defile through the Pyrenees that has been used since earliest times. A few miles below the border is Roncevaux (or Roncesvalles in Spanish), where Roland held off a huge Saracen army in 778 and permitted Charlemagne to withdraw safely into France. This story, which is probably more

Sheep pouring over the mountains

A roadside cross in the Pyrenees

Saint-Jean-Pied-de-Port

legend than fact, is related in the *Chanson de Roland,* the ancient epic that celebrates that mighty hero's last act—the sounding of his horn, the mournful echo of which is a keynote in early French literature.

The narrow mountain road was used by pilgrims for centuries after the battle as they passed on their way to the shrine of Saint James of Compostela in western Spain. They would gather at Saint-Jean-Pied-de-Port in large numbers for mutual protection in the dangerous mountain passes. One of the most picturesque ceremonies of medieval times took place here when the procession was ready to begin its perilous journey. All the town's church bells rang while priests gave their blessings to the gray-clad pilgrims who chanted as they passed through the streets on their way to the shrine that was many days' journey ahead. This same narrow pass made history again in 1813 when the Duke of Wellington drove Napoleon's army out of Spain.

Saint-Jean-Pied-de-Port is now a quiet little place where the walled section of the town is the best reminder of its historic past. Behind the walls, narrow streets wind around the old city on the slopes below the citadel; outside them is the modern town. Part of it is built along the Nive River where houses and gardens line the shores.

Saint-Jean-Pied-de-Port would be a good place to stay in if it had better hotels. The ones it does have are inexpensive but rather primitive.

Route N618 runs on for miles through fine mountain scenery and sparsely settled country until it reaches Arudy. Along the way is Arette where a fine but small Calvary, somewhat like those in Brittany, stands beside the road.

At Arudy you can go north on N134 *Bis* for 25 kilometers (16 miles) to Pau, where Henri IV was born. His tortoise-shell cradle is in the Château there. Pau has a long terrace above the river, from which you can see the Pyrenees on a clear day. It is a pleasant place with many parks and museums, and is certainly more attractive than the commercial city of Tarbes. But Tarbes does have an interesting *haras* (government horse stud farm).

If you stay on N618, it soon begins to climb up the mountain pass, the Col d'Aubisque. Here you are still in the lower Pyrenees, but are high enough to see their high peaks rising along the Spanish border. In the spring or autumn they may have snow on their tops. The Pyrenees' tallest peak, Aneto, is 11,168 feet high.

While you are driving through this mountain wilderness be sure you have plenty of gasoline and oil because service stations are few and far apart.

After a run of 152 kilometers (94 miles) from Saint-Jean-Pied-de-Port you come to Argelès-Gazost, a peaceful little spa with many inexpensive hotels, a Casino, and a thermal establishment. The town is within range of Lourdes (13 kilometers or 8 miles), Cauterets (17 kilometers or 11 miles), or Pau (53 kilometers or 33 miles). From Argelès you can also drive into the mountains to see the spectacular scenery at the Cirque de Gavarnie.

Lourdes

Lourdes was a little-known town in the Pyrenees when Bernadette Soubirous was born there in 1844. She was collecting firewood on February 11, 1858, when she wandered into the Grotto of Massabielle where she said that an apparition of the Virgin Mary spoke to her. This was the first of 18 encounters; during one of them the Lady revealed a spring with waters that are now believed to have miraculously curative powers.

The Grotto became a place of pilgrimage so well-frequented that building after building was erected there, and the little town kept growing until it now has more than 2000 hotel rooms—a far greater number than can be found anywhere from Biarritz to Perpignan. At the time of the annual pilgrimage, which takes place during the week following August 15, all accommodations are ordinarily booked up long in advance. Lourdes has more visitors than the Riviera, but most of them stay for only a few days.

Millions of people, many of them crippled or seriously ill, have come here to pray for the restoration of their health. The Grotto, the huge Basilica, and the milling crowds of worshipers, make Lourdes a remarkable place that is totally unlike any of the other communities in the Pyrenees. You don't have to visit Lourdes during a pilgrimage to see what life is like there; activity goes on all the time.

Zola described Lourdes in a novel in 1874. In 1940, Franz Werfel, after escaping from the Nazis, went there and was in-

Lourdes

spired to write *The Song of Bernadette,* which became a great publishing success during the troubled years of the Second World War.

Cauterets and the Cirque de Gavarnie

Cauterets, like Argelès-Gazost, owes its existence to the presence of mineral springs with supposedly curative powers. But Cauterets is nearer to the high mountains and is located in an area where forests, waterfalls, and spectacular views abound. That it has long been a resort is testified to by the fact that Marguerite of Navarre spent some time there in 1546 and used the town as the setting for the prologue of her *Heptameron.* It has always been a favorite place for writers. Baudelaire, Chateaubriand, Heine, and Dumas are among those who have stayed there.

The journey south on Route N21 can be combined with one to the famous Cirque de Gavarnie, a huge mountain amphitheater where high cliffs and lofty peaks rise above the valley floor. To reach it from Cauterets you have to return to the intersection where N21C and N21 part and then drive south on N21 to the town of Gavarnie, which is 38 kilometers (24 miles) from Argelès-Gazost. On the way you will pass through the little double town of Luz-Saint-Sauveur, which has at least two points of interest. One is the fortified church in Luz, where a special door was built to admit the Cagots who were probably afflicted with leprosy, a disease they may have caught when they went to the Near East as Crusaders. Little is known about these mysterious people, and this is one of the few places that has any associations with them. Saint-Sauveur has the other mystery. One of its springs, La Source des Dames, was long said to have caused women who bathed in it to become pregnant.

Route N21 ends at the town of Gavarnie, and you have to go the rest of the way on foot, mule, or horseback. The Cirque de Gavarnie is a magnificent sight, but it may, of course, be clouded over. Pick a clear day for the journey. High up in the Cirque a jet of water springs into space to fall more than 1400 feet before it hits the ground. The amount that falls depends on glacial run-off, something that naturally varies according to the season.

The noted nineteenth-century artist, Guillaume Chevalier, was so enchanted with the scenery here that he signed his pictures Gavarni and is known to us by that name.

From Luz, N618 runs through many miles of mountain country. You can turn north at the Col du Tourmalet to go even higher by toll road (5.5 kilometers) to the Pic du Midi de Biggore where the altitude is 2865 meters (9400 feet). The last part of the trip to the very top takes about three-quarters of an hour on foot. This is not an easy tour, but the view from the summit is the best of any in the Pyrenees that is even reasonably accessible. You may think that you can reach the top easily on the *téléphérique* which departs from La Mongie, but this is not so. It takes tourists only to Taoulet, 2340 meters (7675 feet) high. There is a good view from Taoulet, but it is not as remarkable as the one from the summit.

If you have had enough mountain driving by this time, you can leave N618 at Sainte-Marie-de-Campan where N134 takes you to Bagnères-de-Bigorre, a well-known spa. From there you go on N638 until you reach N117, the main highway that parallels the Pyrenees at a much lower level.

Whether you maneuver the twists and turns of N618 as it

wanders through the mountains or take the faster route on N117, you will eventually wind up at Saint-Girons, for the two roads come together there and then part again to go their separate ways.

Prehistoric caves in the Pyrenees

Unless you have an insatiable appetite for mountain driving (and there is still plenty of it to do), we suggest that you head for N117 when you leave Sainte-Marie-de-Campan. For one thing, N117 goes past some of the most remarkable prehistoric caves in this part of France. We give a general background description of such caves in our chapter on Périgord.

There are many painted caves in the Pyrenees, but we are going to list only a few that can be visited easily. Some of them are privately owned, practically inaccessible, or both. One is literally both, for you have to get permission to enter it and then go through a water-filled tunnel to reach the decorated part of the cave. Obviously, it has few visitors. You will be near one that is easy to see when you approach Montréjeau on Route N117. This is the Grotte de Gargas, which is south of N117 and quite close to the village of Aventignan. Signs point the way to the cave. A guide will take you through the electrically-lighted passages which may be a bit wet underfoot.

Gargas is best remembered as the cave of the hands because it has an amazing number of them outlined on its walls. Some were made by blowing pigment through a hollow bone to trace a negative impression of the palm and fingers. Others were simply printed on the walls. A good many hands show one or more fingers missing. They may have been cut off as part of a magic ritual, for we know that sacrificial mutilation is common among primitive people. Gargas also has some engravings of animals and some of the finger tracings called meanders.

Although Gargas is easy enough to go through, a prehistoric cave some miles ahead is the simplest of all to visit. This is Mas-d'Azil, a 1400-foot-long, very high natural tunnel which is so big that a stream and the highway run through it. To get there, leave N117 at Belloc a few miles beyond Saint-Girons at the fork where N119 leads off to the left and then goes straight on to Mas-d'Azil. You can park your car inside the cave and go up to the galleries along the side which prehistoric men used for thousands of years. In more recent times these upper levels served as refuges during the Wars of Religion.

In Mas-d'Azil you will see exhibits of objects found there. In some places the bones of long-extinct animals are still in place with large mammoth teeth among them. The town hall in the village also has artifacts on display, although the best of them are in the museum in Saint-Germain-en-Laye near Paris. Toulouse also has some. The mysterious painted pebbles that have puzzled archeologists came from here.

After you leave Mas-d'Azil continue on N119 to Sabarat and turn right there to go to Foix where an early *château fort* with three towers stands on a rocky eminence above the town. It can be visited and has a museum of prehistoric, Gallo-Roman, and medieval art. We found that many hotelkeepers in Foix, for some inexplicable reason, have an exaggerated idea of the value of their rooms. They charge more than those in other towns in this part of the Pyrenees do, and from what we saw of their accommodations, we think you will do better elsewhere.

Montségur

You have to go out of your way to see this tragic reminder of the savagery of religious hatred in medieval times, but it is a place you will never forget. To reach it drive east from Foix on N117 past Celles and Nalzen to the very small village of Les Chaubets, where D9 goes off to the right. It will take you as near to Montségur as you can get. The ruins of this once well-defended citadel stand on the rounded top of a rocky peak nearly 4000 feet high. If you want a close view you will have to climb up the steep mountain path. But even from afar, the bare white summit of Montségur, with its sad ruins, is an impressive sight.

Here, on this lofty eyrie, was played one of the most dramatic scenes in the religious persecution that raged for decades in this part of France. During the early part of the thirteenth century, the Catharists, who were in rebellion against what they considered the too-worldly practices of the Church, were being ruthlessly hunted down by the Inquisition. Thousands were tortured and killed, but the people living on Montségur's practically impregnable location remained untouched until 1243, when the Church's army surrounded the base of the high rock and began a siege that lasted for nearly a year. The fighting was long and terrible, but 210 people on the mountain top held out until March 1244. After the surrender, they walked down to a field where they were tied to long piles of firewood and burned to death in a mass holocaust.

Nothing remains of that dreadful siege except the ruins of the long, narrow church that looks like a huge stone coffin. You can visit it, but there is little to see except walls and staircases. Few people want to make the difficult ascent, so the 700-year-old roofless building usually stands empty and deserted.

Limestone country and its caves

You have to return the way you came on D9, for Montségur is at the end of the road. When you reach Route N117 you have a choice of proceeding east to Perpignan or of going back to N20 and turning south there to Tarascon-sur-Ariège, Ax-les-Thermes, and the high Pyrenees. We recommend the second more roundabout route. Along the way you can visit Andorra, the tiny independent republic that is high up in the mountains on the border between France and Spain.

Tarascon stands above the Ariège River with the older, once fortified section higher than the more modern part. It is a small place, chiefly of interest because of the excursions that can be made from it. A few miles outside the town and a little north of Route N618 is Bédheillac, a cavern so big that the Nazis installed an underground airplane factory in it. Deep in the cave (which has no lights or guides, so you are on your own) are some prehistoric paintings and engravings of horses and bisons. To gain admission, see the Mayor of nearby Bédheillac.

More interesting is Niaux, one of the most important painted caves. It is not easy to visit because you have to make arrangements beforehand at the Syndicat d'Initiative in Tarascon for a guide. Then there is a long climb uphill followed by much walking inside the cave. But Niaux has the Salon Noir with many fine paintings in black outline of horses, bison, ibexes, and one deer. Other parts of the cave have more specimens of prehistoric art. One of the most remarkable is a bison that a clever artist planned so a water spot in the floor serves as an eye while three others represent spear wounds. Farther along the passageway are human footprints thousands of years old.

The limestone rock in this part of the Pyrenees has been so extensively hollowed out by water action that underground streams are common. One of them, Labouiche, which is northwest of Foix on Route D1, runs under the surface so smoothly and so free of obstructions that boats take tourists along it for three kilometers before the water again disappears into the ground.

Some of the numerous caves were used as places of refuge during the religious persecution of the thirteenth century. Lombrive, which is located in the heights above Ussac near Tarascon, is the best-known of these. Here the soldiers of the Inquisition simply walled up the cave and let the people trapped inside it starve to death. When the cavern was opened three centuries later, tradition says that their skeletons were found lying on the ground in a large circle with their feet pointing to the center.

This long-inhabited cave, in which prehistoric and Bronze Age artifacts have been found, is supposed—again according to tradition—to have given the Pyrenees their name. A young princess named Pyrene who lived in it was seduced by the far-wandering Hercules. When he abandoned her, she fled into the countryside where she was eaten by wild beasts. He returned and was so enraged at what had happened that he tore up rocks and threw them into a vast pile of mountains as a memorial to his lost Pyrene.

To Ax-les-Thermes and Bourg-Madame

Route N20 runs along the western shore of the Ariège River. Minor roads lead from it to isolated villages that are seldom visited by tourists although some of them have interesting little Romanesque churches. The one at Verdun is especially good. You can go through this back country by taking D20, which parallels N20 on the east side of the river, but it is a narrow, winding road. A short way beyond Axiat is a path which leads to the isolated ruins of the Château de Lordat, a large feudal stronghold that commanded the river valley.

High up in the mountains near here is a mine from which vast quantities of talc are brought to Luzenac by cars that come down on a cable stretched across the river. Route N20 continues along the Ariège until it reaches Ax-les-Thermes, 26 kilometers (16 miles) southeast of Tarascon.

Ax-les-Thermes is so old that the Romans used it as a spa. From 60 to 80 springs provide hot mineral water for the thermal establishments there. Some people say that the town smells of sulphur from the springs, but we did not notice any odor.

The warm-water pool in the Place du Breilh was built in 1260 by Saint Louis to serve as a basin in which leprous Crusaders could wash themselves.

Ax-les-Thermes is small and unhurried. Like most French spas, it has many hotels, some of which are quite good. They are all fairly inexpensive and give excellent value.

From here Route N20 runs straight south through deep gorges. At the confluence of the Carol and the Ariège, just beyond L'Hospitalet, Route N20B goes off to the right to Andorra. It crosses the frontier and then climbs up to a height of nearly 7900 feet at Port d'Envalira before it drops down again in a long descent to Andorre-la-Veille, the capital of Andorra, even though it has a population of only 2500. Hotels are cheap here, and imported goods are free of duty and taxes. Unless you have an International Driving License you will have to return to France on the same route you came, for the road that runs south of Andorra to France passes through Spain.

This brings us back to France near L'Hospitalet where Route N20B left N20. From this point N20 goes up the mountain pass called the Col de Puymorens (nearly 6300 feet high) and descends to run along the Carol River and the Spanish border until it reaches the cluster of towns around Puigcerda (in Spain) and Bourg-Madame (in France). The entire trip from Tarascon-sur-Ariège to Bourg-Madame (leaving out Andorra) is only 81 kilometers (50 miles), although it may seem longer because N20 goes through mountains all the way. But it is a well-built road that should give no trouble in summer. In winter it is plowed so skiers can reach the high slopes. Skiing in the Pyrenees is not as fashionable as it is in the Alps, but it costs less. Font-Romeu, which is not far from Bourg-Madame, is becoming a popular winter resort although it has no bargains like those in the mountain country just described.

A little bit of Spain

Just before N20 enters Bourg-Madame, which is on fairly level ground, N20C branches off to the left. This is a neutral road which leads to Llivia, four kilometers away. Llivia is a tiny Spanish enclave completely surrounded by French territory. It owes its existence to a treaty of 1659 that ceded 33 villages to France, but Llivia was classified as a "city" so it had to stay with Spain.

This political curiosity, which consists of 12 square kilometers, does not welcome visitors. The red and white bar that ordinarily closes the road to intruders happened to be up when we drove past it, not realizing that we were causing an international incident. We saw what there was to see of unimpressive-looking Llivia in a few minutes and returned. The guard at the gate was waiting for us. "Where is your permit from Perpignan?" he demanded in French.

"We have never been in Perpignan and didn't know you needed a permit."

"I could have shot you," he growled. We showed what we thought was the proper amount of consternation followed by equally proper expressions of regret. Satisfied, but still grumpy, he opened the gate and waved us on. We went gladly and have never had any desire to enter that forbidden little bit of Spain again. But sometimes we wonder how the handful of Spaniards isolated there feel when they compare themselves with the prosperous French people living all around them. The bewigged gentlemen who interpreted a treaty more than three hundred years ago certainly did them no favor.

The Cerdagne

The citizens of Andorra are Catalan, and so are many of the people on both sides of the border between France and Spain.

Two roads lead from Bourg-Madame to Mont-Louis. Route N618 (29 kilometers passes the Chaos de Targasonne with its huge tumbled rocks and goes through Font-Romeu, the resort and winter sports center, but N116 is shorter (23 kilometers). Both skirt the little Spanish enclave, Llivia, and both have fine scenery and good views along the way. They run through

Cerdagne, a region noted for its clear, dry air. The sun shines so often here that the French government has installed its Research Center for Solar Energy in the valley between the two roads, while a solar laboratory is located in Mont-Louis.

Mont-Louis has preserved the elaborate walk built by the seventeenth-century military engineer Sébastien Vauban, who designed more than 1600 French fortresses. This area near the Spanish border always had to be on the alert, and the key road (now N116) that runs along the Tet River to Perpignan has other examples of military preparedness. Villefranche-de-Conflent, near Prades, has defensive walls that are still in perfect condition.

Prades, which has become famous because of the music festivals sponsored by Pablo Casals, is not very interesting for itself, but the nearby Abbey de Saint-Michel-de-Cuxa (a few minutes south on D27) decidedly is. Oddly enough, you may already have seen part of these very early buildings, for some of their stone capitals are in upper Manhattan's Cloisters Museum. Much of the original Abbey, however, has been restored, and it has primitive Romanesque sculpture of a kind you are not likely to see elsewhere.

From Prades, N116 continues on to Perpignan, 43 kilometers (27 miles) away.

Basque cooking

Fortunately for cooking in the Basque country, its sources have come mostly from France rather than Spain. But good as Basque food is, we note that Michelin awards less than a dozen single stars to restaurants in the western Pyrenees, and some of them hardly can be said to specialize in Basque cooking.

Fish from the Atlantic is featured here. *Ttoro* is the Basque version of *bouillabaise* and *cotriade*. And here black inky squids are cooked in their own dark liquid with wine added to it. *Poulet basquaise* (duck cooked with grapes), and *piperade* (eggs with pimentos and tomatoes) are among the more popular specialties. If you can find it, don't miss *pommes de terre à la basquaise,* for these are potatoes stuffed with ham, tomatoes, pimentos, covered with bread crumbs and baked. Fattening? Yes. Delicious? Yes and yes again. *Garbure,* which is popular throughout southwestern France, is a thick soup-stew made of boiled cabbage, many other vegetables, bacon, sausage or ham, and goose fat. The recipe varies from place to place.

Wines: white Jurançon is rather sweet but worth trying. It was a favorite of Henry IV's, whose lips were moistened with it shortly after he was born. Irouléquy (also white) from Saint-Pied-de-Port, is another possibility. Madiran is a red wine produced farther north.

The food and wines of the eastern end of the Pyrenees are treated in the chapter on Roussillon.

16. *Roussillon, the Tarn, and Auvergne*

Traditionalists, who probably winced when we gave the generic term Périgord to a large section of southwestern France that lies far beyond the normal borders of the area that rightfully bears that name, may howl at the grouping of regions covered in this chapter. It is admittedly a huge area that extends for 550 kilometers (342 miles) from the Spanish border to Vichy and is about 125 kilometers (78 miles) wide. There are only two cities with a population of more than 100,000 in it (Clermont-Ferrand and Montpellier); otherwise it is thinly settled and much of it is mountainous, rocky, bare, and barren. Except for Carcassonne, most of its tourist attractions are natural curiosities rather than man-made.

As to places to stay, there are the beaches along the Mediterranean coast, Carcassonne itself, Millau or La Malène in the Gorges of the Tarn, and any one of the Auvergne group of spas—La Bourboule, Le Mont-Dore, or Saint-Nectaire.

During the summer, Perpignan and the roads around it are likely to be crowded with tourists going to Spain. Accommodations may be difficult to get, so make your plans accordingly. The city itself and the small coastal towns south of it on the Côte Vermeille—Argelès, Port-Vendres, Banyuls-sur-Mer, and Cerbère are fairly interesting, but, if it is beaches you want, some of the best in France are located along the Mediterranean here. Route N617 runs from Perpignan to Canet-Plage where there are enormous stretches of white sand. The beaches, however, are far better than the hotels. They are inexpensive enough but not very attractive. Miles of this area are covered by camps, trailers, and rather poor looking summer cottages. Behind much of the shore are large salt-water ponds called *étangs*.

This long-neglected region, with its fine beaches, should have a great future because the French government is planning to develop it into a series of modern resorts that will extend from the Spanish border to Montpellier. It will have the great advantage of being built on land that has never been used before, so hotels, parks, playgrounds, marinas, and sports areas can be constructed inexpensively and operated at a reasonable cost.

Route N9 runs behind the many salt-water ponds to Narbonne, 62 kilometers (39 miles) north of Perpignan. Narbonne's chief attraction is the cluster of buildings around the Cathédrale Saint-Just. The choir is the only completed part of a building which was conceived on a scale so vast that it reminds one of the similarly unfinished cathedral of Beauvais. Saint-Just has a cloister and a small *trésor* designed to house the sacred relics. The Palais des Archevêques is now a museum with early French paintings and ceramics while the Lapidary Museum south of it has many examples of Gallo-Roman and medieval sculpture. A few streets west of this is the Maison des Trois Nourrices, a Renaissance house with elaborately carved caryatids.

Carcassonne

To visit Carcassonne usually requires a special trip because it is located in country that has relatively little else of interest. But the trip is worth it, for this justly celebrated fortified city is a highlight of any tour of France. It is only 56 kilometers (35 miles) from Narbonne, and Route N113, which leads to it, runs through beautiful vineyard country all the way. Carcassonne can, of course, be reached almost as easily from Toulouse, Albi, Foix, or Mont-Louis. But no matter from which direction you come, don't miss Carcassonne. People drive across France to see it. Those who put off making the trip should remember the elderly peasant in Gustave Nadaud's poem. He lived only five leagues away but never saw the fabulous city, much as he wanted to, because he kept delaying the journey and finally died of old age when he at last started out to go there.

Carcassonne is two thousand or more years old, for Roman foundations underlie those built by the Visigoths while medieval walls and towers rise above those. Saracens seized and occupied

Carcassonne

the town in the eighth century, and it was at this time that Carcassonne is supposed to have received its name. According to old wives' tales, the town was besieged by Charlemagne, presumably in 778, and the garrison was reduced to such a state of starvation that it was about to surrender. But a clever woman named Carcas stuffed a pig with the last few morsels of grain left in the town and threw it down to Charlemagne to convince him that the garrison still had plenty of food. The trick worked, and as the army moved off, Carcas sounded the bells of the city—Carcas-Sonne. A crude portrait-statue of the quick-thinking heroine built into the eastern entrance gate would seem to confirm the story. There is only one trouble with it; Charlemagne never besieged Carcassonne. Perhaps it was someone else, because many others did try to capture the fabled city.

Anyway, it was not until the thirteenth century that Carcassonne had fully developed into the magnificent fortified city which became world famous for the strength and perfection of its battlemented double walls, numerous towers, and deep moat. It reached the high point just as stone walls were being rendered obsolete by gunpowder and cannon. Carcassonne remained intact, but only because the currents of history swept around it. Eventually it became so unimportant that it was allowed to fall into decay. Arthur Young, the British traveler, saw the city on August 1, 1787, but it meant so little to him that he merely said that "they carried me to a fountain of muddy water and to a gate of the barracks." But he arrived there on a terribly hot day when he was disgusted by "the myriad of flies ready to devour me," by the difficulty of getting any kind of transportation, and above all by the miserable inns, although he did say that the one in Carcassonne was better than most.

A few years later, during the French Revolution, Carcassonne's beautiful church was used as a warehouse for fodder while munitions were stored in some of the other buildings.

After that, anything thought useful in the dilapidated city was carted away. The lowest point came on July 8, 1850, when an order was given to pull down the ancient walls. Only quick action on the part of a local archeologist saved Carcassonne from being completely destroyed. Prosper Mérimée, who was then the inspector-general of historical remains, and the architect, Eugène Emmanuel Viollet-le-Duc, who had been repairing Carcassonne's Basilique Saint-Nazaire, also helped to save the threatened city.

Viollet-le-Duc

Viollet-le-Duc was an extraordinary man, but he has come in for much criticism. Much of the criticism seems justified, for he admitted that his idea of restoration was "to re-establish [a building] in a state of completion which may have never existed at any given moment in the past." This attitude led him to destroy much that was good, preserve much that was not, and draw upon his imagination when he had no facts. Nevertheless, if it had not been for him, Carcassonne and many other important French historical monuments would not exist today, while others would be in ruins.

Viollet-le-Duc worked for years on Carcassonne. The chief complaint is that he did not merely restore but built anew when something was so far gone that it was impossible to tell what it had been like in the thirteenth century. Nevertheless, this medieval walled city, complete with all the features one reads about in books of history and architecture, is exceedingly interesting to visit. Anyone who is not an architectural purist will enjoy a stay there, so much so, in fact, that we recommend trying to get accommodations in the old city even though the only two hotels there are quite expensive.

Actually, Carcassonne is two towns, the very ancient walled one on a hill and a larger one on the level ground below it. Most of the hotels and restaurants are located in the lower town, which is not as modern as it may seem because it was founded in the thirteenth century and formerly had walls of its own.

Carcassonne as it is today

When you visit the old city on the hill you may find it crowded with tourists, for it is enormously popular. It still has only two entrances, the Porte Narbonnaise on the east side, and the Porte d'Aude on the west.

As you walk around you will see how a medieval city was prepared to defend itself against attack. The double walls have an open space (the Lices) between them so bowmen on the inner one could shoot down at invaders who might breach the outer enclosure. Each tower is an independent unit that could hold out even if others were taken. Anyone seriously interested in the history of warfare can spend days studying this full-scale museum of the art of fortification as it was before explosives made stone walls useless.

The chief points of interest are the great twelfth-century Château Comtal which was built as an interior fort in which the defenders could take refuge even if the rest of the city was taken; the Maison de l'Inquisition; and the Basilique Saint-

Nazaire, which is noted for its fine stained-glass windows. Best of all is the city itself, regarded as a compact unit. Only by walking leisurely around it can you get a good idea of what it is really like. It is best seen at sundown when the western walls and towers are bathed in a golden light that makes them look like an illustration for a fairy tale in which knights and princesses play colorful parts.

If Carcassonne whets your appetite for old towns with big stone gates you may want to drive 65 kilometers (40 miles) north on Routes N118 and N112 to Castres. It is not as impressive as Carcassonne, but it has many admirers. Among other features, it has a Spanish museum with work by Goya and some of his countrymen. Several unexpectedly good hotels and a restaurant that Michelin rates with one star are located there.

From here you can either continue north to the Gorges of the Tarn (described later in this chapter) or return to the Mediterranean by taking Route N112 to Béziers, 102 kilometers (63 miles) away.

On N113, only 11 kilometers (7 miles) south of Béziers, is Nissan-lez-Ensérune. You will pass through it if you are driving north from Narbonne. Here a road leads west over a canal to the Oppidum d'Ensérune, an important archeological site where excavations have been under way since 1915.

It first came to attention when botanists noticed plants growing there that were unknown elsewhere in France although they were native to Greece. When they were dug up, shards of Greek pottery were unearthed. Much digging and research showed that a Greek trading colony had stood on the heights for several centuries before the Christian era. It had been destroyed and the ruined site was then taken over by the Gauls who dwelt there until the Romans drove them out. At one time the town had a population of about 8000.

A museum shows how these early people lived. Among the Greek and Gallic artifacts are many objects of everyday life such as combs, dice, perfume burners, and pottery of all kinds.

Béziers

The modern city of Béziers has only a few reminders of the frightful day on which its entire population—some 20,000 luckless creatures—were put to death. The Albigensian crusade against the Cathars, which ended so tragically at Montségur in 1244, began even more horribly here in 1209. Simon de Montfort, who had been appointed by Pope Innocent III to stamp out heresy in Languedoc, attacked Béziers and demanded that several hundred Cathars be sent to him to be executed. When the townspeople refused, he captured the city on July 21 and turned his soldiers loose upon the populace with orders to kill every living creature. Those who were not hacked to pieces were driven into the churches which were then set on fire.

During the slaughter, one of the officers ran to the Papal legate to tell him that the soldiers were slaying everyone in sight, Catholics as well as heretics. That official's cool reply has come down through the ages: "Kill them all," he said. "God will know his own."

Even more dreadful than the outright murder of the entire population of Béziers is what was done to the Cathars who were captured afterward. They were blinded, deafened by hot wires thrust into their ears, their tongues were cut out, and their hands lopped off. Then these doomed cripples were turned loose on the roads with signs around their necks warning people that it was death to offer them aid. One by one, the miserable creatures died by the wayside where their bodies were left to rot because everyone was afraid to touch them.

Simon de Montfort continued his campaign of terror until the siege of Toulouse in 1218 when a catapulted stone tore his head off. Legend says that his decapitated body quickly turned black.

It took Béziers so long to recover from the massacre of 1209 that only in fairly recent times has it again become a populous city. Arthur Young passed through it in 1787 and commented favorably on the great canal that had been constructed there by Louis XIV.

Nowadays, Béziers has a fine tree-shaded promenade called the Allées Paul-Riquet, the churches that survived the massacre, and a museum of local history and of the wine of the region.

Sète and Montpellier

The best way to reach Sète from Béziers is to take N112 and then N108 along a narrow strip of land between the sea and the huge Bassin de Thau with sandy beaches along the way.

The distance is 45 kilometers (28 miles). At the junction of these two roads is Agde, where twelfth-century Romanesque Saint-Étienne was a cathedral until the time of the French Revolution. It is built of black lava like Clermont-Ferrand's Notre-Dame.

Sète stands on Mont Clair, which rises above the flat land around it. It is an important center for handling the shipment of wine and is also a major fishing port. On July 14 nautical jousts are staged along the waterfront. Since Paul Valéry was born there, the local museum has many of his manuscripts and other memorabilia.

Montpellier is a good-sized city with several museums, some fine old houses, and a university noted for its medical faculty. Doctors who read Latin and French can get a good idea of the way medicine was practiced here in the eighteenth century by referring to the letter written on November 12, 1763, which appears in Tobias Smollett's *Travels Through France and Italy*.

To get from Béziers to Montpellier, one would ordinarily go directly east to Agde on N112 for 22 kilometers (14 miles). But it will be well worth your while to take the longer route (40 kilometers or 25 miles) northeast on N9 and then south on D13 to Agde, for this will enable you to visit Pézenas, which is one of the most attractive unspoiled old towns in France.

Its ancient walls are gone, and its castle was destroyed in 1633 by orders from that habitual fortification wrecker, Cardinal Richelieu, but its seventeenth-century houses remain intact. Here Molière stayed for several years and gave performances. Here is a fourteenth-century Jewish ghetto almost unchanged. And here, the French government, knowledgeable now about its irreplaceable antiquities, has made the town into a classified monument and is spending money to preserve and restore it. Someday, Pézenas will be an important tourist stop. There is still time to see it before the postcard and souvenir shops move in.

At Montpellier you have a choice of going east to Provence or north to the Gorges of the Tarn and Auvergne. The northern trip can, of course, also be undertaken as an extension of your journey through Périgord, in which case you would go east to Millau. But before you enter this rocky wilderness, be sure you have Michelin's Carte Number 80 because the road system is very confusing here.

If you start from Montpellier, the most interesting route is N586 (40 kilometers or 25 miles) to the Grotte des Demoiselles, a big cave which gets its name from the fact that one of its numerous stalagmites looks like a statue of the Virgin and Child. The Cirque de Navacelles can then be reached by a short detour on D25 and D130.

Route N586 ends at Ganges where you have a choice of taking D25 or N99 to the west. The latter goes through Vigan with its fine old high-arched bridge and then on to Millau.

Millau

Millau is an excellent center for visiting many interesting places in the neighborhood. The town of 22,000 people has several fairly good hotels, two of them with one-star restaurants. Ths is not exactly staying in the country, but it is comfortable enough. Nearby Le Rozier has good accommodations in a more rural setting.

Millau is noted for its manufacture of gloves made from the hides of the sheep raised on the *causses*. In Roman times it was an important center for pottery. A small museum has some of the pieces dug up here.

A popular trip from Millau is the one to Roquefort, about 20 kilometers (12 miles) southwest on N592, N99, and D23. Visitors are welcomed to the famous caves where Roquefort cheese is produced.

Roquefort—town and cheese

Again according to legend, which always seems to have an ingenious story to explain otherwise forgotten events, the marvelous properties of the Roquefort caves were discovered by accident many centuries ago when a shepherd boy left his luncheon cheese there by mistake. When he returned some weeks later he found it streaked with green veins. He was hungry enough to taste the odd-looking stuff and found that it had been greatly improved by its stay in the cave. So began an industry that is now famous.

What gives Roquefort cheese its special flavor is the green mold that grows in the caves. Fissures in the rock serve as natural air-conditioning ducts to keep the cheese cool while it absorbs the magic mold.

Nearly everyone in the town of 1500 people earns a living from the product that has brought fame to this isolated place. Cheese takes precedence over everything else, and there is naturally only one kind that matters. It matters so much that the right to use the name Roquefort is jealously guarded and is protected by law in France.

Chaos and caves

Also within striking distance from Millau is the Chaos de Montpellier-le-Vieux. Take D110 for 15 kilometers (9 miles) to an intersection where a road leads southeast to Maubert and the Chaos. You have to park your car at the entrance and go around on foot.

This celebrated Chaos is one of the most widely scrambled assortments of weirdly shaped rocks in France. Parts of it look like a city crowned with a castle; in other sections you will see a giant natural arch and rocks that resemble men and beasts.

From it you can go on to visit several big caves nearby. After the glaring sunlight reflected from the light-colored rocks of the Chaos, their cool interiors will be a relief. In summer this part of France usually has a great deal of sunshine.

Continue on D110 until it ends at D29; then turn right for 8 kilometers to D584 where you turn left to Veyreau; there go right to Dargilan, where a road leads to the cave entrance. Not far from here (on N586) is the Aven Armand, an immense cavern with a huge shaft that plunges straight down for 650 feet. The section the tourist sees, however, is perfectly safe and has a magnificent display of stalagmites lighted by electricity.

You can return to Millau by a different route by going north on N586 for a short way beyond the Aven Armand and then going west on D63, which leads to N596, N107*Bis,* and N9. Allow a full day for such an outing.

The Gorges of the Tarn

From Millau to Saint-Enimie, N9 and N107*Bis* run along the deep gorges made by the Tarn River in a huge mass of limestone. The region west of the river is called the Causse de

Sauveterre, while the eastern section is the Causse Méjean. Actually they are parts of one big *causse,* but they have been given separate names for convenience.

This is a spectacular road to travel, for it runs along a shelf on the limestone cliffs and sometimes cuts through them in tunnels. All around are grotesquely shaped rocks with high pinnacles, towers, columns, crevices, and strange projecting knobs. The road is not difficult, but it requires careful driving. There is so much to see along the way that the person at the wheel may be tempted to look at the scenery—a temptation that must be stoutly resisted no matter how attractive the view may be. Fortunately, there are many good stopping places. Ten kilometers north of Le Rozier a small road leads up to the Point Sublime from which you can get a good view of the Tarn and its rugged gorges. Just beyond this is the Cirque des Baumes and the narrows (Les Détroits). Still farther upstream is La Malène where there are two excellent but rather expensive places to stay. One of them is the fifteenth-century Château de la Caze which was built by a nobleman who had eight beautiful daughters whose portraits are painted on one of the wood-paneled ceilings. The building has moated gardens overlooking the river and an outdoor cocktail terrace.

From Malène you can descend the Tarn by boat, a safe and scenically beautiful ride from which you return by taxi. More exciting—and risky—is to go through the rapids in a canoe.

At Saint-Enimie, a highly photogenic hillside town, 107*Bis* continues along the Tarn to join N107 and go on to Mende by a roundabout way (66 kilometers or 41 miles). You can get there more directly by taking N586 (28 kilometers or 17 miles).

Mende

The cathedral in Mende was built in the seventeenth century to replace an earlier one destroyed by the Protestants in 1579. An odd relic of the original church is the four-foot-long bronze bell clapper that hangs on an inside wall. The town has an interesting museum of Bronze-Age art and a narrow fourteenth-century bridge.

As late as the eighteenth century, the country around Mende was covered by dense forests that provided shelter for wild beasts. One of the numerous wolves that lived there killed so many people that he was called the Bête de Gévaudan. A contemporary description said that it "is the size of a bullock with paws as strong as a bear's. Its jaws are enormous, its breast is as wide as a horse's, its body as long as a leopard's, while its four-foot-long tail is as thick as a man's arm."

This monster became such a threat that regiments of soldiers were sent into the woods to hunt it down. They succeeded in killing a huge wolf, but apparently it was not the right one, for the depredations continued until a peasant shot the beast. It had become so famous by this time that its body was shipped to Versailles so the king and his court could see it. Oddly enough, it proved to be a rather ordinary looking wolf. But it—and no one knows how many others—devoured 92 victims during the years 1763 to 1765. The wolves in this area made out badly, though, for 679 of them were exterminated in the 1760's. The Bête du Gévaudan is so well-remembered in this region that a very modern statue of him stands in a public square in Marvejols, 28 kilometers (17 miles) west of Mende.

Le Puy

It is a long run on N9 from Mende to Clermont-Ferrand (189 kilometers or 117 miles), but we suggest that you take an even longer route by going on N88 in order to visit Le Puy on the way.

You must have seen pictures of Le Puy's Chapelle Saint-Michel-Aiguilhe for it appears on travel posters everywhere. A good many European churches have been built on elevated places, but this one is the most remarkable of all, because it stands on the point of a needle-like volcanic core that is 260 feet high. The church dates from the eleventh century, but the stairway with 267 steps is even older; it was probably hewn out of the rock for the use of the workmen who constructed a Roman temple that stood there before the church replaced it.

Le Puy would be worth going to just to see this church, but it has even more than that. Its huge cathedral is reached by going up the Rue des Tables where lace-makers offer their finely made handiwork for sale. And the twelfth-century cathedral, which seems more Spanish and Oriental than French, has contrasting light and dark facing stones like the Duomo in

FRENCH GOVERNMENT TOURIST OFFICE

Le Puy

Florence. Its Black Virgin, although old, replaces the original one that was destroyed during the Revolution. This huge cathedral covers the table stone of a dolmen which is called the *Pierre aux Fièvres* because people who lie down on it are supposed to be cured of fever.

Behind the cathedral and its cloister rises the volcanic core called the Rocher Corneille with a colossal statue of the Virgin that was cast from the metal obtained from several hundred Russian cannon captured during the Crimean War.

In Stevenson's footsteps

Anyone who has read Robert Louis Stevenson's *Travels with a Donkey in the Cevennes* can retrace that journey from Le Monastier which is 21 kilometers southeast of Le Puy. There

Stevenson and his somewhat difficult companion, Modestine, started out on September 23, 1878, to travel 12 days on a route that took them 120 miles south to Saint-Jean-du-Gard. This was rough country to traverse then, and it still is. In fact, at one place, where the trail leads over the Montagne du Goulet, only donkeys and pedestrians can get through. An automobile cannot; it has to go around.

For those who want to make the trip the itinerary is: Le Monastier, Goudet, Ussel, Bouchet Saint-Nicholas, Pradelles, Langogne, La Bastide, and Notre-Dame-des-Neiges (where Stevenson stayed).

Then the route leaves Michelin map No. 76 to continue on No. 80 as follows: Chasseradès, Lestampes, Le Bleymard, Le Pont de Montvert, Florac, Cassagnas, Saint-Germain-de-Calberte, and Saint-Jean-du-Gard.

Obviously you will take Stevenson's book with you so there is no point in describing his adventures along the way. If you reach Saint-Jean-du-Gard, which is in the country where the Camisards were persecuted after the Revocation of the Edict of Nantes in 1685, you can go a few miles east to see the tiny Protestant museum near Mialet called Le Musée du Désert, where relics of those days are on view.

Auvergne

The great volcanoes in the Massif Central are all extinct now, and only numerous hot springs and the wreckage of their inactive cones remain to testify that fire once reigned here. The biggest crater of them all extended for miles around Cantal's Puy Griou (now 5500 feet high) which marks the approximate center of a volcano that was 10,000 feet high before it blew itself to bits. The Puy Griou was one of its many dykes, and it owes its present existence to the fact that the hard lava core which filled up the vertical throat resisted the weathering that wore down the softer material around it.

You will see many dead volcanoes in the area between the upper reaches of the Lot and Clermont-Ferrand. The northernmost ones around the Puy de Dôme are in excellent condition with many of their craters intact. As you drive through this region, lava, in all its forms, will be everywhere around you. Fortunately, for the economy of Auvergne, decayed volcanic rock makes good soil for grass on which dairy animals can graze.

Except for these peaks, which stand aloof above the countryside, the chief points of interest here are the three famous spas, La Bourboule, Le Mont-Dore, and Saint-Nectaire, which are located along a 32-kilometer (20 mile) stretch of Route N496.

Oddly enough, each town is very different from the other two. La Bourboule is level and open, with many wide streets. Mont-Dore is more compact, with a good part of the town built on the surrounding hills. And Saint-Nectaire, which is the smallest of the three, stands on steep slopes that rise on both sides of N496. The permanent residents of the spas all depend on visitors for a living, so they naturally do their best to please them.

La Bourboule, which calls itself "the capital of allergy," boasts that its springs are "the most arsenical and radio-active in the world" but hastily assures visitors that there is nothing dangerous in their waters. The town favors children and provides many attractions for them. There is a big park with a playground, while ponies and pony carts can be seen everywhere.

Mont-Dore takes its medical treatments very seriously, so much so that you will see patients coming from the thermal establish-

Puy de Dôme

ment dressed in the hooded white costumes required there. You can visit it without having to take the cure. Since the springs were used by the Greeks and the Romans, there are statues and columns from those early times. Nearby Puy de Sancy, which is more than 6000 feet high, has a view over all of central France.

Saint-Nectaire is tiny compared to the other two spas, but is has a fine twelfth-century Romanesque church. The town is divided into two parts, high and low. A "petrifying" spring quickly deposits sodium carbonate on objects immersed in it. The park above the lower town has a fairly impressive dolmen like those seen in Brittany.

Life in the three spas centers around the cures being taken there, but we have found them to be pleasant to stay in. Food is good, and the atmosphere is unhurried. Most of the hotels, except those catering to skiers, are open only from May to September with lower rates offered at the beginning and end of the high season. The free literature available describes everything in great detail and gives exact prices.

If you use one of these spas as a base you can make a number of interesting trips through the countryside. The region has many Romanesque churches built in the style that was developed locally. You can visit three of them while driving to Clermont-Ferrand. The one in Orcival is near, while those in Royat and Orcines are on the route to the city.

The Dordogne River is born in the mountains near Mont-Dore. The nascent stream flows through La Bourboule and then tumbles over rapids in the Gorges d'Avèze. Beyond them it becomes a long, man-made lake with a dam holding back the water at the Barrage de Bort where there is an unusual volcanic formation at Bort-les-Orgues. As the name indicates, the lava there hardened into tall columns that look like huge organ pipes.

Clermont-Ferrand and Thiers

When you travel from any one of the three spas to Clermont-Ferrand, you can go up the road that leads to the top of Puy du Dôme where the ruins of a Roman temple to Mercury stand on the 4800-foot-high summit. From it you can see the black lava cathedral in Clermont-Ferrand.

The city, which is the biggest in Auvergne, is largely industrial with the huge Michelin tire factory dominating the northeastern section. The Basilique de Notre-Dame-du-Port is older than it looks; some parts of it are pre-Romanesque. But the huge black lava Cathédrale Notre-Dame is Gothic with good stained glass in its rose window.

Clermont-Ferrand is not likely to detain a tourist long unless he has business to transact there. Route N9 goes north toward Vichy, passing through Riom on the way. Another well-known spa, Châtel-Guyon, is only a few miles to the west. Riom and Mozac, which are practically one town, are old and picturesque with interesting churches and museums. Just beyond Riom, D211 branches off to the right to Vichy. It becomes D210 and then N493, but it is all the same road.

An alternate but longer route from Clermont-Ferrand to Vichy is N89 which goes east for 42 kilometers (26 miles) to Thiers, where N106 runs north to make a total distance of 48 kilometers (37 miles).

Thiers specializes in the knives it has been making ever since the Crusades. You can visit its small shops and watch their highly skilled artisans put the final sharp edge on cutlery destined for the markets of the world. Old half-timbered buildings testify to the town's great age.

Vichy

Vichy is the most spa-like spa in France. It has so many hotel rooms that it was a natural choice for being the capital of unoccupied France when the Nazis took over the rest of the country. Here you can see how life goes on in a place where the transient visitors have only one interest—their health. They walk around the parks carrying little drinking cups in containers that dangle from one finger and go into glass-covered buildings where mineral water is provided in carefully measured doses prescribed by the spa's doctors. The girls who draw the water swirl it around in the cups with such deft skill that just the right amount is handed to the patient. As diversion, there are concerts, opera, and all kinds of sports.

When you drive east to Lyon, 161 kilometers (100 miles) away, you are entering one of the finest food areas in France.

Roanne, 74 kilometers (46 miles) from Vichy, has two good restaurants. Centered around Lyon are still more eating places which Michelin rates with two or three stars. One-star restaurants are numerous to the west and the north of Lyon.

There are better places to eat in the country nearby than there are in Lyon itself. This is a big industrial city, the third largest in France. It has several good museums and two Roman theaters, one of which is used for outdoor performances during the summer.

When it comes to Roman remains, however, the much smaller city of Vienne, 28 kilometers (17 miles) to the south, has an amazing number of them, for it was an important place in Roman times. There you can see the ruins of temples, a big theater, and other monuments of antiquity. As is so often the case, much of the Roman city is covered by modern buildings that must be removed if the ancient ones are ever to be brought to light.

Vienne has one of the best restaurants in France, the Pyramide. It is expensive, but so renowned for its food and pleasant outdoor terrace that many travelers go miles out of their way to dine there.

Vichy: serving mineral water

FRENCH GOVERNMENT TOURIST OFFICE

Gallic statue

As is indicated by what we have already said, this part of France is heavily industrialized, so much so that the nearby city of Saint-Étienne is a tangle of factories and mills that can be of interest only to those whose work takes them there.

Food and wine

Since the enormous area covered in this chapter stretches from the Spanish border to Vichy and Lyon, its food and wine vary greatly. Except at its upper end, where the food is superb, the best restaurants are rated by Michelin with only one star.

In the eastern Pyrenees and Roussillon you can get fish from the Mediterranean. There a fish stew called *bouillinade* is the local *bouillabaisse. Civet de langouste,* salt codfish from the North Atlantic prepared in several novel ways, and small Mediterranean tuna cooked fresh, are among the widely varied fish dishes available here.

Perhaps the most popular dish is *cassoulet,* which consists of white beans, bacon, sausage, and other pork products all cooked in an earthenware casserole with onions and herbs. In some places mutton or even goose is added. *Ouillade* is similar, but haricot beans, cabbage, carrots, and stronger herbs are used.

As to wines, Banyuls, the sweet dessert *Vin de Liqueur,* comes from Roussillon. Plenty of warm sunshine gives it a high alcoholic content which is then fortified by adding brandy. Sweet Muscat is also produced here. But far more important to the economy of France is the vast amount of cheap table wine made from grapes grown in the huge crescent that stretches along the Mediterranean from the Rhône to Spain. A few better wines with *Appellations Controlées* come from the area between Béziers and Montpellier, but the entire region is better known for quantity rather than quality. Those who are satisfied with table wines can get plenty of them at low prices, while those who want fine vintages can order them in good restaurants that bring them in from Bordeaux and Burgundy.

Farther north, where the mountains begin, few wine grapes are grown. The *causse* country, as we have said, produces Roquefort, which the famous British gourmet, P. Morton Shand, once called "the most famous cheese in the world." Bleu d'Auvergne is less salty and far less expensive. Cantal, also from Auvergne, is dry, not soft, and very delicate.

Auvergne has cabbage soup and several kinds of *potées.* Stuffed sheep feet (*tripoux*) are a specialty of the region. Potatoes are cooked with cheese, pork, or cabbage to make different kinds of *truffades. Coq au vin,* although hardly peculiar to Auvergne, is popular there.

Some Auvergne local wines are produced in small quantities. Here you will do best to ask your restaurant keeper to recommend what he thinks is best.

Once you get to Vichy you can eat well. And in the Lyon area and in Vienne, you can, of course, dine like a king—if you have a king-sized wallet.

17. *Provence*

When we recall the various regions of France we have visited, each one seems to have its own color. Normandy is luxuriantly green, Brittany mottled gray, the Château Country white and gold, the Atlantic Coast greenish-blue, the Pyrenees dark green spotted with red and gray, Auvergne brown and black, Corsica reddish-brown, Burgundy royal purple overlaid with green, Champagne off-white, Jura brown and green, and the Alps blue, white, and luminous reddish-gold. With few exceptions they all seem colorful enough, but Provence seems to be the most vivid of them all. Van Gogh saw it truly when he squeezed out tubes of startling yellow, brilliant orange, all kinds of reds, some greens, occasional blue, and then hardly bothered to mix the pigments on his palette before spreading them with quick, heavily-painted strokes on neutral canvas which he transformed into a more-than-real landscape that blazed with Provence's magic light.

Undoubtedly the sun shines just as brightly on the Riviera, the western Mediterranean, and Corsica, but it bathes Provence with color even when the cold winter mistral blows.

Of course, Provence lacks many things which some tourists seem to think essential. It has no great luxury resorts, no first-rate beaches, little night life, and no fashion at all. Nor is it the posh sort of place that name-droppers like to boast about. Its qualities are so special that you have to seek them out, for no one will insist that you simply must see this, that, or the other thing.

But if you like bleak, bare, long ridges of white rock outlined against a bluer-than-blue sky; the lustrous shadows that strong sunlight makes on old stones shaped by the hands of long-dead masons and sculptors; the strange contrast of barren desert that suddenly becomes fertile ground for growing some of France's finest fruit and vegetables; the charm of small towns hidden away and seemingly unchanged, then you may enjoy a trip through Provence. But you must travel around to appreciate it fully. Too many tourists go only to Avignon, Arles, Aix-en-Provence, and Marseille and then think that they have seen all that this endlessly fascinating region has to offer. Actually, some of its most interesting places are small and out of the way.

Undoubtedly Provence's chief attractions are its climate, its Roman and medieval antiquities, and its excellent food. Its area is so small that one—or at most two—bases in which to stay are all that one needs to explore it. We recommend Arles, Saint-Rémy, or Avignon as centers for the western part and Aix-en-Provence for the east.

Aigues-Mortes

When you come in from the western Mediterranean coast the first place of interest is Aigues-Mortes, a medieval walled town that rises about the flat marshes near one of the mouths of the Rhône. It was that swift flowing river which created the land here, for it brought down stones and mud from the Alps to deposit them in this vast delta with its many brackish ponds and lagoons.

Aigues-Mortes (dead waters) is a superb example of a medieval walled town because it was built all at one time and has come down through the ages without any major alteration or restoration. It came into being in 1240 when Louis IX (Saint Louis) purchased the area so he could build a port to launch the Seventh Crusade against the infidels who were holding the Holy Land. He enlarged an existing tower until it became the massive Tour de Constance that now stands at the northwest corner of the rectangular walled town.

He departed for the East in 1248 with 30,000 men and sailed from Aigues-Mortes again in 1270 on an expedition from which he never returned, for he died of the plague in Tunis that year.

Louis never saw the walls of Aigues-Mortes. Only the donjon tower of Constance was completed in his day. The fortified town was built by his son, Philip the Bold. It is the best example of a Crusader's stronghold in Europe, for the others have been destroyed wholly or in part.

The walls and towers of Aigues-Mortes are as good as the day they were built. The town itself has shrunk in population; in medieval times it had 15,000 people; today, only 4200.

The Tour de Constance can be visited. On the inside of its 18-foot-thick walls you will see inscriptions made by the Huguenots who were imprisoned there for decades after the Revocation of the Edict of Nantes in 1685.

Aigues-Mortes' defenses may seem impregnable, but they were not. In 1418, during the civil war between the Burgundians and the Armagnacs, a Burgundian army captured the town. They did not hold it long, for the Armagnacs overwhelmed the men who were guarding one of the gates and swept through it to massacre the Burgundians. There were so many corpses that they were piled up in the southwest tower and covered with salt. This sepulcher still bears the name, La Tour des Bourguignons Salés.

When you walk through the streets of Aigues-Mortes, the town looks very much like any other French community of the same size. But it has been inhabited continuously for 700 years, and even though some of the store fronts are modern, the streets have seen a processional of history that runs from the time of the Crusaders to our own.

Les-Saintes-Maries-de-la-Mer

Aigues-Mortes is old, but Saintes-Maries-de-la-Mer (34 kilometers or 22 miles away on N579, D58, D85, and D38) is even older. According to tradition, a group of people who had been close to Christ came here by boat about 40 years after the crucifixion. Some traditions say that one of the Marys was Mary Magdalen; others that they were relatives of the Apostles, but all versions of the legend agree that their black servant, Sara, accompanied them. When they died, their tomb became a celebrated place of pilgrimage. But this isolated spot on the shore was always open to attack from the sea, so the primitive church was strongly fortified in the thirteenth century. It stands there today, looming up over the flat lands and lagoons, complete with stone machicolations and crenelated walls.

It comes to life twice a year: once, on May 24 and 25, when Gypsies arrive from all over Europe to honor their patroness, black Sara; and again, on the Saturday and Sunday after October 22, when local people hold a religious festival there. At such times you can see cowboys from the Camargue with their horses and bulls. Music and dancing follow the religious ceremonies, and for a little while the ordinarily desolate village takes on the animation it had during the Middle Ages.

The Camargue

North of Saintes-Maries is a zoological park where you can see flamingos, egrets, and other water-loving birds as well as some wild animals. Beyond this is the Étang de Vaccarès which is now a huge wild-life reservation. The extensive marsh area called the Camargue surrounds this.

Until quite recently, the Camargue was largely given over to the raising of half-wild horses and cattle. Skilled horsemen called *gardians* rode across the wide stretches of marshland and were very much like the cowboys of the Old West or the gauchos of South America. Some of them still exist, but the horses and cattle are no longer wild. We stopped our car where a few white horses were grazing in a field and offered them some sugar candy. They approached us warily but took the sweets from our hands.

Large-scale cultivation has converted this once wild land into a vast rice farm. As you drive along the road you can see carefully tended little rice plants sprouting inside flooded enclosures. Riding camps, equipped like Western ranches, are numerous. And here and there are some of the old houses built in an architectural style peculiar to the Camargue. They are little whitewashed buildings with thatched roofs. And they all have rounded ends on the north to ward off the cold mistral that blows from that direction in winter. Each one has a white conical top surmounted by a small wooden cross. And each one is exactly like the next, for they are all built from the same time-honored pattern.

At Albaron, N570 runs east for 16 kilometers (10 miles) to Arles. If you have time, you can visit Saint-Gilles-du-Gard by making a detour for 11 kilometers (7 miles) north on D37. It has a twelfth-century Abbey church with a fine sculptured portal and a vast crypt in which there is now a lapidary museum. Behind the church is a spiral stairway called the Vis de Saint-Gilles.

From Saint-Gilles N572 goes east for 19 kilometers (12 miles) to Arles.

Arles

Arles stands on the site of a Roman city, and the ancient and modern buildings are so intermingled and pieced together that it is hard to tell where the old parts end and the modern begin.

Ales grows upon you. We have been there often and have found something new each time. One note of warning, though: be sure you have confirmed hotel reservations if you plan on staying in town, because bullfights, theatrical performances, and other public spectacles attract more people than the hotels can accommodate. Before you start out to see the sights, buy a combination ticket to visit all the places that charge entrance fees. You don't need a car; the town is small enough to be explored on foot.

Wherever you go, the past is very much in evidence. Dominating everything is the huge Roman arena which could hold more than 20,000 spectators in the days when gladiatorial combats were staged in it. It is still used. When a bullfight, with matadors and the famous black animals from Spain, is announced, people travel hundreds of miles to see it. And in the great arena, before a noisy crowd, the drama of life and death is again staged as it was 2000 years ago.

During the Middle Ages the arena was put to a new use when a village of several hundred houses grew up inside its protecting walls. Three of the towers built at that time still project above the outermost rim.

The arena has withstood the ravages of man and weather far better than the Roman theater next to it. Its fine marbles, statues, and square-cut stones were pillaged for centuries until now only two columns and parts of the stage and seats remain. Some of the statutes that once adorned it can be seen in the Musée d'Art Païen, although the best of them, the Venus of Arles, is in the Louvre. The local museum has only a cast of it.

As you walk around Arles you will constantly be reminded of the Roman city that preceded it. In the present Place du Forum two ancient columns have been built into a modern wall. Near the river are the remains of the Roman baths that were constructed later than most of the other monuments. They are not easy to visit and may prove to be disappointing because a good part of them still has to be excavated.

The ruins of Roman Arles are underneath the modern town. You can enter this underground city by going down a staircase in the Musée d'Art Chrétien. A guide will take you through dark passages and into chambers that were long used for grain storage. Further excavation is under way, and new and remarkable discoveries may be made in subterranean areas that have remained untouched for nearly 2000 years.

Bridging Roman times to medieval are Les Alyscamps, which is a vast cemetery on the edge of the city where a long alley lined with ancient sarcophaguses leads to the ruined Church of Saint-Honorat. All around it are evidences of burials that continued in this honored place for centuries. Near the church some of the big stone coffins are stacked together like crates in a warehouse. Gauguin and Van Gogh painted Les Alyscamps, and both gave it more color than one ordinarily sees there.

Also medieval is the Church Saint-Trophîme, which faces the Place de la République. In the square is an obelisk that once stood in the Roman circus of Arles where chariots were raced

Arles: a bullfight in the Roman arena

as recklessly as they were in Rome itself.

The sculptured façade of Saint-Trophîme is a fine example of Romanesque decoration. So are the cloisters with statues carved on some of the supporting pilars. If you look carefully when you go through the interior of the church you will see ancient stonework incorporated into it, for Roman marble and early sarcophaguses have been used as building material.

The Musée Arlaten was founded by the poet Frédéric Mistral with money awarded him when he won the Nobel Prize for literature in 1904. This museum specializes in the costumes, furniture, and peasant art that were characteristic of Provence only a few generations ago.

Van Gogh went to Arles in February 1888 when he had only two years to live. Yet it was during this period, while he was becoming more and more insane, that he did some of his best work. In Provence, he said, "the vault of sky is a marvelous blue and the sun is pale sulphur." The yellow house in which he lived and of which he painted a picture, was destroyed by a bomb in the Second World War.

Gauguin joined him here in October and it was in this house that Van Gogh cut off his ear and gave it to a prostitute. Some months later he voluntarily entered an asylum near Saint-Rémy. He remained in it for a year, industriously painting all the while. He left there to go to Auvers (near Paris), where he shot himself and died on July 29, 1890, at the age of thirty-eight.

Route N570 goes north from Arles to Tarascon and Avignon, but we advise you to take D17, D78F, and D27, for they run through more interesting country. Just outside Arles is the deserted and partly ruined Abbey of Montmajour. It was a victim of the French Revolution and was sold to be torn down for building material. Fortunately, the work of destruction was never completed, and much of the original Abbey still exists. The solid rock foundation on which it was built has coffin-shaped holes cut into it. They are empty now, but they were made as sepulchers for the monks who died there.

A little farther on are the two Roman aqueducts of Barbegal, one of which brought water to Arles while the other supplied power to operate eight pairs of mills of which the foundations are still in place.

Then, on a hill near Fontvielle, is Alphonse Daudet's windmill, which gave the title *Lettres de Mon Moulin* to the book that made him famous in 1866. The carefully restored mill is now a museum in which the author's manuscripts and memorabilia are on display.

Les Baux

Beyond Fontvielle, D27 leaves D78 to go north to Les Baux. You will soon see a long ridge of fantastically carved white limestone stretching from west to east. Partially hidden in the rugged crags are the ruins of Les Baux, a hilltop town that was once celebrated for its Courts of Love and for its troubadours who praised the objects of their affection in Provençal verse. In their time Les Baux was the capital of a barony that ruled more than 70 other towns. Its name is known today throughout the world because the aluminum ore found in the vicinity is called bauxite.

Les Baux

When you park your car and walk up to explore Les Baux you will understand why this lofty spur of rock has been inhabited from prehistoric times. It was a superb defensive position that in theory could never be taken. But the community was destroyed twice, and then, as the present ruins attest, was wrecked forever by gunpowder in 1632 when Richelieu gave orders to blow it up.

Les Baux is remarkable because its buildings were carved out of limestone rock which is so dazzlingly white that you need sunglasses to protect your eyes from the glare.

The street that leads up to the once-flourishing town passes the empty shell of a Protestant oratory on which the words "Post Tenebras Lux" (after the darkness, light) are carved. Then it goes up to a broad plateau from which there is a panoramic view over the flat marshes that stretch south to the Mediterranean. After you leave this plateau you can spend hours roaming around these photogenic ruins.

When you return to the entrance you will see a swimming pool filled with bright blue water. This belongs to the Hotel Baumanière, which has a restaurant that Michelin rates with three stars. And as you drive north after leaving Les Baux you will go through weirdly twisted white rocks that give this section its name—Val d'Enfer, the Valley of Hell. Cut like deep caves into some of the limestone hills are recently-made but now deserted quarries from which slabs of this fine white building material have been taken.

Saint-Rémy and Glanum

At the intersection of D27 and D31 turn right to go to the little town of Saint-Rémy, which is an excellent place to stay in and from which you can make day trips to all of central Provence.

Saint-Rémy has two museums next door to each other, so if you visit one you can visit both. The Musée des Alpilles specializes in regional material while the Musée de Sade is devoted to archeology and has the artifacts found in the excavations of the nearby Greco-Roman city Glanum. No, the notorious Marquis de Sade did not live here. The sixteenth-century building belonged to a collateral branch of his family.

Excavations of the Greco-Roman city of Glanum

If you drive through the fertile country north of Saint-Rémy you will see how vegetables are raised for particular French buyers. Small, level pieces of ground are shielded from the cold mistral by elaborate screens of evergreen trees, shrubs, and rush fences to permit the tender plants to be started early in the season. The warm sunshine of Provence then quickly makes them ready for the market. Saint-Rémy is a shipping center for growers who specialize in fine fruits and vegetables.

South of Saint-Rémy is the former Monastery of Saint-Paul-de-Mausole, which was made into an asylum in the nineteenth century. Van Gogh was confined there in 1889–1890. Very near it are two large Roman monuments called Les Antiques. One is the lower part of an arch; the other is an almost intact memorial to the dead.

The arch probably served as an entrance to the Greco-Roman town Glanum which has been undergoing excavation since 1921. As yet only a small part of this ancient community has been uncovered, but what can be seen is impressive because many walls and pillars are still standing. Before it became a Roman town, Glanum was a Greek settlement called Glanon. Underneath the Greco-Roman ruins are evidence of a still earlier Gallic village.

Since excavation work will be going on here for years to come, there is always a chance that you may see an interesting discovery being made. In the already uncovered section you can wander around streets that were paved more than 2000 years ago. Some of the house foundations were built in the Greek style, which is exceedingly rare in France. Glanum was destroyed in the third century by a barbarian invasion. Then, over a long period of time, it was gradually buried under wind-swept soil and concealed from view.

Tarascon and Beaucaire

Before going back to the Rhône River you may want to explore Les Alpilles, the limestone hills east of Les Baux. This picturesque outcrop of white rock has many surprises. You can see isolated chapels, piles of ruins, and at Castelas de Roquemartine, which crowns a small hill, you can investigate the remains of a deserted town and enter an abandoned church that is now falling into ruin. Beyond it, across the Durance River, is Cavaillon, where the delicious melons come from. It also has a fifteenth-century church, an ancient synagogue, a Roman arch, and two museums.

When you drive west on N99 from Saint-Rémy, Tarascon is only 15 kilometers (9 miles) away. This riverside town's outstanding attraction is the massive twelfth-century Château that stands on the eastern shore of the Rhône. It is a fine example of an early fortification so strongly built that it could defy invaders in the days before explosives made stone defenses obsolete.

Tarascon plays a part in French literature because Alphonse Daudet named his boastful Provençal character Tartarin de Tarascon. And Aucassin and Nicolette lived across the river in Beaucaire where their castle was the setting for their thirteenth-century romance. The building was partly destroyed by orders from Richelieu who feared that such strongholds might shelter his religious and political enemies. One tower of Beaucaire remains. It can be visited for its view over the Rhône valley.

For six centuries, Beaucaire was the scene of a great fair that was attended by people who came from all over Europe to buy merchandise there. The broad field on which the fair was held lies between the Château and the river. A modern arena has been built there so bullfights can be staged in competition with those put on in Arles, Nîmes, and other southern French cities.

Nîmes

When you leave Beaucaire you can easily go to Nîmes which is only 24 kilometers (15 miles) away on Route N99.

The Roman arena there is similar in size to the one in Arles, but it is in even better condition and the upper ranks of its walls are nearly complete. As was the case in Arles, it housed an entire village in medieval times.

Also in the center of the city is the Roman-built Maison Carrée, which is remarkably well preserved although it is not quite as perfect as the very similar Roman temple in Vienne. The Maison Carrée is now a museum of Roman antiquities. This building, which is obviously patterned after a Greek temple, had an enormous influence on Greek Revival architecture in America, for Jefferson admired it so much that on his recom-

Nîmes: the ancient Roman arena

FRENCH GOVERNMENT TOURIST OFFICE

Nîmes: the Maison Carrée

FRENCH GOVERNMENT TOURIST OFFICE

mendation it was used as the model for the state capitol in Richmond, Virginia. And the great Boston architect, Charles Bulfinch, visited it on his grand tour of Europe. Hundreds—perhaps thousands—of banks and other public buildings in the United States are the architectural offspring of the Maison Carrée.

There are more Roman ruins near the Jardin de la Fontaine, which is on the site of the baths and theater that once stood there. Only the Temple of Diana remains; all the other buildings have been replaced by terraced gardens and fountain-fed pools constructed in the eighteenth century. On the crest of the hill above them is the Tour Magne which is probably of Roman origin. Steps lead to a platform on the top of the tower from which there is a wonderful view over the country for miles around.

The Pont du Gard

In addition to the museum in the Maison Carrée, Nîmes has an archeological museum with much Gallo-Roman material, a museum of old Nîmes where objects of local history are displayed, and a Musée des Beaux-Arts.

The Pont-du-Gard

In order to supply Nîmes with water the Romans built an aqueduct to springs 30 miles north of the Gard River. In order to bring water across the deep ravine through which the river flows, they constructed a great aqueduct-bridge that is now almost 2000 years old.

This huge masonry structure, which is 160 feet high and 900 feet long, consists of three series of arches, the upper one of which supports the conduit that carried the water. The squared-off stones, some of them weighing more than 13,000 pounds, were put together without mortar. Time has weathered them to a rich yellowish-orange color. When the sun is setting, the Pont-du-Gard looks as if it were made of gold instead of stone.

The visitor who wants to appreciate this outstanding example of Roman engineering skill should spend several hours walking across and around it. The best view is from upstream, but to get a good photograph from there requires late afternoon sunlight. When you walk across the bridge, examine the massive stones and you will see initials, names, and dates that were carved there many centuries ago. Even the lower bridge that flanks the larger one to carry traffic across the river on Route N581 is more than 200 years old.

Alongside the Hôtel du Pont-du-Gard is a large, low-ceilinged cave which is now used for a garage. It sheltered man long before the Pont-du-Gard was built, and many prehistoric remains have been taken from it. Some of them can be seen in the Musée Archéologique in Nîmes.

Avignon

Avignon would have been just another Provençal town if an accident of history had not made it a papal residence in the fourteenth century. In 1305, when Italy was torn apart by internal conflict, the French king Philip the Fair succeeded in persuading the newly-elected Pope, Clement V, to remain in

France where he had been born. Four years later, Clement V made Avignon the papal seat, and Rome was left without a Pope. For seven pontificates, Avigon remained the papal residence except for one brief period when Urban V went to Rome in 1367 but returned to Avignon in 1370. The situation was still further complicated in 1378 when Urban VI became the Pope in Rome while Clement VII was the antipope in Avigon. The last antipope did not leave Avignon until 1403. For nearly a century the formerly obscure Provençal town had been growing until it became a city with far more population than it has now.

Enormous wealth poured into the papal treasury in Avignon. So much money was available that it was possible to build the huge Palace of the Popes in less than 20 years. Then it was magnificently furnished so the Pope and the cardinals could live in it in great luxury. After 1403 Avignon declined, and its tremendous palace was stripped of its finery. At one time it was used as a barracks for soldiers who removed pieces of its celebrated frescoes from the walls and sold them.

The town is now only a shadow of what it was in the fourteenth century, but it is still a lively place and one that no tourist should miss.

The encircling defensive wall built by the Popes still stands although the moats in front of it have long ago been filled in. The Rue de la République leads to the central Place de l'Horloge; beyond that is the Palace of the Popes. Between it and the Rhône is the hilly Promenade du Rocher des Doms which has a view over the river and of Villeneuve-lès-Avignon on the other side of it.

The Rocher des Doms is now a beautiful park where swans glide around a pond in the shadow of an artificial grotto. These heights commanding the river have been lived in ever since prehistoric men dwelt there and left some of their flints and stone axes behind. A Roman fort and then a medieval castle stood here. At the beginning of the seventeenth century a powder magazine in the castle blew up and scattered fragments of rock around. The castle was then replaced by four windmills and a cemetery. In the nineteenth century the modern park gave the Rocher des Doms a new aspect, but many relics of its ancient past are probably still lying under the soil where grass and flowers now grow.

When you look down from the Rocher des Doms, you will

see what is left of the Pont d'Avignon, which was made famous by a song for children. Actually, the dancing described in the song was done on the island under (*sous*) the bridge and not on (*sur*) it. Only part of the once long span remains. The Pont Saint-Bénézet no longer crosses the river but it still leads to a small double chapel, double because the older Romanesque one has a slightly more recent Gothic chapel built on top of it. For many centuries this bridge was the only solid and dependable one that crossed the Rhône between Lyon and the Mediterranean. As you stand on the Rocher des Doms and look down at the river's fast-rushing water—so fast that ships going downstream seem to be racing while those headed up make hardly any progress—you will understand how important this ancient bridge was. The primitive ferries used before it was built must have had a hard time returning to their starting places when they had to cope with such a current.

In the southwest corner of Avignon is the Rue des Teinturiers where the narrow Sorgue River is confined between stone embankments. Huge wooden paddle wheels are mounted across the stream, which ran bright with color when the dyers washed superfluous tinting materials out of their cloth.

Avignon lost much of its importance after the Popes left it;

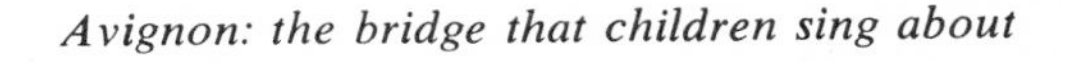

Avignon: the bridge that children sing about

then it suffered another loss during the French Revolution when many of its numerous churches were demolished. A great deal of fine sculpture was also destroyed at that time. The cathedral, which predates the Palace of the Popes alongside it, has been marred architectually by a too-large statue of the Virgin that was perched on top of it in the nineteenth century.

The city's museums preserve relics of its remarkable past. The Musée Calvet has a huge collection of beautifully wrought ironwork and a noteworthy series of fourteenth-century paintings of the Avignon School. It also has pictures by noted nineteenth- and twentieth-century French artists. The Musée Lapidaire contains many pieces of ancient stonework dating back to pre-Roman times. There are several important pieces of Gallo-Roman sculpture here, some of which depicts ships and horse-drawn vehicles of the period. Here too is the grotesque man-eating monster of Noves holding two severed Gallic heads in its paws while it munches a severed arm.

Across the river is Villeneuve-lès-Avignon where many of the fourteenth-century cardinals built luxurious homes. Commanding the heights above the town is the powerful stronghold called the Fort Saint-André from which there is a sweeping view over Avignon and the country around it. This is best seen late on a sunny afternoon.

Also in Villeneuve-lès-Avignon is the Chartreuse du Val de Bénédiction, which is a vast conglomeration of churches, chapels, cloisters, and other ancient religious buildings. The frescoes in the Chapel of Innocent VI are especially worth seeing. And the Musée de l'Hospice has many fine pictures among which the Coronation of the Virgin, painted in 1453 by Enguerrand-Charonton, is outstanding.

The Rhône Valley

Heavily traveled Route N7 leads north from Avignon. We suggest that you leave it at Sorgues, 10 kilometers above the city, and go left on D17 to Châteauneuf-du-Pape. This was once the summer palace of the Avignon Popes, but it is now best known for its vineyards, which produce an excellent red wine of high alcoholic content. When phylloxera hit France in the nineteenth century and ruined the vines, the growers here carefully removed the stones from their fields so they could

FRENCH GOVERNMENT TOURIST OFFICE

Orange: the Roman theater

be planted with wheat. Then, when it was found that phylloxera-free American roots could have French vines grafted on them, the growers put the smaller stones back in place to conserve heat and moisture for the plants. The Châteauneuf vineyards are unusually stony, which is supposed to be an advantage, although rocks still under the surface make plowing and cultivation of the soil difficult.

Wine grapes are grown on both sides of the Rhône, with most of the better vineyards located fairly near the river. Tavel, noted for its good rosé wine, is just across from Châteauneuf-du-Pape, while L'Hermitage and Côte-Rôtie are much farther north.

Orange

When Orange was a Roman city called Arausio (from which its modern name is derived), it had a full-sized stadium for chariot racing, baths, temples, and a capitol which are now either in ruins or are buried beneath the modern town. Only a big stone arch and the theater remain relatively intact. But they are truly important examples of Roman architecture, for the arch is the third largest one in existence while the theater is the most complete one left from Roman times. They owe their good state of preservation to the fact that they were incorporated into later defenses of the town.

The arch stands by itself now with Route N7 circling around it. Some of its reliefs have been worn down by time and weather, but enough of them remain to show how impressive it must have been when it was new. Its carvings illustrate the wars against the Gauls and are an important source of information about costumes, weapons, and early naval vessels.

The enormous backstage wall of the theater, which is 338 feet long, 124 feet high, and 13 feet thick, was once covered with marble and had statues in niches above the stage. One of them (a portrait of Emperor Augustus) has been found and put back in place.

Seats for the audience were cut into a rocky hill and could accommodate eight or ten thousand people. They were sheltered from the hot Provençal sun by a huge awning, the supports for which are still in place. You can see them projecting high up on the exterior wall. The stage, which is now covered by a wooden platform, has been used for modern theatrical performances since 1894.

Next to the theater are the ruins of a great temple and a large gymnasium. It was in front of these that the former stadium stretched for hundreds of feet to the shores of the little Meyne River.

At the height of its glory Orange probably had four times as many inhabitants as it has now. Only its Roman remains make the town worth visiting. If some of the modern structures are ever removed so more of the buried city can be uncovered, Orange will be even more of an attraction to tourists than it is at present. And what lies underground may prove to be more valuable than some of the mediocre buildings that stand on the site now.

Nyons

From Orange you can go 42 kilometers (26 miles) on Routes N576 and N95 to Nyons. This little town with fewer than 5000 inhabitants, is more interesting than it might at first seem. First of all, it is reputed to have the best and most dependable climate in France. Sheltered by mountains from the unpleasant mistral, Nyons boasts that it has 2600 hours of sunshine a year

—which is just about what Nice has.

Its climate makes Nyons a center for raising olives, almonds, figs, and other warm-weather plants. Truffles grow there too, and also various kinds of fruit from which preserves are manufactured locally. The mild climate has attracted so many retired people that the town has nearly doubled its population since the war.

The old part of Nyons, which is called the Quartier des Forts, stands on a hill above the more modern section. Up there you will find narrow, winding streets and picturesque houses built centuries ago.

Only 23 kilometers (14 miles) west of Nyons on N541 is the little town of Grignan which readers of Madame de Sévigné's letters may want to visit. She went there several times to see her daughter who had married the Comte de Grignan. His château is open to the public. Madame de Sévigné died there in 1696 and was buried in the Église Saint-Sauveur. Her tomb, however, was robbed during the Revolution. Outside the town is the grotto of Rochecourbière which the Marquise described in some of her letters.

Vaison-la-Romaine

South of Nyons (16 kilometers or 10 miles) on Route N538 is Vaison-la-Romaine, which has two separate parts. The lower one was originally a Roman settlement while the upper town came into being during the early Middle Ages when people sought the heights on the other side of the Ouvèze River for protection. The ruins of a thirteenth-century castle stand on the hill above the town. After the Middle Ages, many of the inhabitants returned to the site of the Roman city to build their houses on top of it. Only in recent years have excavations brought the long-buried ruins to light. And, as is the case in Orange, much of the ancient city still lies underneath the modern buildings.

Yet Vaison-la-Romaine is even more interesting to the layman than Saint-Rémy's Glanum is, for it has more to see. The theater, which is smaller than those at Orange and Arles, is reached by going through a tunnel under a hill that separates it from the city.

So many statues were found during the excavation work that

some of them were re-erected in recesses in the walls. Others are in the local museum. Much original pavement is still in place. So are sewers, some of them with public latrines built over them. The foundations of private houses show how the rooms were arranged. And huge jars for storing grain and wine stand where the Romans put them.

There are two excavated sections (Puymin and Villasse) separated by a parking area. Be sure to see them both. The bridge used by traffic going south from the modern Grande Rue was built by the Romans. It leads to the medieval town on the heights.

From Vaison-la-Romaine, N538 goes south to Malaucène. Just beyond the town, on N54, is a spring-fed pool surrounded by a beautiful tree-shaded area which we found ideal for an outdoor lunch. There is even a *buvette* to supply drinks.

Mont Ventoux

Route N574 will take you to the summit of Mont Ventoux, the highest mountain in Provence (1912 meters or 6270 feet). The top is covered with small white stones that make it look as if it has snow on it even in summer. In winter, snow does make ideal ski slopes here. From the Observatory you can see the Alps on a clear day.

Route N574 circles the mountain for 55 kilometers (34 miles), then goes southwest to Carpentras, where there is a notable Roman arch with figures of manacled barbarians on it. It is now located in the rear courtyard of the Palais de Justice. Near it is the interesting fifteenth-century church of Saint-Siffrein. This town of 15,000 people has four museums and the oldest synagogue in France.

Route N538 runs south from Carpentras for 17 kilometers (11 miles) to L'Isle-sur-la-Sorgue, which, as its name indicates, is literally an island, for branches of the Sorgue River flow around the town. There is so much water here that canals, mills, and fountains abound.

The Fontaine de Vaucluse

Water—and lots of it—is also the reason for the fame of the nearby Fontaine de Vaucluse. You have to park your car and walk for some distance to see the spring that gushes with great force out of a cave to feed a stream that surges violently alongside the path.

The Fontaine de Vaucluse is associated with Petrarch, the noted Italian poet who had grown up in Avignon when his exiled father settled there in 1313. It was in a church in that city that Petrarch first saw Laura, the young girl whose name he was to make immortal in his verses. He wrote many of them about her while he was living near the Fontaine de Vaucluse in the 1330's.

He would not find the place suitable for quiet meditation and writing poetry if he returned there now. The powerful spring still continues to pour out great quantities of cold, pure water, but the shores of the stream that flows from it have been desecrated by commerce and industry. A big factory stands on one side while the other has souvenir shops, eating places, and summer shacks.

Eastern Provence

Route D24 leaves the Fontaine de Vaucluse and joins N100 which goes direct to Apt. The less popular D2 will take you to two exceedingly interesting small towns, Gordes and Roussillon. (Roussillon has nothing to do with the ancient province with the same name.) The mountainous area (Luberon) south of here was the scene of the terrible mid-sixteenth-century religious massacres in which several thousand Vaudois (a later name for the earlier Waldenses) were put to death in the most horrible ways imaginable.

Gordes, fortunately, was not harmed by these massacres. It seems almost untouched although part of it was demolished by Nazi tanks. You will come upon it suddenly. Stop as soon as you catch sight of it, for the best spot to see it is from D15 just before it enters the town. Like many such places, this hilltop village is more beautiful when seen from far away than it is when you view it closely.

Beyond Gordes, D102 branches off to the right from D2 to go to Roussillon, the bright red and yellow town that gets its color from the ochre deposits around and underneath it. In 1950–51, Laurence Wylie, the American sociologist, made a study of this community which was published under the title

Village in the Vaucluse. His book goes more deeply into the roots of French small-town life than anything else we have read. Roussillon (which Wylie calls Peyrane) was then poor and backward. When he returned to make another but briefer study in 1961, he found that the village had become much more prosperous. Artists, writers, and summer people had purchased vacant houses and redone them. The town has gained even greater prosperity since then. It now has an excellent hotel and a restaurant starred by Michelin.

As you drive through this part of Provence you will occasionally see small stone windowless houses made by piling up flat rocks with such skill in placing them to curve the walls into a semispherical roof that no mortar is needed. They are called *bori*. Most of them were intended to be storage huts or shelters for farm animals but some have been used at times as dwellings for people. And some are so old that Neolithic and Bronze Age artifacts have been dug out of their earthen floors.

Gordes

Aix-en-Provence

From Apt, Route N543 goes south through the Luberon Mountains to Aix-en-Provence, 51 kilometers (32 miles) away. This small but truly elegant city is worth a protracted visit. Its Cours Mirabeau, with four rows of tall plane trees that make a great archway over the wide thoroughfare, is a sight to remember. This splendid street was named after Honoré Gabriel Riquet, Count Mirabeau (1749–1791), the eloquent orator who played an important part in the early years of the French Revolution when he was elected to the States-General as the representative from Aix.

Mirabeau's stormy life seems strangely out of place with the quietly beautiful avenue that bears his name. The street is short, for it leads only from the big fountain in the Place de la Libération to the Place Forbin where a statue of the Good King René stands above a much smaller fountain. You will hear a lot about René in Aix. As a good king he deserves to be remembered.

The Cours Mirabeau has two fountains besides these. One is the Fontaine des Neufs Canons with three basins mounted one over the other. The second is a strange, stubby, moss-covered, almost shapeless lump down which water drips. Lean over and test its temperature with your hand, and you will find that it is noticeably warm, for this is the Fontaine Chaude, one of the many mineral springs that gave the city its name (Aix=*aquae,* from the Latin plural for water) and made it celebrated even in Roman times. A fountain with four dolphins is located three streets south of the Cours Mirabeau in a square at the intersection of the Rue Cardinale and the Rue du Quatre Septembre. There are still more fountains, for Aix has plenty of water and uses it freely to beautify its streets and public squares.

The Cours Mirabeau is lined with fine seventeenth- and eighteenth-century houses. These were formerly private mansions, but they have now been converted into apartments or made over for commercial use. Benches stand at regular intervals along the wide sidewalks where bright shafts of sunlight filter down through the trees. And there are cafés and restaurants that serve as meeting places for students who come here from all over the world to attend the University. The presence of this important seat of learning, founded in 1409, has made Aix a cultural center that has more museums, stately buildings, and fine old churches that one would expect to find in a Provençal town with a population of less than 75,000. And it has so many bookshops that there seems to be one everywhere you turn. In recent times the University has been combined with the one at Marseille so its official name is now Aix-Marseille. It also has several specialized schools in Nice.

Most of the University buildings and the older part of the city are north of the Cours Mirabeau. There, too, are the Hôtel de Ville and an early sixteenth-century clock tower with four mechanically operated wooden figures representing the four seasons. The upper stories of the Hôtel de Ville house the Bibliothèque Méjanes which began with a fine collection of books and manuscripts left to it in 1786 by the Marquis de Méjanes. It has grown until it now has 2000 manuscripts and 300,000 books.

Beyond this is the truly remarkable Cathédrale de Saint-Sauveur, a composite of many styles that go back through the years to the baptistery which was built at the end of the fourth century with eight Roman colored marble columns to support its domed roof.

The cathedral consists of an early Romanesque church which has been incorporated into a later Gothic structure. No architectural masterpiece because of its too-disparate elements, its best features are its cloisters and its many fine sculptures, tapestries which were originally made for England's Canterbury Cathedral, and the "Burning Bush" triptych painted in 1475 by Nicolas Froment. This was done at King René's command and is placed over an altar that contains part of his remains.

René, who lived from 1409 to 1480, was the non-resident king of Naples, Sicily, and Jerusalem. (The title of king was evidently spread around freely in those days of tiny kingdoms.) In France, René was the Duke of Anjou, where he was born, and also the Count of Provence. He was a gifted and talented man who was interested in painting, poetry, and the mystery plays that then represented the theater. Among other good works he introduced Muscat grapes to France. The right-hand panel of the "Burning Bush" triptych portrays him as a kneeling figure.

Aix has many fine paintings although it regrettably has nothing important by Paul Cézanne, who was born there in 1839, and who died there in 1906. Like Arles with Van Gogh and Cagnes with Renoir, Aix cannot afford to buy the works of its best-known artist because they have become so astronomically expensive. Cézanne's "Houses at l'Estaque," which is certainly not one of his greatest works, brought $800,000 in 1965.

Aix has some good older paintings. In the Église Sainte-Marie-Madeleine is the central panel of a triptych illustrating the Annunciation that was painted by an unknown artist (probably of the Avignon School). And the Musée Granet has a superb portrait by Ingres of the artist after whom the museum is named. Ingres' "Jupiter and Thetis" and one of Rembrandt's self-portraits are also there.

The archeological section of this museum has an outstanding collection of sculpture and other artifacts made by the pre-Roman Gauls who lived north of Aix on the plateau of Entremont. What was found in the excavations there has given us wholly new ideas of what these hitherto little-known people were really like. Posidonius, the Greek writer (*c.*100 B.C.) who had made a study of the Mediterranean world of his time, said that the Gauls were head-hunters; the excavations at Entremont and Roquepertuse have proved that he was right, for stones were found there with niches for skulls. The Musée Granet has several grim-looking sculptures of severed heads that show what important trophies these were for the ancient Gauls. And in the museum in the annex of the Château Borely in Marseille you can see a stone door-frame with cavities for skulls cut into it.

Cézanne's studio is on the road to Entremont (north on D14, then the right fork to Avenue Paul Cézanne). He, too, collected human skulls, for he owned seven of them as models to paint. His studio can be visited, although it is closed on Mondays and for two and a half hours at lunchtime. Cézanne lived in Aix at 28 Rue Boulegon, but he used this out-of-town studio for his daily work. His clothes are still hanging on the wall; his easel, palette, and the gear he used when he went out on painting expeditions are also there.

The country for miles around Aix was Cézanne's most often painted subject. His pictures have made the names of obscure local places like Les Lauves, Bibémus, and Sainte-Victoire known throughout the world. Émile Zola went to school with him in Aix, and the two young men used to go on walking tours through the countryside.

The Field of the Dead

A vast horde of Teutonic tribes came swarming into Gaul about a century before Christ. They defeated a Roman army near Orange, but hesitated to march on Rome itself. Instead, they overran Spain and then in A.D. 102, flushed with victory and rich with spoil, marched toward Aix determined to conquer Rome. The Roman general Marius, hastily summoned from Africa, awaited the oncoming barbarians who were so numerous that it took six days for their columns to pass the general's observation post. Then he attacked, first at a point west of Aix; and again farther to the east on the plain south of Mont Sainte-Victoire. His troops slaughtered the tribesmen until the ground was littered with 100,000 bodies. There were too many corpses to bury so they were left on the field. The present-day village Pourrières, which is near the battleground, derives its name from Campi Putridi, the fields of putrefaction. A monument was erected to Marius, but it is now only a pile of stones, and nothing remains of the terrible battle that was fought here nearly 2000 years ago.

Marseille

Route N8 goes from Aix-en-Provence for 31 kilometers (19 miles) to Marseille. Part of this highway is a modern auto route. If you have the time, however, you may want to turn off to the west to see the wide lagoon called the Étang de Berre. It has two passageways from the Mediterranean; the one to the west is an open canal, but the eastern one is a four-mile-long tunnel big enough for ships to pass through it. This Souterrain du Rove can be visited by boat from Marseille. Near the tunnel's northern terminal is the Marignane airport. And the mountainous area under which the ship tunnel runs is the Estaque where Cézanne painted many of his best-known canvases. The Estaque is no longer as wild as it appears in the pictures he painted several generations ago. Its shores are lined by huge petroleum refineries and other industrial installations.

Marseille is France's second largest city. It is also its oldest, for it was founded about 600 B.C. by Greek sea-venturers from Phocea in Asia Minor. They settled on the shores of this excellent natural harbor and used it as a base for operating what was actually an extensive export-import business. These early traders penetrated deeper and deeper into France and made that still primitive country known to the more advanced peoples who lived at the eastern end of the Mediterranean.

Marseille has always been an important maritime base, and the city grew up around the Vieux Port, which is still a center of activity even though large ships no longer enter it but dock in the artificial basins along the coast to the north.

Before the Second World War an unusual type of bridge, the Pont Transbordeur, carried passengers on a moving platform over the water in the Vieux Port, but it was blown up by the Germans so there is now no way to cross except by ferry. As a result there is always a traffic jam in the streets in and around the wide harbor. A tunnel is under construction, but it will not be finished for several years.

The big steel Transbordeur bridge was not the only thing the Nazi invaders destroyed in Marseille. They found themselves unable to cope with the unruly denizens of the tough quarter on the north side of the Vieux Port, so they drove them out and dynamited the area. Modern buildings were constructed there after the war, but behind them is what remains of the old section with its narrow streets lined with ancient tenements. Occasionally there is a once-aristocratic mansion with an inner courtyard, but it, too, has been converted into a rookery of the meanest kind with an outdoor faucet to supply water to the poverty-stricken people who inhabit the decaying building.

Running through the city to the head of the Vieux Port is the Canebière, a wide avenue that is to Marseille what the boulevards around Montmartre are to Paris. This lively street bubbles with activity day and night. It is representative of Marseille, because the city is noted for its animation. The Vieux Port is equally busy; little ferry boats shuttle back and forth, while the stone piers along the sides are populated with fishermen, sailors, and tourists.

South of the Vieux Port rise the heights dominated by the

Basilique de Notre-Dame-de-la-Garde. This vast church, which is now a century old, was damaged in the fighting of the Second World War and still bears the marks made by shells and bombs. From the terrace around it is a magnificent view over the entire city and the sea. On the nearest island to the west is the famous—or infamous—Château d'If.

Between Notre-Dame-de-la-Garde and the Vieux Port is Saint-Victor, a very old church that looks more like a fort than a religious building. Its crenelated towers and sturdily built walls are all that remain of the abbey of whch it was once a part. Even older than the church itself is its crypt dating back to the fifth century. A Roman temple probably stood there before that. This area near the entrance to the harbor had to be strongly held from earliest times. Near Saint-Victor is the massive Fort Saint-Nicolas which faces Fort Saint-Jean across the water.

Another huge church, which was built in the same style and at about the same time as Notre-Dame-de-la-Garde, is the Cathédrale de la Major on the north side of the city near the modern ship basins. More interesting is the smaller twelfth-century church next to it which is now being made into a museum of Christian art.

Marseille has museums that specialize in ships, furniture, old musical instruments, numismatics, and natural history. Its Musée des Beaux-Arts has something that you may not know exists—Daumier's caricatures in sculptured form. It has other interesting works of art, but the Daumier room alone is worth the price of admission.

You can go by excursion boat to the Château d'If, the island fortress that was used for many years as a prison. In it was confined the Man in the Iron Mask, whom you will encounter again on the island of Sainte-Marguerite near Cannes. This mysterious prisoner was moved from place to place for 40 years until he died in the Bastille in 1703. Alexandre Dumas wrote a novel about him. He also wrote one about the fictitious character, Edmond Dantès, the self-styled Count of Monte-Cristo who escaped from the Château d'If to become enormously rich so he could take revenge on the people who had caused him to be imprisoned.

While you are in Marseille you will undoubtedly want to taste *bouillabaisse,* the fish soup for which that city is famous.

It is very good indeed while you eat it, but it may have an unfortunate after-effect on tender stomachs. If you are willing to risk the possible digestive upset, by all means try it. It will be prepared especially for you—which takes time—and it is a meal in itself, so don't fill up on too many other things while you wait for it to be brought to the table. Thackeray wrote a ballad about *bouillabaisse* in which he called it a noble dish, a "hotchpotch of all sorts of fishes." But two of the three he named (roach and dace) are fresh-water varieties. Genuine *bouillabaisse,* of course, is made only from salt-water fish, preferably from the Mediterranean.

If you are headed for the Riviera when you leave Marseille, take the Corniche (now named after the late President John F. Kennedy). It goes along the sea to the Parc Borely. The Musée Lapidaire, which is in an annex of the Château there, has a notable collection of Gallic artifacts found in the excavations at Roquepertuse (west of Aix).

If you will drive east a few streets from the Parc Borely to the Boulevard Michelet, you will see the 17-story apartment building designed by Le Corbusier to be part of his Cité Radieuse. If it no longer seems as novel as it did when it was put up in 1952, that is because many of its outstanding features have since been incorporated in other apartment houses.

After visiting the Corbusier architectural landmark, keep going south on the Boulevard Michelet which is part of N559, the road that runs along the shore of the Riviera.

Food and wine

Provence ranks high for its food, but it is not particularly French. Nor is it really Italian; let's say that it is Mediterranean—with olives, garlic, tomatoes, and salt-water fish as prominent ingredients. It has a great number of fine and very fine restaurants, more than 20 of them according to Michelin. Two of them have three stars.

The garlic used here is said to be milder than that encountered elsewhere. But it is characteristic of Provençal cooking, and *à la provençale* means that the food has been prepared with garlic (*ail*). You will find it in local mayonnaise (*aïoli* or *ailloli*), and also in some of the soups. The very best *potage* we ever had in France had a garlic sauce that was served separately so you could use as much or as little of it as you wished.

We have already mentioned *bouillabaisse.* Marseille specializes in it, but it is by no means the only place that features it. Squids (*poulpes*) are favored here as they are all along the Mediterranean. Except for lamb and pork, the meats of Provence will win no prizes. The free-ranging beef from the Camargue is tough and is best eaten as *estouffade de boeuf, daube de boeuf,* or *boeuf bouilli* in which cooking makes it tender—or at least less tough. The better restaurants serve beef that has been shipped down from the north. They also have local game birds, both large and small.

Among the vegetables of the region artichokes take a high place. So does eggplant (*aubergine*), which is the outstanding ingredient in *ratatouille,* although tomatoes, onions, pimentos, garlic, and herbs are also needed. The Cavaillon melons (as their name indicates) come from the area around Cavaillon east of Arles and Avignon. You can get them all over France, but they are at their best when they are picked ripe here. Figs, almonds, and other warm-weather fruits and nuts grow in Provence. The *calissons* of Aix-en-Provence are small, sweet almond cakes. This is not cheese country, but some is made, mostly from goats' milk.

The wines of Provence are better than one would expect from this warm climate. We have already discussed the Rhône Valley's Châteauneuf du Pape, Hermitage, Côte-Rôtie, and Tavel. Other fairly good to very good ones are *blanc de blancs de Provence,* Bandol rosé and white, Cassis rosé, and Bellet and Palette both red and white.

18. *The Riviera*

The Mediterranean coast of France runs from Spain to Italy, and nearly all of it is lined with beach resorts. The Riviera, however, is the best-known part of this long coastal strip. Oddly enough, there is much disagreement as to just how much of it can rightfully be called the French Riviera (Côte d'Azur). Local people say that Fréjus marks the western end, but for convenience we are going to include all the area between Hyères and Menton. Beyond Menton is a long stretch of the Italian Riviera.

In recent years would-be sophisticates have been saying that the Riviera has lost much of its glamor and that it has become overbuilt, overcrowded, and overpriced. There is some truth in these charges, but it is still possible to have a fine time there at reasonable prices if you know where to go. If you want to splurge, you can do that easily, for this celebrated resort area has some of the most expensive hotels in France. According to the red Michelin guide, however, it does not have a single three-star restaurant, and less than half a dozen two-star ones. This does not mean that you can't eat well there. You can, for the Riviera has plenty of good eating places.

Those who take malicious delight in running down the Riviera are more justified when they say that it is not what it used to be. If they mean that it is no longer devoted exclusively to entertaining wealthy people, they are right. It has become more democratic, although there are still many luxurious estates on its sunny slopes. But most of them are concealed behind high walls and thickly planted shrubbery, so the casual tourist does not see them. There is no doubt, though, that the Riviera is no longer the wealthy man's paradise it was before the First World War when kings, princes, lords, and millionaires flocked there to spend money recklessly.

Many French people of ordinary means are in revolt against the high prices demanded by some Riviera *entrepreneurs*. As a result, 1965 was a poor year with hotels less than full, streets not crowded, and beaches that charge admission not well patronized. Restaurant receipts declined, and rentals asked for villas had to be reduced. But the Rivera was not the only French resort area that showed a decrease in revenues that year. Camping has everywhere become a direct competitor for the money vacationists set aside for their annual flight to the provinces. And they are spending much less for food. A widely circulated French newspaper said that the 1965 visitor to the Riviera was being called "Monsieur Sandwich."

British sun seekers

Although this sun-blessed land has been settled since earliest times—as the prehistoric caves near the Italian border show—it was supposedly "discovered" by Lord Brougham, after whom a once well-known closed carriage was named. In the 1830's, when he was prevented from going to Nice by a cholera plague that caused that city to be quarantined, he went instead to Cannes, and was so enchanted with the little fishing village that he built a house there. His presence attracted other English people to the Riviera where they could escape British winters. (Nice has nearly twice as much annual sunshine as London has.) This strip of Mediterranean shore soon became a popular winter resort for wealthy people of all nations.

At least that is how the story goes. Certainly, Lord Brougham did build a house in Cannes. In fact, he died there in 1868 and is buried in a local cemetery. But some English people—and other foreigners—knew about the Riviera's mild winter climate long before Lord Brougham went there.

Tobias Smollett visited the Riviera in the early 1760's and wrote an excellent book about it—*Travels Through France and Italy, 1776*. Among other things, he described the difficulty women had when they wanted to bathe in the Mediterranean:

> If a lady should be at the expense of having a tent pitched on the beach where she might put on and off her bathing-dress, she could not . . . go into the sea without proper attendants; nor could she possibly plunge headlong into the water, which is the most effectual . . . way of bathing. All that she can do is to have the sea water brought into her house and make use of a bathing tub.

And this was in the licentious eighteenth century!

The Riviera climate

The Riviera's good climate has many causes. One of them is that it is on the northern shore of the Mediterranean reasonably far—but not too far—away from the dry, hot deserts of North Africa. This great landlocked sea, which is almost tideless, is very deep. But even at the bottom, its water is far warmer than that in comparable ocean depths. Below the 200-fathom line, the Mediterranean is almost uniform in temperature—about 55 degrees all the way down, which is more than 20 degrees higher than deep ocean water. Above the 200-fathom line, much sunshine, winds from the Sahara desert, and the enormous amount of heat stored far below the surface of the water all tend to keep the top layer at a relatively constant high temperature—more than 62.6 degrees from May to October.

This makes for good swimming and boating. It also tempers the Rivera's climate so its winters are mild and its summers not too hot. But don't be deceived about its supposedly dependable winters. We have seen several inches of snow on the palm trees. It melted quickly, but it did seem out of place on tropical plants.

Tropical vegetation the Riviera does have in abundance. Flowers begin to bloom late in December and continue in riotous profusion all summer long. Oranges, lemons, almonds, and olives grow there. So do century plants, cactuses, and other shrubs and flowering trees that require fairly warm weather all year around. This part of France is a gardener's paradise. Some of the great estates, like the one formerly owned by Ephrussi de Rothschild at the entrance to the Peninsula of Cap Ferrat, are open to the public. These expertly tended gardens are glorious and always green.

Rich people, however, no longer flock to the Riviera for

the winter as they used to. Fast jet planes now take them to places that are really warm when Europe is cold. As a result, summer has now become the Riviera's big season.

Where to stay

Choosing a place to stay depends largely on what you want—and can afford. If you prefer to be in a quiet, uncrowded, and inexpensive area, you will do best in the section west of La Napoule. The shore from La Napoule to Antibes is more fashionable and costly although you can find some reasonably priced hotels there. A wide, rather desolate highway runs along the coast from Antibes to Nice. Then the stretch from Nice to Cap Martin again becomes fashionable and expensive. Menton, which used to be both, is now a family resort—and a rather pleasant one.

Generally speaking, hotels in the interior charge less than those along the shore do, although there are exceptions.

If you want to be located where the most interesting spots in the Riviera can be reached by car in less than an hour, we suggest that you stay on Cap Ferrat to be within striking distance of the eastern part of the Riviera, or on the Cap d'Antibes in order to cover the western part. Actually, the whole area is so small that any centrally located hotel can be used as as a base.

You may wonder why we recommend the two most celebrated and presumably expensive places in the Riviera. We do so because they are both very beautiful (rich people naturally pick the best locations) and because you can find any kind of hotel or *pension* you want there.

The shore road

If you are coming from Provence and have the time, we suggest that you take Route N559, which follows the shore. It passes through every town and village and is therefore exasperatingly slow, but it enables you to see the Rivera close-up. If you are in a hurry take the new, very good fast toll road that runs through the interior from Fréjus to Nice.

Assuming that you are going along the coast from Marseille, you will pass through such resorts as Cassis, La Ciotat, Cap

Gros Nez, and Bandol before you reach the naval port of Toulon. With the Riviera acting as an almost irresistible magnet, few people, except the French who know their way around, bother to stop in these little-known places, although they have their attractions. Most of their hotels are reasonably priced; some are quite cheap. Cap Gros Nez is expensive. And the little island of Bendor near Bandol caters to a well-to-do clientele. It can easily be visited for the day by ferry if you don't want to stay in one of its high-priced hotels.

Although Toulon played an important part in Napoleon's career and in the Second World War, it has little of interest for the tourist except its museums. Access to the modern naval installations is forbidden, and no photographs may be taken anywhere near them.

East of Toulon you have a choice of continuing on N559 or of taking the faster inland route to Hyères.

Hyères is an ancient town, as you will see if you visit the old part of the city. The long peninsula that projects into the sea south of the town is filled with rectangular shallow ponds for evaporating sea water to make salt. From it you can take a boat to visit the Ile de Porquerolles, Ile de Port-Cros, and Ile du Levant. They can also be reached by excursion boats from Le Lavandou.

The three islands have many advantages such as good bathing, peace and quiet, and lush semitropical foliage, but you had better inspect them on a day trip before you decide to stay. Porquerolles, the largest one, has a number of hotels, most of which are fairly expensive. Port-Cros has only two, both rather dear. The Ile du Levant is somewhat special, for the French Navy has taken over a good part of it while much of the rest is occupied by nudists who don't welcome unsympathetic visitors who insist on wearing clothes.

The Maures and Saint-Tropez

The region between Hyères and Saint-Raphael is called the Massif des Maures. The rocky area behind the coast is thinly settled and has few attractions for the average tourist, but the little shore resorts have good sandy beaches and quiet family hotels. There are bargains to be had in some of the more modest places, but Le Lavandou, Aiguebelle, Cavalaire, Val-

D'Esquières, and Saint-Tropez are more expensive.

To reach Saint-Tropez (the "z" is silent), you have to leave the main coastal road and take N98A for five kilometers. The town is located on the southern side of a big gulf so it faces north and can be cold when the mistral blows. Across the bay is the much quieter resort Sainte-Maxime.

Many people think that Saint-Tropez' rise to fame as a vacation center for playboys and girls started after the Second World War. Actually, it began in the mid-twenties, was given an impetus by the Duke of Windsor's visits there, and was in full swing by 1939. Charles Graves said that in that year it was "crowded with semi-nude girls burnt almost black, their young men stripped to the waist, drinking through straws . . . while big cars with foreign number-plates crawled past."

As evidence of the way recent dates are easily forgotten, another author, writing about Saint-Tropez, said that he had first seen bikinis there in—well, what year? In 1950. And then he commented, "All the rage last year, this season, regrettably, they are not so popular." Add this to the famous wrong guesses of history.

Saint-Tropez is very old. It was founded by the Greeks about 2500 years ago. When the saint of that name was beheaded in Pisa, his body was placed in an open boat which was cast adrift. Guided across the water by angels, they say, the boat came ashore at the place where Saint-Tropez is now located. Every May 16 to 18 the citizens celebrate his name (and also the repulse of a Spanish fleet in 1637) by holding a picturesque outdoor ceremony called a *bravade*.

Paul Signac was the first of the many painters and writers who came to Saint-Tropez before the turn of the century. Noted modern artists left it a valuable legacy of paintings which are in the Musée de l'Annonciade. But Saint-Tropez has long ceased being a gathering place for serious artists. Film stars, starlets, models, fashion editors, and beach boys have taken it over. It figures largely in the news these days but as a source of gossip and scandal rather than as a place where new ideas in writing or painting originate.

You will undoubtedly want to see this world-famous resort, but a quick look is all it deserves unless you are professionally interested in beach fashions or the sociology of the international young climbers set. If you stay on, you will need someone

Saint-Tropez

who is "in" to show you around or you will be very much "out." And you will find hotels overcrowded and expensive—as is everything else.

The little harbor, which was once solely used by fishermen, is now jammed with pleasure craft. The beaches are outside the town, three miles or more away. Life is regulated by a routine that compels the "in" and would-be "in" people to move from place to place at exactly the right moment like mechanical dolls operated by clockwork.

Sainte-Maxime, which is only three kilometers from Saint-Tropez by water, is 14 kilometers away by car. It is a pretty beach resort with a tree-shaded promenade. It is smaller, less crowded, less expensive, and far less competitive than its better-known neighbor across the bay.

Only 8 kilometers beyond Sainte-Maxime is Val d'Esquières with its luxury hotels and some less expensive ones. Then the shore road runs along a coast where there are few resorts of any consequence except Saint-Angulf which has a sandy beach and a number of modestly priced hotels. At Fréjus (the "s" is pronounced) and Saint-Raphael the Maures ends and the Esterel begins. S. Baring-Gould described the region by saying that its

> porphyry assumes the boldest and most fantastic shapes, and the gorgeousness of its colouring defies description. These flame-red crags shooting out of a sea the colour of a peacock's neck, or out of dense woods of pine, afford pictures where form and colouring are alike of sovereign beauty. It is a region unique in Europe, extending something like twelve English miles from east to west, and as much from north to south. The medium height of its summits is 1500 to 1800 feet, so that the elevation is not great, but it is cleft by valleys that abound in scenes of the finest order of picturesqueness. Here and there the granite and gneiss appear; elsewhere serpentine, trap, basalt, and blue quartzite prophyry. Beside this is the new red sandstone and the Bunter sandstone. Variety of soil gives variety of vegetation; plantations of mimosa . . . thrive on the primitive rocks, and are mixed with cork trees, umbrella pines, oaks, bushes of cistus, laurestinas, myrtle, rosemary, heath, broom, and in the spring gleam the white spears of the asphodel.

The Esterel

Fréjus (Forum Julii) was founded by Julius Caesar and soon became a Roman naval port with a population that was twice what it is at present. The town is now more than half a mile from the sea because the Argens River has silted up the former harbor. Nor is that the only damage this trouble-making river has done; in December 1959 it broke through a dam farther upstream, flooded the lower part of the town, and drowned more than 300 people.

The ruins of a Roman arena that once could seat 10,000 people, a theater, and the arches of an aqueduct that brought water from 20 miles away are located on the edge of the modern town. There is also an archeological museum. In addition to its Roman remains, Fréjus has a cathedral, a baptistery with eight ancient columns taken from a Roman building, and cloisters that are worth seeing.

The road from Fréjus-Plage runs along the sea to the port of nearby Saint-Raphael, which was once a bathing resort for wealthy Romans. Today Saint-Raphael is a pleasant town with old streets around its twelfth-century Church of the Templars. It also has many modern buildings, for part of it had to be rebuilt after it was badly damaged during the Second World War when the Nazis held out there.

La Napoule

The shore road now goes on for a long way (34 kilometers or 21 miles) along the foot of the Esterel Mountains until it reaches sea level again at La Napoule. A few small resorts are scattered along the coast at places where one can get down to the water's edge, but most of this stretch has few houses or hotels.

La Napoule marks the end of the Esterel and the beginning of the 67-kilometer (42-mile) strip of shore that is the heart of the French Riviera.

La Napoule itself is more interesting than it may seem to be at first glance. It has three sandy beaches, one of which (La Ragouette) is tiny. If you look sharply there you will see that the Nazis built two concrete pillboxes in the rocks at one end of the little beach to defend this possible landing place against the inevitable invasion they dreaded so much. Today La Ragouette is a family beach where children play.

La Napoule has a fourteenth-century château that was restored shortly after the First World War by the American sculptor, Henry Clews. It is now a museum with many examples of his work.

The town is also noted for its good food, although its better restaurants are rather high-priced.

Cannes

Beyond Napoule the road runs for 8 kilometers along the shore to Cannes, which, after Nice, is the Riviera's largest resort. For many years its activities centered around a yacht harbor in which the boats were so closely packed together that owners hesitated to move them. A new marina with space for 450 more boats has recently been opened to take pressure off the old one.

Although Cannes prides itself on being one of the most fashionable and luxurious resorts in the Riviera, part of the town is quite old and very much down-to-earth. West of the yacht harbor, narrow streets lead to the public market and go up Mont Chevalier to the section called Suquet. Here is the seventeenth-century church Notre-Dame-de-l'Espérance. Here also are the Musée de la Castre and the tower of Mont Chevalier from which there is a fine view of the town and its waterfront. You can see La Croisette where some of Cannes' best hotels face the sea. Beyond it is the Cap de la Croisette, which is elegant on the western side and less so on the eastern side where there are public beaches and less expensive places to stay.

The yacht harbor is Cannes' biggest attraction. Anyone interested in boats can spend hours there looking at all kinds of craft from every major port in Europe.

The town is almost as crowded with people as the harbor is with boats. Parking a car anywhere near the center is a major undertaking when the season is in full swing.

Beyond the town the ground rises until it reaches the observatory of Super-Cannes, 770 feet above the sea. The tree-shaded groves on the hills have many fine homes hidden in them. Cannes is seen at its best in the suburbs. They, even more than the city itself, are truly luxurious and elegant.

Iles de Lérins

Excursion boats from Cannes to the Iles de Lérins run at frequent intervals from the Gare Maritime near the Casino. They are literally brother and sister islands, for the larger one, Sainte-Marguerite, was named for a devout nun who lived there during the fifth century, while her brother, Saint Honorat, dwelt in a monastery on the smaller island that bears his name. Honorat permitted himself to visit his sister only when the almond trees flowered. But a tree, before which his lonely sister prayed, bloomed by a miracle more than once a year, so the two were able to be reunited more often than the ascetic saint had expected.

Most of the island of Sainte-Marguerite is state property and is still a well-preserved wilderness area. It is best known for the fort in which the Man in the Iron Mask was imprisoned from

1687 to 1698. His identity is still unknown, although there are many romantic theories about it. His mask, incidentally, was probably made of black velvet which the few people who ever saw him—and from a distance—thought was iron.

Saint-Honorat has a fortified monastery that was built long after the saint lived there. L'Abbaye can be visited, but only by men, and not even by them on Sundays. This small island was once an important and well-populated religious community. Ireland's Saint Patrick was educated there.

It is possible to stay on Sainte-Marguerite, but the number of hotel rooms there is very limited. The islands are usually visited only for day trips. The bathing in the clear, clean water is very good.

A very private village

About six miles north of Cannes, on a small and unobtrusive road leading west from D3, is a remarkable village that you are not likely to be able to see unless you know someone who lives there. This is Castellaras, an experiment in modern building that would be a tourist attraction if strangers were permitted to pass the guard at the gate. But they are not, because Castellaras is a highly exclusive community for people who can afford to own one of the very expensive and luxurious architectural novelties there. Each house is unique, and in the newer part of the village the dwellings are built in "Geological" style. This means that they have no straight lines or flat surfaces; everything is curved, and windows are small and irregular in shape. The houses blend in with the landscape and seem to be part of it with their roofs repeating the curves of the hills behind them.

Grasse

There is nothing exclusive about Grasse, and you will be welcomed there, especially if you visit one or more of its perfume factories. Grasse is only 17 kilometers (less than 11 miles) inland from Cannes. Route N567, which leads to it, is very fast, but we suggest that you go at least one way on the little country roads that parallel N567. In this way you will see some of the small villages in the back country.

Grasse calls itself the perfume capital of the world. A guide will take you through one of the factories, but your tour of inspection will end in the manufacturer's salesroom where he hopes to sell you some of his products.

Besides its much-touted *parfumerie,* Grasse has a picturesque old section where narrow streets and stone stairs wind around the steep hills. The eighteenth-century French painter, Jean Honoré Fragonard, was born here in 1732. One of the perfume factories is named after him.

Vallauris

On your way back to Cannes you can visit Vallauris, a small town that has been making decorative pottery for centuries. Picasso gave the native industry a sudden boost to fame when he went there shortly after the Second World War to design his own ceramics. Examples of his work can still be bought at Madoura's salesroom. (It is closed from 12 to 2.) The medieval chapel attached to the Château has Picasso's "War and Peace" on display.

Many people seem to think that because of Picasso's connection with Vallauris, the town sells nothing but fine art pottery. That is not so; dozens of shops line the streets, and nearly all of them display the kind of brightly colored, notably ugly ceramics which tourists (French tourists included) buy as souvenirs. Pottery cats climb on the walls, green frogs sit waiting to be put in someone's garden, and hideous little bits of molded clay of all kinds bid for the attention of unsophisticated purchasers. More than 95 percent of the ceramic objects offered for sale in Vallouris are no better than those sold in roadside shops in the United States. And most of them are far worse than what you can buy in comparable towns in Mexico.

The shore road leads to Golfe-Juan, which has a good beach, and then goes on to Juan-les-Pins, a resort that owes its existence to the American millionaire, Frank Jay Gould, who, in the 1920's, bought up as much land as he could get along the coast west of Cap d'Antibes. There are long white sand beaches, but the railroad and the main highway both run behind them to make the narrow strip seem even more constricted than it actually is. The town itself is closely built up, and its streets are crowded with cars and people. It has several expensive hotels near the Casino and some less expensive ones farther away. The quieter places that charge reasonable prices are some distance inland.

Antibes

East of Juan-les-Pins, Cap d'Antibes juts southward into the sea. The town of Antibes, which is north of it, is very different from the elegant peninsula, which is one of the most beautiful seacoast areas in France. Antibes (from the Greek name Antipolis) is a very old town with extensive fortifications along the water's edge. An interesting new museum has been built into the ramparts. More important is the Musée Grimaldi in the château of that name. It is noted especially for its collection of Picasso's paintings and ceramics, but it also has works by other noted modern artists.

Cap d'Antibes, as we have already said, is one of our two favorite places on the Côte d'Azur. It has few—very few—relatively inexpensive places in which you can stay, but they are worth seeking out.

For those who can afford it, Cap d'Antibes has everything money can buy. The spacious Hotel du Cap, although built in the nineteenth century, is magnificently located in a large park. Attached to it is Eden Roc, which you have undoubtedly seen in pictures with stars and starlets draped around the edges of the pool cut out of the solid rock lining the shore. Since you can use the restaurant, the swimming pool, and other facilities of Eden Roc without staying at the Hotel du Cap, you can have a very pleasant vacation by booking a room nearby and paying a fee to use this justly famous swimming pool. It is not too expensive. In fact, Eden Roc gives good value for what it has to offer.

Nearby is the Batterie de Graillon, an ancient fort that now houses a naval museum of the Napoleonic period. This is not easy to visit because it is open only in summertime from 3 to 6 P.M.

On the eastern side of the Cap d'Antibes is the well-sheltered Plage de la Garoupe which is lined with bathing places, restaurants, and hotels. This section is upper middle-class. It lacks the lush elegance of the other side of the Cap, but it is not without attractions of its own. Few hotel rooms are to be had. If you are lucky enough to get one, take it. And if you can obtain one that overlooks the sea, you can consider yourself luckier still.

The best thing about Cap d'Antibes is its magnificent rock-lined shore, a good bit of which is taken up by private estates. This is also true of the tree-shaded interior where you can walk along the pleasant roads but see very little of what goes on behind the walls and hedges that insure privacy.

In the center of the peninsula the century-old Jardin Thuret, now owned by the French government, has a large collection of trees and plants gathered from warm countries all over the world. Near it is the 245-feet-high Plateau de la Garoupe where there is a chapel with maritime votive offerings. A fine view over the coast can be had from there.

Biot and Cagnes

The coast road from Antibes to Nice is fast but not very interesting. The interior, however, decidedly is. At Biot is the museum built by Fernand Léger's widow to house a huge collection of the various kinds of work done by the artist who was one

Cap d'Antibes: Plage de la Garoupe

Biot: the Leger Museum

of the founders of Cubism. A dramatic and brightly colored mosaic runs across the entire front of the 130-foot-long building. Facing the entrance is a big stained-glass window. And on the lawn a massive, brilliantly colored ceramic sculpture called the *Jardin d'Enfant* rises against a background of trees.

A few miles beyond Biot is Cagnes where you can visit the house in which Renoir spent his last days. Here, in a fine grove of gnarled and twisted olive trees, where flowers grow in sunny spots, the painter who loved sunlight, vibrant colors, and robust women, had his studio. Here you can see his easel, his palette, and the wheeled chair in which the aging man sat with a brush strapped to his rheumatically crippled hand while he painted some of his best pictures. Very few of his works are here; they have become so enormously valuable that this city-owned establishment cannot afford them.

The Château of Haut-de-Cagnes in the old part of the city has a collection of modern paintings. The 600-year-old building itself is architecturally interesting, with medieval rooms, some remarkable decorated ceilings, and a display of objects associated with the local olive oil industry.

And just west of Cagnes is Villeneuve-Loubet, the birthplace of the great French chef, Georges Auguste Escoffier. A museum dedicated to his memory has recently been opened there.

Saint-Paul de Vence and Vence

Route D36 leads from Cagnes to these two interesting towns. Saint-Paul-de-Vence is a well-preserved hill village complete with ancient ramparts from which there is a good view over the surrounding countryside. In the tiny square an old fountain with four spouts supplies water for the townspeople. The narrow streets have small shops which offer for sale the objects that the artists living there have created. And just outside the walls is the Auberge de la Colombe d'Or with many modern paintings collected by its former owner, who accepted some of them in payment for board and lodging from the then-indigent artists who have since become famous. A number of these pictures were stolen in 1960, but they were recovered soon afterward. This elegant and expensive hotel-restaurant has a pleasant outdoor dining terrace overlooking the valley north of it.

One of the most remarkable museums in southern France opened in Saint-Paul-de-Vence during the summer of 1964. This is the Fondation Marguerite et Aimé Maeght (pronounced "Mag"), which has works by Chagall, Miró, Braque, Matisse, Giacometti, Kandinsky, Calder, and other modern artists. Some of the sculpture is displayed outdoors, while the building has been designed to illuminate the interior with cool, natural daylight that shows its important pictures at their best. The museum is open only on Mondays, Wednesdays, Saturdays, and Sundays.

Four kilometers beyond Saint-Paul is the somewhat larger town of Vence. As you make your way toward it you can see a dramatic monument left from the fighting in the Second World War. This is a single, very high shaft that once supported a bridge which spanned a deep valley. The bridge was blown up, and this tall ruined column is all that remains of it.

Vence has an old section which very sensibly does not permit automobile traffic, so you have to wander around there on foot. Fortunately, the town has a large public parking place where you can leave your car under the trees. At one end of it is a small fountain that supplies free mineral water. A plaque gives you the chemical analysis of it.

Inside the walls is the Place du Peyra where a tall urn-shaped fountain sends cheerfully splashing jets of water down into the basin below it. Nearby is the Place du Frêne with an enormous ash tree.

Vence is worth exploring. You will find stones with Roman inscriptions built into the walls, and the cathedral, although not remarkable, has examples of styles that evolved over a period of more than 14 centuries.

D. H. Lawrence came to Vence to stay in a hotel-sanitorium in February 1930. In one of his last letters he said, "The mimosa is all out, in clouds . . . and the almond blossoms [are] very lovely." He died here on March 2 at the age of 44.

Henri Matisse also came to Vence in a search for health. As a tribute to the Dominican nuns who took care of him, he designed a small modern Chapelle du Rosaire which was built in 1950. It is outside the town and is open only on Tuesdays and Thursdays with a three-hour midday closing period. The interior blazes with light on a sunny day, and Matisse's very simple decorations in primary colors are truly impressive. Some of his preliminary sketches are displayed in a side gallery; the Matisse Museum in Cimiez near Nice has more of them.

The hills and steep cliffs beyond Vence are often crowned with villages like Tourettes-sur-Loup, which has strong walls as well as height to defend it. West of it, the Loup River turns north and runs through deep gorges with several waterfalls along the way. You have to go up the east side for several miles before you can turn south to visit the spur-top village of Gourdon, which was once a Saracen fort. It is noted for its spectacular panoramic views.

Even farther north than Gourdon is the holiday village of Tintinville at Coursegoules which children love to visit. There you may think you are back in America, for the riding school has a saloon and a sheriff's house that look as if they came from the set for a Western movie. But there are swimming pools and tennis courts too.

Nice

Nice is the fifth largest city in France, and it is growing all the time. It differs from other big French cities in that it has very little industry. But it does not depend entirely upon tourism, for it is also a place where people go to live after they retire.

When Tobias Smollett visited Nice in 1764 it consisted only of what is now called the old city. This is the section between the river and the steep hill on which the ruins of the Château stand. All the rest is modern; much of it recently built. Even the river is largely covered over.

Smollett had come to Nice for its good climate, and on January 15 could say:

> The plain presents nothing but gardens full of green trees loaded with oranges, lemons, citrons, and bergamots, which make a delightful appearance. If you examine them more nearly, you will find plantations of green peas ready to gather; all sorts of sallading, and pot-herbs in perfection; and plats of

Nice

> roses, carnations, ranunculas, anemones, and daffodils blowing in full glory with such beauty, vigor, and perfume, as no flower in England ever exhibited.

Nowadays when you drive from Antibes to Nice, you pass the big airport, and as you approach the city you see modern buildings rising against the background hills. Late in the afternoon, when the sun gilds the white structures, the scene is truly magnificent. Some of this magnificence remains when you drive along the four-mile Promenade des Anglais with its palm trees and green parks, but once you leave the seafront, the streets are narrow, filled with shops and pedestrians, and as commercial-looking as they are in any other French city.

Nice has many advantages, although we prefer to stay outside and drive in for the day. Parking there has become so difficult that when we do find a place to put the car, we leave it and walk. This is no hardship, for the city has all kinds of restaurants, interesting shops, and parks in which you can rest if you get tired.

The Promenade des Anglais, where the best hotels are located, was begun in 1822 with money supplied by the English to give employment to the poor. The beach below it is likely to be a disappointment because it is covered by good-sized stones that make barefoot entry into the water uncomfortable. At the eastern end of the beach is a bathing platform cut out of the rocks. From this you can go into the water without having to step gingerly on the stones.

But bathing in the sea is not Nice's greatest attraction. The streets behind the waterfront are. The old city should be visited, as should the tree-shaded Jardin Albert Premier, which has an open-air theater and a children's playground.

The carnival, with its gigantic *papier-maché* figures that are paraded through the streets, takes place in February or March, and culminates on Shrove Tuesday when the big manikin that is supposed to be the King of the Carnival is burned with much ceremony.

Nice has several museums, the most interesting of which is not in town but up in the hilly suburb of Cimiez near the ruins of the Roman arena there. This is the Matisse Museum which has many works by that artist. It is particularly rich in sketches and other objects that show his development as a painter, a sculptor, and a designer. On the ground floor Roman artifacts dug up in the surrounding area are displayed. This was the site of the ancient Roman city, Cemenelum, which is now just beginning to be excavated. It was described in January 1764 by Tobias Smollett who said that it was "a rich mine of antiquities, which, if properly worked, would produce a great number of valuable curiosities."

North of Cimiez is the charming hilltop village of Falicon where many artists live. At its highest point is a tree-shaded bench from which you can see Nice and the Mediterranean.

The Three Corniches

When you go east from Nice you have a choice of three routes. The one along the sea, the Corniche Inférieure (N559) is slow because it runs through the towns along the shore. The middle one, the Moyenne Corniche (N564), is higher and has some views of the coast. But the Grande Corniche (N7) deserves its name, not only for its height but for the splendid panorama of the coast that is spread out below it. It goes over the mountains to Menton, whereas the Middle Corniche joins the lower one at Cabbé.

People who drive over the Grande Corniche for the first time think it is a modern road. Actually much of it was laid out by the Romans as part of the Aurelian Way that ran from Rome to Arles. The Romans often placed their roads on mountain ridges where their marching legions could survey the landscape for miles around and be sure that no one could make a surprise attack.

A reminder of the Roman conquest of this area is at La Turbie where the impressive ruins of the Trophée des Alpes stand high above the hills. This was built in 5 B.C. during the reign of Augustus to proclaim the victory of Rome over 44 Gallic tribes. A small museum near it has interesting documents and a model of the monument as it was in Roman times. Funds for the restoration of the Trophée and the building of the museum were supplied by Edward Tuck, a New Hampshire banker who spent much of his life in France.

Beyond La Turbie, the Grande Corniche passes the remarkable new hotel, Le Vistaëro, which is perched high on the edge of a cliff. It is an expensive place to stay in, but you may want to visit the terrace to have drinks there and admire the view.

The Grande Corniche runs past Roquebrune before it descends to sea level. It is difficult—and sometimes impossible—to find parking space in this tiny mountainside village, but it is worth trying to stop there long enough to see its odd streets and terraces. It was in this remote community during the late 1930's that Hans van Meergeren, the Dutch forger, painted "Christ at Emmaus" in such perfect imitation of seventeenth-century Jan Vermeer's style that his picture deceived some of the greatest art experts in Europe until the truth about its origin was revealed after the war.

The Middle Corniche is less interesting than the upper one, but it passes the ancient hilltop village of Èze, which has one of the best restaurants on the Riviera, the Chèvre d'Or. The dining terrace has a justly celebrated view.

Èze is a two-part village with its lower half (Èze-Bord-de-Mer) at the edge of the sea. Only a mule path connects the two communities. Èze-Village, the upper one, cannot be reached by car. You have to park below it and walk up the steep streets that lead to the walled town.

The higher Corniches are beautiful to drive on, but it is the lower one that goes to the places you are most likely to want to visit or stay in.

Villefranche is the first town after you leave Nice. Its well-sheltered harbor has long made it a favorite anchorage for vessels from the United States Mediterranean fleet.

Cap Ferrat

Near the Port de la Santé is the tiny Chapelle Saint-Pierre, which was decorated by Jean Cocteau. It is easier to visit than the Matisse Chapel near Vence, but it closes for three hours at lunchtime. And you have to pay an admission fee.

Beyond Villefranche is Cap Ferrat, our favorite place on the Riviera. One of its greatest assets is that it is a peninsula, so no through traffic goes into it. It has two fingers that stretch far out to sea. Down the middle of the larger one runs a long, high ridge, the very top of which is a military zone.

The town of Saint-Jean-Cap-Ferrat has a little port that was once used by local fishermen but which is now filled with sports craft. They are fairly modest ones, though, not at all like the elaborate yachts that tie up at Cannes, Saint-Tropez, and Monte Carlo. That doesn't mean that Cap Ferrat is not affluent. It is—very—as you will see as you pass its many fine estates.

You can get glimpses of them if you walk along the Maurice-Rouvier promenade that leads along the eastern side of the peninsula from the harbor to Beaulieu. There is another interesting path along the shores of the promontory that ends at the Pointe de Saint-Hospice. Near this is a huge copper statue of the Virgin. It overlooks a small cemetery in which are buried a number of Belgian soldiers who came here to be hospitalized after being wounded in the First World War.

The new lighthouse and its beautiful garden can be visited. From it you will see—among other things—the Olympic-sized pool belonging to the Grand Hotel. You can bathe in this shoreside pool without being a guest of the hotel. Outsiders are charged an admission fee.

We have already mentioned the gardens on the Rothschild estate. The mansion is a museum which displays the kind of costly and elaborate art that millionaires favored at the turn of the century.

Saint-Jean-Cap-Ferrat: a pension *garden*

Children—and many adults—will want to visit the outdoor zoo where rare birds, wild animals, and amphibians are kept. It also has a "school" for chimpanzees where trained apes perform their tricks.

People hesitate to plan on staying on Cap Ferrat because it seems to be solely for millionaires. Fortunately, there are inexpensive places, hotels and *pensions,* although most of them are in the center of the peninsula without a view of the sea. But they may have tropical flower gardens as compensation, and freedom from traffic noise is assured. There are several public beaches and a section set aside for campers.

Beaulieu is a small but fashionable resort noted for its luxury hotels and its Casino which is more like what you think Monte Carlo ought to be than Monte Carlo actually is. You are more likely to see fine clothes and costly jewels here than in the more famous establishment.

Monte Carlo

You will soon be able to make a comparision because the Monte Carlo Casino is only a few minutes away. Actually, Monte Carlo is part of Monaco, the tiny independent state that is only 370 acres in extent although 46 more acres are being added by filling in part of the seafront. Monaco has a population of 21,783, of whom only 3266 are citizens. They pay no taxes and are not subject to military service.

The Grimaldi family has ruled this little state since 1308. It was reduced to its present size in 1861 when France purchased Roquebrune and Menton from it. Shortly after this, the Société Anonyme des Bains de Mer et du Cercle des Étrangers à Monaco was founded with money supplied by François Blanc, who had successfully operated a casino in Bad Homburg. There had been gambling in Monte Carlo before this, but it had not amounted to much. Blanc put the new Casino on its feet financially and soon made it world famous.

There is much more to this interesting little principality than gambling. In fact, gambling, which was once the source of more than 75 percent of Monaco's income, now provides only 4 percent. When the Monte Carlo Casino began operating it had no rivals anywhere in France. The numerous casinos which opened there in the 1920's have cut into what used to be a monopoly.

The decline in gambling income has brought new problems to Monaco, but they are being tackled with imagination and forethought by Prince Rainier III, who realizes that his country needs more than gambling profits to keep it going. He has taken many steps to make it self-supporting. In addition to the extended seaport, the railroad tracks are being built over, and every inch of scarce space is being ingeniously utilized for tourism and international industry.

His wife, the former American motion picture actress, Grace Kelly, is a definite asset to the little country. She has provided a gracious image—no pun intended—for Monaco that has earned good will throughout the world for a state that was once known only for gambling.

Monaco

When you enter Monaco you will see that it consists of three towns: Monaco itself, the rocky eminence on which the very old 250-room Grimaldi palace is located: the middle part, La Condamine, with a yacht harbor and the Olympic-sized swimming pool; and Monte Carlo, where the Casino dominates the heights above the shore.

Monaco is a tourists' Mecca. They come there to stand in front of the palace perhaps hoping to catch a glimpse of the beautiful princess who lives behind its closely guarded walls. Their chance of seeing her, except on public occasions, is very slight. But they like to watch the uniformed guards and stroll around the wide terrace that overlooks the sea and the other two towns. Near the palace are tropical gardens, prehistoric grottoes, and a zoo, all of which can be visited. Below it is the aquarium and the Oceanographic Museum founded in 1910 by Prince Albert I, who was so interested in marine zoology that he went on many specimen-gathering voyages. His second wife, the former Alice Heine, was Monaco's first American-born princess.

La Condamine's harbor shelters some of the finest and largest yachts in the Mediterranean. Behind it is a valley where shops and commercial establishments are located. Then, on the hill to the east, are the modern office buildings and apartment hotels that surround the Casino, the Opera House, and the other buildings owned and operated by the consortium that has the

Monte Carlo gambling concession. Below and beyond the Casino are the new beaches, some of which are still unfinished.

The Casino

Despite the fact that gambling at the Casino has lost much of its glamor, it is still the one place every visitor to the Riviera wants to see. You will have to be over twenty-one years old, and you will need your passport to enter. Local citizens are not allowed to gamble there. And you should be dressed respectably, although evening clothes are no longer required. Ian Fleming once said: "Do not approach casinos with timidity or reverence. They are simply fruit-machines tended by bank clerks and mechanics. . . . They are very pleased to see you come in and will be sorry to see you go."

If you have been to Las Vegas, Monte Carlo may seen old-fashioned and rather tame. The Casino, which has no comparable bargains in food or drink, is hardly ever crowded. But for a serious gambler it has one notable advantage: its roulette wheels have only one zero, not two, so you get better odds than you do in America.

You will be reminded of American gambling places when you enter because slot-machines have been installed in an anteroom since the war. And you can play craps at a table where American terms are used. But old Monte Carlo, the Monte Carlo of E. Phillips Oppenheim, goes on largely unchanged except that many of its roulette tables now stand idle much of the time.

The room to which an ordinary ticket admits you is the Salle Schmidt (called the "Kitchen"). This is the one where most tourists are satisfied to stay because the stakes are lowest there. Beyond it are the *Salles Privée,* for which a higher admission fee is charged and larger stakes are played. Still more exclusive is the Sporting Club which is in another building that is open only during the high seasons.

Although roulette is not the only gambling game played in Monte Carlo it is that hypnotically spinning wheel with a little white ball bouncing around it that gives the Casino its special fascination. The faces of the people seated or standing on three sides of the table intently playing or looking on are worth studying. Most interesting of all is the superlative skill of the *croupiers* as they put the wheel in motion, handle the chips, and supervise the playing. They are highly trained men for whom their well-paid work is a lifetime career. Note how the one who operates the *cylindre* puts it into motion with his forefinger and middle finger and then holds the ball between his thumb and forefinger before sending it clicking around the rapidly revolving wheel. Listen to the French phrases that control the play: *"Messieurs, faites vos jeux,"* begins the game, and then, as the wheel begins to slow down, *"Rien ne va plus"* ends the players' chance to place bets. But you will need a knowledge of much more French than that to risk putting any appreciable amount of money on the table. English is not unknown at Monte Carlo, however, so you can risk small sums without having to understand French or the fine points of roulette. You will probably lose unless you have incredible luck.

If you have some knowledge of roulette and want to play in earnest, spend some time studying the Monte Carlo routines before you buy chips. When you begin, be sure to get a seat at a table. You are likely to do better if you are next to one of the *croupiers* and give him a chip each time you win. He will drop it into a slot in the table called the *cagnotte* so the collective tips can be divided among the employees. Tell him where you want your chips placed. He will do a precise job, and there will be no argument as to whose winning counter belongs to whom. He will not offer advice, but he is helpful to have around.

Although it has been said that the ornate Casino looks as if it had been put up temporarily for an international exposition, it was built in 1878 after designs made by Charles Garnier who was responsible for the even more ornate Opéra in Paris. A photograph of it taken about 1910 showed that nothing has changed since that time except that the big automobile parked in front of the palm trees would now be a valuable museum piece. The more than ample costumes worn by the men and women in the picture would also qualify for being displayed in glass cases.

Like most things that do not change with the times, the Casino has not been doing well in recent years, although it still takes in far more money than any of its French competitors. The key property owned by the Société des Bains de Mer is important to the economy of Monaco, but Prince Rainier and the Société's major stockholder, the multimillionaire Greek shipowner, Aristotle Onassis, have not been able to reach an agreement about the way the principality should develop. The Prince wants to go ahead rapidly with ambitious improvements, but Onassis is more cautious. The outcome is still unsettled at this writing. But we hope that Monaco, which is very prosperous and Monte Carlo, which is not, continue to be as important as they have been for more than a century. It would be unthinkable to visit the Riviera without stopping to see them both. We have always liked this little principality that has maintained its independence for centuries in a world in which small states are often crushed beneath the might of big powers.

Menton

We like Menton, too, although there has been an effort to disparage it as a resort. Certainly its warm climate is in its favor. It is sheltered by a wall of high mountains that block off cold winds from the north. As a result Menton has become a famous lemon-growing area. Since lemons are even more susceptible to frost than oranges are, their presence is a fair guarantee of mild winters.

Menton has two distinct parts—the new section along the seafront and the older one on a hill in the eastern part of the town. The new part is very much like other small Riviera resorts, but the old city was built by Italians when it was part of Italy.

Menton's town hall has a wedding chamber decorated with murals by Jean Cocteau. And there are many art galleries and print shops.

We remember fondly an August evening spent in the old section's Parvis Saint-Michel during one of the annual Chamber Music Festivals. This was an outdoor concert in which Isaac Stern was the featured player. The façades of the two churches facing the square were lighted by hundreds of candles. All the seats had been sold, but we found places on the steps outside the enclosed area and listened to the music with the townspeople who had gathered there. Children and dogs went about their usual business, but a strict ban of silence was imposed upon them. Wooden beach sandals that ordinarily clatter loudly on the stones were removed for the occasion, and people walked on bare feet while the music was being played.

Beyond Menton is the Garavan quarter with the magnificent Colombières gardens. And beyond this is Ventimiglia and the

Italian border.

Very near the border are a number of caves that were used as dwelling places by prehistoric men. Unfortunately they were excavated in the nineteenth century before modern methods of archeological digging were known, so much valuable material was lost or destroyed. The deposits were 30 feet deep with numerous artifacts and animal and human bones imbedded in the magma. Some of the more important discoveries may be seen in the Anthropological Museum in Monaco.

Mountain villages

You may want to return by one of the many interesting inland routes. The country behind Menton and Nice is especially rich in picturesque hilltop villages that were built for protection against the marauders who menaced this area for centuries. Castellar, Castillon, Peille, and Saorge are especially good examples of these villages. There are also deep gorges and much rugged country to explore. The best way to go about it is to start north from Menton on Route N566, turn briefly off course to Castellar, and then continue to Castillon and Sospel, after which you take N204 to Saorge. From there you may or may not want to go on to Tende and Italy. If you swing south again to Sospel you can work your way west to Peïra-Cava and finally reach N202 which leads to N207 and then N555 to Castellane. Beyond this are the gorges of the Verdon River. South of the river D71 is called the Corniche Sublime because it runs along the very deep gorge that has been named the Grand Canyon. Route D71 then becomes D19; it joins N557 on the south shore of the river, and at this point you can return to the Riviera or cross the bridge and go north to Digne and the Alps.

Food

What we have said about food in Provence applies also to the Riviera, although the Italian influence is stronger in the section from Nice to Menton. *Soupe aux poissons,* which is more like Italian *zuppa di pesce* than *bouillabaisse,* begins to make an appearance. Nice has given its name to delicious *salad niçoise* which has become so popular that it has spread across the world.

Since the Riviera lies between Provence and Italy, which are both great originators of food, it has been content to follow their lead. It has few specialties, and its best restaurants serve food that is more in the tradition of Paris than it is local.

Nor does the Riviera have any remarkable cheeses or wine. Its table wines come from the Midi or Algeria; its better ones from the Côte du Rhône; and its finest ones from Bordeaux, Burgundy, and Champagne.

19. *Corsica*

Unless you just want to stay in one place for a rest—and Corsica is very good for that—we suggest that you tour the island. On your way around you may want to stop off for a while at L'Ile-Rousse, Calvi, Porto, the shore towns near Ajaccio, or Propriano—all on the west coast. For the interior, Corte is a convenient center. For modern accommodations on or near a fine beach, we think that L'Ile-Rousse or Propriano are the best possibilities. Bonifacio is a spectacular town to visit but not to stay in. The flat east coast south of Bastia can be traversed rapidly; it is the least pleasant part of this pleasant island.

Corsica is the one place in France where the duration of your stay is important. Fortunately, you can arrive at a positive answer by the use of simple arithmetic.

You can go to Bastia or Ajaccio by ship or air from Nice or Marseille. (The trip from Nice costs less.) You can also go overnight by rail and air from Paris. If you want to take your car, you have to send it by ship. That is not as simple as it sounds. The available cargo space is pretty well booked up for June, July, and August. The charge for automobile freight is high, and you will need special insurance for your car while it is on the ship. It may therefore pay you to leave your car at the airport on the mainland, fly over, and rent an automobile if you are going for a short visit. Here is where arithmetic comes in.

Transportation rates for accompanied automobiles are figured by weight. The Compagnie Générale Transatlantique will tell you what the sea voyage costs, and Air France will let you know how much it is to fly. Then find out what the terms for car rentals are in Corsica. You now have the necessary data to make cost comparisons for the number of days you want to spend there. Since automobiles come in all sizes and weights and the charges for transportation of vehicles and passengers keep changing, we cannot give you any figures here. We can only say that when we went to Corsica, we took our car on a ship because we were staying on the island for more than a week. For a shorter visit, we would have done better to fly and rent. There is no universal answer; each prospective visitor has to figure out his own.

We took the night run which proved to be a mistake; we would have done better on a day ship. The time required for loading and unloading lost us half a day or more. The night ship arrives at dawn, but it is many hours before your car is put ashore.

Since we wrote this, a new ship, the *Comté de Nice,* was added to the fleet. You can drive your own car on and off this one if you are lucky enough to be booked on it.

When to go

Getting to Corsica is a bit of a nuisance and is fairly expensive, but a visit to this remarkable island is worth the trouble and money involved. Relatively few tourists go there, although more and more of them are visiting it each year. Nowhere in France can you be as sure of good weather as on this sunny isle.

The season begins early, and spring is by far the best time to be there. That is when the *maquis* is in bloom, and the perfume of the wild mountain flowers pervades the air. Napoleon, who is Corsica's most famous son, said that he could tell when his ship was approaching the island, because the sweet odors drift out to sea.

From April 6 to June 6—and in some cases to the end of June—sizeable discounts are offered from the regular prices for transportation by ship or air, hotels, and car rentals, provided that your stay is from 6 to 30 days during this bargain period.

If you are going to Corsica to tour the entire island, Bastia is the best point of arrival; otherwise land at Ajaccio, which is nearer most of the places you are likely to want to visit.

Corsica was Italian until 1768, when it was purchased by France—just in time to give French citizenship to Napoleon, who was born at Ajaccio the following year.

The island has been settled since earliest times. It has fascinating prehistoric remains, notably at Filitosa, and many reminders of the various peoples who struggled for possession of it over the centuries. Greeks, Romans, Vandals, Lombards, Saracens, Pisans, Genoans, and Milanese followed one another in successive waves of occupation from 560 B.C. to the time when the French took possession. War, revolution, and worst of all, the Black Death, which wiped out two-thirds of the population in 1347, made life hard on this rocky island where good soil is scarce.

Corsica entered the mainstream of literature in 1829 when Prosper Mérimée wrote *Mateo Falcone* and again in 1840 with his even better-known *Colomba*. Both deal with the Corsicans' delicate sense of honor and the terrible vendettas that arose when vengeance was called for to satisfy a family that felt it had been wronged. The vendettas are gone, but tourists can buy souvenirs of them in gift stores that sell pocket knives of various sizes with the words *Vendetta Corsa* engraved on their blades.

Banditry, which developed from the vendettas and was of a rather special kind because it was directed only at marked victims and not at strangers, gave Corsica a bad name. But it was finally put down in the 1930's, and you are probably safer there than in most other places. We found the people to be unusually helpful, always courteous, and apparently as honest and decent as you can find anywhere.

French is the language, although some of the older people still speak Italian. Nearly all place names are Italian, but they are pronounced in the French manner, so Ajaccio is Ajaseeo rather than Ajacheeo as the Italians would say.

Just as Americans living on Puerto Rico and the Virgin Islands refer to people from the American mainland as "Continentals," so do the Corsicans call the French from the mainland *"les continentaux."* Don't even hint that Corsica is in any way separate from France. Corsicans are very sensitive about their country. Dorothy Carrington, the British travel writer who has lived on the island for more than ten years, says in her fine book: "Refrain from criticizing Corsica to the Corsicans; they simply can't bear it. . . . The Corsicans are constantly criticizing Corsica to each other in conversation and in the local press. But they are deeply offended if foreigners do. . . . Try to like the Corsicans; they will repay you prodigiously. If they feel you like them they will do everything in their power to facilitate your journey and ensure that you leave with a good opinion of their island; and always remember, they want you to become fond of it too."

It is not hard to like the Corsicans and their ruggedly beautiful island. We were enchanted with both.

Getting around

Bastia, the northernmost good port of arrival, is 230 kilometers (143 miles) across the water from Nice. Except for the fast, new *Comté de Nice,* which takes only 5 hours, the older ships require 6½ hours to make the crossing. This means that the night run is inconvenietly short. Planes fly over in 40 minutes.

The population of Corsica, according to the 1962 census, is 280,000. It is one of the few places in the world that is losing population, for the 1896 census enumerated 290,000 inhabitants. This trend, however, will probably soon be reversed because the country is rapidly being developed.

It is the third largest Mediterranean island and is 114 miles long by 52 wide. This makes it comparable in size with Long Island although that sea-girded bit of New York State with its teeming millions is slightly greater in length but is much less in width. Except for a few low-lying hills, Long Island is rather flat, while Corsica is mountainous with peaks rising so high (8000 or 9000 feet) that we have seen snow on them in the middle of June.

The mountains make driving difficult in some places where the roads are just shelves cut out of cliffs towering above the sea. But while driving is tiring because of the constant shifting and turning, it is not really dangerous if you pay close attention to the road and sound your horn when you approach a blind curve.

Timorous drivers may prefer to leave their car on the mainland and tour the island by bus, but that is not really necessary. Just be extra careful and don't try to go fast because goats, cows, and donkeys are seldom fenced in and may be encountered in unexpected places. And be sure to keep your gas tank well filled, for service stations are often a long way apart.

We drove all around the rim of the island, exploring the middle, and had no trouble anywhere. Except for a few clouds in the high mountains, we had brilliant sunshine every day.

Corsica, however, is still rather primitive compared with most other sections of France. Good modern hotels are scarce,

Erbalunga, a seaside village

but most of those that do exist have spectacular views over the water. And the magnificent sandy beaches are never crowded. In fact, some of them are deserted most of the time.

The food does not come up to average French standards, and the wines are full-bodied and potent in alcoholic content, but in no way distinguished. Prices in general are higher than on the mainland because most things have to be shipped in. On some items you pay heavily for the freight. A bottle of Évian water, for instance, costs just twice as much as it does in Nice. Hotel rooms, however, are priced about the same as they are in the rest of France.

Northern Corsica

Bastia, which has about 50,000 inhabitants, is Corsica's biggest city. Originally it clustered around the narrow Old Port which is dominated by the Citadel, but it has spread out to include the more efficient but less interesting New Port where passenger ships from the mainland dock. Between the two is the long, tree-shaded Place Saint-Nicholas. Here the townspeople come to sit at the tables of the many outdoor cafes and watch the strolling crowd. Everyone seems to know everyone else.

Bastia is not too bad a place to stay in, but there are good country hotels nearby. See our hotel list for recommendations.

When you start out from Bastia you have a choice of going around Cap Corse on N198 or of proceeding west to L'Ile Rousse and Calvi on N189. If you want to visit Cap Corse we suggest that you go there first. You will find its rock masses and vistas of deep blue sea spectacular, although they may seem less impressive after you have seen the rest of Corsica.

Cap Corse is one of the most primitive parts of the island. The towns are small, hotels few and very simple, while eating places are exceedingly plain. But you can make the trip in about six hours, including stops, so you can return to Bastia or go on to the west coast resorts the same day.

The east side of the cape is almost treeless, but forests cover the west. More people live there, and it is obviously the better side to be on. But one of the most picturesque towns in Corsica is on the east coast, only 10 kilometers (6 miles) north of Bastia. This is Erbalunga, which is built on a rocky spur that sticks out into the sea. Water washes over ledges on the southern side, and the village itself is tightly knit together on the slightly higher ground above them. A half-ruined watch tower rises above the rooftops.

The Genoese built 67 of these towers that encircle the island. They are near enough to each other to enable a signal to be sent rapidly down the line if a suspicious-looking vessel approached. In those days, Barbary pirates from North Africa made sudden raids on places that were open to attack.

As you drive north to Macinaggio and then west to Centuri you will pass several small fishing ports and see villages perched in the hills above them. This juxtaposition, which occurs all along the shores of Cap Corse, is not accidental. In the days when the island was subject to invasion, the ports were used during the day and then were abandoned at night when the workers went up to sleep in their well-protected homes on the heights.

From the loftier points along this coast you can see several distant Italian islands. When the weather is right, they are capped with clouds and seem very unreal as they rise above the deep-blue water.

The coastal road does not go all the way to the tip of the cape but turns west a few miles south of it to lead to Centuri. Young James Boswell landed there in 1765, only two years after he had met Samuel Johnson, whom he was later to immortalize. He spent some time with Pasquale di Paoli, who was then planning to build a man-of-war at Centuri in order to attack the Genoese on the nearby island of Capraja. Boswell was greatly taken with the people he had encountered and returned to London to write his *Account of Corsica,* which appeared in 1768. The period he deals with is of especial interest because Paoli's capture of Capraja led to the French purchase of Corsica. And Boswell describes the island as it was just before Napoleon was born there.

Today Centuri is a sleepy little fishing port with fewer than 300 inhabitants. The underwater rocks provide good shelter for shellfish, and skin-divers as well as natives come here to catch them.

As you drive down the west side of the cape you will see tiny villages, an occasional castle high in the hills, and the watch towers that ring the island. The sea is nearly always visible; it usually lies so far below you that you cannot hear the sounds of the waves you see breaking on the rocks along the shore.

The trip from Bastia to the junction of N198, N189, and N199 at the western foot of Cap Corse is 115 kilometers or 71 miles. It may seem longer because there is much to see and much work to do as you swing the car around curve after curve. But the scenery is always impressive, and the side roads are worth exploring, although most of them are better suited to four-wheel jeeps than ordinary cars. They are narrow winding tracks that lead up to settlements in the mountains where you have to turn around and come back down again over the same route you drove up.

At this road junction you can return to Bastia on N189 which zigzags up the Col de Teghime or go on to Saint-Florent and L'Ile-Rousse.

As you approach Saint-Florent you will see beyond it the barren rocky wastes of the Désert des Agriates which is one of the wildest stretches of coastal land in Corsica. It can be traversed only on foot, and the going is hard.

Saint-Florent is a charming small town which is so well located on the gulf of that name that it may someday be a fully developed resort. There are a few modest hotels there now.

The 46-kilometer (29-mile) run to L'Ile-Rousse passes through part of the Désert des Agriates. You get occasional glimpses of the sea through breaks in the sun-baked rocks, and the distant water seems bluer than ever by contrast with the light color of the stone.

L'Ile-Rousse and Calvi

L'Ile-Rousse, which gets its name from three pink-granite islets near the shore, has nearly 2000 inhabitants, an impressive covered market, and fine beaches, some of which are private. Most of the summer visitors are well-off and well-behaved so the atmosphere is quiet and even a bit reserved. It is an excellent place for an extended stay. The hotels in the town and around it run from quite inexpensive to the high priced.

From L'Ile-Rousse to Calvi is 24 kilometers (15 miles), and the shore road, N199 and N197, has some resorts strung along it. Calvi has only a thousand more inhabitants than L'Ile-Rousse, but it seems much more like a city.

The center of interest is the photogenic, high-walled citadel located on the tip of a rocky bit of land that projects out to sea on the west side of the gulf. This grim fortress has twice been attacked by invaders, unsuccessfully by the Turks in 1553 and successfully by the English in 1794. Horatio Nelson, who was second in command of the British fleet, lost the sight of his right eye when it was struck by a piece of gravel driven into it by the impact of a cannon ball that hit the ground near him.

One of the reasons for the fall of the citadel was that its garrison not only ran out of food but was seriously reduced by the malarial fever that made Corsica a place to be avoided during the summer. The mosquitoes that bore the disease have now been exterminated, and malaria is no longer a threat. The only reminder of them are the huge eucalyptus trees—especially numerous on the east coast—which were thought to have a beneficial effect upon malarial-ridden country. Actually, they did serve some purpose, for they require lots of water and helped to dry out the swamps.

While L'Ile-Rousse seems to appeal to a somewhat older,

better-fixed clientele, Calvi is a young persons' town with nightlife, several modern hotels, and a long strip of sandy beach backed by pine groves. The water is shallow, but good swimmers and divers can find greater depths on the sea side of the Citadel.

The younger crowd does not mean that Calvi is even remotely like Saint-Tropez. It is a favorite with middle-class—and middle-aged—English people who come to stay in its better hotels and spend a leisurely vacation on its beaches where they can be sure of having plenty of warm sunshine.

South to Ajaccio

From Calvi you may want to go inland to Corte on winding mountain roads through the wilderness. Corte is noted for its ancient citadel which is perched on an almost impregnable rock peak. The town, which has several inexpensive hotels, is a good place to visit if the weather gets hot along the coast, for it is high enough to be fairly cool. From there you can reach the west side of the island again by taking N193 to Vizzavona and

Calvi: the Citadel

The old man, a wind-sculptured rock *Wind-carved rocks*

Ajaccio (83 kilometers or 52 miles). But if you do, you will miss some of the best scenery on this scenic isle. Route N193 is beautiful, but no road in Corsica compares with the brief stretch of the coastal one (N199) which passes through the wind-carved rocks of the Calanques south of Porto. You can get to the shore road from Corte by going 8 kilometers out of your way on D18 to the downhill road that eventually runs through the Spelunca Gorge to meet N199 at Porto.

If you are willing to miss Corte you can save a lot of mileage and hard driving by taking N199 along the coast from Calvi to Porto (81 kilometers or 50 miles instead of 179 kilometers or 111 miles).

Porto has a superb sandy beach in a protected cove where great red rocks come down to the sea. A Genoese watchtower overlooks the bay while a grove of eucalyptus trees shades the valley behind the shore. It is amazing that so glorious a spot should remain relatively undeveloped, but so far it has. Its hotels are all rather modest (none is close to the water), and many of its visitors are campers who pitch their tents in the woods and spend their daytime hours on the beach.

Just beyond Porto, N199 enters the famous Calanques and for a short distance is lined with reddish-colored, grotesquely shaped rocks. Examine them carefully, and you will see human and animal figures, weird abstractions, and almost anything you want to make out of them. They are worth coming back to study more than once, for they change in appearance from hour to hour as the sun moves across the sky.

It is 83 kilometers or 52 miles from Porto to Ajaccio, and once you reach the sea again at Cargèse, N199 runs along the shore for miles. Here you will pass one splendid beach after another and find them nearly all deserted. Corsica has more good beaches than it has people to enjoy them. This will change, but right now you can have the place pretty much to yourself.

Ajaccio

Ajaccio, the capital of Corsica and a city of more than 40,000 inhabitants, is still dominated by the figure of the man who was born there nearly 200 years ago. The house in which Laetitia Bonaparte gave birth to a commoner who was to have as much effect on the course of French history as any of its kings is larger and finer than you may expect. It was refurbished in order to be in proper condition to receive the rising young conqueror when he returned from Egypt in October 1799, but it was probably a rather impressive mansion even before that. It is located on a narrow street in the center of the old city, and the growing boy must have roamed around the nearby waterfront until he was nine years old. Then he was sent to a school in Autun on the mainland to learn the French language.

A successful search was made for the family's furniture, so much of what you see is original. The bed on which Napoleon was born almost surely is, and so are some of the other pieces. But beyond doubt these are the rooms which the Emperor knew as a boy. That he went so far from these middle-class beginnings in remote Corsica was possible only because he was born into the Revolution that overthrew the nobility and enabled a professional soldier to rise to supreme power.

Napoleon's name and image occur and recur throughout the city, most notably on the wide plaza facing the gulf where he and four of his brothers are immortalized in bronze as Roman citizens. The Musée Napoléonien in the Town Hall has relics of the family.

But there is much more to Ajaccio than its association with Napoleon. It is the liveliest place in Corsica, with crowds surging through streets where some of the shops stock merchandise that would be hard to find elsewhere on the island. And Ajaccio, which is protected from the north by mountains, has even more hours of sunlight during the year than the rest of sunny Corsica.

The shore of the beautiful gulf on which Ajaccio is located is lined with fine homes and interesting small towns. You may, in fact, be better off staying in one of the hotels on the outskirts than in the city itself.

A favorite drive is the 12 kilometer (7 mile) one along the western shore to the Tour de la Parato from which you can get a good view of the Iles Sanguinaires. The best time for this is at sunset when the rocky islands take on the deep reddish hue that gives them their name. You can also visit them by boat.

If you are interested in the history of Paris you can see a fragment of it by driving 13 kilometers (8 miles) up D61 to the Château de la Punta. This is a replica of the Palace of the Tuileries which connected the two wings of the Louvre until this section was burned down in 1871 during the violent days when the Commune was repressed. The present structure was built of stones taken from the ruins.

The so-called *Grotte de Napoléon* near the city was built after he had left Corsica as a boy. He may, however, have visited it when he stopped off at Ajaccio on his way back from Egypt.

Route N199 ends at Ajaccio; N196 then goes south from there. Since it soon turns inland to run through the mountains on its way to Olmeto and Propriano on the shore, you can save mileage by taking N851 (a perfectly good road) which rejoins N196 a few miles north of Olmeto.

Propriano and Filitosa

Propriano is a small town that was formerly an active port serving Sartène. It is no longer active, but its location on a big sheltered bay with fine sandy beaches and clear, clean water, makes it one of Corsica's most attractive resorts.

From Propriano you can make excursions into the interior, the most interesting of which is to Filitosa where there are some remarkable stones that date back to prehistoric times. At Baracci, only 3 kilometers away, is a hot sulphur spring with waters that are supposedly good for people suffering from rheumatism or skin ailments.

You can easily visit Filitosa from Propriano by driving north along the shore of D157 and then turning east on D57. Or you can stop off there on your way down from Ajaccio. To do this you leave N851 before you reach Sollacaro and go west on D57.

The entrance to the site is clearly marked. You pay a small admission fee and walk for several hundred yards to the ancient sanctuary. On the way you will pass two carved menhirs. The first one has arms and ribs carved on it; the second has a face surmounting a long sword and a dagger.

When you reach the actual site, you will see why it was regarded as a sacred place even before men began to erect stone monuments there. Huge rocks, strangely shaped by nature, are tumbled all around in the shadows of trees that add to the eerie quality of a bit of land that seems set apart for religious purposes. At least two—and probably more—separate civilizations used

Filitosa: a carved menhir

this place as a sacred grove.

The one that created the carved menhirs may have been the outgrowth of an earlier group that marked the spot with plain menhirs, now fallen, but these creators of the sculptured menhirs were the luckless victims of invaders who broke up many of their statues and used the fragments as building material for the circular towers they erected here.

The site is a spur of elevated land that overlooks a valley where five carved menhirs stand. The tower-building invaders blocked access to the spur by walling it off and erected two stone structures and some houses in the protected enclosure. A small museum has relics of the people who once lived and died here.

Many of the broken carved menhirs have been recovered and piled up around the central monument. Several of them are obviously phallic, while others are anthropomorphic.

There are other menhirs and dolmens in Corsica, but the heavy concentration of them in Filitosa and the Taravo River valley indicates that this was the religious capital of the people who inhabited the island in early times. South of Propriano and near the point where the road crosses the Rixxanèse River on a bridge are two isolated menhirs which legend says are the petrified figures of a monk and a nun who were fleeing from Sartène when they were turned to stone.

From Propriano you can visit the village where Prosper Mérimée's Colomba lived. Take N196 south for 1.5 kilometers, then turn left on D19 to Fozzano (15 kilometers or 9 miles) where you will find her house and the little chapel in which she is buried. This story of a Corsican vendetta in the early nineteenth century was not invented. Actually, the truth was more terrible than Mérimée's telling of it, for not just two but four people met their death on the day the quarrel between families erupted into violence.

Sartène and its ancient feuds

Route N196 south from Propriano goes inland 13 kilometers or eight miles to Sartène, a town of 4000 inhabitants which was once divided into two warring factions by a vendetta that involved nearly everyone who lived there. In 1830 the feud became so intense that parts of the town were barricaded, and all communication between the hostile sections ceased. This state of affairs went on for four years during which there were many street battles in which a number of citizens were killed. A formal treaty at the end of 1834 ended the intra-urban war. Since then, Sartène has been quiet and is now a very peaceful place with no remainders of those violent days except the fortress-like dwellings with their strong protective walls.

South of Sartène, N196 passes through rock-strewn land where some remarkable stone formations can be seen. The most famous of them is the Lion of Roccapina, which is west of the road. This gigantic beast is very lifelike, even to its color. Nearer the road is a rock elephant that is best viewed in early or late sunlight when the level rays make its trunk stand out sharply from its body. There are other natural rock figures along here. One of them has the face of an old man with a sharp pointed nose.

Bonifacio

This southernmost settlement in Corsica is 54 kilometers or 34 miles from Sartène on N196. There are two parts to Bonifacio—the new lower town which is located on a long, narrow strip of water, and the older fortified section on a plateau 210 feet above it.

Part of the upper town is built up to the very edge of the limestone cliffs that rise out of the sea. You can get partial glimpses of this from points along the shore, but the best way to see the houses that seem to hang precariously over the water is from one of the small excursion boats that take short trips along the coast to visit the caves that have been hollowed out of the soft limestone by the waves. These boats depart from a wharf in the inlet.

Despite the fact that the French Army maintains a garrison in the Bonifacio Citadel, the town now has only 2600 inhabitants, 1000 fewer than it had 50 years ago. There is a certain amount of animation along the waterfront where the hotels and restaurants are located, but the streets in the upper part are very quiet, and some of the churches are no longer used for religious purposes. But there is a splendid view from the heights. Sardinia is only seven miles away, and you can go there by boat if you want to spend some time on that Italian island.

A few miles southeast of Bonifacio is Cape Pertusato with a

lighthouse from which you can see two small islands. The more southernly one is Lavezzi, which was the scene of a dreadful shipwreck in 1855 when the frigate *Sémillante* foundered on a reef. Nearly 800 French soldiers, who were on their way to the Crimean War, were drowned and their bodies were washed ashore. A memorial pyramid marks the spot where the disaster occurred. The other island is Cavallo. Both were used as quarries by the Romans, and some unfinished stone columns are still there. The two islands are now used as nudist camps.

Bonifacio has withstood attack from land and sea. A well more than 200 feet deep was dug through the rock beneath the Citadel to supply water if the upper town was cut off. And a flight of 142 steps leads down to the Mediterranean. According to legend, it was constructed in one night during the terrible five-month siege in 1420. Few people believe this incredible story about the stairs now, but details of the siege that Alphonso of Aragon launched against the little town are well substantiated. Eighty ships bombarded the coast while a determined army pressed the assault from the land side. Help for Bonifacio was expected from Genoa whose people had founded the town, and a small ship, which had been built on the heights and lowered down to the sea at night, was sent to urge the relief fleet to hurry. But it was a long time coming, and a 40-day truce, after the end of which the Bonifacians had agreed to surrender, was about to expire. On the fortieth day the invaders saw the walls of the city suddenly manned by what appeared to be Genoese soldiers carrying the flag of their Republic. But Alphonso saw through the trick, for the "soldiers" were townswomen who had made themselves Genoan uniforms. He attacked, but Bonifacio held out for four more days—and then the relief fleet did appear. A fierce battle followed, and the Spaniards were compelled to withdraw.

Perhaps it was because this much-attacked town always had to be on the defensive that its people became gentler and more peace-loving than most Corsicans. The vendetta was unknown there, and the present-day Bonifacians are hard-working, simple citizens who get on well with each other and with visitors from the outside world.

Corsica is one of the major sources for the millions of corks needed for French wine bottles. Bales of cork-tree bark are piled up on the wharves of Bonifacio.

Porto-Vecchio

Route N198 goes north for 27 kilometers (17 miles) to Porto-Vecchio, which is on the well-protected gulf of the same name. The town, with its now little-used stone docks, was formerly a much busier port than it is today, although it is one of the few Corsican communities that have gained in population (5600 compared with 3200 in 1900). More people live there now for the simple reason that Porto-Vecchio is a more healthful place to be in during the summer than it was in the days when malaria was rife there. A British visitor who was in Porto-Vecchio in May 1908 wrote:

> During the greater part of the summer months it is deserted by the majority of its 3000 inhabitants, who depart for the healthier uplands. In May the exodus had not yet begun, but fever has put its stamp indelibly on the place. Inhabitants of the port are lacking in the fine Corsican physique to which one becomes accustomed in rambling through the island. One feels sorry for the little children playing around the poor, tiny fountain in the market place with its slight flow of water, which in summer one would scarcely dare to drink. The youngsters look as though they had fever in their blood already. The houses in the few tortuous streets have a deserted appearance; many are quite in ruins and it is often difficult to tell from the outside whether a dwelling is occupied or vacant.

This state of affairs, fortunately, was changed at the end of the Second World War when a massive chemical assault was made on the mosquitoes that were responsible for spreading malaria. Today, Corsica is free from the disease. The British visitor seemed to think that drinking water caused malaria. He was wrong, of course, but in Corsica it is still inadvisable to use tap water anywhere except in the larger cities. You won't get malaria from it, but it may carry other unpleasant germs.

The Ospedale Mountains and Col de Bavella

After N198 leaves Porto-Vecchio it runs north along the shore to Bastia which is 143 kilometers or 89 miles away. If you are in a hurry you can cover this distance quickly, for the road is straight and level. But there are very few interesting places along it. We suggest that instead of taking this rather dull coastal route you make an expedition into the Ospedale Mountains, which are very beautiful and almost unspoiled by modern civilization. The journey through the mountains from Porto-Vecchio to Solenzara is just about twice as long as the coast road, but it is more than twice as interesting.

The ascent up RF11 is not difficult, and when you come to Zonza 40 kilometers or 25 miles) you can cross over to the west coast and go to Ajaccio from which you can return to the mainland by ship or air just as easily as you can from Bastia. But the second half of the mountain journey—39 kilometers from Zonza to Solenzaro on RF4—is even more scenic than the first part.

When you reach the Col de Bavella you will find a mountain meadow with high, sharp-pointed rocky peaks on both sides. Standing in the grassy meadow are huge, wind-distorted trees that show how powerful the air currents are when they sweep through the pass. Here, too, is a cairn surmounted by a statue of the Virgin. Just beyond the pass are numerous cabins for vacationers.

The road going down is a succession of rapid twists and turns on slopes that are always steep. It is easier to negotiate than it looks. All you have to do is stay in low gear and keep a sharp lookout ahead. The descent from the Col de Bavella may be a bit hard on the driver, but it passes through some of the finest mountain and forest scenery in Corsica. Cliffs, boulders, trees, flowers, ferns, and numerous tumbling streams are all mingled together in a memorable wilderness panorama that keeps changing every few feet. Tarffic is almost non-existent so you can make stop after stop to look at the great spectacle that unfolds along the route.

At the bottom is a deep valley that was once a glacial lake. The road crosses this, climbs up out of it, and then goes steadily downhill again—but more gradually—until it reaches the lowlands along the coast to join N198 at Solenzara.

The east coast

From Solenzara to Bastia is 103 kilometers or 64 miles. You pass a new French airbase a few miles above Solenzara, and then at Aleria, a road goes off to the west to the ruins of a Roman city that replaced an even earlier Greek settlement. Outside the ruins, which are now being excavated, is a large brick building that was once an elaborate Roman bath. North of these ruins is the *Étang de Diane,* the former harbor for the Roman fleet. And there is a museum of antiques nearby.

Still farther north, between the Bastia airport and the sea, is the site of another Roman settlement, Mariana. Little of it remains, but towering above the site is the Canonica, an impressive Pisan-type cathedral that is now in ruins. Twenty kilometers beyond the airport is Bastia. There your circular tour of Corsica ends.

Food and wine

Except for one place in L'Ile-Rousse, Michelin does not give any stars to the restaurants of Corsica, although fish and seafood on that sea-girt island are very good. *Langoustes* usually cost less there than they do on the mainland. Sea urchins, which you may have tasted on the Riviera, are highly regarded here, especially when they contain roe. The fish soup that is called *bouillabaisse* in Marseille is called *ziminu* in Corsica where *langoustes,* pimentos, and red peppers, add novelty to this Mediterranean dish.

Pork, mutton, and goat meat are preferable to beef because cows are scarce on this rocky island, and the few it does have are likely to be tough. Game, such as wild boar, is found more often here than in France, although it is not met with ordinarily. *Merle,* a blackbird, is served in pies as *pâté.*

Cheese is made either from sheep's or goat's milk. One is famous, but it won't keep and has to be used on the day it is made. This is *brocciu,* which is boiled in milk before being served. It has the consistency of cottage cheese and may be accompanied by chestnut fritters or figs.

Some Corsican wines are better than you may expect; certainly they are cheaper than those imported from the mainland. At least one, Patrimonio, is shipped to Nice to be served in some of the restaurants there. Don't expect anything great, and you won't be disappointed.

We remember Corsica very fondly and can enthusiastically recommend going there. The ideal trip would consist of about a week's inspection tour after which you can head back to the place you liked best and stay there for a while. Just make sure you can get in because good accommodations are booked up during the season. On your way, stop off to examine hotels and then phone for reservations in the one you like best. Propriano would be our first choice.

20. *The Alps*

What you need to know about the French Alps cannot be learned from an ordinary two-dimensional map. The truly wonderful mountain country that stretches from Lake Geneva to the Mediterranean has so many ups and downs that only a relief map can give you a good idea of what it is like. On the two-dimensional map you will see a curiously twisted network of roads that looks as if someone had dropped tangled string on the paper. Only when you study the roads of this section on a relief map do they make sense. Then you will note that they usually follow the valleys and avoid high places as much as possible. In some spots the heights cannot be avoided; there cars have to go up or down on a series of hairpin turns called *lacets* (literally shoestrings), that make the otherwise impossibly steep grades possible.

For more than 400 kilometers (250 miles) this tremendous chain of snow-topped mountains serves as a border between France and Italy as well as Switzerland. Highest of all the many lofty peaks is Mont Blanc with an elevation of 15,777 feet (4807 meters). And this impressive mountain is not only high; it is ideally located for distant viewing, for visiting with a minimum of effort, or for exploring with climbing equipment and a guide. All around it are other great peaks, so many of them in fact that Mont Blanc is just the culmination of a massive, eternally snow-covered chain that is incredibly beautiful and that momentarily changes with every alteration of light and weather.

Mountains attract clouds; as a result Mont Blanc is said to be clearly visible for only about 60 days a year. We have been fortunate because we have seen it in bright sunlight day after day nearly every time we have gone there. In any but hopelessly bad weather (we have seen that too, in winter), the Mont Blanc area is a photographer's dream. Color pictures taken at sunset on a fine day show the snowy peak changing from white to yellow to gold and then to violet, reddish-purple, and purplish-blue until all the light fades and night takes over.

Routes through the Alps

Although Mont Blanc is the crown jewel of the Alps, there is much more to them than this famous mountain, splendid as it is. As you come up from the Mediterranean you can drive through the high Alps all the way by taking N202 which runs along the Italian border and passes through Barcelonette (160 kilometers or 100 miles from Nice), Briançon (another 102 kilometers or 63 miles), Val d'Isère (158 kilometers or 98 miles more), and which then, after another 28 kilometers or 17 miles, meets N90. At this junction, N90 to the east leads to the Little Saint-Bernard Pass and Italy, while N90 to the west goes to Albertville (56 kilometers or 35 miles), where you can turn off to the northeast on N212 to Megève (31 kilometers or 19 miles) and Chamonix (35 kilometers or 22 miles) on N506. Most of these places, except Albertville (which is an industrial town), are noted ski resorts where the winters are long and the snows deep.

At Albertville, N90 and then N6 continue to Chambèry (50 kilometers or 31 miles), at which point both N201 and N491 go north to Aix-les-Bains on the Lac du Bourget (14 kilometers or 9 miles). There N201 leads to Annecy and its beautiful lake (33 kilometers or 21 miles).

N202, the route through the high Alps, is scenically magnificent, but it is slow, hard driving, and parts of it can be difficult to get through in winter. Sometimes it becomes temporarily impassable until snowplows clear the road. Snow haunts this part of France. At Val d'Isère, for instance, enough sometimes falls in August to make the roads slippery.

An easier, faster, yet scenically attractive route north is N85 which goes from Cannes to Grasse to Digne to Sisteron (173 kilometers or 107 miles). A little beyond Sisteron you have a choice of continuing on N85 to Gap and Grenoble (140 kilometers or 87 miles) or of taking N75 over the Col de la Haute Croix to Grenoble. We have been on both routes and prefer N75 for its fine scenery.

If you stay on N85, however, you will be taking the route Napoleon followed in March 1815 when he returned from exile in Elba to meet final defeat at Waterloo in June.

South of Grenoble, N75 passes along the east side of the high plateau called Le Vercors which was a major center of resistance against the Nazis and the scene of much bitter fighting. This wild mountainous country is cut by deep gorges; it also has many waterfalls and some underground streams. Hotels are scarce except in Villard-de-Lans which is only 31 kilometers (19 miles) from Grenoble. This town of 3700 people is a noted resort in summer as well as in winter. A road marked by memorials to the martyrs of the Resistance leads from it.

North of Grenoble, in equally mountainous country is the Massif de la Chartreuse. There the world-famous liqueur by that name is distilled by Carthusian monks at the monastery of Grand-Chartreuse. They were twice expelled but were allowed to return in 1938 to continue to produce the liqueur that brings in revenue to the French government. The extensive monastery buildings are in a walled enclosure on the side of a valley dominated by rocky heights. It cannot be visited.

Throughout this section you will find roads that cling to rock ledges and sometimes go through tunnels cut into the cliffs. Rapid flowing streams, gorges, cascades, mountain lakes, and hilltop villages make the countryside beautiful.

Grenoble

Grenoble, a city of 163,000 inhabitants, is the capital of this mountainous area. Although Grenoble itself is level enough, a steep escarpment rises on the other side of the Isère River. On top of this is a citadel which can be reached by *téléphérique*. The cable car swings out over the river and mounts swiftly to the heights above. On clear days you can see Mont Blanc from there.

Grenoble is noted for its many museums, its library, and its University, which is attended by a large group of American students. The city is surrounded by mountains, and you can often catch glimpses of them at the end of a street. Sometimes you can see clouds streaming off their tops like masses of windswept hair.

Just outside the city, 6 kilometers on Route N531, is Sassenage, where there is a series of grottoes and the exit of a good-sized underground stream. An attractive tree-shaded area here is an ideal place for a picnic. Michelin gives two stars to The Rostang restaurant in Sassenage.

Route N90 goes north to Chambéry (57 kilometers or 35 miles) which is best remembered for its odd-looking elephant fountain where four huge beasts (which are all fronts joined together with no rears) face in four directions.

On the outskirts of Chambéry (N512 going south) is

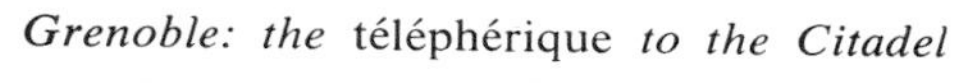

Grenoble: the téléphérique *to the Citadel*

a place that no reader of Jean-Jacques Rousseau will want to miss. This is Les Charmettes, the country villa where the young writer spent several years with the pretty widow Madame de Warens whom he had already known in nearby Annecy. Les Charmettes is now the property of the city of Chambéry and is kept as a museum to preserve the memory of the famous author who once lived there.

From Chambéry to Aix-les-Bains is a short run (14 kilometers or less than 9 miles). The celebrated spa has the attractions typical of French resorts of this kind, and there are some Roman ruins as well. Hotels of all grades line the streets, but the central part of Aix-les-Bains is not near the lake. Grand Port, however, is right on the water. Long rows of big trees line the shore at this point, and there are several excellent restaurants and modern hotels.

For some reason, perhaps because they are so bleak and desolate, we have never been able to work up much enthusiasm for the southern part of the Alps and greatly prefer the section north of a line drawn between Lake Annecy and Saint-Gervais. This would include the charming resorts along the lake, the great peaks around Mont Blanc, and the towns on the south shore of Lake Geneva. There is so much to look at and do in this relatively small area that we see no point in roaming around the mountains east of Grenoble. They are doubtless fine for skiers, but so are the slopes above Chamonix. Three beautiful villages with good hotels serve as bases in this time-tested triangle. They are Talloires on Lake Annecy, Combloux overlooking Mont Blanc, and Yvoire on Lake Geneva. We have been going back to them for years and enjoy every minute we spend in them. Obviously, there are plenty of other fine places, but we like these best.

Annecy and Talloires

One reason why we have spent relatively little time at Aix-les-Bains and the Lac du Bourget is that we have fallen in love with Lake Annecy which is only about half an hour's drive away (33 kilometers or 20 miles). Annecy, a town of 46,000 people at the northern end of the lake, is a small French version of Venice. Canals, lined with ancient houses where housewives do their laundry on platforms suspended above the water, run

Lake Annecy

through the old part of the city while a properly grim Château rises above the rooftops. But the glory of Annecy is its extensive parks, which line the lakefront and are complete with playgrounds, boats, and flower gardens. Swans glide over the surface of the water, speedboats will take you for a short, fast run, and large, comfortable excursion streamers tour the lake.

Annecy is a wonderful place to visit. It has hotels of all grades, but we prefer to stay in the nearby country. If you go around the lake by boat or car you will see why.

Lake Annecy is 9 miles long and is at the bottom of a deep basin that was scoured out by a glacier. Around it a ring of stark, white rocky peaks add to its scenic beauty. It is fed by several small streams and springs far below the surface that pour vast quantities of clear, clean water into the upper end of the lake. Near the middle is a shallow part where prehistoric lake dwellers once lived.

We think that the eastern shore is the better one on which to stay because it has less heavy traffic and more of its hotels are located directly on the waterfront. We especially favor

Talloires, a tiny village with hotels and restaurants of all sorts from very inexpensive ones to noted luxury resorts. You can also rent furnished rooms there.

Talloires' roots go far back in time. In the eleventh century, the ascetic St. Germain (the third of that name to be sanctified) spent the last forty years of his life in a shallow cave high on a hill above the town. It can still be seen in the cliffs below the chapel bearing his name. To reach it you go down a path lined with stations of the cross.

Life in Talloires was closely connected with the Church for many centuries. The important Abbaye Royale was large and flourishing, and its Benedictine monks were the mentors and administrators of the community. The French Revolution ended their rule on June 30, 1793, when the last seven monks left the Abbey, and citizens from Annecy took over. They burned the ecclesiastical relics, books, and manuscripts, destroyed the church, and threw down its huge bronze bells. When they proved to be too massive to be broken up, they were sunk in deep water. They ring again, the villagers say, on stormy nights when the wind blows across the lake.

Present-day Talloires is built around activities for summer tourists. The old village is a few hundred feet above the water, but the resort centers around a little bay that is sheltered on the north by a high promontory. The ancient Abbey has been made into a luxury hotel with its own bathing area. A public beach with boats and *pédalos* to rent separates it from one of the few restaurants to which Michelin grants its top rating of three stars. (Paris has five; the Riviera has none while the others are scattered along the main routes N6 and N7 that run from Paris to Provence.)

Despite the air of opulence and luxury that dominates Talloires, you can stay in this exceedingly pleasant resort and have practically all its advantages for relatively little money. The Monk's Walk, an ancient walled right of way, connects the bay with some of the hotels along the lakefront. There are many good places to go walking in the area, although most of them are rather hilly. Especially steep is the rock-paved path that leads up to the Cascade d'Angon.

A much easier walk from Talloires—and on level ground—is the one to the village of Angon. Here you can see some fine examples of very early Alpine domestic architecture. In these

The boat landing at Talloires

combination farmhouses and barns, which are built solidly of stone, a hayloft covers the entire structure and insulates everything under it. Below the hayloft are the family's living quarters. Underneath them is the stable where the cattle radiate heat to the rooms above. The living quarters should be warm enough even on bitter cold nights because enormous stacks of wood are piled up around the walls to feed the stoves within.

One of the many advantages of staying in Talloires is the fact that you can tour the lake on one of the excursion steamers. You can visit Annecy or go to the top of Mont Veyrier (4100 feet high) by *téléphérique* and perhaps see Mont Blanc, if the weather is clear. In fact, Talloires is one of the few places where you don't need a car because you can do very well by boat. You can thank the Empress Eugénie for this. She was so enchanted with Lake Annecy when she visited it in 1860 (to celebrate the return of Savoy to France after its annexation to Italy in 1815) that she donated the money needed to buy the first lake steamer.

Fishing in France

When you are staying at a lakeside or mountain resort you will see fair-sized fresh-water fish brought to the table. This gives visitors the idea that they can catch some themselves, and the French stubbornly keep trying to do so. They have good equipment, and they work hard at what they evidently consider a sport. But they are easily satisfied and will keep anything they catch, no matter how small, to be cooked and eaten as *friture du lac.*

The good-sized fish served in hotels and restaurants have almost surely been caught by professionals who use nets of nylon trot-lines baited with hundreds of hooks. The chance for an amateur to get anything of consequence is very slight, so slight that we think that lake fishing in France is a waste of time.

Trout fishing in the more remote mountain areas is somewhat better. Fingerlings are raised in government hatcheries and when large enough are released to restock the streams. But fishing is so intense that your chance of making a good catch is less than fair.

As to salt-water fishing, the heavily populated Mediterranean has been over-fished for years, and wartime bombing there took a further toll. So do skin-divers now. Professional fishermen still bring in some rather small fish, but amateurs are not likely to do well, even though fairly big tuna are caught there.

Only in the Atlantic Ocean are there likely to be fish worth catching. But the facilities for going out after them are almost nonexistent. Party boats are unknown, and charter boats are so scarce that we have never seen one. You probably have to make private arrangements with someone who owns a boat and is willing to rent it.

We like fishing and have done a great deal of it in America. But we have never bothered to drop a line in French waters; it just didn't seem worthwhile.

French fishing equipment, however, is excellent. You will see many novelties that are unknown in America, so you may want to buy some to take home.

Excursions from Talloires

There are all kinds of automobile trips you can take from Talloires. Driving around the lake is always interesting; so is exploring the small roads that lead up into the hills. Some of them were built for lumber trucks and go nowhere except to a clearing where wood is being cut. It is better to avoid them, for you may meet one of the big *camions* coming down the narrow road, and this means that you will have to back up to let it pass.

If you leave early in the morning you can make day trips to Megève and Chamonix, Geneva, Aix-les-Bains, and even go to Lyon or Grenoble if you don't mind getting back late.

One nearby trip is to a mountain-top battlefield of the Second World War. At Menthon take N509 east. You will soon pass the impressive-looking Château de Saint-Bernard, which can be visited only on Sundays. Beyond this you will see looming up in front of you a mountain crowned with steep white cliffs. On the top of this is the high plateau of Glières which was an active center of resistance against the Nazis and the scene of a battle that deserves to be better known.

Resistance forces began to be organized there at the end of January 1944. The local people fed them, and the British supplied them with arms dropped in by parachute. They fought off several minor attacks by Vichy police and militia, and their members increased until there were about 500 men on the snow-covered heights.

The Nazis soon became suspicious and began to send scouting planes over the area. These were followed by bombers on March 23. Then 8000 troops, cannon, and airplanes moved in against the 500 men who were holding the heights. The odds were overwhelming. By March 26 the one-sided battle was over. A few of the Resistance fighters managed to escape, but many were killed in combat or were ruthlessly executed after being captured. Some were taken to Annecy and were sent from there to German concentration camps where many of them died.

Today more than a hundred of the Resistance fighters are

buried in the little military cemetery of Morette-Glières. There a waterfall tumbling down the mountain serves as an eternal memorial.

Near the cemetery is a *chalet* built in 1794, which houses a collection of objects found on the battlefield. It also has posters of the time, German orders, correspondence, and many photographs. In the basement is a crypt where the original wooden crosses taken from the first hurried graves are kept.

From here you can go on to Chamonix by turning left on D12 to Bonneville where you turn right on N506 to Cluses. This is the gateway to the truly thrilling area around Mont Blanc. At Cluses go south on N202 towards Sallanches. If you approach Sallanches on a clear day you will see Mont Blanc rising above the town. The snow on its dazzling white peaks defies the sun, for it is always winter up there.

You can also get from Talloires to Chamonix by taking N509A to the southern end of the lake. There you continue on N508 to Ugine and then on to N212 to Megève, where you go through Saint-Gervais to reach N506 which is the big highway that leads to Chamonix. This way is shorter, but we think that the first route is easier and more interesting.

Mont Blanc

We have spent a good deal of time exploring the country around Chamonix to find a place to stay where you can see Mont Blanc clearly. The closer you get to that huge mountain the more difficult it becomes to catch a glimpse of the summit because foothills and lower mountains shut off the view. In really good weather Mont Blanc is visible from places as far away as Geneva and the Citadel above Grenoble, but in Chamonix, which is in a deep valley, the topmost peak cannot be seen. If you want to stay in a hotel with a view of Mont Blanc, you have to be farther away from it. When writing for reservations, ask for a room that faces the mountain.

Here are the results of our survey of places with good views:

SALLANCHES itself is unattractive, but the heights above the town, especially at Cordon, have superb views of the entire Mont Blanc chain. See our list of hotels for recommendations.

PLATEAU D'ASSY. The roads going up to this level bit of ground (especially D43) have fine views. The very modern church Notre-Dame-de-Toute-Grâce d'Assy, which was decorated by Léger, Lurçat, Matisse, Chagall, Braque, Bonnard, Lipchitz, and other contemporary artists, is up here. It should be visited on a bright sunny day when the interior is well lighted. There are many sanatoriums but relatively few hotels on the heights above the church.

COMBLOUX. This is our first choice for a place to stay because it has several hotels with a panoramic view of the Mont Blanc chain. And all around it are pleasant Alpine farms where the cowbells never cease tinkling. The hotels with the best views are booked up so early that it took us three summers to get into the one that has become our favorite.

OTHER PLACES. The terrain in this section is so complicated that it is hard to tell beforehand just where the good views are. Sometimes you come upon one unexpectedly. A hotel situated far back from a main road may have an excellent location. Some of the *téléphériques* go up to hotels with fine views, but you can't reach them by car.

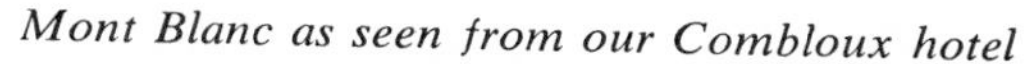

Mont Blanc as seen from our Combloux hotel

Chamonix and the country around it

Chamonix (the name, according to the people who live there, may be pronounced either with or without sounding the terminal "x") is the capital of the high French Alps, a world-famous winter sports center, and a resort that is popular all year. It is a very lively town, and one of the few in France with large areas of municipal parking space. Chamonix owes its existence to tourists and makes every effort to please them. Its Information Office is a model of its kind. There are many hotels in the town and in the little settlements around it.

Even though you can't see the summit of Mont Blanc from the bottom of the deep valley in which Chamonix is located, there are many other interesting sights there. Glaciers come down the steep slopes, a mountain stream fed by melting ice rushes through the town, and every now and then you catch sight of high, sharp-pointed rock pinnacles standing aloof from all the works of man.

One thing you will have to get used to—and, if you have never been in high mountains before, it may seem incredible—is that everything you see up there is much bigger and much farther away than it seems. The glaciers are wider, the peaks higher, and the snowfields vaster than they appear to be.

The Mer de Glace

Two easy excursions can be made to the glaciers by train. The one to Montenvers, which overlooks the Mer de Glace, is the more interesting. Montenvers has a restaurant with a dining terrace, and you can even stay overnight in the hotel. The ride up is thrilling, and you can stroll about Montenvers in perfect safety and comfort to examine the enormous body of ice that is several hundred feet below you. The glacier's progress is far too slow to be noted while you watch, but at various times stakes have been driven into the ice in a straight line across the glacier; after a few months the line becomes bow-shaped with the arc pointing downward. Further proof of the glacier's motion was noted dramatically in the nineteenth century. In 1820, three men walking on the Mer de Glace were crushed under an avalanche that swept their bodies into a deep crevasse. By figuring the rate of the ice flow at 225 feet per year, it was estimated that their remains should arrive at the tip of the glacier in about 40 years. In 1861, parts of the bodies, which had been torn apart by glacial action, began to appear there as predicted.

Montenvers is a geologist's paradise, for this easily reached place is a fine observation post for inspecting a classic glacier. Here you can see this huge river of ice flow down the valley from the snowfields higher up on the mountain where thousands of years of snowfalls have been packed down under each new deposit until pressure hardened the soft flakes into ice. And then this compacted ice, pulled by the force of gravity, descends with majestically slow but enormous power to carry boulders, stones, and gritty sand along with it. This never-ceasing grinding action keeps wearing away the solid rock walls, rounds them, and in places even polishes them. The net result is to widen and deepen the valley. And the stones brought down by the glacier are deposited at its tip to form a terminal morraine.

You can go down from Montenvers to the Mer de Glace on foot or by *téléphérique*. Or you can walk down and ride back. Once you reach the surface, you will notice that it is very uneven and that it is covered with small fragments of stone and grit. These are bits of rock that have fallen down from the surrounding peaks and walls. They provide good footing on the slippery ice, but only young, active people should venture out on the glacier—*and never alone*. It has many deep crevasses, some of which are hidden.

The Bionnassay Glacier

The tramway ride from Saint-Gervais to the Nid d'Aigle, which overlooks the Glacier de Bionnassay, is more interesting for the trip than it is for the view of Bionnassay, which is far less impressive than the Mer de Glace. But all along the way are many striking panoramas of superb mountain scenery. The terminal area, however, is small and constricted in comparison with Montenvers.

At Montenvers you will see many people equipped with rudimentary climbing outfits. They have no intention of going up on the high peaks but are merely out for a walk along the paths that lead in many directions on the lower slopes. To climb Mont Blanc or any of the surrounding mountains requires a guide and thus becomes a rather formal affair that should be undertaken only by those qualified by physique and experience for the ascent. The Information Office in Chamonix will tell you how to go about this.

You can, however, see a good deal of the higher Alps in ordinary clothes and without effort because a number of *téléphériques* will take you up many thousands of feet. The most remarkable of them is the one that goes up by two stages to the Aiguille du Midi to an altitude of more than 3800 meters (12,563 feet). And from there you can swing out over the Vallée Blanche and go across the Alps to the Italian side of Mont Blanc. This is a fairly expensive trip, but it is worth it. People with bad—or even faint hearts—are advised not to try it. The journey takes hours, and you can't get down in a hurry. If you go, dress warmly.

Summertime skiing

Sportsmen, of course, know that Mont Blanc is one of the great ski capitals of the world. But they may not know that they can practice their favorite sport there even in summer. Again the Chamonix Information Office can tell you where to rent equipment and hire a guide for this. The high slopes, which are used then, are suitable only for those who have had a great deal of experience.

Summer skiing is possible not only on the slopes above Chamonix but also in the Val d'Isère and L'Alpe-d'Huez. But in summer neither of these places has snow-covered runs as long as those at Chamonix.

Less ambitious skiers will probably want to visit Megéve in summer in order to find out what it has to offer during the winter. They can see the ski lifts and perhaps go up the *téléphériques* to Mont Arbois, the Croix de Rochebrune, or Jaillet. They were built to carry skiers and may be disappointing to summer tourists. Megéve itself has no views of the high mountains, and even the *téléphériques* do not necessarily take you to a place where you can see them. You may have to do quite a bit of walking after leaving the *télécabine* if you want a good view of the snow-clad peaks that rise beyond and above these lower mountains.

Megéve is not very interesting in summer, but it is a sort of winter version of Saint-Tropez. It is expensive all the year around and has one of the most luxurious—and high-priced—hotels in this part of France. Good skiers who go to Chamonix for strenuous sport on the very steep slopes there look down on Megéve as a place that appeals more to people who are interested in the fashionable life than in serious skiing.

Walking around Mont Blanc

There is more to Mont Blanc than peaks and glaciers. You can spend days exploring the country around it. One of the most interesting trips is from Saint-Gervais down the long valley in which the village of Contamines-Montjoie is located. This, incidentally, is a very charming, quiet, and relatively inexpensive area in which to stay although it has no views of the high mountains.

The lower part of the valley is heavily wooded, and rushing streams run through its floor. At the far end is Notre-Dame-de-la-Gorge, a small church with colorful baroque decorations. Near it is a waterfall and beyond that an ancient rock-paved road that goes uphill. When Francis Trench walked around the massive base of Mont Blanc in 1847, he came this way and wrote:

> I had now to pursue a very singular road—if road it might be called—and yet it deserved the appellation, for it was much broader and more brought into form than a common mule-track, and evidently had had much labour employed upon it at some time or other. It was, however, a mere succession of slabs of rock, some being the general and natural foundation, and others (in some instances of very large size) added, as occasion required, in order to form the causeway as a passable track.

This mysterious roadway is still there, untouched and unchanged after more than a century. Who built it and why? It would be interesting to know.

Since there is no outlet for cars at the southern end of the valley, you have to turn around and go back the way you came.

People still walk around Mont Blanc. It takes about eight days to make the journey through three countries—France, Italy, and Switzerland. The trail is marked, and there are refuge cabins in which you can sleep. Since much of the route is on high, snow-covered slopes, no one should start out who is not in physical condition to keep going for at least 52 hours of walking at the rate of four to ten hours a day over some of the world's harshest terrain. Those who have made the trip say that the experience—and the magnificent views—are worth the effort. One drawback, of course, is that it is impossible to predict mountain weather for eight days ahead, so pedestrians who start out in bright sunshine may encounter fog or storms along the way.

The Mont Blanc tunnel

The area around Chamonix, which has been popular with tourists for many years, recently became even more popular. After six years of cutting through solid rock, the Mont Blanc Tunnel, which goes from France to Italy, was opened on June 16, 1965, at a cost of one hundred million francs. Work took longer than was expected because of unusual difficulties encountered under the mountain. The enormous pressure exerted by millions of tons of rock made it dangerous to extract stone that was suddenly released from the crushing weight that had been resting on it ever since the mountains were formed. Worst of all was an underground stream fed by water from the glaciers overhead. This rushed by with incredible force that made it hard to divert the mad course of the torrent away from the straight line the rock-drillers had to follow.

But the highly successful tunnel now shortens the road from Paris to Rome by 150 kilometers (93 miles). It begins at the village of Les Pèlerins near Chamonix and runs for 11.6 kilometers (7.3 miles) to Entrèves near Courmayeur in Italy. Even at the carefully controlled speed of 70 kilometers (43.5 miles) an hour it takes only a few minutes to go from one end of the tunnel to the other. Rates run from $3.20 for a small car to $8 for a big one. This may seem high, but the saving in time—as well as in the gas needed to go over a mountain pass—is considerable. And it makes it possible to cross the Alps in winter. The customs offices for both countries are located on the Italian side.

Lake Geneva resorts

When you leave the Chamonix area the easiest way to go is to double back the way you came—through Sallanches and Cluses to Bonneville where you can turn northwest on N203 and then N505 to Annemasse and Geneva. If you want to visit the charming French resorts on the south side of Lake Geneva, stay on N203 and at Machilly take N203B to Messery and the shore. From there you can go along the coast to Nernier and Yvoire which are excellent places to stay, with good swimming and boating. The hotels in these towns are relatively inexpensive, but this section is so beautiful that it deserves to have better accommodations.

Yvoire is a medieval walled village complete with castle, tower gates, narrow streets, and ancient houses, many of which have been taken over by artists and city people who have renovated them and decorated them with flowers. There is a boat landing here from which you can go on one of the lake steamers to Geneva or to the Swiss and French towns along the shore. Study the printed schedules carefully, though, or you may not be able to get back the same day.

As you drive east along the lake you will pass many good

Yvoire

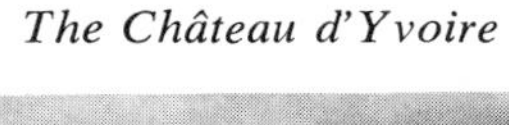

The Château d'Yvoire

beaches and camping sites. Thonon-les-Bains is an upper middle-class spa with all kinds of activities. It has a fine view over the water, an interesting museum, and several beautiful parks, one of which has a trout hatchery.

Évian-les-Bains is a fashionable resort with a number of fine and expensive hotels in town and in the country around it. The lakefront is especially pretty with many trees and brightly colored flowers in the gardens. It is from here that the universally distributed Évian bottled water comes.

Le Chablais

From Évian, the lakefront road goes to the Swiss border, and then on to Montreux and Lausanne. The whole area running south from the French shore deep into the mountains for 25 or 30 kilometers is called Le Chablais. It abounds with interesting places to visit, and has many byroads that lead through gorges to mountain passes and high meadows. N202 goes south from Thonon through the Gorges de la Dranse, the Gorges du Pont du Diable, and on to Morzine where a winding mountain road with many *lacets* circles around the little Lac de Montriond and then goes downhill to rejoin N202.

An easier and much shorter excursion is the one to the Château des Allinges which is just south of Thonon on N203 and then left on D12. Here, only a few hundred feet apart, are the ruins of two early castles that face each other across a tiny valley. Their people spent years in bitter combat and were so near to each other that the huge stone balls used as missiles for their primitive cannon were fired back and forth until they broke up. Some of them still exist, however, and serve as tops for the gateposts. This senseless fighting went on until 1355 when the Château Neuf overcame the Château Vieux and destroyed it so that only part of its shattered walls remain.

When you leave the Alps you may want to go into Switzerland to visit Geneva, which is a good city for shopping and for stocking up on high-quality canned goods for picnics. It is also an excellent stopping place for receiving or sending airmail, because international jet-planes land there.

The city is noted for its beautiful lakeside parks, its museums (one of which is devoted to Voltaire), and its institutions, such as the Red Cross and the International Labor Office.

Food and wine

Michelin awards from one to three stars to a dozen and a half restaurants in this area, so the food must be good. But the native ingredients are limited. They consist chiefly of cow's milk from which cheese is made, fresh-water fish, nuts, fruits, mushrooms, chickens, and eggs. The mountain meadows on which cattle feed provide some beef. Cheese is the Alps' great specialty. Reblochon and Tome rightfully come from the French Alps, but Emmenthal is produced across the border in Switzerland. Gruyère is made in both countries. One fine Alpine cheese dish is *Gratin Dauphinois,* which consists of potatoes, milk, cheese, flour, breadcrumbs, and butter. Yes, regrettably, it is fattening.

Trout from mountain streams and *omble chevalier* from the lakes are among the best fish of the world, and they are cooked in a dozen different ways. Crayfish are found here; so are snails. Pike is the basis for *quenelles de brochet.*

Potatoes and omelettes are especially good in the Alps where they are almost invariably prepared with cheese.

There are no great wines in this region, but there are many very pleasant ones, mostly white. Seyssel, Crépy, Frangy, Chignin, and Apremont are some of the best.

21. *Burgundy*

Burgundy is, of course, most famous for its wines, but it also has superb food and some of the most beautiful Romanesque churches in France. The province is so big that you will need at least four bases from which to explore it. We suggest that you use the following centers of operation: Cluny (or Solutré) for the south; Beaune for the Côte d'Or; Avallon or Vézelay for the west; and Châtillon-sur-Seine for the north. They all have excellent hotels and eating places. And each one is a charming town with attractions of its own.

If you are coming from Geneva, you will pass through Nantua on N84 and Bourg-en-Bresse on N79. They are not in Burgundy but serve as a gateway to it. We remember Nantua for its pretty lakefront park which is a fine place for a picnic lunch. You can feed your leftover bread to the swans. Travelers who prefer to eat in restaurants will find several good ones in the town. Incidentally, the signs on N79 warning drivers about the long hill ahead are unnecessarily frightening. It is not bad at all.

Bourg (pronounced Bourck) is widely known for its food, and the plump chickens raised in Bresse are highly regarded everywhere. Here, too, are several first-rate restaurants. You will eat well in Burgundy and can start sampling its delicacies even before you enter the region.

The road from Nantua, N79, leads to the center of Bourg. But instead of going straight ahead we suggest that you turn left shortly before you reach the city and then go right on N75. This will bring you to the little town of Brou with its remarkable late flamboyant Gothic church which has an art museum installed in its cloister. N75 will take you into Bourg which is more celebrated for its food than for its sights although it does have some attractive old houses.

Pérouges

You can go from Bourg directly to the Beaujolais vineyards by driving west on N436 and D17 to Belleville. But a more roundabout way, south on N83 and D22 through Chalamont, will give you a chance to see Pérouges, a remarkable, very ancient town which tourists have now "discovered." South of Chalamont, go left on D22A which will take you to Meximieux. Pérouges is practically next door.

The little town stands on a hill which is supposed to have been settled more than 2000 years ago by Italians from Perugia, which explains how Pérouges got its name. It had lost so much population early in the twentieth century that it was about to be abandoned, but antiquarians and artists from nearby Lyon came to its rescue and helped to save it from destruction. Now it is a flourishing little village with artisans' shops, well-restored houses, a fortified church, and a very attractive restaurant that Michelin rates with one star.

The Beaujolais vineyards

To get from Pérouges to the Beaujolais vineyards go northwest on little back roads through Joyeux, Villars-les-Dombes, Saint-Trivier, and Chaneins to Belleville.

Some of the very best Beaujolais wines are produced in the country beyond Belleville. A wide swing west to Brouilly and then north on D68 and the other minor roads that wind through the vineyards will take you through the heart of the region from which Morgon, Chiroubles, Fleurie, Moulin-à-Vent, Chénas, Juliénas, and Saint-Amour come.

As you drive around the seemingly endless vineyards, you will see that Moulin-à-Vent really does have an old windmill standing up above the well-tended vines. And in every village you will note that the production of wine dominates the life of the people.

Just north of the red-wine district of Beaujolais, where the

Gamay grape is grown, is the Mâconnais region where Chardonjay grapes produce white Pouilly-Fuissé. This carefully developed grape is responsible for some of the finest white wines of France.

Solutré

In the midst of the Pouilly-Fuissé vineyards a huge rocky spur rises above the rolling land. This is Solutré, a name which those familiar with mankind's early history will recognize. It is only 9.5 kilometers (6 miles) west of Macon on Routes N79 and D54.

Solutré was a natural hunting ground that was used for 10,000 years or more by prehistoric tribes who banded together to drive a now-extinct breed of wild horses up the narrow spur from which there was no escape. The frenzied animals were forced to jump off the rocky cliff to fall to their deaths. (Lascaux has a painting of a horse plunging down like this.) Their shattered bodies were quickly cut up for meat by big flint knives made by the Solutréans.

So many horses were driven over this cliff for so many years that the ground below it was littered with the broken bones of more than 100,000 animals. (Simple arithmetic shows that only 10 horses a year over the course of 10,000 years were needed to make 100,000 victims.) The bones are still there, tons of them, covered by a thin layer of soil. They are almost never intact because our hungry ancestors broke them open to extract the marrow.

This vast boneyard has been excavated—but only in part. From it came examples of the finely made laurel-leaf flint cutting instruments that are called Solutréan. Some of them, along with other interesting finds, can be seen in the tiny local museum.

Perhaps one of the reasons for the high quality of the Pouilly-Fuissé wines is the fact that rain which falls on high ground filters down through soil fertilized by the bones of all those slaughtered wild horses.

Northwest of Solutré are the places that were dear to the Romantic poet Lamartine. He spent his childhood in Milly and lived in châteaux in La Roche-Vineuse and Saint-Point.

Cluny

Only a few miles from Solutré, going northwest on N79 and N80, is the truly fascinating old town of Cluny. Still farther west on N79 is Charolles, the center of the area where the handsome white cattle of Burgundy are raised. Charollais steaks are highly thought of throughout France. Just beyond Charolles is Paray-le-Monal with a renown twelfth-century church and a Renaissance Hôtel de Ville that was built as a private residence.

The enormous Benedictine Abbey of Cluny, which once made this remote part of Burgundy a religious center of far-reaching importance, is only a fragment of its former self, but enough of it exists to indicate how vast it was. In the eleventh century it was the head of 1500 dependencies scattered throughout Europe, and the Abbey was so extensive that in 1245 the King of France, the Pope, the Emperor of Constantinople, and dozens of lesser rulers and prelates were able to use it for a conference. The Wars of Religion took their toll and then, during the Revolution, the Abbey was sold to some merchants in Macon to be torn down for its stones. Demolition went on until 1823, when only a part of the huge Abbey church, which had once been the largest in Christendom, was left standing.

When you visit Cluny today you pass through a modern engineering school that occupies some of the restored buildings. When you reach what remains of the Abbey church you will get an idea of how big it was before the wreckers removed whole sections of it. You then go through the gardens to the thirteenth-century *farinier* that has been converted into an architectural museum. This, too, is very large and has a high wooden roof that must have been constructed by ship carpenters.

The Musée Ochier, which is near the entrance to the Abbey, has some Romanesque sculpture that was preserved when the church was wrecked. And also nearby is one of the most interesting *haras* (horse stud farms) in France.

Tournus

If you take D15 to the east when you leave Cluny you can visit a grotto at Azé which has many traces of the giant cave bears that once inhabited it. D15 ends at N6 which goes north to Tournus where there is another unusually beautiful Romanesque church, Saint-Philibert. It is particularly impressive because it is in fine condition. Large, round, very tall pillars of pink stone support the roof and permit the interior to get more light than most buildings of this period do. Attached to Saint-Philibert are a cloister, a refectory, and a building formerly used as a lodging place for pilgrims. All these, of course, belonged to the Abbey as did the church.

Tournus has another early church, La Madeleine, which is located in the southern part of the town near the river. It is small and is often overlooked, but it is worth visiting.

Since Jean-Baptiste Greuze, the eighteenth-century painter, was born in Tournus, the town has a museum containing some of his work. The same building also has well-arranged exhibits of local history.

Going farther north on N6 you come to Chalons where Nicéphore Niepce, one of the inventors of photography, died in 1833. The Musée Denon has some of his apparatus. If you are not interested in going into town you can drive around Chalons, for it has one of the few by-pass roads in France.

The Côte d'Or and Beaune

At Chagny, Route N6 turns toward the northwest to go to Saulieu and Paris while N74 leads northeast to Beaune and Dijon. Here the gentle slopes of the Côte d'Or begin to rise along the west side of the road. To drive along this section of N74 is like reading the labels in one of the world's best-stocked wine cellars. One great name after another is encountered: Montrachet, Meursault, Volnay, Pommard, Beaune, Aloxe-Corton, Nuits Saint-Georges, Vosne-Romanée, Vougeot, Chambertin, and Fixin are only some of the better-known vineyards near the main road. Many of them are combined with other names of which Chassagne-Montrachet, Puligny-Montrachet, Romanée-Conti, and seven or eight combinations with Chambertin are a few examples.

As we have explained in the chapter on wines, the slopes on the west side of N74 have the kind of soil, drainage, and exposure to the sun needed to produce the grapes from which some of the world's best wines are made. As you drive by, you

Vineyards in Burgundy

will note that a few pieces of land on the slopes have not been planted with vines. They have not been overlooked; centuries of experience have taught the growers that the soil there is not good enough to produce first-rate wine. You will also note that most of the hilltops are covered with trees. They were planted there because their roots retain enough moisture to provide water in dry weather for the vines lower down on the slopes. And the fact that there are many stones on the soil is not accidental. They absorb the heat of the sun during the day and keep the vines warm during the night. Nothing has been overlooked; nothing has been left to chance, except the weather. Science, art, skill, and long experience all go into the making of wine in the great Burgundy vineyards.

A visit to Beaune shows how important the production of wine is to the economy of this region. You will see stores that sell the specialized hardware and pesticides needed in the vineyards. They also have casks, corks, and bottles in stock.

In the summer the grapes slowly ripen, and everyone even remotely connected with the wine trade prays for enough sunshine to bring them to early maturity. This is the big topic of conversation. "So far, so good," the growers say cautiously during the first weeks of August. "One never knows, of course."

And they never do know, because storms—and hail—can ruin the grapes before they are ready to be picked. Like all people whose livelihood depends on good weather, the growers go from year to year, always uncertain of what the next season will bring. Most of them seem to do very well though.

The Hôtel-Dieu

Even the local charities profit from wine, for the Hospices de Beaune are supported by revenues obtained from the famous vineyards it owns. The Hôtel-Dieu, which was founded in 1443 and opened in 1451, still functions as a hospital. (There is an even more ancient one in Tonnerre, but it is no longer

Beaune: wellhead in the courtyard of the Hôtel de Dieu

active.) Beaune's Hôtel-Dieu is a fine example of Flemish architecture in France, for it was designed and built by men imported from the Low Countries. It does not seem remarkable when viewed from the street, but when you go inside to see the huge courtyard with its hanging balconies, checkered tile roofs, and big wellhead, you find yourself looking into a world where everything is just the same as it was more than five hundred years ago. But the medicine practiced here is very modern, for this is a wealthy institution that can afford to have the best doctors and equipment.

The hospital, and even the patients' ward, is open to visitors. Some of its most interesting features are its ancient pharmacy, its big kitchen (shown only in the afternoon), and its museum, which has one of the outstanding works of art in art-rich France—the Last Judgment, which Roger van der Weiden painted in 1443.

The Hôtel-Dieu draws a crowd of tourists every day, but on the first Sunday after November 11, when the wines of the Hospices are auctioned, the town is so crowded that you may do better to stay elsewhere and drive in for the day, because all the available rooms will have been booked for months in advance. Some of the visiting wholesale buyers reserve them from year to year for this important occasion.

Beaune is also overcrowded in the spring when a fair is held there during the week between the first and second Sundays in June.

Some of the town's chief attractions are grouped around the church of Notre-Dame which is notable for its high porch. At the end of the *impasse* to the right is a collection of ancient tapestries. Here, too, is the Musée du Vin where you can trace the history of the grape from earliest times.

Beaune was a walled city, and many of its ramparts and bastions are now used as wine cellars. Inside their enormously thick walls, where the temperature hardly ever varies, casks are stored until their contents are ready for bottling. The stone walls are covered with a half-inch layer of green fungus that flourishes only in the presence of wine.

Around the town are many *caves* where visitors are invited to enter and taste the wine. *Dégustation* is the magic word. Wherever you see it, it means, "Come in and taste our wine." The owner naturally hopes you will order some. French people can, but visitors from other countries may have trouble if they try to ship it home. Alcohol often has a harder time crossing borders than people do.

The Côte d'Or

If you make Beaune your headquarters you can take several interesting trips from there. To explore the many little villages with world-famous names in the Côte d'Or drive along N74 toward Dijon but turn off to the west on the minor roads that lead through the vineyards. Stop at Nuits-Saint-Georges and walk around the western part of that celebrated wine-making town. Just beyond it a well-marked road leads to the Clos de Vougeot, which is open to visitors. This Renaissance château is surrounded by vineyards that stretch away on every side. It

Beaune

The Clos Vougeot and its vineyards

has been kept just as it was when the monks worked there. Enormous wooden presses, fermentation vats, and other crude apparatus show how wine was produced then. The Confrérie des Chevaliers du Tastevin now owns the Château and meets there in the autumn to dine and taste the wines of the region. They do not own the 124 acres of vineyards which are entitled to use the name Clos de Vougeot. This precious bit of land has 65 proprietors.

Just beyond this point another little road (D122H) leads west to Vougeot where D122 parallels N74 and goes through one famous vineyard after another until you reach the outskirts of Dijon.

Before you enter the city, stop in Chenove, which is the northernmost town on the Côte d'Or. There you can see what must be the oldest continually used mechanical device in the world. They are two gigantic wine presses that were built in 1238 and are still in operation.

Dijon

Dijon has much history, several fine museums, streets lined with old houses, and three noteworthy churches, the Cathédrale Saint-Bénigne, Saint-Michel, and Notre-Dame. But in re-

Autun: Gislebert's Last Judgment,Cathedral of Saint-Lazare

cent years it has become an industrial center with heavy traffic and few places for parking. Again the best way to see it is to leave your car and stroll around on foot.

This is not difficult, for the most important buildings are located between the Cathédrale Saint-Bénigne on the west and the Église Saint-Michel on the east. In between is the archeological museum next to the cathedral while others are grouped around the Place de la Libération where the Palais des Ducs de Bourgogne and the Musée des Beaux-Arts are located. Behind them is Notre-Dame, which has a façade with ranks of slender columns supporting small arches—an arrangement seldom seen in France. The front of Saint-Michel is also very unusual.

The Musée des Beaux-Arts is noted for its primitives painted in France, the Low Countries, Germany, and Italy. And it has some good medieval and Renaissance statuary.

Autun

Also within an easy drive from Beaune is Autun, which is 48 kilometers (30 miles) to the west on Route N73. Here are several Roman structures of which a theater, two large stone gates, and a Temple of Janus (outside the city) are the most notable. The Musée Lapidaire has many Roman statues and carved funeral steles.

Autun's twelfth-century Cathedrale Saint-Lazare brings visitors to this part of Burgundy. Its most interesting feature is a richly decorated porch which has marble columns taken from one of the gates of the old Roman city. Far more important, however, is the tympanum over the doorway. It is not only a masterpiece of Romanesque art but is signed—something that was almost unknown at a time when a sculptor was looked upon as nothing but a good stonemason. This tympanum of the Last Judgment, which was carved during the years 1130 to 1135, carries the name of the man who created it. You can see his name on a panel below the feet of Christ. There, chiseled in block letters, are the words: Gislebertus Hoc Fecit (Gislebert made this).

Although Saint-Lazare was begun in the Romanesque period, it has many later additions that make its exterior look more Gothic than Romanesque. Its spire is even more recent, for it was added in the fifteenth century to replace an earlier one struck by lightning.

Alongside the church is a handsome sixteenth-century fountain with streams of water falling quietly from a bowl set inside its classic columns.

The Musée Rolin has some truly fine Romanesque sculpture One piece expresses a tenderness seldom seen in those harsh times. It portrays a winged angel carefully spreading a coverlet over the sleeping forms of the three Magi who were on their way to pay homage to the new born Christ. In this museum is a painting that goes well with the sleeping Magi even though it is of a somewhat later date. It is the very handsome Nativity painted by an artist known as the Maître de Moulins.

A circle tour of northern Burgundy

Burgundy is so large that a good part of it can be covered only by driving from place to place in a long swing around the province. Avallon is a good base of operations for the southern part of this northern section. If you are starting out from Beaune or Autun, N6 takes you through Saulieu where there are several excellent restaurants. The Romanesque Basilique Saint-Andoche and a little museum of local history and art are the town's chief attractions.

From Saulieu, Route N80 goes north for 29 kilometers (18 miles) to Semur-en-Auxois, a town of 4200 inhabitants that stands on rocky heights in a curve of the River Armançon. With the four massive round towers of its castle and the spire of its Gothic church of Notre-Dame outlined against the sky, this ancient Burgundy community looks like a museum piece. Its remarkable portal has a strange tangle of sculpture looking down from it. Inside are carvings and stained-glass windows that depict medieval tradesmen at work. This extraordinary little town has a museum and a library with illuminated manuscripts and incunabula. A pleasant promenade overlooks a curve in the river.

Only a few miles east on Route N454 and D103 is the even smaller town of Alise-Sainte-Reine where a big statue of the Gallic chieftain Vercingetorix stands on the summit of Mont Auxois. Here Caesar and his legions reduced Gaul to a Roman province. These now quiet fields and slopes were the scene of a decisive battle in 52 B.C., for it was here that Vercingetorix surrendered and was taken to Rome where he was executed six years later.

Caesar's *Commentaries,* Book VII, gives a graphic account of the battle. With a copy of it in hand you can locate the places mentioned. One of them, where Caesar stood dressed in a scarlet cloak, is now Flavigny-sur-Ozerain, southeast of Mont Axois. Another, where the Romans had a camp, is Mussy-la-Fosse, which is farther away to the southwest.

Napoleon III wanted to make Vercingetorix better known as a French hero and was responsible for erecting the statue on the hill. He also had the area excavated in the early 1860's when many relics of the battle were found. They can be seen in the two museums.

After the victory the Romans built a good-sized town on the site. Some of it still exists.

Fontenay and Montréal

Northwest of Alise-Sainte-Reine on N5 and D32 is the former Cistercian Abbey of Fontenay. Built in the twelfth century as a self-sustaining religious community, it did well for four hundred years but then began to decline and was sold off during the French Revolution. It was made into a paper factory and was used as such until 1906 when it was carefully restored. Today it stands isolated in the midst of great forests, but it can be visited.

You can cut through back roads from Montbard to reach N457 which goes southwest to Avallon and Vézelay. This road passes through the small fortified town of Montréal which has a twelfth-century church noted for its pictorial wood carvings that portray scenes with Biblical characters modeled after the people who lived there centuries ago. The one that shows the infant Jesus playing on the floor of his father's carpenter's shop is especially moving.

Avallon

Avallon has much charm and is a good center for visiting this part of Burgundy. Its Hôtellerie de la Poste is one of Michelin's three-star restaurants and is an excellent place to stay if you can afford it. The British writer George Slocombe described it vividly:

> Swinging signboard from a gibbet of wrought iron, galleried courtyard, massive hand-carved wooden staircase, old timber, dormered roofs of small brown tile, flowers in pots, panelled dining room, a kitchen of shining red copper pans, old well, a garden of lilacs—the whole gamut of the picturesque inn of tradition is satisfied in this place. . . . The shadow of the great Napoleon broods over Avallon and over the inn. He came there in that impetuous flight of his, from Elba. He had marched northward in that epic adventure of the Hundred Days. . . . In the sleepy little town of Avallon, on the threshold of the inn, the disturber of the peace of the world had just stepped from a dust-covered post-chaise drawn by sweat-lathered horses whose master, for sole remuneration, humbly begged "the enormous favour" of being permitted to embrace the Emperor. The inn which welcomed the exile gave him respite from the wakeful night which is the privilege of inns. Napoleon slept badly. A heavy storm raged outside. The house was full of noises. The ardent Bonapartists of the region, among them many women, encumbered the corridors. The stables were full of the drenched and exhausted horses of his escort, and his men slept with the horses. He rose, lit a candle, and wrote feverishly at a small table. On the result of his midnight labours—whether battle orders, edicts, letters to his Empress, or merely the melancholy thoughts of a man alone, at night,

> on the eve of his destiny, with a storm beating at the windows —history is silent. But for that prodigious night in history, the inn holds his portrait entire—his portrait as posterity was to see it; that of a man devoured by a fever of living, vigilant, sleepless, magnificent in victory, invincible even in death.

Even if you can't afford to dine or stay in this historic inn, Avallon has plenty of other less expensive places. The old part of the town is still surrounded by ancient walls, and its main street runs through an archway under a clock tower. It then passes the Église Saint-Lazare which has two beautifully decorated doorways, one of which has a small tympanum over it. All but one of the eight elongated statues on the sides have been destroyed and replaced by slender stone columns.

Beyond the church is the tree-shaded Promenade de la Petite Porte which overlooks the little Cousin River and is a pleasant spot for a picnic lunch.

Avallon has many very old houses and a museum containing some of the Roman remains found in the area. Its paintings, too, are better than you would expect to find in so small a town.

The police here are kind to tourists. We had evidently parked our car in a forbidden area, but the paper stuck under the windshield-wiper was not a ticket. It was a map showing where the legal parking places were. On it was a polite request to move our car to one of them.

If you use Avallon as a base, the little roads south of it are fun to explore. You can just roam around on them or head for Quarré-les Tombes, 19 kilometers (12 miles) to the south on D10. There you will find a church surrounded by more than a hundred empty sarcophaguses neatly arranged in rows.

A medieval song leads to a discovery

From Avallon to Vézelay is only 13 kilometers (8 miles) on Route N457. This approach takes you close to the Fontaines-Salées on N458 where excavations have been under way since 1934 to uncover an area that goes far back into the history of France.

The story of the discovery is a fascinating one, for it came about through a medieval *chanson de geste*. This ancient song said that a great battle had been fought in the ninth century at a place called Vaubeton and that in the course of it Girart de Roussillon (who founded the Abbey of Vézelay) had descended from his horse at a large block of stone where a stream flowed past an old building. With this as a clue, a young professor from Auxerre named René Louis succeeded in locating the stone in a meadow south of Saint-Père-sous-Vézelay. Excavations revealed one surprise after another. An important Roman thermal establishment had stood on the site to utilize the salt water from springs that surfaced there. Then it was found that the Gauls had used the springs before the Romans did and had utilized hollowed-out tree trunks to collect and distribute the water. A Gallic necropolis with many urns containing the ashes of the dead stood nearby. The old building mentioned in the *chanson de geste* was one of the ruins that had stood in the meadow until the monks of Vézelay leveled them.

The Fontaines-Salées can be visited, but it is best to go first into the little museum in Saint-Pére-sous-Vézelay to see the many objects found on the site.

Near the museum is the charming Gothic Église Notre-Dame which is overshadowed by the larger and more famous church on the hill. Statues decorate its façade, and its porch is most unusual.

Vézelay

Some French towns are visited because their churches are great masterpieces of art. Chartres, Bourges, and Moissac come readily to mind. Vézelay ranks with them, for its Basilique Sainte-Madeleine is one of the most beautiful of all French churches. And it is important not only for its architecture and sculpture, but for the part it played in medieval history.

The great Abbey church is a complicated structure standing on the foundations of an earlier Carlovingian building. Parts of it are Romanesque while later sections, particularly the choir and the transept, are transitional Gothic. Only one of the two original towers remains; the other was destroyed by lightning in 1819. The century during which the basic church was being built was the time the Crusades began. The Second Crusade was launched here in 1146 when Saint Bernard preached on the eastern slope of the hill crowned by the church. Louis

VII, the King of France, who was present, was won over by his passionate persuasiveness, as were a host of lords, knights, and common people who could serve as soldiers. The Second Crusade, despite the fervor of its beginnings, was a failure. The Third Crusade did not start at Vézelay, but the King of France, Philippe-Auguste, and the King of England, Richard the Lion-Hearted, met there during the planning stages. Their armies then marched past the church.

Because of its close connection with the Crusades and because the relics of Mary Magdelen were supposed to be in the church named after her, Vézelay became one of the major stops on the pilgrimage routes that led through France to Spain and Italy. When doubt was cast on the authenticity of these relics, Vézelay began to lose its importance. The fine old building was in danger of collapsing in 1840 when Viollet-

Vézelay

FRENCH GOVERNMENT TOURIST OFFICE

le-Duc came to its rescue. The big white church is now in excellent condition and is most impressive to visit. Much of it, however, has obviously been restored.

It has two tympanums, one outside and one over the interior doorway leading from the narthex to the nave. The first is beautiful, but the second is magnificent. Fortunately for posterity, its position indoors protects it from the weather.

We have seen many *Son et Lumière* performances in France, but the most moving of them all was the one we watched in Vézelay in July 1960. It was marvelously effective because not only time but space was utilized. Sounds came from the hillside, the woods, the valley, and finally from the church itself. Villages far away on the horizon blazed with flames when invaders sacked them. As a grand climax, the doors of Sainte-Madeleine swung open to reveal an interior glowing with light. While the organ pealed—and an unseen choir sang ancient liturgical music—we all marched in to admire the great spectacle that was being staged around us and in which we were playing the role of congregations that had preceded us there in ages long past.

Splendid as it is, this magnificent church is not all that Vézelay has to offer. The hilly streets in front of Sainte-Madeleine are lined with interesting old houses, while the area behind it is a parklike woods. The walls that once protected the town no longer exist, but some of their gates do.

Treasure after treasure

Age sits heavily on this part of France. Only a few miles north on Route N6 (west of Saint-Moré) are a Roman road, the remains of a Gallo-Roman camp, and the prehistoric site of Arcy-sur-Cure where recent excavations in the caves there show that they had been continuously occupied by men for nearly 100,000 years.

Route N151 and N6 go north to Auxerre (pronounced Ausserre) which is 53 kilometers (33 miles) from Vézelay. Here the late Gothic Cathédrale Saint-Etienne looks unfinished in the same way that the earlier one of the same name in Sens does. Auxerre has only a left-hand tower, while Sens has only a right-hand one.

Auxerre has another religious monument—the former

Abbey church of Saint-Germain which is built over two crypts that date back to the ninth century. One of them is decorated with some of the earliest Christian murals yet discovered in France. The church itself is much later—thirteenth to fifteenth century.

There is an archeological museum with many of the Gallo-Roman artifacts that Burgundy is so rich in. The Musée des Beaux-Arts, in addition to its paintings, has a collection of Napoleonic relics.

At Auxerre you can continue north on N6 to Sens, 57 kilometers (35 miles) away, where the cathedral was not only patterned on England's Canterbury but is associated with Thomas à Becket, for he took refuge there after his quarrel with Henry II.

Then from Sens you can drive east on N5 and N60 for 65 kilometers (40 miles) to Troyes where there are nearly a dozen fine old churches. The Église Sainte-Madeleine has a beautifully carved rood-screen that was installed there several centuries after the church was built. In Troyes you will see ancient clock towers and half-timbered buildings that lean at twisted angles over some of the very narrow streets.

When you leave Troyes, N71 will take you south for 68 kilometers (42 miles) to Châtillon-sur-Seine. You can go on N65 from Auxerre through that other part of Burgundy's famous wine country where the Chardonnay grape produces a number of white varieties. The little town of Chablis is the center of the district. There you can sample the various kinds of wine that bear that label.

Still farther east is Tonnerre, which is also in the Chablis wine region. When we described the Hôtel de Dieu in Beaune we said that there is an even earlier hospital in Tonnerre. There is also a natural spring that supplies large quantities of water for the Fosse Dionne in which housewives wash clothes.

The Trésor de Vix

Route N65 continues east to Châtillon-sur-Seine which also has another spring with a copious flow of water. This one is in a little park where the emerging stream courses through a beautifully landscaped area.

Châtillon is an important stop on any tour of this part of

France, for its museum has on display the famous Trésor de Vix that was discovered near here in January 1953.

Vix is a small village six kilometers north of Châtillon-sur-Seine. It is located at the base of a long, low hill called Mont Lassois where great quantities of shards from a Gallic oppidum have been found. Among them, strangely enough, were a few bits of pottery that were clearly of Greek origin. Vix is believed to have been on the route by which tin from the British Isles was transported across France in ancient times.

The tomb that was uncovered in an open field contained archeological surprises which startled the world. About 2500 years ago a princess, who had been traveling in a large hand-drawn four-wheel cart, had died and been buried there with many objects of great value. Encircling her skull was a golden diadem, and scattered around her bones were bracelets and other jewels. The wheels of her cart had been placed against one wall of the tomb, but only their metallic parts have survived. There were several bowls made of silver or bronze together with an Etruscan jug and two Greek pottery cups, one of them decorated with battling warriors and Amazons. But the real treasure was a huge bronze vase.

Around the neck of this big wine crater is a decorative frieze of beautifully sculptured bronze horse-drawn chariots and helmeted soldiers that are unquestionably Greek. The vase evidently had been on its way from Greece—or from one of the Greek colonies in the Mediterranean—and was doubtless intended to be a present for some important person.

The vase came from Greece, the jug from northern Italy, while the golden diadem with tiny long-haired winged horses at its tips is believed to have come from Scythia in southern Russia. How all these things of such widely scattered origins got to France is an unsolved mystery.

The vase stands in the middle of a good-sized, well-lighted room where its lustrous green patina, marching figures, and Medusa-headed handles can be inspected at close range. We urge you to see it. Michelin says that three-star restaurants are "worth a special journey." So is the Trésor de Vix.

Food and wine

Our tour of Burgundy ends here. This rich province has more than the food and wine for which it is famous, but they are of a very high order indeed. We have discussed its wines; here are a few words about its food:

There are probably more good to supremely good restaurants in Burgundy than in any other part of provincial France. Here fine wine and fine food are really wedded. There are so many excellent restaurants scattered across the land from Macon to Châtillon-sur-Seine that they are sometimes only minutes apart when you go by car. And they don't have to have several stars to be good. One reason for their multiplicity is that travelers from Paris bound for Lyon, Geneva, or the Riviera pass through Burgundy and like to stop to eat on the way. Another reason is that this is a naturally bountiful land that produces great wine, fine beef cattle, and wonderful cooks. Its natives enjoy eating well and have done so for centuries, so they have built up a tradition for fine food.

Both the food and wines of Burgundy are rich, too rich perhaps for those who are not hearty trenchermen. But you can, of course, get anything you want, even plain boiled chicken. And don't sniff at that, especially if it's a *poulet de Bresse.*

Those who can eat anything will delight in *pâtés* served in a hot crust, tripe cooked in Chablis wine, duck with cherries, or a truffled *fondue.* Local cheese is not outstanding, but most restaurants will have a *plateau* of varieties brought in from the top cheese-producing regions of France.

Whatever you do, be sure to try Charollais beef. Even Texans will approve of it. And if you want mustard with it, that too will come from Burgundy, for Dijon is the center for it. You can see acres of its yellowish-green flowers covering the fields around that city.

Beef can be had in many forms in Burgundy, but the most distinctively local one is *boeuf à la bourguignonne,* rich, dark, and reddish brown. You may have had it before, but don't miss it here. This applies also to snails. They seem to have a special quality in Burgundy.

There is also a superb fish dish—*Pôchouse* (or *pauchouse*) —which is made from six or seven fresh-water varieties all cooked together and covered with brandy which is then ignited. A cream-and-egg sauce is added; so are poached mushrooms and *quenelles de brochet* as garnishes. Properly prepared, this can qualify as one of the great fish dishes of the world.

If you have to skimp your way in other sections of France, save your pennies to spend them for food in Burgundy. Even its less expensive restaurants are marvelously good.

22. *The Jura, Alsace, and Lorraine*

We have put these three regions together because they form a geographical unit in the northeastern corner of France. Relatively few tourists—American especially—go to them, although Alsace has a fair number of visitors. The Jura and Lorraine are largely rural with relatively little to see except for some not very exciting mountains in the Jura and Joan of Arc's birthplace in Lorraine. Nancy, however, is well worth a visit; while Alsace is a must.

There are very few good hotels in the Jura; not many in Lorraine, except in Nancy; but Alsace has a large number of them and some excellent restaurants too.

As a result, we suggest that you drive through the Jura and Lorraine and spend most of your time in Alsace. People seeking a quiet and inexpensive vacation in a country hotel, will do well in the Jura. Note what we say about Arbois.

We are not giving any bases of operation in Lorraine or the Jura. For Alsace we suggest Les Trois-Épis, Sainte-Odile, and perhap Strasbourg itself, although its hotels do not offer good value and are certainly not quiet.

The Jura Mountains

The Jura Mountains extend from a point west of Aix-les-Bains to the Rhine near Bâle (Basel). The department called Jura is much smaller than this; it covers only the section between Saint-Claude and Dole. But the folded mountains run for

300 kilometers in a crescent-shaped curve along the western shores of Lakes Bourget, Geneva, Neuchâtel, and de Beinne. They are not very high compared to the Alps or the Pyrenees (5652 feet at the Crêt de la Neige near Saint-Claude), but many people like this quiet rural area where cows graze on lush pastureland against a background of dark pine trees.

Because of the well-defined folds in the mountains most of the roads run from southwest to northeast along the valley floors, but a few cut across from west to east. These have to go over the high folds and are naturally located where they can take advantage of the lower gaps.

The Jura Mountains lie along the Franco-Swiss border, and their crests are the dividing line except in the area west of Geneva where French territory comes down to within a few kilometers of the lake. This isolated bit of France has two interesting places: the stylish and expensive resort-spa Divonne, and the very simple little village of Ferney-Voltaire. Divonne is a bit out of the way if you are going over the Col de la

Jura: Baume les Messieurs

FRENCH GOVERNMENT TOURIST OFFICE

Faucille to Saint-Claude, but the main road passes through the town that Voltaire made famous.

He purchased a small château, enlarged it, and spent the last 18 years of his long life there; he died in Paris in 1778 when he returned to the capital to see one of his plays performed. In Voltaire's time, the village bustled with activity. Distinguished visitors came to see him, and there he wrote thousands of letters to people all over Europe. His castle is not ordinarily open to tourists, but anyone with a serious interest in Voltaire should stop in at the local Syndicat d'Initiative which may be able to arrange a short tour.

Saint-Claude

The road goes up the mountainside in sharp *lacets* until it reaches the Col de Faucille, 4343 feet high. There is a splendid view over Lake Geneva and the Alps from a parking place along the way. Beyond the summit the road descends to Saint-Claude which is in a narrow valley on the east side of the Bienne River.

Several towns in the Jura are highly specialized manufacturing centers. Saint-Claude carves briar pipes while Morez has been making eyeglass-frames since the eighteenth century. Clocks and watches are manufactured in some of these remote mountain communities. All kinds of small industries flourish here: plastics are molded, diamonds are cut, and native woods are turned or carved.

Saint-Claude lies deep in a valley so narrow that the town is stretched out along the river. Here are stores and cafés to which people come from farms that may be miles away. The late Gothic Cathédrale Saint-Pierre has some open ground near it so you can park there while you go in to see the carved wood stalls and the sixteenth-century retable.

As you drive north from Saint-Claude, you will note that the Jura is sparsely settled and that towns of any size are few and far apart. There are no luxury accommodations to be had anywhere except in Divonne. But the hotels are clean and pleasant, and you will eat well in the restaurants even though none is rated by Michelin with more than one star. Hard-pressed gourmets will do best at Arbois which has two such restaurants.

You can drive directly north from Saint-Claude to Belfort by taking N437 which runs along the Lac de Saint-Point and goes through Pontarlier. Only 14 kilometers beyond this is Montbenoît where the Abbey church has some really amusing sixteenth-century carved wood decorations. One shows two women pulling each other's hair; another is called the Humiliation of Aristotle; while a third portrays Delilah cutting Samson's hair.

Another possible route is to leave N437 at Saint-Laurent to take N5 through Champagnole and then, just beyond Montrond, go right on N469 to Arbois with its good restaurants.

Arbois is a pleasant little town, located in wine country. Louis Pasteur, the great nineteenth-century chemist, spent most of his life there, and his early work on fermentation was undoubtedly influenced by his surroundings.

Arc-et-Senans

Salins-les-Bains, only a few miles to the east, has a salt works that has been in operation for centuries. Even more interesting, however, is the ghost of a salt works, an eighteenth-century one at Arc-et-Senans, which is a remarkable example of the way factories could be built in those lavish days. It is north of Arbois and not easy to find. Take N83; at Monchard go left at N72 and almost immediately to the right on D121. At Cramas turn right, go through the village, and then left on D17 which crosses the Loue River. Arc-et-Senans is on the other side with the great forest of Chaux north of it.

Here, in 1775, construction of this truly impressive group of buildings began. The gifted architect, Claude-Nicolas Ledoux, a true eighteenth-century Romantic, had persuaded Louis XV that it was worth building a truly magnificent royal salt works and that vain and unthinking monarch gave him the order to proceed. He died the year before construction started, but his successor, Louis XVI, was certainly not going to be concerned about anything so trivial as the building of a salt factory on the other side of France.

The location of the new plant had been determined by the fact that there was plenty of firewood near it to provide heat for evaporating the salt out of water which was to be brought in two lead pipes from the springs at Salins-les-Bains, 23 kilometers away.

But what was unusual about Ledoux's plans was that they called for a splendid city to be built in the midst of an uninhabited wilderness. The factory, the administration office, houses for workers, and some other subsidiary buildings were constructed in four years out of quarried stone, and the elaborate installation actually began to produce salt. But the circular city that was to surround the factory never got started. Before long the conduits carrying saline water began to be corroded, and then the Revolution put an end to all such ambitious schemes.

Today, the salt factory and its garden city, which were so substantially built nearly two centuries ago, still stand and can be visited. Fire and deliberate destruction have taken their toll but enough remains to show how a creative architect could dream and almost see his dream come true.

Besançon

Any competent geographer can take a good relief map of a country he knows nothing about and quickly point to probable locations for its cities. Some of the best possibilities are at the confluence of two or more rivers (Lyon, Tours, Grenoble) or in the bend of an important one (Poitiers, Cahors, Périgueux).

Besançon belongs in the second category. It is situated in a curve of the Doubs, which makes a nearly complete circle as it swings around the city. The Romans, who were experts in selecting good sites, founded a settlement here. Some of its remains, including a small arch of triumph, are still there.

Besançon has a cathedral, most of which is rather late, and a very elaborate astronomical clock which shows how skillful the people of the Jura are when it comes to building any kind of mechanism that measures time. The Musée des Beaux-Arts has a room devoted to local clockmaking. There is also a collection of prehistoric and Gallo-Roman artifacts of the region. The museum, which is far better than most in towns of this size, has many eighteenth-century French drawings and a collection of Impressionist and Fauve paintings. It also features work by Gustave Courbet who was born in nearby Ornans. In the seventeenth-century Hôpital Saint-Jacques, there is a beautifully equipped and decorated pharmacy of the period.

Although the Doubs seems to be a most unlikely stretch of water to inspire an inventor to build a pioneer steamship, one actually ran at Besançon in 1776, long before Robert Fulton's experiments began. This was the brainchild of Claude de Jouffroy d'Abbans, whose 36-foot-long vessel was propelled by oars rowed by a steam engine. It was a crude affair, as most prototypes are. He made a big step forward in 1783 when his 135-foot sidewheeler was able to move upstream at Lyon. But the members of the French Academy of Science were so little interested that they refused to send an observer from Paris, and the poor inventor's new scheme died young. Fulton, however, gave him due credit when he built his own steamboat.

Besançon is also noted for the fact that Victor Hugo was born there on February 26, 1802. But this was merely a matter of chance because his soldier-father happened to be stationed in the city at the time. After a few months the family moved on. The birthplace, at 138 Grande-Rue, is marked with a plaque.

Belfort

From Besançon, N73 and N83 go on to Belfort 90 kilometers (56 miles) away. The city is noted for the important part it played in military history, particularly in the Franco-Prussian War of 1870 when Belfort held out long after Napoleon III surrendered at Sedan. A huge lion, the work of Frédéric August Bartholdi, the sculptor who designed the Statue of Liberty in New York Harbor, commemorates the bravery of the soldiers and citizens who withstood a 104-day siege. It is carved out of a red sandstone cliff on the eastern side of the city.

Students of architecture, particularly those interested in the work of Le Corbusier, may want to drive from Belfort for 21 kilometers (13 miles) west on Route N19 to see the very modern Chapelle Notre-Dame-du-Haut near Ronchamp. Built in 1955 to replace an earlier one destroyed in the Second

World War, it exemplifies Le Corbusier's basic ideas of solid simplicity by the use of massive concrete walls without any kind of ornament. The roof, with its darker color and upward sweeping curves, gives the church a unique appearance among religious buildings.

Alsace

Belfort is the gateway to Alsace, the northeastern section of France, that has been under alternating German and French rule for so long that its people speak both languages. The half-timbered architecture, the food, and many of the place names are German, but Alsace, throughout war after war, has remained consistently loyal to France.

Alsace is interesting to visit. Its food, wine, and beer are very good, and its little villages are a constant delight. Most of its hotels, however, are higher priced than comparable ones in the Jura. But bargains can be found in some of the smaller villages where there are attractive country inns.

The hurried traveler will probably head for Mulhouse and then drive fast along the main highway to Colmar and Strasbourg. Those two cities have many attractions, but anyone who sees Alsace only from its main thoroughfares is going to miss a great deal.

We therefore suggest that from Belfort you go north on N465 which climbs up the Ballon d'Alsace on a series of *lacets.* The several round-topped mountains in Alsace are called "balloons" because they look like the huge, gas-inflated spheres that were mankind's first airships. The Ballon d'Alsace is only 4100 feet high, but there is a good view from the summit where a big statue of the Virgin stands.

From there you can drive over the Vosges Mountains to Colmar, or, if you don't mind making a detour, go out of your way to see Gérardmer and its lake. This pleasant-looking resort town is all new because the older one was blasted apart and burned by the Germans when they were driven out of it in November 1944.

Route N417 runs east for 52 kilometers (32 miles) over the mountains from Gérardmer to Colmar, which is one of the essential places to see in Alsace.

Colmar

Colmar is a small city, small enough to explore on foot. There is street after street of old half-timbered houses, some of them with decoratively carved beams. Outstanding are the Maison des Têtes (which has a good restaurant), the Maison Pfister, and the Ancienne Douane.

Near them is the Musée d'Unterlinden which was formerly a convent. In the garden is the statue of the mustached dog (with two conflicting dates) we mentioned in the Introduction. The museum has many early paintings, and a world masterpiece, the Retable of Issenheim. This elaborately conceived and executed altarpiece, which consists of several large panels, each one of which is a major work of art, was painted by Mathias Grünewald about the year 1500. Another great religious picture is Martin Schongauer's "Virgin with the Burning Bush" which is in the cathedral.

Colmar

A street scene in Colmar

Colmar has so much to offer that one leaves it reluctantly. But the best part of Alsace is just ahead. Resist the temptation to hurry on to Strasbourg by taking Route N83 which goes north in a way that is reminiscent of N74 in Burgundy's Côte d'Or; in both regions the main highway parallels the vineyards that lie on slopes west of it.

And, as was the case in Burgundy, you will do well to take the little roads that run through the wine country to one lovely village after another. Some of them were damaged or destroyed during the Second World War. Ostheim, which straddles Route N83 north of Colmar, was so completely wrecked that only one wall remained standing. This has been carefully preserved as a memorial. On top of it is a huge stork nest.

The storks of Alsace

That brings us to a subject which seems to be very important to people visiting Alsace for the first time. "Are there really storks there?" they ask.

Yes, there really are, although they are not always easy to

find. And they are present only during the season that begins in March, when the males arrive, and that ends in mid-August when all the storks in the region, including those hatched in Alsace, congregate in a small area north of Colmar. From there they fly to Africa to winter in a warm climate.

If you want to see storks—assuming that you are in Alsace during the nesting period—keep looking up. Before long you will see one of their enormous circular nests on a chimney top, a church roof, or some other elevated place. It is not hard to find a stork's nest, but it is much harder to find a stork. The nest may be an old one, not occupied this season. Or there may be no sign of life while you are looking at it. But before long you will come across one that is bustling with activity. One of the parents, seeing a mate approaching with food for the young ones, flies off to continue the ceaseless search for frogs, lizards, mice, or insects. Fledgling storks require a lot of nourishment to enable them to grow large enough to go thousands of miles to Africa. Everyone is standing by ready to applaud and help them in every way possible, but Alsace is slowly losing its storks. Some say that the land is drying up so that the supply of frogs is diminishing. Others believe that fumes from industry and automobile traffic are the cause. Whatever it is, storks are becoming scarcer every year. And that is a pity, because Alsatians and tourists hate to see them go.

Unspoiled Alsace

We first saw storks in action in a walled village that tourists haven't discovered yet. There are such places if you hunt for them.

We entered this one by going under a tall thirteenth-century clock tower and then along a street where water runs in a stone channel to provide a lengthy basin for washing clothes. A little square paved with cobblestones is surrounded by some highly photogenic old buildings. But what immediately attracted our attention was a stork nest on the church roof. While we watched, frogs and other delectable morsels were carried through the air by devoted parents to the insatiable small mouths hopping around in the nest.

Stork's nest

The townspeople saw how eager we were to get a photograph. Some suggested this vantage point, some that. "Here, I'll show you a good spot," said the town cesspool cleaner, not in German but in French. "Follow me. I know the place well."

We dutifully accompanied him and his foul-smelling cart. He was right. He did know the town well, and he led us to a spot where we could get a clear view of the goings and comings of the parent storks and were able to take a picture of them.

If you want to go on a hunt for villages unknown to tourists, there is one very simple way to tell whether your hoped-for discovery is genuine or not. Find out whether picture postcards or souvenirs are for sale. If they are, you will know you are too late; commercialization has begun.

Some of the most interesting places in Alsace are in the hills west of N83. D11 leads from Colmar to Turckheim, which preserves much of its old charm and still employs a night watchman to call out the hours. The road then continues to Les Trois-Épis, which is 2300 feet high and has a wide view over the surrounding mountains. North of this are Ammerschwihr and Kaysersberg, while still farther north are the three exceedingly picturesque towns of Riquewihr, Ribeauvillé, and Bergheim. Then, high up in the hills and standing clear against the sky so it can be seen from far away, is the Château of Haut-Koenigsbourg which was destroyed in 1633. The ruin was presented by the town of Sélestat to Kaiser Wilhelm II at the turn of the century when Alsace was part of Germany. He ordered the castle to be restored, and it was rebuilt in the solid style he liked. It is open to visitors who can see the Kaiser's own quarters there.

Still farther north is the pleasant mountain resort Le Hohwald where there is not much to do except rest and take long walks through the pine woods. Near this idyllic place is one of the most terrible reminders of the Second World War.

A German death camp in France

Few people—even French people—seem to know that it exists, but there is a German concentration camp in the beautiful Vosges Mountains. The Nazis, arrogant with success, evidently felt that conquered Alsace would remain part of the Third Reich for the thousand years its archdemonic Fuehrer predicted for it. They therefore went ahead and built Natzweiler-Struthof, which is located on D130 south of Schirmeck.

Part of the camp was burned at the time it was captured, but much of it remains as it was in those terrible days. It is open to the public. Despite the fact that many French visitors take their children through it, you may not want to expose impressionable youngsters to the dreadful things that are to be seen there.

Standing on a hill above the camp is a truly magnificent memorial to the thousands who died in Struthof. It looks like a giant airplane wing on which is drawn the emaciated figure of a prisoner. Around it are numerous graves.

The camp is still enclosed in barbed wire which was electrified to discourage all hope of escape. Both men and women met their deaths here, executed by machine-gun bullets, by the gallows (which still stands), and by gas chambers in which the naked victims huddled together for mass extermination. Even the crematorium is intact.

Moving as the sight of the death camp is, the group of buildings to the west of it is even more horrible, for among them is a small experimental chamber where observers could study the effect lethal gas had on its victims. And there also are three deep tile-lined tanks in which corpses were kept before being sent for dissection in the medical schools of Germany. Incredible as it may seem, across the road from this concentration of horrors, is a hotel recommended by Michelin as "pleasant, quiet, and well-situated." Ghouls may want to stay there. More normal people usually want to get out fast, terribly shaken by their experience in viewing this reminder of the grisly power the Nazis had over the helpless people of Europe.

Route D130 and N426 go east to Sainte-Odile where a visit to this 2300-feet-high haven of peace and quiet may enable you to recover from the emotional shock of Struthof. The convent is located on a mountain top which is one of the oldest inhabited places in Alsace. It got its name in the seventh century from a girl who was born blind but miraculously became able to see when she was baptized. The building is now used as a non-commercial lodging place with more than a hundred simple, modestly priced rooms.

Enclosing the top of the mountain is a very long curving wall called the Mur Païen which is so old that no one knows whether it goes back to Gallic times or beyond them to the prehistoric era. It would take hours to follow the wall as it courses around one slope after another, but part of it can easily be seen near the convent.

Strasbourg

Strasbourg is only 42 kilometers from Sainte-Odile. This Alsatian city, with its vast Gothic cathedral, its old streets, fine restaurants, and excellent food, calls for a fairly extended visit.

Ordinarily we try to avoid the larger French cities (except Paris), but Strasbourg is worth the trouble it takes to get through the traffic on its exasperating tangle of one-way streets. Fortunately, the section where the cathedral is located is less crowded. It is sometimes even possible to find a place to park there.

Only by looking at a map can you realize that Strasbourg is an island which was once the site of a Roman city. Two branches of the Ill River flow around this island while numerous bridges cross these and the little canals at the western end of the city. Strasbourg is located on the left bank of the Rhine, but you will see that famous river only if you go looking for it. Huge waterfront industrial areas shut it off from the part of the city that is of interest to tourists.

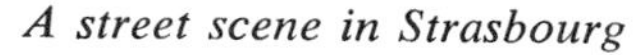

A street scene in Strasbourg

FRENCH GOVERNMENT TOURIST OFFICE

Strasbourg: the Cathedral of Notre-Dame

Strasbourg has twice missed having world fame thrust upon it. It was there in 1436 to 1444 that Gutenberg began the experiments which led to the invention of printing. But his native city of Mainz got the glory, for he returned to it to do the final work. Then again in 1792, Strasbourg, by a fluke, was deprived of having the French national anthem named after it. Rouget de Lisle wrote the famous war song for the Army of the Rhine while he was in Strasbourg. But soldiers from Marseille chanted the popular new refrain while they were marching toward Paris, so it became known as the Marseillaise, and Strasbourg lost the credit that rightfully belonged to it.

A rose-red cathedral

Since France has many superb cathedrals, it is hard to choose the outstanding ones. Strasbourg's Notre-Dame is surely one of the most impressive. It is so tall that its single lacework steeple can be seen towering over the city. And the Vosges *grès* of which it is built is not gray but red, so the entire structure seems warmer in feeling than most of the more austere cathedrals do. The building is kept in perfect condition, so perfect that if a chip drops off, a stone mason is apparently standing by to make an immediate repair.

The interior is vast and rather dark with much fine old glass left after the bombardment of 1870 when workmen kept removing it even while German shells were bursting outside. Some damage was done at the end of the Second World War, but no sign of it can be seen now.

The best time to visit the cathedral is before noon. At 12:30 the big astronomical clock goes into action. Death strikes the bell, and the Apostles move in a solemn procession to greet the figure of Christ while the cock crows as it did when Peter renounced his Master.

Near the clock is the very beautifully carved thirteenth-century Pillar of the Angels which is the work of the unknown sculptor who created some of the figures on the exterior of the cathedral of Chartres.

Strasbourg has many fine museums. One of them belongs to the cathedral; next door to it is the Château de Rohan where there are many Alsatian and German primitive paintings as well as exhibits of archeology and the decorative arts.

On the other side of the Ill River is the Musée Alsacien which shows how people dressed and lived in this part of France in the not-too-distant past. Near it is the Cour de Corbeau where you can see an entire street lined with very old half-timbered buildings.

The bridge in front of this, the Pont de Corbeau, was used for the punishment of criminals. It got its name, they say, because crows came here to feast on the bodies of the executed men.

If you walk west along the river you will pass the Protestant

One of the decorative statues on the Strasbourg Cathedral

Église Saint-Thomas where Marshal Saxe is buried in an imposing mausoleum. Beyond this church are some of the most interesting old streets in Strasbourg. Many of them are in or near La Petite France where there are so many ancient half-timbered houses that no one seems to care much about them, for we saw wrecking crews pulling some down.

This section has several good restaurants. Near the cathedral is a world-famous one, the Maison Kammerzell which is housed in a high-peaked, elaborately carved structure, part of which was built before Columbus discovered America.

Nancy

Route N4 leads west from Strasbourg to Nancy, 154 kilometers (96 miles) away. The road is good and very fast so the run is easy to make. Watch out though after you leave Lunéville, for 10 kilometers beyond that city N4*Bis* branches off to the left to bypass Nancy, while N4 goes to the center of town. Don't miss Nancy. It is a beautiful small city, particularly around the Place Stanislas which has gold-tipped eighteenth-century wrought-iron fences and gates.

Stanislas Leszczynski was the father-in-law of Louis XV. When Stanislas lost the Polish crown he was given the throne of Lorraine as a face-saving gesture. He spent a great deal of money to induce some first-rate architects and wrought-iron workers to come to Lorraine and beautify his domain.

The buildings that extend north from the Place Stanislas to the Palais du Gouvernement are all noteworthy. And the large green park to the east adds to the charm of the city.

From Nancy you can drive north for 57 kilometers (35 miles) to see the interesting Gothic cathedral of Metz which was made by combining two earlier churches into one building. And beyond Metz is the small independent state of Luxembourg. But the road from Metz to the Luxembourg border is lined with smoke-belching industrial plants and is part of the highly profitable but rather grim-looking manufacturing and mining area that runs across northern France.

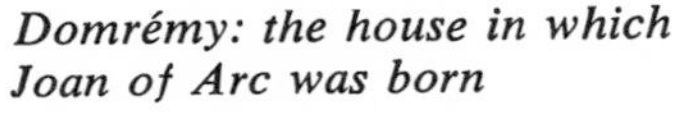

Domrémy: the house in which Joan of Arc was born

The fat statue of Joan

Joan of Arc and Domrémy

You may therefore prefer to go southwest from Nancy on N74 to visit Domrémy where Joan of Arc was born. To reach it leave N74 just below Autreville where D19 goes off to the left to run through countryside that has changed very little since this remarkable young girl lived here in the early years of the fifteenth century.

Domrémy was a small and undistinguished looking village when Joan was born there on January 6, 1412. It still has fewer than 300 inhabitants, and its houses are the homes of the rural poor. Joan's birthplace is a slant-roofed stone building with thick walls, tiny windows, and an earthen floor. Some changes were made in it in 1480, but there seems to be no doubt that this is pretty much how the humble cottage looked in her day.

Over the doorway is a fat and rather absurd statue of Joan clad in armor of the wrong period. And it shows her wearing a ruff, which is also out of period, and with long hair although it is known that she had cut her hair off when she started out to travel in men's clothing. Unfortunately, except for one tiny, very crude sketch drawn in the margin of a report on the siege of Orléans, no portrait made in her lifetime exists.

Because she lived so long ago and because we know so little of what she really looked like, there is a tendency to think that Joan is a rather shadowy and remote figure. This is not true. The testimony taken down at her trial is so detailed that we know more about her than we do of the kings and noblemen of her time. Joan was a very real person, and here in the town where she grew up you can see some of the things associated with her. One is the stone font at which she was baptized. Here too you can wander around in the fields and woods where she walked and first heard her "voices." And if you are lucky enough to find the little Chapel of Notre-Dame de Bermont (north of Greux), you will see a tiny church that stands on the site of the one in which Joan worshipped. The bell that hangs above it is the original one; so is the ancient crucifix before which she used to pray. Here in Lorraine you are more likely to see Joan's world as she saw it than anywhere else along the route that took her to her death in Rouen.

The big modern Basilique de Bois-Chenu south of Domrémy represents Joan in her official capacity as a saint of the Church. There is very little, if anything, of the simple country girl there.

The first stop on the way that Joan took to meet the Dauphin at Chinon is Vaucouleurs, which is 19 kilometers (12 miles) north of Domrémy on N64. But you will find little there that has to do with her except the ruins of the Sire de Baudricourt's castle. He was the man she had to convince in order to get started on her way. Near the castle is a rebuilt chapel which replaces the one she prayed in while she waited for Baudricourt's answer. The broken statue of Notre-Dame-des-Voûtes is the original one.

A forgotten Roman city

Before you leave Domrémy, however, you may want to make a side trip (12 kilometers or 11 miles) to see one of the least known, yet fascinating, Roman sites in France. This is the village of Grand with a population of only about 600. But this obscure little town has as the remains of an amphitheater that could seat 15,000 spectators. Near it is one of the largest mosaic pavements ever uncovered in ancient Gaul. The settlement was a rather late one, for it dates from the second or third century after the birth of Christ. It is believed that a temple dedicated to Apollo stood there and that the Emperor Constantine may have had some connection with the city.

To reach it, go south from Domrémy on D53 (which passes the Basilique de Bois-Chenu), then west on D3 and D71E to Grand. Seven roads come together at this village, but it has long ago lost the importance it had when it was a Roman community. There seems no reason for a city to be built in such a remote forest unless it had a shrine that drew pilgrims to it from afar.

Food and wine

Food in the Jura is so much like that in the Alps that there is no point in describing it in detail. Comté cheese is the best known of the region, but *bleu de Gex,* which comes from the eastern slopes facing Lake Geneva, ranks high among the blue cheeses of the world.

The wines of Jura are good but not great. Perhaps the best are the rosé of Arbois and the white from the village of Château-Chalon, which is a bit of an oddity because it comes in stumpy-shaped bottles called *clavelins* and is produced very much as sherry is although it is not fortified with extra alcohol. *Vins de Paille,* which are made from grapes laid down on straw, are produced in the Jura. They are white, sweet, and high in alcohol.

As must be expected, Alsatian food is more German than French, but it seems less stolid and heavy than it is in Germany itself. French imagination and know-how in cooking have added a certain amount of Gallic magic to it.

Pork products, geese, sauerkraut, dumplings, and noodles are its mainstays. Sausages of all kinds are highly prized, and *pâté de foie gras* is the great specialty of the region. Sauerkraut (*choucroute*) comes plain or fancy, i.e., cooked in Riesling wine or even in Champagne.

Munster is the best-known cheese; it is often—but not necessarily always—made with caraway seeds in it.

We described the fine wines of Alsace in our chapter on wines, so there is no need to talk again about them here. But a word must be said about Alsatian beer, which is probably the best in France although the dark beer brewed along the Belgian border is also very good.

Lorraine has given one famous food to the world—*quiche lorraine* which is an untopped crust filled with strips of bacon covered by custard. Bacon soup, blood pudding, and *potée lorraine* are great favorites here. Gérômé cheese, which is made near Gérardmer, only a few miles west of Munster in Alsace, also may have seeds in it, although these are likely to be fennel, anise, or cumin.

Lorraine does have some wines, but with Alsace, Burgundy, and Champagne so near, most of the better restaurants prefer to offer you the vintages from those great wine-growing districts.

23. *Champagne and the Battlefields of the First World War*

Unless you are interested in exploring battlefields or in seeing champagne made, northern France is not going to have much to offer you although it does have some fine cathedrals, notably in Reims, Laon, and Amiens. Since this book does not deal with Paris and its environs, we do not cover the many tourist attractions that can easily be reached in day trips from that city. You may, however, want to visit some of them while you are so near. If so, Pierrefonds, Compiègne, Senlis, Chantilly, and many other places are certainly worth seeing. So is Beauvais with its huge, unfinished cathedral.

We cannot recommend northern France as a vacation place. Except in the area near Paris, good places to stay are scarce —and out in the country practically nonexistent. Your best chance of finding reasonably pleasant hotels is to try Verdun, Reims, and Amiens in that order. Verdun has two hotels with well-rated restaurants; Reims has one restaurant in the city and one just outside to which Michelin gives a star, but its hotels, at any price, are in no way remarkable; Amiens has three one-star restaurants and an indifferent lot of hotels. Laon's hilltop location with its views cries out for a good hotel with terraced gardens, but it has none we can recommend.

Bar-le-Duc and the Voie Sacrée

When you drive northwest from Vacouleurs you are entering a vast battlefield area that stretches for 300 miles to the English Channel. Nearly every foot of it was bitterly contested for during the First World War. Most of the damage has been repaired, but some can still be seen in a few places. War memorials dot the land, while everywhere are the sad, lonely cemeteries with the graves of men who died young.

From Vaucouleurs you have a choice of going to Verdun by way of Bar-le-Duc and the dramatic French supply route called La Voie Sacrée or through Saint-Mihiel, where an independent American army went into action for the first time. American troops had fought in the war before this but only as supporting units.

Bar-le-Duc consists of two towns, an upper and a lower one. The Église Saint-Pierre in the upper section has one of the most gruesome funeral monuments in France. Signs with the words *Le Squelette* point the way to it. When the Prince of Orange was killed in a siege in 1544, it was found that he had left instructions for a memorial to portray him as he would look three years after he had been buried. The life-sized stone image on the church wall shows his partly decayed cadaver.

From Bar-le-Duc, the Voie Sacrée runs for 56 kilometers (35 miles) to Verdun. In the early spring of 1916, when this sector was under attack, this vital artery was the only route over which essential supplies and ammunition could be brought to the front. It had been so heavily used that it was no longer passable, but it was quickly repaired by a concentrated effort that never ceased even when shells tore up sections that had just been completed.

Saint-Mihiel

If you go to Saint-Mihiel you will see the little town that gave the famous salient its name. The Germans had pushed forward to it in 1914 and were still holding this advanced position. It was a constant threat to Verdun, although the Germans had never taken full advantage of it. The American First Army attacked on September 12, 1918, and in one day captured the big salient. Route D119 goes east from Saint-Mihiel for 15 kilometers (9 miles) to the colonnaded circular American war memorial which stands on top of the Butte de Montsec. From it is a view over the battlefield. Farther east, near Thiaucourt, is the American Cemetery with the graves of 4152 soldiers who died in the fighting around Saint-Mihiel.

Verdun

The battle for Verdun began on February 21, 1916, with a tremendous bombardment from some of Germany's heaviest guns. Shells fell by the thousands, churning up the soil and everything growing in it. The terrible assault went on for months, during which hundreds of thousands of men were killed on the fields north of the city.

The town has a monument with a wide flight of many stairs leading up to a colossal statue of a helmeted knight. There is an interesting little museum of war relics in the Hôtel de Ville. The Citadel vaults, which served as wartime shelters, are open to the public.

The battlefields of 1916 can be visited by driving east for 5.5 kilometers on N18 and then going off to the left on N403. Dead-end side roads lead from this to points in the field. N403A goes to the Fort de Vaux, and N403D to the Fort de Douaumont. Photographs taken during the war show that these massively constructed cement blockhouses were battered by so many shells that they lost all shape and finally became the rounded hillocks they are now. So many million small shell fragments cover the ground near these forts that they are almost as common as pebbles. As you drive through this terribly torn-up terrain you will see that scrub growth has sprung up to hide the countless shell holes and trenches. Occasionally you will pass monuments to villages that no longer exist because they were blasted to bits.

Near the base of 403D another road leads to the Ossuary of Douaumont, a tremendous monument to the hundreds of thousands of unidentified French soldiers who were killed at Verdun. The 450-foot-long vault contains tons of bones that were picked up on the battlefield. Small porthole windows make it possible to see the dreadful contents of this vast necropolis.

Just beyond the Ossuary is one of the world's most remarkable war monuments. This is the Trench of the Bayonets where French infantrymen were buried alive when shells caused the earth to collapse. Their bayonets still project in a row above ground while the undisturbed corpses remain in place below it. A concrete vault now preserves this dramatic incident of battle.

Route N403 curves around and goes west until it meets N64 at Bras where a bridge crosses the Meuse River to Charny. From there D38 leads to Mort-Homme. A dead-end road goes to the top of Hill 295 where desperate fighting took place in 1916. A grim-looking monument with the legend "They have not passed" stands on the summit. West of this is Hill 304 with a tall shaft to commemorate the 10,000 French soldiers who died there.

From this point D18 goes north to the area where American troops fought in September 1918. At Romagne-sous-Montfaucon is the biggest American military cemetery in Europe with 14,246 graves.

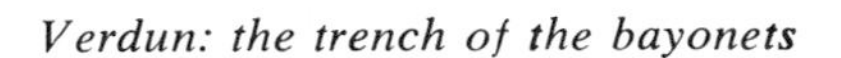

Verdun: the trench of the bayonets

FRENCH GOVERNMENT TOURIST OFFICE

The battlefields around Reims

Reims (spelled Rheims in English) is pronounced Hranss with the "a" sounded as it is in add.

Routes N3, N31, and N44 connect Verdun with Reims, which is 118 kilometers (73 miles) to the west. As N31 approaches the town it joins N44. Just beyond the point where the two roads meet, the Fort de la Pompelle rises to the south.

We first saw this shell-smashed fort in 1923 when we walked from Reims to visit it. It was only five years after the war then, and the fields were still crisscrossed by trenches and barbed wire, while rusted corrugated iron served as roofs for dugouts. Even a few wrecked automobiles and trucks littered the roadside. War relics were so common that German helmets could be picked up along the way.

The fort was open to anyone who wanted to visit. it. We wandered around to inspect the underground shelters and long passages that wound around below the surface. Bedding and discarded clothes, wet and crumpled, were still there.

From the upper part of the fort we could see endless fields that had been so badly scarred up by shellfire that the chalky undersoil lay upon the surface, presumably making it unfit for anything ever to grow in it.

We returned to the Fort de la Pompelle in 1962, nearly 40 years later. Farmers had reclaimed the soil, and crops were flourishing. All signs of war were gone except at the fort itself. It had been made into a National Monument in which everything remains just as it had been at the end of the war.

Ventilation pipes still stick out of the ground from underground shelters, and barbed wire can be found if you search for it. But much of the area is now blocked off with signs warning visitors not to pass the barricades because live shells may still be buried in the earth. The deep galleries that we had explored so heedlessly in 1923 are all closed. Carefully marked paths lead around the fort to sections that are regarded as safe.

Reims

When we saw Reims in 1923 more than 80 percent of the city was in ruins, and the great cathedral had been hit by hundreds of German shells. Today there are few evidences of First World War damage. Reims was also a center of activity in the Second World War, for it was here, in a red-brick schoolhouse, that the German army surrendered on May 7, 1945. The room in which the ceremony took place has been kept as it was on that historic day.

Another, and more tragic reminder, is a very ordinary looking house on a side street which has a large plaque that reads:

> French people: Never forget that for the four years of occupation (1940–1944), the Gestapo tortured hundreds of patriots in this building. They suffered and died to defend your liberty.

The Second World War left its mark on Reims; but it was the earlier conflict that will be forever associated with the city, for then the Germans shelled it for four years and destroyed or damaged nearly every building in the town. What they did to

Reims: the ventilator of a First World War bunker

the glorious Gothic cathedral took 20 years to repair, for fire as well as shells had wrought havoc upon this priceless treasure of medieval art.

It was a gaunt wreck when we saw it in 1923. Many of the statues on the front of the church had been smashed, stones were missing from the towers, and flames had melted the lead roof so that the empty rose window framed the sky behind it.

The well-restored cathedral shows no major war damage now. It was essential that this building be saved, for it has played a key role in the history of France. Here kings were crowned for centuries, and here Joan of Arc stood at the altar on July 16, 1429, to watch Charles VII be made the King of

Joan of Arc's statue in front of the Reims Cathedral

France. Only six months before, she had left Lorraine as an unknown teenage girl, and in that incredibly short time had changed world history. Reims was the high point of her career, but it was also an ending, because the miserable creature being crowned there was already turning against her. After the coronation her downward path to the marketplace in Rouen would begin. Remember Joan as she stood here in Reims at the height of her glory. They say that she wanted to return to Domrémy at this time because she knew her work was done. But she was destiny's child who had to complete the legend she had begun.

The fame and importance of its cathedral have overshadowed

The façade of the Cathedral of Reims

FRENCH GOVERNMENT TOURIST OFFICE

everything else in Reims, which is a pity, for the Basilique Saint-Rémi is a fine building in its own right, and the best Roman arch in northern France is in this city. The Musée des Beaux-Arts has a number of good Corots and one of Renoir's most charming portraits of women.

Champagne

The grapes for making champagne are grown south of Reims in an area that centers around Épernay, where the vineyards stretch east and west along the Marne River, and south as far as Route N33. Between Reims and Épernay, the vineyards swing around in a wide semicircle on the slopes of the Montagne de Reims. Everywhere the soil is chalky white, while down below the surface are 120 miles of tunnels used for storing the wine—and for shelters in both World Wars. The Romans began this vast underground labyrinth when they quarried the soft limestone for building purposes.

Although some white grapes are used for making champagne, most of it comes from the same Pinot Noir that produces the fine red wines of Burgundy. To get pale champagne from dark grapes requires a very light pressing with the wine removed quickly before the skins can color it. The white grapes (Chardonnay and Pinot Blanc) are grown south of Épernay; the red along the Marne or on the slopes of the Montagne de Reims.

The *caves* can be visited, and in their cool depths you can see how champagne is produced. More than a dozen firms will welcome you to their establishments. Two of them, Taittinger in Reims and Mercier in Épernay, are open every day of the year, Sundays and holidays included. Most of the others can be seen only on working days. Mercier takes guests through the long tunnels on an electric train.

The newly pressed champagne is allowed to stand for about 12 hours to clear. Then, after a little sugar and tartaric acid are added, the wine is put into wooden casks or glass-lined vats to ferment until the end of the year, at which time cold air is introduced to stop the process.

After this the champagne is racked three times to clear it of impurities. It is then blended with other new pressings, and older vintages may be added if needed. In March it is bottled with a small amount of sugar and is laid flat for the second fermentation, which starts in the spring. The bottles are allowed to lie on their sides for several years. Then they are thrust at a slant and with necks down into oval openings in racks called *pupitres*. For three or four months highly skilled workers shake and turn each bottle a little every day in order to get the sediment down into the very bottom of the neck. After this *remuage* is completed, the bottles remain upside down until they are to be shipped. At this time the sediment is expelled by a process called *dégorgement*. The most modern way of doing this is to freeze the neck of the bottle so the deposit can be blown out as an icy plug. But many firms prefer the traditional method which calls for an expert to uncork the bottle, let the sediment pop out, and quickly cover the mouth with his thumb until he can seal it temporarily in a machine that brings a rubber nipple down to keep the champagne under pressure for a few moments.

The slight empty space is now filled with champagne of the same kind with just the right amount of sugar added to make the the finished product *Brut, Extra Dry,* or *Sec*. The final cork is inserted and wired into place to prevent internal pressure from blowing it out.

You can now see why champagne is expensive to produce. And it is even more expensive outside France because many countries, the United States and Great Britain among them, charge high duty on all sparkling wines.

Chateau-Thierry and Belleau Wood

From Épernay, N3 runs west along the Marne to Château-Thierry, 48 kilometers (30 miles) away. This part of the Marne was bitterly fought over during the First World War. The area is of particular interest to Americans, for the impressive United States Aisne-Marne memorial stands on a hill two miles west of Château-Thierry, while seven miles to the northwest is Belleau Wood, the only place in France where evidences of American fighting in the First World War still exist. Trenches, cannon, and shell-scarred trees mark the scene of the battle. Nearby is the Aisne-Marne military cemetery.

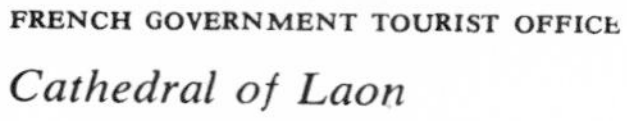

FRENCH GOVERNMENT TOURIST OFFICE

Cathedral of Laon

FRENCH GOVERNMENT TOURIST OFFICE

The interior of the Cathedral of Laon

We are now only 56 miles from Paris, but to complete our circular tour of France we will turn north and avoid Compiègne, which can easily be visited in a day trip from the capital.

Route N37 goes from Château-Thierry for 41 kilometers (25 miles) to Soissons where the beautiful Cathédrale Saint-Gervais was seriously damaged in the First World War. Here, too, is the former Abbey of Saint-Jean-les-Vignes where Thomas à Becket stayed for nine years. The façade of its church was hit by German bullets not only in 1914–1918 but in 1870 as well.

Laon

Still farther north and a bit out of the way on Route N2 is Laon, another great cathedral city. It is remarkable not only for its huge church but for its location, for it stands on a curiously shaped hill that rises several hundred feet above a flat plain. Laon has changed very little over the centuries, because there is a limited amount of space on the high plateau. At the eastern end are the Citadel and the cathedral; from there the town curves west and south to end on a spur where an arsenal and former abbey buildings stand. Several roads lead up from the railroad station and the industrial area to ascend the heights in *lacets*.

The cathedral is noted for its lantern and four towers which rise above the city and can be seen from far away on the wide plain. The two western towers have commemorative sculpture of the oxen that hauled the heavy stones up the hill. The present church replaces an earlier one which was burned during an insurrection in 1112.

The battlefields of the Somme

Northwest of Saint-Quentin, the triangle marked by Péronne, Albert, and Bapaume was the scene of the worst of the battles of the Somme, which followed Verdun in 1916. This section north of the Somme River is seldom visited now, but in those terrible days it was crowded with British, French, and German soldiers. On both sides of Route N338—and far to the north of it—are vast areas where mine craters, shell holes, and trenches mar the peaceful land. So many projectiles buried themselves into these quiet fields that men still make a living going over the ground with mine detectors to reclaim pieces of metal. They are not hard to find, even on the surface. In 1964 we saw an unexploded shell lying untouched in a sheep pasture. When the Paris-Lille highway was being built near here in 1965, bulldozers dug up live shells at the rate of one in every cubic meter of earth.

On these fields slaughter reached such intensity that on a single day—July 1, 1916—there were 57,000 British casualties. This was the time when generals sent whole battalions into machine-gun fire to die in windrows. And it was here, in September, that tanks first went into action. History was made on these now-deserted fields where grass grows on mounds of earth that were thrown up in the heat of battle. Few monuments are to be seen, but there are many cemeteries for the French and British soldiers whose lives stopped suddenly in 1916. Otherwise nothing remains of all that concentrated fury except torn-up ground that time and weather will eventually level.

The Cathedral of Amiens

Amiens

Route N29 goes southwest to Amiens, which has the largest Gothic cathedral in France. If you examine the dates when some of the churches were being built in the area around Paris you will see that nearly all of them were under construction during the year 1220 when Amiens was started. This meant that skilled laborers were scarce, that architects were in great demand, and that raw material was being competed for. But Amiens' very lateness worked to its advantage because its builders had a chance to observe what was being done in other cities only a short distance away. They did well, for Amiens is one of the most beautiful of all the French cathedrals of this period. Its interior, which is unusually well lighted by tall windows, is even more impressive than its exterior.

North of Amiens the industrial area along the Belgian border begins. It is so thickly settled and so filled with the smoke and haze of factories that a tourist traveling for pleasure is not likely to be attracted to it, although Arras and Lille are worth visiting. If you are headed for Brussels we suggest that you go through Cambrai and Valenciennes, which are both small enough to cope with and are not overindustrialized.

Food and wine

It has often been said—and we too have said it—that a region that produces fine wines will have good food to go with it. Champagne, however, is a very special wine—white, sparkling, and expensive—so it is hardly the sort that local cooks would use in their kitchens. Nevertheless, some dishes are cooked in champagne. Chicken done that way is heavenly. And potato salad made with champagne is very special, but you are not likely to come across it in any of the restaurants here.

Potée champenoise is a hearty dish, but it is very similar to the *potées* of Lorraine and Alsace. That great French favorite, *andouillettes* (tripe sausage) are popular from the Loire Valley through Burgundy to Champagne.

Wine, of course, is another matter. There is always champagne . . . and more champagne . . . .

24. *The North Channel Coast*

At the beginning of our chapter on Normandy we said that we assumed that your trip through France would probably start from Paris, so we omitted the northern part of Normandy and all of the ancient provinces of Flanders, Artois, and Picardy. But travelers coming from England or Belgium will enter France here. If they are not in a hurry, they may want to spend some time on the Channel coast. It lies open to the sea and the sky with sand dunes and beaches stretching along its western edge. Except in its few thickly settled communities this whole area has a feeling of spaciousness. Many of its roads run through wide fields with nothing in sight for miles. Its major drawback is the fact that the weather may be cool and cloudy. People who have been brought up in the same kind of climate in England don't seem to mind the lack of sunshine. They flock to the sandy beaches and are happy to be able to get good French food and wine. Restaurants here serve pretty much what those in the southern part of Normandy do.

The resorts along the shore are patronized mostly by tourists from England, some from Paris, and a few from cities in the interior of northern France. Since the area's attractions are slight compared to those on other French coasts, anyone who has the time to drive on for another day or two will do much better in Brittany or farther south.

There is no point in trying to find bases here from which to explore the nearby country, for the land behind the coast has little of interest. Along the shore we would recommend Le Touquet-Paris-Plage and Étretat as being better than most. We mention some pleasant small resorts later in the chapter. This part of France has many close associations with England, the most recent of which was at Dunkerque where 350,000 soldiers were evacuated under fire in May and June 1940 when the Nazis overran northern France. The port of Dunkerque (or Dunkirk as it is spelled in England) is behind the beach with canals leading to its docks. At the time of the evacuation, the Nazis held everything except this tiny pocket from which thousands of troops were moved across the Channel. The part that hundreds of small boats played in that tremendous drama will never be forgotten.

Only a few miles west of Dunkerque, Thomas à Becket came ashore at Gravelines more than 800 years ago when he had to leave England to escape the wrath of his former friend, King Henry II.

This is a battle-haunted corner of France, for it was at Crécy in 1346 and again at Agincourt in 1415 that British longbowmen stood off superior numbers of the French and won unexpected victories. These battles are remembered for the deadly work done by arrows; far more important, however, is the fact that they saw the introduction of gunpowder—an innovation which was to change the art of warfare.

Dunkerque: the port

FRENCH GOVERNMENT TOURIST OFFICE

These once-famous battlegrounds are not easy to find. Agincourt (spelled Azincourt in French) is now a tiny village east of Route N28 a few miles north of Hesdin. Crécy appears on the map as Crécy-en-Ponthieu. It is farther south and is located on Route N338 which runs west from N28 at an unnamed crossroads 18 kilometers (11 miles) north of Abbeville.

The coast road

The coast road along the Channel is N40. After leaving Dunkerque and Gravelines, it passes through Calais and Boulogne where ferries from England bring tourists and their cars to France. We suggest that you avoid N1. Route N40 has less traffic and cuts through wide green farm fields that often stretch down to the sand dunes behind the beaches. Many Nazi blockhouses, some partly destroyed, others still intact, are scattered along this vital coast. Near Cap Gris-Nez, the local people have erected a large crucifix with a colorfully decorated wall behind it to mask the sinister-looking cement reminder of the years when the country was occupied by a ruthless enemy.

Le Touquet-Paris-Plage

N40 passes through Le Touquet-Paris-Plage, where you can find accommodations at any price you are willing to pay. There is a big swimming pool on the beach, and the town has two Casinos, horse racing, a tennis club, and a golf course. This is a popular place with Parisians because they can get there quickly by plane.

You leave Picardy and enter Normandy at Le Tréport where N40 becomes N25. Just before Dieppe, you may want to visit Puys, the small town in which Alexandre Dumas died in 1870. The little resort there was founded by his son.

Dieppe, noted for its fishing boats and commercial shipping, is more interesting to visit than to stay in. It was the scene of a disastrous commando raid on August 12, 1942, when 15,000 soldiers, mostly Canadian, tried to seize the port. About half of them were killed or captured.

West of Dieppe, scattered along D75 and D68, are many

isolated and attractive little resorts that are often located where ancient watercourses have carved their way down to the sea. Veules-les-Roses and Saint-Valéry-en-Caux are on N25; beyond them you have to take less-traveled D79 to reach others like Veulettes-sur-Mer and Les Petites-Dalles.

Fécamp is a smaller version of Dieppe with its own fishing fleet and boat basins. Only 10 miles farther on is Étretat, our favorite resort on this coast.

Étretat

The edge of the sea here is very much the same as it is on the British side of the Channel. High white chalk cliffs rise abruptly from the water with narrow beaches below them. Since the full sweep of the Atlantic crashes against the French coast when the winter storms come in, the powerful waves and gnawing winds have carved the soft chalk into grotesque shapes Tall rock arches rise from the sea and must eventually be over-

Veules-les-Roses

FRENCH GOVERNMENT TOURIST OFFICE

FRENCH GOVERNMENT TOURIST OFFICE

The white chalk cliffs of Étretat

thrown by it.

Étretat first became a resort for city people when artists came from Paris in the 1840's to paint the spectacular cliff scenery. Others followed, and the previously unvisited fishing village soon developed into a fashionable summer place.

Monet made many paintings of Étretat and the area around it. One of his pictures of the wave-cut arches along the shore is in the Fogg Museum in Cambridge, Massachusetts. The Louvre has Courbet's dramatic painting of the cliffs at Étretat after a storm. Scenes along the coast from Fécamp to Honfleur were favorite subjects of several Impressionists.

Along the beach at Étretat fishermen use old boats turned upside down as shelters to protect their nets and equipment. Some of these ancient dories may have served as models for the paintings that Monet and Courbet made of this area.

Étretat is so small that you can cover the town on foot in a few minutes. It takes more time to explore the endlessly fascinating cliffs. They were well guarded during the Second

World War when the Germans built camouflaged defenses on them. The forts are still there with the ground around them torn up by shells from Allied warships.

The beach itself is covered with pebbles, some of which have holes bored through them.

Étretat is very quiet and is ideal for a rest after a long journey. Here our in-and-out, often roundabout circular tour of France approaches its end unless you want to visit Le Havre, 28 kilometers (17 miles) away on N40. That big port was so thoroughly smashed up in the Second World War—and so completely rebuilt afterwards—that it is a modern commercial city where few tourists stay longer than they have to.

Paris is now beckoning, drawing everyone to it like a powerful magnet. From Étretat it is 224 kilometers (139 miles) away. There are a dozen routes to return on, but most of them lead through Rouen or across that overpriced Tancarville Bridge. If you are in no hurry, we suggest that you go by way of Forges-les-Eaux with its pretty Parc Thermal. You can also stop off to inspect the royal tombs in Saint-Denis at the very gates of Paris. It is surprising how many people who have spent a good deal of time in that city have never traveled to the industrial suburb to visit this important church. You may find it easier to spend some time there on your way into Paris rather than to make a special trip out.

At any rate, Paris is now very near, and there our long tour of France comes to an end.

L'Envoi

After re-reading the text, we realize that we have constantly stressed the idea that America and France are very different, and that their people are too. This is true, of course, and it is these differences that a traveler goes abroad to see.

But if he is observant and sensitive enough, he will soon note that the differences are largely on the surface and that they are not basically important. Underneath, the peoples of these two countries have much in common, for they are both the inheritors of Western civilization, and although they may not always agree about which aspects of that civilization they think are best, they do share what it has to offer.

One incident comes to mind that has some bearing on this. While we were traveling through Brittany, an old peasant woman stopped us when she saw the U.S.A. plaque on the back of our car. In rapid French she said: "Oh, you are Americans! I like Americans! Our people must always be friends as they have been in the past. That is important for the peace of the world."

She went on to explain what two World Wars had meant in her life. She told us about the American soldiers she had met, and how the second generation of them had called her Mother when they were billeted in her home.

We talked for about half an hour and heard a great deal about life in her village and about the fast-vanishing customs of old Brittany. When we parted, her last words were: "When you get home, please tell your friends that America and France must stand together. We are the old world, and you are the new. From both of us the future must come, but it will be a good future only if we remain allies and let no one come between us."

When we drove away, heading toward the hilly interior of Brittany as twilight came on, the old woman's words went with us: "America and France must always be friends." We hope they will.

Books and pamphlets about traveling in France

We have included books in French as well as in English. Since England has always published many more titles about France than the United States has, you will find a preponderance of British books here.

We have listed only those works that are reasonably up to date but have put in a few older ones that we found exceptionally interesting. Most books published between 1914 and 1950 now seem outmoded, whereas those issued before the First World War have taken on a curiously timeless quality. You may be able to find copies of some of these in your library.

Ask any French Government Tourist Office (addresses on page 30) for a free copy of their excellent pamphlet, "The Key For Your Trip to France." Also request a free map and illustrated pamphlet for the areas you are going to visit. They are available in English for Normandy, Brittany, the Château Country, the Southwest, Pyrenees, Auvergne, Provence, the Riviera, Corsica, the Alps (Savoy), Alsace, and Champagne.

The best-known general guidebooks to France are: Baedeker's (Macmillan), Nagel's (Taplinger), Fodor's (McKay), and *Le Guide Bleu*, in French and English editions (Hachette, Paris). *Les Albums des Guides Bleus* are picture books of the various provinces. Horizons de France also publishes some in its *Visages du Monde* series.

More specialized and available only in French are the *Guide Artistique de la France* (Hatier, Paris, 1964), and the

Guide Littéraire de la France, Paris, 1964. Zodiaque has a series of picture books on Romanesque art in eight provinces.

Not guides but travel books are: *All the Best in France* by Sydney Clark, New York, 1966 (new edition); *The Land of France* by Ralph Dutton and Lord Holden, London, 1952 (fourth edition); *Unknown France* by Bernard Newman, London, 1963; and *The Splendour of France* by Robert Payne, London, 1963. In French, the multi-volumed series *La France Inconnue* by Georges Pillemont, Paris, 1959 and v.d., covers out-of-the-way places.

Henri-Paul Eydoux specializes in writing about little-known antiquities. His three books, *Monuments et Trésors de la Gaule*, Paris, 1958; *Cités Mortes et Lieux Maudits de France,* Paris, 1959; and *Promenades dans la France Antique,* Paris, 1965, all have a great deal of information about some truly fascinating places.

René Joffroy has written *Le Trésor de Vix,* Paris, 1962, about the remarkable ancient Greek trove he found in northern Burgundy.

Guide de la France Mystérieuse, Paris, 1964, and *Guide de Provence Mystérieuse,* Paris, 1965, have many attractive old pictures but miss many places that should have been included in such big volumes.

A fine picture book (with text in English) by Marcel Pobé and photos by Jean Roubier is *The Art of Roman Gaul,* London, 1961.

S. Baring-Gould, the long-lived British author who wrote many books about travel, did several on France that are hard to find but are worth having. Among them are *In Troubadours' Land*, (Provence), London, 1890; *The Deserts of Southern France*, New York, 1894; *A Book of the Riviera,* London, 1905; *A Book of the Pyrenees,* London, 1907; and *A Book of the Cevennes,* London, 1908.

France by Peter Latham, London and Glasgow, 1964, has concentrated information on travel, business, study, and art.

Helpful when you travel by car are: *Motoring Holidays in France* by Alison Lascelles, London, 1962; *With Your Car in Southern France* by Dudley and Marianne Noble, London, 1959; and intended for all of Europe but fairly useful for France is *Enjoy Europe by Car* by William J. Dunn, New York,

1962. The pamphlet, "Driving Abroad," can be obtained gratis from the California-Texas Oil Corporation, 380 Madison Avenue, New York, N. Y., 10017. More complete is the booklet *La Code de la Route*. It can be had in English from Louis Rousseau, Les Sables d'Olonne, (Vendée) or in French from Flammarion in Paris.

Anyone who takes pictures will want "Notes for the Photo Traveler Abroad," Kodak Pamphlet No. C-17, which can be obtained free from the Sales Service Division of the Eastman Kodak Company, Rochester, N. Y.

As a safeguard for physical well-being send 35 cents to the Superintendent of Documents, Washington, D. C. 20402, for the U. S. Public Health Service pamphlet, "Immunization for International Travel." More general advice will be found in "Health Guide for Travelers" which is sold for 50 cents by Consumers Union of U. S., Inc., Mount Vernon, N. Y.

Books about food and wine

Except for cookbooks, the literature on French food is far less extensive than it is on wine. The good ones are expensive. Among them, *The Food of France* by Waverly Root, New York, 1958; *Bouquet de France: An Epicurean Tour of the French Provinces* by Samuel Chamberlain, New York, 1952, and *Gastronomic Tour of France* by Jean Conil, New York, 1960, rank high.

Authoritative and outstanding is *Wines of France* by Alexis Lichine, New York, 1963 (fourth edition). Revised and brought up-to-date is the great British classic, *A Book of French Wines* by the late P. Morton Shand, London, 1964. This is available as a Penguin paperback. Expensive but impressive is *The Noble Grapes and Great Wines of France* by André L. Simon, New York, 1957. Very detailed and complete is *Vignes et Vins de France* by Louis Jacquelin and René Poulain, Paris, 1960. An English edition of this was published in London in 1962 under the title of *The Wines and Vineyards of France*. *The French Vineyards* by Dennis Morris, London, 1958, is about a British wine expert's tour of the French vineyards. It is a book to read and treasure if you can get a copy.

Not specifically about French wines but about wine generally are *Wines and Spirits: a Complete Buying Guide* by William E. Massee, New York, 1964. The author collaborated on Lichine's book, so he must have a good background. Frank Schoonmaker's *Encyclopedia of Wine,* New York, 1964, is alphabetically arranged to cover the world.

Two useful paperbacks (not specifically on French wines) are *The Vintage Wine Book* by William S. Leedom, New York, 1963, and *Wines and Spirits,* a Penguin Handbook, by L. W. Morrison, London, 1962.

Normandy

The *Guides Bleus* cover every region listed and so will not be mentioned each time.

The Michelin Green Guide (available in English)

A. Houghton Brodrick, *Normandy*, London, 1947

Vivian Rowe, *Return to Normandy,* London, 1951

Henry Adams, *Mont-Saint-Michel and Chartres,* Boston, 1905

Yvan Christ, *Mont-Saint-Michel,* Paris, 1962 (pamphlet)

Dawson Gratrix, *The Holiday Beaches of Northern France: Picardy, Normandy, and Brittany,* London, 1958

Patrice Boussel, *Guide des Plages du Débarquement,* Paris, 1964

Information on both *Normandy and Brittany* can be found in the book by that title written by Ralph Dutton, London, 1953.

Brittany

The Michelin Green Guide (available in English)

Alan Houghton Brodrick, *Brittany*, New York, 1951

George Millar, *Oyster River*, New York, 1964. A yachtsman's experiences on the Auray River and the Gulf of Morbihan.

Eleanor Clark, *The Oysters of Locmariaquer,* New York, 1965. Now in a paperback.

Glyn Daniel, *The Megalith Builders of Western Europe,* London, 1958 and 1963, has a great deal of information about the megalithic monuments of Brittany.

Henri Queffélec, *L'Evangile des Calvaires Bretons,* illustrated, Paris, 1957

V.-H. Debidour, *Grand Calvaires des Calvaires,* Châteaulin, Finistère, 1960. This is one of many pamphlets and monographs that are illustrated with photographs by Jos de Doaré on various aspects of Brittany.

The Château Country

The Michelin Green Guide (available in English)

Alan Houghton Brodrick, *Touraine: with Anjou and Maine,* London, 1950

Philippe Lannion, *Châteaux of the Loire,* illustrated, B. Arnaud, Grenoble and Paris, 1962 (available in English) Arnaud publishes more than a hundred picture books on various regions of France all illustrated by photographs printed in heliogravure or color.

Short illustrated monographs on the great buildings of France —cathedrals, churches and chapels, abbeys, and castles are published by Henry Laurens in Paris. Among them are Amboise, Chambord, Chenonceaux, Chinon, Loches, and Valençay, while *Châteaux de Touraine* covers some of the minor castles.

Old and hard to get but exceedingly useful is Theodore Andrea Cook's *Old Touraine,* New York, 1908 (3rd edition). Two volumes.

The Atlantic Coast

The Michelin Green Guide (in French only)

One area is covered in Roger Galy's *Promenades Pittoresques dans Bordeaux et autour du Bassin d'Arcachon,* Paris, 1962

Périgord

The Michelin Green Guide (entitled *Dordogne* in English)

For general background reading we recommend:

Philip Oyler, *The Generous Earth,* London, 1951; Penguin Paperback edition, 1961. Oyler, a British agriculturist, visited Périgord and fell in love with it. His book is a minor classic of travel literature.

Freda White, *Three Rivers of France, the Lot, Dordogne, and Tarn,* London and New York, 1962. Périgord seems to inspire good writing. This excellent book was written by a Scottish woman who spent many months in Périgord and knows the region well.

Joan Grant, *A Lot to Remember,* London, 1962. The author is a clairvoyant, but her factual information on Périgord is down-to-earth and interesting.

Peter de Polnay, *An Unfinished Journey,* London, 1952. This deals mostly with the area around Souillac where the author lived for some time.

200 Châteaux de l'Auvergne au Quercy, illustrated, Paris, n.d. but recent

For the prehistory of the region, Ann and Gale Sieveking's *The Caves of France and Northern Spain,* London, 1962, is a very useful guidebook with maps of many important caves.

Geoffry Grigson, *Painted Caves*, London, 1957, is more general.

E. Peyrony, *Les Eyzies and the Vézère Valley,* an illustrated pamphlet, Montignac, 1959. Available in English.

The Pyrenees

The Michelin Green Guide (available in English)

Andrew Shirley, *South from Toulouse,* New York, 1959. Informative also for parts of Périgord and Roussillon

Out-of-print but worth trying to get are:

Hamilton Jackson, *Rambles in the Pyrenees,* New York, 1912

Regina Jais, *Legendary France and the Basque Country,* New York, 1931

Roussillon, the Gorges of the Tarn, and Auvergne

The Michelin Green Guide for the Pyrenees also covers Roussillon; separate ones are *The Gorges of the Tarn* and *Auvergne.* All in French only.

Freda White, *West of the Rhone: Languedoc, Roussillon, and the Massif Central,* London and New York, 1964. By the author of the excellent *Three Rivers of France*

Bryan Morgan, *Fastness of France,* London, 1962, deals with Auvergne

Provence

The Michelin Green Guide (in French only)

Alan Houghton Brodrick, *Provence and the Riviera,* London, 1952

James Pope-Hennessy, *Aspects of Provence*, London, 1952. A first-rate travel book—one of the best

Laurence Wylie, *Village in the Vaucluse,* Cambridge, Mass., 1957. We described this in our chapter on Provence. It is only about one village but is an outstanding work.

Douglas Goldring, *The South of France,* London, 1952

M. F. K. Fisher, *Map of Another Town: a Memoir of Provence,* Boston, 1964. The author, who is famous for her books on food and cooking, lived in Aix-en-Provence for two years.

Monica Krippner, *Discovering the Camargue,* London, 1960. Illustrated

Michel Droit, *Camargue,* Chicago, 1963. A picture book

The Riviera

The Michelin Green Guide is available in English.

General travel books are:

- Peter Churchill, *All About the French Riviera,* London, 1960
- Charles Graves, *The Riviera Revisited,* London, 1948. This tells what the area looked like after the devastation of the Second World War.
- Eric Whelpton, *The Road to Nice,* London, 1955
- Ethelind Fearon, *Without My Yacht: How to be at Home in the South of France,* London, 1959
- Warren Hall, *Azure Coast: My Diary of the French and Italian Rivieras,* London, 1952

Out of print but entertaining is C. B. Black's *The Riviera,* an old-fashioned and highly detailed nineteenth-century guidebook.

More specialized are:

George W. Herald and Edward D. Radin, *The Big Wheel: Monte Carlo's Opulent Century,* New York, 1963

General Pierre Polovtsoff, *Monte Carlo Casino,* New York, n.d. but c. 1937 (out of print); written by the man who was then the president of the International Sporting Club.

Jacques Thirion, *Les Peintres Modernes dans les Musées de la Côte d'Azur, La Revue Française,* Paris, 1962; large illustrated pamphlet

Corsica

Michelin has not yet published a guidebook on Corsica, but it covers the hotels and restaurants under the listing "Corse" in its red guide.

The outstanding current book in English is:

Dorothy Carrington, *This Corsica, a Complete Guide,* London, 1962. This is a first-rate book by an author who has lived on the island for nearly 10 years and knows it well.

George Renwick, *Romantic Corsica,* London, 1909, is long out of print but worth trying to find. The author toured Corsica on a bicycle in the days before automobiles reached the island.

Antonie-Marie Pietri, *La Corse.* Hachette's *Encyclopédie par l'Image,* Paris, 1963. An illustrated pamphlet. In French only.

The Alps

The Michelin Green Guide is available in English.

The first of the elaborate and rather expensive *Guides d'Or* to be published by Arthaud is *Savoie* by Bernard Willerval, Paris, 1965. It is exceedingly good. Others on Provence, the Riviera, Brittany, and the Château Country are scheduled to appear later. Arthaud, probably because of its location in Grenoble, has issued several big and expensive picture books on the Alps, *Mont Blanc* and Grenoble among them.

Burgundy

Historical literature on Burgundy is extensive, and there are plenty of books about its wines. But travel writing on the region is regrettably scarce.

The Michelin Green Guide is available in English.

Horizons de France has a text-and-picture book, *Bourgogne,* Paris, 1963.

Evelyn M. Hatch, *Burgundy, Past and Present*, London, 1927, is out of print but your library may have it.

The Jura, Alsace, Lorraine

Two Michelin Green Guides cover this area: *Jura* and also *Vosges, Lorraine, et l'Alsace.* They are available only in French.

Literature on the Jura is scant. It is also scarce for Lorraine except for works about Joan of Arc. The most readable one is *Saint Joan of Arc* by V. Sackville-West, New York, 1936. Intended for young people but with a good short text and superb illustrations is *Joan of Arc* by Jay Williams, New York, 1963.

Most of the books about Alsace deal with its complicated wartime history. Roger Pilkington's *A Small Boat to Alsace,* New York, 1961, may be of interest even to those who go there by automobile.

Champagne and the battlefields of the First World War

The Michelin Green Guides do not cover these areas.

The American Battle Monuments Commission's *American Armies and Battlefields in Europe,* Washington, 1938, gives a thorough account of the part which United States armed forces played in the First World War. Many maps and illustrations. The Commission will supply pamphlets on the Military Cemeteries in France.

The now out-of-print and now eagerly sought-after *Guides Illustrés Michelin des Champs de Bataille* will interest military historians. They were published in French in the early 1920's. Their many illustrations and detailed maps are useful even to those who can't read the language.

Books dealing with the Northwest Channel Coast will be found near the beginning of this list under Normandy.

A list of recommended hotels and restaurants

Since this book is based on the idea of staying in pleasant, well-located central bases while you tour France, we concentrate on hotels that fit into this plan. Places in between, where you are not likely to be staying longer than one night, are not important so we make no suggestions for them unless we know of one that is exceptionally good.

Remember that we usually favor quiet country hotels. Generally speaking, they charge less than city hotels. But this does not apply to fashionable resorts where the most luxurious hotels may be very expensive indeed.

The following table translates our comparative cost ratings into the actual price ranges charged in dollars per day for a room for *two* people with bath and toilet, service and taxes included. This usually means the most expensive room in the house; others naturally cost less. These are 1966 prices and are subject to change. Food and wine are extra.

A bargain—less than $4.00
Low-priced—$4.50 to $7.00
Medium-priced—$7.50 to $12.00
Expensive—$12.50 to $18.00
Very expensive—$18.50 to $30.00
De luxe—more than $30.00

These are high-season prices and will usually apply all year in non-resort areas. In resorts, you may be able to get a reduction during the off-season.

If you find a hotel you like very much and want to stay on

The Manoir du Stang
*Forét-Fouesnant, Brittany**

Château Hôtel du Pray
*Amboise, Château Country**

Hôtel du Bon Laboureur
*Chenonceaux, Château Country**

Hôtel le Vieux Logis
*Tremolat, Perigord**

Hôtel Bonnet
*Beynac, Périgord**

Château de la Caze
Gorges of the Tarn

Rena Bianca
Propriano, Corsica

Baumanière
*Les Baux, Provence**

Hôtel Plein-Soleil
The Alps

Hôtel Saut du Prince Charles
*Saverne, Alsace**

Hôtel Beau-Site
Talloires, the Alps

Château Hôtel de Couvrelles
*Champagne**

* FRENCH GOVERNMENT TOURIST OFFICE

longer than you had planned to, don't wait until the last minute to ask for an extension of your reservation. If you do, you may then find out that your room is booked the day you are expected to leave.

If this happens in an area where the surroundings are more important than the hotel, ask the proprietor to help you find quarters in a place he recommends.

Restaurants

We see no point in telling you about the many excellent low or medium-priced restaurants that can be found almost everywhere in France. In most cases you will probably be dining in your hotel anyway.

The ones we do mention are included because we think there is something outstanding about their quality of food, attractiveness of decor, or superb location. Such restaurants tend to be expensive because good food is dear in France; superlative food, great wines, fine service, and beautiful surroundings cost as much there as they do anywhere in the world.

The fact that a top restaurant is located in the country does not mean that it will necessarily charge less than if it were in a big city. French people will go miles out of their way—or even make special trips—to dine at these noted restaurants. Some gourmets make a tour of them and relish their recollections almost as much as they did the meals they enjoyed there.

You may want to economize on other things and occasionally treat yourself to a meal in one of the really fine restaurants. See, however, our chapters on the food and wines of France, because a reasonably well-trained palate is required to appreciate these at their best. They will be lost on the American steak-and-potatoes man or on his British counterpart who prefers cabbage to artichokes and trifles to truffles. Readers whose doctors have forbidden them to eat rich food or touch any kind of alcoholic beverage are entitled to feel sorry for themselves. Others have a chance to learn how wonderful food and wine can be when served in restaurants that are judged daily by the world's most critical gourmets—their French patrons.

Normandy

East: The better hotels around Honfleur are expensive and are getting more expensive every year. The Roche Vasouy and the Ferme Saint-Siméon, both west of the town, are very good, but they have tripled their prices during the last six years. The Ferme de la Grande Cour on D62 is still in the medium-priced range.

Deauville is even more expensive, but a few places like the Océan and La Fresnaye are medium-priced, while Le Paradis is very reasonable.

Trouville costs less than Deauville, but it is no longer the bargain it used to be. Some medium-priced places are Les Roches and La Maison Normande, both only a block from the beach.

People with plenty of money can get top accommodations in Deauville. Budget travelers are advised to try elsewhere, say in nearby Cabourg or Dives. Except for Cabourg's Grand Hotel, the other hotels there are medium-priced, and some are bargains. The Grand Balcon, where we once stayed, is still low-priced.

West: Carteret's two best hotels are the medium-priced Angleterre and the low-priced Marine.

Mont-Saint-Michel lacks good hotels. We think that the medium-priced Du Gueslin is the best buy there. It is very small and may be booked up.

South: Le Pin-au-Haras has the tiny, very beautiful, but expensive Tourne-Bride. Bagnoles-de-l'Orne has many hotels that range from the expensive Bois Joli to some real bargains. There are even better bargains outside the town where the Manoir du Lys on D235 and the Vallée da la Cour on D387 are best buys.

Restaurants: Normandy's best restaurants are in the interior.

Rouen: La Couronne, La Marée, and the Relais Fleuri
Caen: Le Rabelais and the Alcide
Orbec (20 kilometers or 12 miles southeast of Lisieux on N819): the Canneton, superb and reasonably priced

Alençon (48 kilometers or 30 miles east of Bagnoles on N807 and N12): here the Petit Vatel is another good buy in provincial restaurants.

Brittany

North: Perros-Guirec has two more expensive hotels, but we prefer the medium-priced Roseraie for its quiet location with a view over the beach. Ker-Mor also has its own grounds above the beach and charges the same price. Michelin ignores the Hotel du Sphinx although it is noted for its food. Hotels in some of the smaller towns nearby may cost less than those in Perros-Guirec.

In Roscoff, the low-priced Angleterre has a garden. The Belle-Vue is a bargain.

Central: Huelgoat does not have much choice. The low- to medium-priced Angleterre is the best bet.

West: Morgat has two medium-priced hotels, the Mer and the Grand Hôtel de la Plage, both on the beach. Lower-priced possibilities are the Sainte-Marine, the Julia, and the Baie.

Sainte-Anne-la-Palud has only one hotel, the Plage, with a wide sandy beach and gardens. It is on the high side of medium-priced but is in an attractive and quiet location.

South: Saint-Guénolé on the Penmarc'h peninsula is a low-priced area with half a dozen small hotels. The Saint-Guénolé is the prettiest-looking one of them. The others all fall into the bargain class. The Mer has a one-star restaurant.

Lesconil, a few miles to the east and also on the shore, is another bargain area. The Manoir de Kerlut there, with gardens and a view, is a best buy.

Bénodet is rather expensive for what it has to offer. So is Beg-Meil. As we said in the text, there are far better buys on the Penmarc'h peninsula.

About a mile northwest of La Forêt-Fouesnant is the Manor du Stang which we think is the most beautiful hotel in Brittany. It is an old manor house, well-restored and surrounded by extensive gardens. It is expensive and likely to be booked up.

Carnac's most expensive hotel, the Brittania, is modern and

right on the beach. Michelin stopped listing it in 1966, perhaps because it charges far more than any hotel in the area. The Tumulus is medium-priced, not near the water, but with a good view. The Ker Ihuel, new and on the beach, offers good value.

Le Trinité-sur-Mer has the Voyageurs, which is right in town, but it is known for its good food. Some parts of it have been modernized; some have not.

A bargain can be had in the Gulf of Morbihan area where Larmor-Baden has the fairly new, very plain little Hôtel-Restaurant des Iles with a terrace facing the water. On the Ile aux Moines, which can be reached only by ferry, are the San Francisco and the Hôtel de la Brise; the latter is the better and somewhat more expensive.

Belle-Ile-en-Mer has more than a dozen hotels, nearly all of which are bargains. For the best accommodations try the medium-priced Manoir de Goulphar.

La Baule: what we said about Deauville applies here.

Nantes has the Duchesse Anne where we have stayed several times. The restaurant is excellent.

Restaurants: Brittany has few outstanding restaurants and those it does have are often clustered close together.

North: The Lorand-Barre, with two stars, is on N786, 13 kilometers (8 miles) east of Saint-Brieuc. It is attractively decorated in the old Breton style.

West: The charming little town of Locronan, 10 kilometers (6 miles) east of Douarnenez at the junction of D63 and D7, has the Auberge Saint-Ronan with one star.

South: Pont-Aven, on N783, 15 kilometers (9 miles) east of Concarneau, has the Moulin Rosmadec. And only 5 kilometers east of this, at the junction of N783 and D104 is Riec-sur-Bélon with the restaurant Chez Mélanie. Michelin gives them both two stars.

East: Nantes has several excellent hotel restaurants and La Rôtisserie. Basse-Goulaine, 8 kilometers east of the city on the south shore of the Loire (N751), has two good restaurants, Mon Rêve and the Parc.

The Château Country

West: A very beautiful but expensive place is Le Prieuré in Chênehutte-les-Tuffeaux located on the river 8 kilometers (5 miles) west of Saumur.

Chinon's Boule-d'Or and the Gargantua are low-priced.

Central: De luxe in every way is the Château d'Artigny located in a large park 2 kilometers west of Montbazon. Slightly less expensive is the Domaine de la Tortinière, a castle 1.5 kilometers north of Montbazon. Expensive but not quite as much so is the Choiseul just outside Amboise.

Medium-priced and very good is the Château de Pray in its own park 2 kilometers east of Amboise. Also the Bon Laboureur et Château in Chenonceaux.

Low-priced but likely to be booked up is the little Château de la Haute-Borde on the Loire 13 kilometers (8 miles) east of Amboise.

East: Medium-priced and right across the way from Chambord is Saint-Michel. Also medium-priced and on the Loire is the Château des Colliers in Muides, which is 8 kilometers northeast of Chambord.

Low-priced are La Motte and the Plage (a bargain) in Saint-Dyé, 4 kilometers west of Muides. Both have gardens.

Restaurants: The best ones are in and around Tours where you will find the Barrier and the Lyonnais in town, while the renowned Le Nègre is across the Loire in Saint-Symphorien. Bourges has the Jacques Coeur. Some of the hotel restaurants in this region are excellent.

The Atlantic Coast

North: Les Sables-d'Olonne has many medium-priced hotels and a fair number of inexpensive ones. In the medium range, the Beau Rivage faces the sea and has a good restaurant.

We think that budget travelers will do better in the smaller resorts north and south of here. Saint-Jean-de-Monts has some good buys; Sion-sur-l'Océan is even less expensive. Southward, Jard-sur-Mer, Saint-Vincent-sur-Jard, and La Tranche have great bargains although the accommodations are rather primitive.

Royan has many hotels, but most of them are near the southern beach where the water from the Gironde is muddy. North of the town, in the Conche de Nauzan, is the very beautiful but fairly expensive Résidence de Rohan.

Central: Bordeaux is one of the few large French cities that offers the traveler better than a fair deal. Even its top places are not terribly expensive. Lower-priced possibilities are the Faison (which has recently been modernized), the Français, and the Balzac.

Alouette, 8 kilometers southwest on N650, has the Réserve Etche Ona, which is primarily a good restaurant, but it has some rooms (expensive). In the city, the Dubern and the Château Trompette are the outstanding restaurants, but the Clavel and the Toque Blanche are also very good. The famous Chapon Fin has gone out of business.

Arcachon has all grades of hotels but is on a landlocked bay; east of it is Pyla-sur-Mer on the ocean near the entrance to the bay. It has the medium-priced Beau Rivage and La Guitone, which is a good and not expensive restaurant with some low-priced rooms.

South of this is Pyla-Plage, also on the ocean and much higher priced. Those who don't mind paying top rates may want to investigate Les Brisants which has bungalows in the pines.

South: Mimizan-Plage and Vieux-Boucau have some of the most astounding bargains in France. Naturally, the hotels are very modest. Soustons (inland on a lake) is still low-priced, and it has an excellent and not expensive restaurant, the Pot de Résine. The hotels, La Bergerie and La Pesquite, both have gardens.

Hossegor's best hotels are on the lake although a few low to medium-priced ones are on the ocean beach. Some of the prettier medium-priced ones on the lake (with gardens) are the Parc and the Hermitage, while the Hortensias du Lac (also with a garden) can qualify as a bargain. The Cap-Breton hotels run from bargains to low-priced.

Hotels in the coastal area from Biarritz to the Spanish border cost more than they do farther north. The best ones are de luxe and exceedingly expensive.

One of the best restaurants in this region, the Darroze in Villeneuve-de-Marsan, is far in the interior on N134 at the intersection of D1. You can get there by driving north from Pau or by taking N124 northeast from Bayonne. It is fairly expensive; so are its rooms.

Périgord

West: Les Eyzies-de-Tayac has the well-known medium-priced Cro-Magnon. Try to get a room in the new annex on the side *away* from the railroad. Les Glycines, slightly cheaper, is also very good. Michelin gives a star to the restaurants in both hotels.

Farther west, in Tremolat, is the very expensive Hôtel le Vieux Logi's with garden and all kinds of luxuries—but no stars for its food. South of Les Ezies is Beynac et Cazenac, where the low-priced Hôtel Bonnet has a one-star restaurant.

East: Alvignac-les-Eaux is a small, peaceful country village with several hotels. We prefer the cottage rooms at the low-priced Hôtel du Parc which has a large tree-shaded terrace.

If you don't mind getting up to the cliffside locations, the Belvédère and the Sainte-Marie at Rocamadour are both low in price if not in altitude.

Still farther east, Saint-Céré has the Touring Hôtel in the medium-priced range, while the pleasant Parc et Nord is almost a bargain.

South: In the Cahors area the medium-priced Ambassadeurs is in town; in Larroque-des-Arcs, 5 kilometers east on N653, is the Beau Rivage, which is also medium-priced. It has a garden overlooking the Lot River. The Château de Mercuès, was sold in 1966 to be made into a training place for executives. During its summer vacation, it may have rooms available to the public. Hotels of any kind are scarce south of Cahors, although Montauban and Moissac have a few inexpensive ones.

Restaurants: Despite the fact that Périgord has a justified reputation for fine food, the region has no great—or even fairly great restaurants. You can, however, eat very well in some of the better hotels and sometimes surprisingly well in very modest ones.

Cahors has La Taverne; Souillac, La Vielle Auberge; and Toulouse, La Séville (rather expensive): Michelin rates all of them with one star.

The Pyrenees

West: Saint-Jean-Pied-de-Port is all right for an overnight stay, but its hotels do not amount to much. You will do better at Argelès-Gazost where the most expensive hotel in town is in the lower medium-priced range. Real bargains are the Miramont (new) and the pleasantly decorated Marie-Bernadette.

Luchon is much more expensive. Its hotels are nearly all in the upper ranges. And at nearby Superbagnères they cost even more.

East: Tarascon-sur-Ariège is a good center, but its hotels will win no prizes. The Poste is medium-priced; the Francal is less expensive and well-located on the river but rather old-fashioned in equipment and decor.

Ax-les-Thermes' hotels are in the lower medium-priced range. It also has some bargains. But so does the nearby little republic of Andorra, where only the Parc in Andorre-la-Vielle has recently entered the expensive class by doubling its prices. The Roc Blanc (in Les Escaldes) is in the upper medium-priced range, but all the other Andorra hotels are low-priced and many are bargains or near bargains.

Font-Romeu's Grand Hotel (and others of its class) is on the upper edge of the medium-priced class, and there are few if any bargains there. Tiny Molitg-les-Bains' Thermal Hotel is very expensive indeed.

Roussillon, the Gorges of the Tarn, and Auvergne

South: Although we did not like Collioure, if we had to stay there we would choose the Auberge la Balette, a low-priced hotel that is not near the beaches but has terraces with a fine view. The Casa Païral, medium-priced with a garden, is another possibility.

At Canet-Plage, the best hotel is the medium-priced Mar-I-Cel; the Font et Patio is half the price, while the Regina is a bargain.

In Carcassonne, if you can possibly afford it, stay in the old city, for the hotels in town are overpriced and not very good. The Cité is beautiful and quite expensive; the little Donjon, also in the old city, is in the upper medium-priced range.

Central: The two hotels in Millau with one-star restaurants are the Commerce and the Moderne, both in the heart of the town. Two kilometers west on N592 is the small Château de Creissels with a garden. The Commerce is medium-priced; the other two are on the upper range of being low in price. The Hostellerie du Crès (with a garden) is still lower-priced. The town also has a one-star restaurant, the Capion.

Those who want de luxe accommodations can find them at the fine old Château d'Ayres in Meyrueis, 42 kilometers (26 miles) east of Millau. This twelfth-century castle has a garden and a swimming pool. It is very expensive.

Le Rozier, 21 kilometers (13 miles) northeast of Millau on Route N107*Bis,* has the medium-priced Grand Hôtel du Rozier et de la Muse with a terrace overlooking the Tarn.

La Malène, farther up the Tarn on N107*Bis,* has two fine but expensive places, the Manoir de Montesquiou and the even dearer Château de la Caze.

North: The spas around Mont-Dore have so many hotels that it is hard to choose among them. This is a middle-class area where only two places are above the medium-priced range. And bargains can be had.

La Bourboule's two top hotels are the Ambassadeurs and the Iles Brittaniques, both well inside the medium-priced class.

Mont-Dore's old-fashioned Metropole is expensive, but the Bardet et Régina (with a one-star restaurant), the Thâvenin and Les Sapins (both with gardens) are medium-priced. The very modern Panorama, up on a hill, has balconies with good views and is not expensive.

Saint-Nectaire has the most expensive and luxurious place in this area. This is the sixteenth-century Manoir de Viginet, which is outside the town in its own park. It has only 10 rooms so reservations are essential. The Modern-Hôtel has a one-star restaurant and gives good value to those who stay there *en pension.*

East: Since we do not consider the Lyon-Vienne area to be a desirable base, we are ignoring the many city hotels there and are discussing its restaurants only. See below.

Restaurants: The whole region from the Spanish border north to Roanne has no outstanding restaurants. Michelin awards one star to a few, but that is all. At Roanne, 87 kilometers (54 miles) northwest of Lyon on N7, the Troisgros, with two stars, has some medium-priced rooms. Then, as you approach Lyon, restaurants rated with stars are thicker than in any other place in France (except Paris).

There are two with three stars, Paul Bocuse, 9 kilometers north of Lyon at Collonges-au-Mont d'Or, and Mère Brazier, 21 kilometers west at the Col de la Luère. Mère Brazier also has a place in town to which Michelin gives two stars. Other two-star restuarants in or near Lyon are: Mère Guy, Nandron, Chez Juliette, and La Sauvagie.

There are many with one star. All these ratings, of course, are subject to change from year to year.

At Vienne is the world-famous three-star Pyramide which has a beautiful tree-shaded terrace. For the convenience of its guests, the expensive Résidence de la Pyramide is nearby.

And 11 kilometers south of Vienne on N86 is the two-star Hôtel Beau Rivage at Condrieux on the western shore of the Rhône. It has medium-priced rooms.

Provence

Central: The area here is so small that you can stay in one place and easily cover it all in day trips. Avignon is the most centrally located, but there is much to be said for Arles, Saint-Rémy, and Les Baux.

People who don't care about the expense can stay at Le Prieuré in Villeneuve-lès-Avignon, a very beautiful old building with a central court and gardens, or at Baumanière in Les Baux. It has a three-star restaurant. Under the same ownership is the nearby medium-priced Cabro d'Or.

Villeneuve-lès-Avignon also has the somewhat expensive Hostellerie Provençale du Vieux Moulin with a terrace overlooking the river.

In Avignon the Europe charges as much as Le Prieuré and Baumanière, but it is not so well located or attractive. In this luxury class, the pretty and very quiet Auberge de Noves, near the place where N7 crosses the Durance River, is the best buy. It has a three-star restaurant and rooms that cost less than those in the other top establishments do.

Also in Avignon is the low-priced Auberge de France with a one-star restaurant.

The budget traveler no longer has an easy time in Provence. He can find some hotels—not very attractive ones—in the cities, but he will do better in small towns like Carpentras, Cavallon, Châteaurenard, or in somewhat larger places like Tarascon or Beaucaire.

There are reasonably priced but old-fashioned hotels in Saint-Rémy, but the modern *pavillons* in the garden of Les Antiques are now on the expensive side.

In Arles, the top place is the Jules César, a rather elegant and fairly expensive hotel and restaurant. The medium-priced Touring Hotel (with no restaurant) has some very attractive newly decorated rooms and baths.

North: Vaison-la-Romaine has the very pleasantly located medium-priced Hostellerie le Beffroi, a sixteenth-century house with tree-shaded terraces, a view, and a good restaurant. Bargains, or near-bargains, can be found in town.

East: Roussillon has come up a long way since Laurence Wylie wrote about it in *Village in the Vaucluse* in 1957. It now has the upper medium-priced Rose d'Or and the David, a restaurant that Michelin rates with a star.

Aix-en-Provence has a number of quite expensive hotels. In the medium range are the Nègre-Coste and the Moderne. Bargains exist but are hard to find. One near-bargain is the Hôtel Saint-Victoire. Meyrargues, 15 kilometers (9 miles) north of Aix on N97, has the Château de Meyrargues with a two-star restaurant, a garden, and some expensive rooms.

Marseille is a good place to visit and to eat in, but is too big, noisy, and traffic-jammed to use as a base.

Restaurants: All the better hotels we have listed have good restaurants, some of them very good indeed. In addition to these, Avignon has the two-star Hiély-Lucullus. In Orange, the Provençal has one star.

In Châteauneuf-du-Pape is the well-known Mule du Pape,

to which Michelin gives one star. It gives none to Chez la Mère Germaine which has a small terrace and a view.

Aix-en-Provence's Le Vendôme is a beautiful pavilion surrounded by a terrace. Michelin gives it only one star, but it is very good.

In Marseille, Guido's specializes in *bouillabaisse*. Michelin gives it one star as it also does to the New-York, Calypso, Michel-Brasserie des Catalans, and Chez Fonfon. Panoramique Saint-Georges has no stars, but it is nicely located with a view.

The Riviera

West: Le Lavandou's Auberge La Calanque, with a garden, is medium-priced. Slightly cheaper and also with a garden is La Bastide in nearby Saint-Clair. Sur le Port is a not too expensive one-star restaurant.

The Saint-Raphael area has many medium-priced hotels and some lower-priced ones. In the medium range are: Saint-Raphael's Ile d'Azur (with a garden), nearby Boulouris' La Potinière (with a terrace), and Agay's Baumette. Agay (11 kilometers east of Saint-Raphael) also has some bargains, notably the Beau Site, the Robinson Crusoë, and the Hôtel du Débarquement.

Central: La Napoule, which used to be a good medium-priced resort, has recently become expensive. It now has two two-star restaurants, Mère Terrats and L'Oasis.

Cannes has hotels of all grades, most of them expensive, although a few are medium priced. You will have to hunt for bargains in areas far from the beach.

Antibes' best hotel, the Royal (on the water) is medium-priced. The others charge even less.

Antibes is a middle-class resort, but Cap d'Antibes is one of the most fashionable and expensive places on the Riviera. Its Hôtel du Cap d'Antibes is fantastically dear, but you can use its celebrated and luxurious Pavillon Eden Roc restaurant and seaside pool by paying an entrance fee while you stay in a less costly hotel nearby. There are several good ones, most of them inland, but a few are on the water at the Plage de la Garoupe.

Nice has plenty of famous, very expensive hotels on The Promenade des Anglais. Not far away and also on the sea are the medium-priced Beau-Rivage and the Suisse. There are low-priced hotels—even bargains—in the town, but we hesitate to list any. With a car, you will do better outside.

Cap Ferrat, like Cap d'Antibes, is a fashionable resort, but it has several good places that are not expensive. The medium-priced Résidence de la Robbia, although not near the sea, has a garden and a one-star restaurant. It is small, so reservations well in advance are essential. Even less expensive is Le Clair Logis, a pension in a large and beautiful garden.

For those who can pay the very high price, this area has some top hotels: the Grand on Cap Ferrat with a seaside swimming pool; the very fine Réserve with a two-star restaurant, and the Métropole, both in Beaulieu. And Monte-Carlo's famous Hôtel de Paris, with a two-star restaurant, is only 11 kilometers away.

Monte-Carlo also has some good medium-priced hotels, notably La Réserve et Suisse, the Alexandra, and the Helder. The Hôtel de la Poste is a bargain.

East: Menton's relatively new and very pleasant medium-priced Vendôme is on the water. The Hôtel du Parc, also medium-priced, is located in a large and quiet garden. If you want a fine view and don't mind the very steep road going up to it, the Pins, high up above the town, is another medium-priced hotel.

Inland: Vence is interesting, but its hotels are not. On a hill north of the town is the very beautiful and super de luxe Château du Domaine Saint-Martin.

Saint-Paul-de-Vence has many good hotels, some inexpensive ones in the walled village, and more expensive ones just outside. The Auberge Colombe d'Or is costly but worth it. In the same price class is La Résidence, while Les Oliviers, with a one-star restaurant, is just above the medium range.

Restaurants: The better hotels, particularly the Réserve in Beaulieu, the Paris in Monte-Carlo, and the Colombe d'Or in Saint-Paul, all have noted restaurants.

Eze has the Chèvre d'Or with a panoramic view over the

coast. At La Brague, 4 kilometers north of Antibes on N7, is La Bonne Auberge with two stars.

Corsica

Some of the small Corsican towns have little hotels where the rooms are amazingly cheap. Pension rates may be triple the cost of the room. This usually means that the accommodations are very primitive. Examine the rooms carefully before you commit yourself.

North: Miomo, 5 kilometers north of Bastia on N198, has the new medium-priced Sablettes with a terrace overlooking the sea.

West: L'Ile-Rousse has the very modern La Pietra in the upper medium-priced bracket.

Calvi's Grand Hotel is expensive, but its Résidence des Aloës, the Kallisté, and the Clos des Amandiers are medium-priced, new, and very good.

Porto has many small hotels, many of them in the lower-priced range, but you should examine them and see for yourself whether any of them is what you want. The Kallisté and the Marina are somewhat better than most; they are in the medium-priced range.

Ajaccio's in-town hotels of all prices are old-fashioned and unattractive. With a car you can stay in one of the new hotels along the coast near the city. The Hotel du Cap at Porticcio, 18 kilometers south on D55, is very beautiful—and very expensive. Nearer are the new and very good upper medium-priced Dolce Vita and the Cala di Sole on the Route des Sanguinaires (N193B). Budget travelers should shop in town for inexpensive hotels.

Propriano's Arena Bianca is new and right on the beach. The Roc é Mara is also. And across the bay is the equally new beach hotel, Marinca. They are all in the medium-priced range and offer good value.

Inland: Corte is a small and inexpensive resort where the low-priced Hôtel de la Paix is the best in town. There are a few others which are still cheaper.

Restaurants: In Corsica, you will usually do best to dine in your hotel. L'Ile-Rousse has L'Auberge-Chevallier which Michelin gives one star. It is the only restaurant on the entire island so honored. But we ate well in Bastia's La Concorde.

The Alps

South: Although we don't think that Grenoble is a good base, it is an interesting city with several excellent restaurants in the vicinity. We stayed at the modernized, medium-priced Angleterre. Lesdiguières is more expensive, but it may be of interest because it is a training place for students of the École Hôtelière des Alpes Françaises.

Central: Talloires, in addition to being a superb base in which to stay, has hotels of every kind and price from the Père Bise with a three-star restaurant and the big, plush Abbaye with a one-star restaurant, to low-priced small hotels like the Auberge Chamois, Ma Campagne, and the Dents de Lanfon. Medium-priced and beautifully located on extensive grounds running down to Lake Annecy, is the Beau Site, one of our favorites.

The Sallanches area, with its superb views of Mont Blanc, is fine for budget travelers. In Cordon, Les Sonnailles is a real bargain. The Roches Fleuries costs a little more but not much. On a steep road just outside Sallanches is the Crémaillière, also a bargain.

But Combloux, we think, has the best views of all. There the Plein Soleil is a modern, medium-priced hotel built in the Alpine style with balconies running around it. Some Combloux hotels have no views; this one has—and a very fine one.

Both Megève and Les Contamines-Montjoie are down in valleys from which you cannot see the mountains. Megève is a high-priced area where most of the hotels give poor value. If you want luxury accommodations you can get them there, especially at the super-de-luxe Mont d'Arbois. Les Contamines-Montjoie is a middle-class resort with medium-priced hotels and even a few bargains.

Chamonix has hotels of all grades, mostly in the medium or upper-price ranges. There are lower-priced hotels but practically no bargains. In quiet areas of the town the Mont-Blanc would be our choice for a fairly expensive hotel, and La

Savoyarde for a medium-priced one. The Savoy is the top luxury place.

North: Yvoire's best bet is Les Flots Bleus, a low-priced hotel right on the lake. It is usually well booked up. Les Falaises et Plage is on the heights above the lake. It is not expensive, but its restaurant is better than its rooms. The little Hôtel et Restaurant du Port was being renovated when we saw it last.

Restaurants: The best restaurants are in and around Grenoble, where the two-star Rostang is in nearby Sassenage, while the one-star Poularde Bressane is in town. The Bec Fin is also very good. Varces, 13 kilometers south on N75, also has a two-star restaurant, the Brunet.

On Lake Annecy you have, in addition to the fine hotel restaurants, the two-star Pavillon Ermitage in Chavoire, the one-star Garcin in Talloires, and the Auberge de Savoie in the city of Annecy.

Megève has two one-star restaurants, The Toque Blanche and La Gérentière which is a Relais de Campagne with some expensive rooms. In Chamonix the Relais Carlton also has a star.

Yvoire has no outstanding place to eat, but in nearby Messery is the one-star Terrasse Fleurie; in Thonon, the one-star Clos Savoyard; and in Evian, the Bourgogne.

Burgundy

South: Solutré is 9 kilometers west of Macon on N79 and D54. The medium-priced Relais Solutré is a former vineyard manor house which was recently modernized and converted into a small hotel. The restaurant is a *rôtisserie* with an enormous charcoal grill built along one wall.

Cluny's medium-priced Hotel Bourgogne is on the square next to the Abbey. Michelin rates the similarly priced Moderne higher and gives it one star, but it is less well located and is near the railroad station.

Central: Beaune's Hôtel de la Poste, with a one-star restaurant, is quite expensive. Medium-priced places are the Marché, also with a one-star restaurant, and Le Home, outside the town and newly renovated. The Auberge Bourguignonne is in town and a bargain.

Avallon has the famous and very expensive Hôtel de la Poste with a three-star restaurant that people travel far to get to. The medium-priced Chapeau Rouge gives good value while the Centre is in the near-bargain class. In nearby Vézelay, the Poste et Lion d'Or, with a one-star restaurant, has raised its prices every year until it is now almost as expensive as Avallon's Poste. Châtillon-sur-Seine's Côte d'Or, with a two-star restaurant, is expensive, but not terribly so. The Sylvia, located outside the town in a walled garden, is still medium-priced. It has no restaurant, so you can dine at the Côte d'Or.

In addition to these centers, good hotels can be found in Tournus, Verdun-sur-le-Doubs, Arnay-le-Duc, Saint-Honoré-les-Bains, and Autun.

Restaurants: Except for Paris and the region around Lyon, Burgundy has more excellent eating places than any other part of France. Avallon has its only three-star restaurant, but the Côte d'Or in Saulieu is very good. It recently lost its three-star rating when there was a change in management so it now has only two. Other two-star restaurants in Burgundy, in addition to those listed with hotels, are the Gare in Montbard, the Paris et Poste in Sens, and the Auberge Bressane in Brou (near Bourg).

One-star restaurants are so numerous in Burgundy that there is no point listing them. And there are so many good, plain little restaurants that some towns have three or four of them.

The Jura, Alsace, and Lorraine

The Jura: Arbois has two excellent low to medium-priced hotels with one-star restaurants, the Messageries and the Hôtel de Paris. The restaurant called La Balance recently lost the star which Michelin had given it, but you can probably still eat well there.

Alsace: There is no shortage of good country hotels in Alsace, but we are mentioning only a few. Les Trois-Épis has the medium-priced Marchal and the Grand Hôtel, while the Croix d'Or is a bargain.

Three kilometers west of Saverne on N4 is the Hostellerie Saut du Prince Charles, which is a bargain in every sense of the word.

In Sainte-Odile, the big convent Hôtellerie du Mont-Sainte-Odile is beautifully located and gives great value for its plain but comfortable rooms.

Strasbourg is a problem. It is a best buy for restaurants where the food is as good as the prices are reasonable. But hotels are another matter. There are four expensive ones (of which the Sofitel is the newest), a dozen or more medium-priced ones, and scores of bargains or near-bargains. We didn't care for any. If you concentrate on food rather than on accommodations, you will get good value.

Restaurants: In Strasbourg, the beautiful, richly decorated, and very old Maison Kammerzell is the place to start even though Michelin gives it no stars. But it does to the famous Crocodile, the fairly-expensive Rôtisserie Aubette, the Valentin-Sorg, the Zimmer, the Bristol, and the Gourmet Sans Chiqué. We like the handsome old Maison des Tanneurs and the Petite France.

In Colmar, the Maison des Têtes and Chez Albert are good places to eat. And 8 kilometers to the northwest is Ammerschwihr with the two-star Aux Armes de France. Another, the Auberge d'Ill, is at Illhaeusern, 17 kilometers north of Colmar.

Lorraine has Les Vannes, a two-star restaurant in Liverdum, 15 kilometers northwest of Nancy. And Nancy has the expensive two-star Rôtisserie des Cordelières and the less costly one-star Capucin Gourmand.

Champagne and the Battlefields of the First World War

East: Verdun's Hôtel Bellevue and the Coq Hardi both have one-star restaurants. The first one is rather expensive, while the second is medium-priced. There are no real bargains here, but there are a few low-priced hotels.

Central: Reims has no fine hotels—only medium-priced and inexpensive ones. The Univers is as good as any. The old-fashioned Bristol, where we once stayed, is slightly less expensive. Épernay's Royal Champagne is 21 kilometers south of Reims. It is small and expensive—but good. And it has a restaurant to which Michelin gives one star.

Between Reims and Soissons, on Route 31 near Braine, is the Château de Couvrelles with only 10 rooms, but they are medium-priced.

West: Amiens, like Reims, has no really fine hotels. Its best, the Grand Hôtel, is in the medium-priced range and should get credit for not having raised prices as much as most French hotels have. There are numerous low-priced hotels but few bargains here.

Restaurants: Amiens has three to which Michelin gives a star, the Godbert, the Joséphine, and the Royal. Reims has the Florence with one star. And 2.5 kilometers south on N51 is La Chaumière also with one star. And, as we have said, Épernay's Royal Champagne has a star.

The North Channel Coast

North: Le Touquet-Paris-Plage has several very expensive hotels, the Westminster and the Mer among them. Nearby is Manoir Hôtel et Golf Club. It is expensive but not terribly so. The Motel du Touquet, which is also near the golf course, charges more. Facing the sea is the relatively modern Hôtel de la Plage which is in the lower medium-priced range.

South: At Puys, 3 kilometers east of Dieppe on D113, is the small, quiet, medium-priced Auberge du Vieux Puits. Budget travelers should try Veules-les-Roses, Saint-Valéry-en-Caux, Veulettes-sur-Mer, or Les Petites-Dalles. Most of the hotels there are no longer true bargains, but they still offer good value.

Étretat has the medium-priced Golf Hôtel-Dormy House with a fine view of the sea. In town is the Rôtisserie de la Résidence, big and old-fashioned but with good food. It is medium-priced—or was when we were there. It no longer posts its prices.

Restaurants: Le Touquet's Flavio-Club de la Florêt has one star and is in a good location. Fécamp's one-star Auberge de la Rouge specializes in seafood. Yport, which is between Fécamp and Étretat, also has a one-star restaurant, Le Deun.

Index

Abbeville, 482
Abélard and Héloïse, 202
accidents on the road, 110-12
Adams, Henry, 134, 156, 159
Agincourt, 481
Aiguebelle, 357
Aigues-Mortes, 323
Aiguille du Midi, 416
airplane baggage allowance, 49-51
Aisne-Marne military cemetery, 475
Aix-en-Provence, 214, 323, 345-48
Aix-les-Bains, 403, 406, 411
Ajaccio, 382, 390-93
Albert, 477
Albert I, Prince of Monaco, 376
Albertville, 403
Albi, 133, 253, 255, 282-83
Albigensian crusade, 307-8
Aleria, 399
alignments of menhirs, 191-92, 195-97
Alise-Sainte-Reine, 434
Aloxe-Corton (wine), 426
Alpe-d'Huez, L', 416
Alphonso of Aragon, 397
Alps, the, 402-21
  cheese of, 421
  description of, 402-3
  food of, 421
  wines of, 95, 421
Alsace, 118, 450-61
  bases to stay in, 444
  description of, 444
  food of, 464
  Nazis in, 450
  storks of, 452
  wine of, 93-94, 465
Alvignac, 255, 272-73
Alyscamps, Les (cemetery in Arles), 327
Amboise, 210, 212
American cemeteries (*see* cemeteries)
Amiens, 466, 478
Ammerschwihr, 455
Andelys, Les, 143
Andorra, 286, 296, 298
Angers, 210-12
Angon, 408
Angoulême, 243
Anne of Brittany, 205-6, 219, 220, 222, 223
Annecy, 403, 406-7, 409
Annecy, Lake, 406, 407, 410
Antibes, 356, 365-66, 371
antipope in Avignon, 336
Apt, 343
Arbois, 444, 447
Arc, Jeanne d' (*see* Joan of Arc)
Arc-et-Senans, 447-48
Arcachon, 247
architecture, 131-35 (*see also* Gothic and Romanesque architecture)
Arette, 290
Argelès, 302
Argelès-Gazost, 291
Argentau, 164
Arles, 189, 323, 326-29, 333
armagnac, 242-43
Arras, 479
Arromanches, 152
Artois, 480
Arundy, 290
association as a memory aid, 129
Atlantic Coast, the, 235-52
  central bases of, 236
  description of, 235
  food and wine of, 251-52
Aubusson, 243-44
Aucassin and Nicolette, 332
August, traveling in, 64, 121-22
Auray, 190, 203

Autoire, 274
automobiles, 100-13
  accidents, 110-11
  average daily mileage, 106
  baggage in, 56, 64
  buying, leasing, or renting, 46-48
  driver's licenses for, 48
  driving at night, 112-13
  expenses for, 36
  gasoline (*essence*), 113
  headlights, 113
  hierarchy of the road, 104-5
  horns, 113
  insurance for, 46
  nationality plaques for, 45
  number of, 111
  parking, 111-12
  police and, 109-10
  right of way, 103-4
  road repairs, 109
  road signs, 101-3, 107
  roads, 106-7
  second-hand, 47
  shipping, 45
  speed, 105-107-9
  traffic, 109
  travel, 126
Autun, 432-33
Auvergne, region of, 302, 315-17
Auxerre, 439-40
Avallon, 422, 433, 435-36
Avignon, 323, 328, 335-38
  Popes and antipopes of, 336-38
Avignon School of painting, 336-38
Avranches, 156-57
Ax-les-Thermes, 286, 296, 298
Azay-le-Rideau, 212
Azé, 425

baggage, 49-51, 56, 63
  camera gear, 57
  in car, 64
Bagnères-de-Bigorre, 293
Bagnoles-de-l'Orne, 165
Baker, Josephine, 266
Ballon d'Alsace, 450
Balzac, Honoré de, 209, 221, 237, 243
Bandol, 357
banks
  business hours of, 39, 120
  keeping an account in France, 40
Banyuls-sur-Mer, 302
Bapaume, 477
Bar-le-Duc, 467
Baracci, 393
Barcelonette, 403
Baring-Gould, S., 360
Barsac, 246
Bartholdi, Frédéric August, 449
Basques, the, 287-88
  food of, 300
Bastia, 382, 385-88, 399
Bastia airport, 400
bastides, 264-65
bathing, 148-49
bathing suits, 55
Battlefields of the First World War, 466-79
  bases to stay in, 466
battles of the Somme, 477
Baudelaire, Charles, 292
Baugé, 214
Baule, La, 204-5
Baux, Les, 217, 329-30
Bayeux, 142, 161-64
Bayonne, 248
Beaucaire, 332-33
Beaugency, 211, 230
Beaujolais, 91
Beaujolais vineyards, 423-24
Beaulieu, 374, 375
Beaune, 99, 422, 426-30, 433, 440
Beaune (wine), 426
Beauregard, 228
Beauvais, 466
Becket, Thomas à, 157, 164, 216, 272, 440, 476, 481
Belfort 447 449, 450
Belle-Ile, 200
Belleau Wood, 475
Belleville, 423
Bergerac, 255
Bergheim, 455
Bernadette of Lourdes, 161, 291
Besançon, 448-49
Bête de Gévaudan, 313
Beynac, 255, 265, 267
Béziers, 307-8
Biarritz, 249-51
bicycles, 109
Biot, 366-67
Blanc, François, 375
Blois, 212, 213, 226-28
bocage, 160
Bonifacio, 382, 396-97
Bonnard, Pierre, 413
Bonneville, 419
Bordeaux, 236, 244-46, 251
Bordeaux (wines), 89, 99

bori, 344
Bort-les-Orgues, 317
Boswell, James, 388
Boudin, Eugène Louis, 147
bouillabaisse, 350, 380
Boulogne, 482
Bourboule, La, 302, 316
Bourdelle, Antoine, 280-81
Bourg-en-Bresse, 422
Bourg-Madame, 298, 299
Bourges, 232, 437
Braque, Georges, 368, 413
bread, 74-75
Bresse, 422
Bresse, poulet de, 442
Brest, 182-84
Briançon, 403
Brittany, 167-209
  bases to stay in, 167
  calvaries of, 167
  climate of, 167-68, 191
  description of, 167-70
  food and wine of, 207
  megaliths of, 191-97, 201-2
  pardons of, 181, 183, 203
  people of, 168-69
  place names of, 170-71
Brocéliande, Forest of, 204
Brou, 422
Brougham, Lord, 354
budget travel, 37
Bulfinch, Charles, 334
bullfights, 326
Burgundy, 422-43
  bases to stay in, 423, 433
  description of, 433
  food of, 442-43
  Romanesque architecture in, 131
  wines of, 91, 442
buying in Europe, 51-52

Cabbé, 372
Cabourg, 142, 150-51
Cabrerets, 276
Cadillac, 246
Caen, 142, 161-63
Caesar, Julius, 360, 434
Cagnes, 367
Cahors, 255, 256, 279-80, 448
Calais, 482
Calanques, rocks of the, 391
Calder, Alexander, 368
calvaries, 177-79
  Brasparts, 179
  Confort, 186
  Guehenno, 203
  Guimiliau, 179
  La Martyre, 179
  Pencrau, 179
  Pleyben, 179
  Plougastel-Daoulas, 179, 183
  Plougonven, 177
  Plovau, 187
  Quilinen, 184
  Saint-Thégonnec, 179
  Saint-Vennec, 184
  Tronoën, 187
Calvi, 382, 387, 389-91
Camargue, 325
  beef from, 352
Cambrai, 479
cameras, 57
camping, 72, 354
Candes, 215
Canebière (Marseille), 349
Canet-Plage, 287, 302
canned food, 76
Cannes, 354, 361-62, 374, 403
Cap-Breton, 248
Cap Corse, 387, 388
Cap d'Antibes, 364, 366
Cap de la Chèvre, 183
Cap de la Croisette, 362
Cap Ferrat, 355, 356, 373-75
Cap Fréhel, 173
Cap Gris-Nez, 482
Cap Gros Nez, 356-57
Cap Martin, 356
Capraja, 388
Carcassonne, 302, 303-5
Cargèse, 392
Carnac, 191, 194-96, 201, 203
carnival, 371
Carpentras, 342
Carrenac, 274, 285
Carrier, Jean-Baptiste, 206
Carrington, Dorothy, 384
carte verte (automobile insurance), 46, 111
Carteret, 142, 156
Cartier, Jacques, 147
Casals, Pablo, 300
cashier's checks, 39
Cassis, 356
Castellane, 380
Castellar, 380
Castellaras, 363
Castelnau, 274
Castillon, 380
Castres, 307

Cathars, the, 295, 308
cathedrals, 133-35
  Agde (Saint-Étienne), 309
  Aix-en-Provence (Saint-Sauveur), 346
  Amiens, 478
  Autun (Saint-Lazare), 433
  Auxerre (Saint-Étienne), 439
  Bayeux, 164
  Beauvais, 303
  Bordeaux (Saint-André), 244
  Bourges, 232
  Cahors (Saint-Étienne), 280
  Chartres, 459
  Clermont-Ferrand (Notre-Dame, 318
  Coutances, 156
  Dijon (Notre-Dame), 431
  Dijon (Saint-Bénigne), 431
  Evreux, 161
  Laon, 477
  Lisieux, 161
  Marseille (Major), 350
  Narbonne (Saint-Just), 303
  Orléans (Saint-Croix), 231
  Perigueux (Saint-Front), 256
  Poitiers (Saint-Pierre), 236
  Puy, Le (Chapelle Saint-Michel-Aiguilhe), 313
  Reims, 472
  Saint-Claude (Saint-Pierre), 446
  Saint-Lô, 160
  Saintes (Saint-Pierre), 240
  Sens (Saint-Étienne), 439
  Soissons (Saint-Gervais), 476
  Strasbourg (Notre-Dame), 459
  Tours (Saint-Gatien), 222
  Tronoën, 187
causse, 255, 270, 272-73, 310
Cauterets, 291, 292
Cavaillon, 332
Cavaillon melons, 352
Cavalaire, 357
Cavallo, 397
caves, 253, 256
  Arcy-sur-Cure, 439
  Aven Armand, 311
  Bédheillac, 296
  Cap Blanc, 261
  Combarelles, Les, 260-61
  Cougnac, 264, 269-70
  Domme, 267
  Font-de-Gaume, 259, 260
  Gargas, 294
  Labouiche, 297
  Lascaux, 253, 262, 278, 424
  Lombrive, 297
  Mas-d'Azil, 294-95
  Menton grottos, 380
  Mouthe, La, 259, 260
  Niaux, 296
  Pech-Merle, 264, 276-78
  Rouffignac, 256-58
cemeteries, military (U. S.)
  Aisne-Marne, 475
  American Cemetery (near Thiaucourt), 468
  Romagne-sous-Montfaucon, 469
  Saint-Laurent, 153
central-base hotel system, 13-14, 141-42
Centuri, 387, 388
Cerbère, 302
Cerdagne (region), 300
Cézanne, Paul, 347, 348
Chablais, Le, 420
Chablis, 91, 440
Chablis (wine), 91, 442
Chagall, Marc, 368, 413
Chalons, 426
Chambertin (wine), 426
Chambèry, 403, 405, 406
Chambord, 210, 212, 213, 220
Chamonix, 403, 406, 411, 412, 414, 416
Champagne (region), 466, 474
Champagne (wine), 90, 92
  making of, 474-75
Champagnole, 447
Champlain, Samuel de, 147
Chanteloup, Pagoda of, 224
Chantilly, 466
chaos, 184
Chaos de Montpellier-le-Vieux, 311
Chaos de Targasonne, 299
chapels (*see* churches and chapels)
Charlemagne, 288, 304-5
Charles VII, 211, 217, 221, 223, 472
Charles VIII, 219, 220, 222, 224
Charles Martel, 236, 273
Charolles, 425
Chartres, 231, 437
Château Country, the, 131, 209, 210-34
  food and wine, 233-34
  list of its châteaux, 214-32
château de plaisance, 211
château fort, 211, 295

Château Lafite-Rothschild (wine), 246
Château Latour (wine), 246
Château Margaux (wine), 246
Château Mouton-Rothschild (wine), 246
Château-Thierry, 475-76
Chateaubriand, François René, vicomte de, 172, 292
Châteauneuf-du-Pape (wine), 338, 339
châteaux
  Allinges, 420
  Amboise, 210, 212
  Angers, 210-12
  Azay-le-Rideau, 212
  Baugé, 214
  Beaugency, 211, 230
  Beauregard, 228
  Blois, 212, 213, 226-28
  Caze, de la, 312
  Chambord, 210, 212, 213, 220
  Chaumont, 226
  Chenonceaux, 210, 212, 213
  Cheverny, 212, 213, 228-29
  Chinon, 211-13
  Clos de Vougeot, 430
  Gaillard, 143-44
  Gien, 210, 232
  Gontaut-Biron, 276
  Haut-Koenigsbourg, 455
  If, 350
  Labrede, 246
  Langeais, 144, 211, 212
  Loches, 211, 212
  Lordat, 297
  Montal, 274
  Montsoreau, 215
  Plessis-Bourré, 214-15
  Plessis-lès-Tours, 212, 222
  Punta, 393
  Saché, 221
  Saint-Bernard, 411
  Saumur, 210, 215
  Sully-sur-Loire, 232
  Ussé, 220
  Valençay, 229
  Vendôme, 213
  Villandry, 212
  Yquem, 246
Châteaux-Hôtels, 67
Châtillon-sur-Seine, 127, 422, 440-41
Chaumont, 226
cheese, 83, 85, 165
Chenonceaux, 210, 212, 213
Chenove, 431
Cherbourg, 156
Chevalier, Guillaume, 293
Cheverny, 212, 213, 228-29
Chinon, 211-13, 463
churches and chapels, 55
  architecture of, 131-35
  Arles (Saint-Honorat), 327
  Arles (Saint-Trophîme), 328
  Aix-en-Provence (Sainte-Marie-Madeleine), 347
  Auxerre (Saint-Germain), 439
  Avallon (Saint-Lazare), 436
  Bar-le-Duc (Saint-Pierre), 467
  Beaune (Notre-Dame), 429
  in Brittany, 181
  Caen (Saint-Pierre), 163
  Candes (Saint-Martin), 215
  Cannes (Notre-Dame-de-l'Espérance), 362
  Clermont-Ferrand (Basilique de Notre-Dame-du-Port), 318
  near Contamines-Montjoie (Notre-Dame-de-la-Gorge), 417
  Dijon, 431
  near Domrémy (Basilique de Bois-Chenu), 463
  Evreux (Saint-Taurin), 161
  as fortresses, 133
  near Greux (Notre-Dame de Bermont), 463
  Loches (Saint-Ours), 223
  Marseille (Basilique de Notre-Dame-de-la-Garde), 350
  Marseille (Saint-Victor), 350
  Moissac (Saint-Pierre), 132, 255, 268, 280-82, 437
  Orcines, 317
  Orcival, 317
  Poitiers (Notre-Dame-la-Grande), 236
  Poitiers (Saint-Jean), 236
  Poitiers (Sainte-Radegonde), 236
  near Ronchamp (Notre-Dame-du-Haut), 449
  Royat, 317
  Saint-Benoît (Saint-Benoît-sur-Loire), 231-32
  Saint-Giles-du-Gard, 325
  Sainte-Mère-Église, 154-56
  Saint-Nazaire (Basilique), 305
  Saint-Père-sous-Vezelay (Notre-Dame), 437

Saint-Piérre (Villefranche), 373
Saint-Pol-de-Léon (Kreisker), 176
Saint-Raphael (Templars), 360
Saint-Savin-sur-Gartempe, 325
Saintes (Saint-Eutrope), 240
Sarlat, 265, 267-68
Saulieu (Basilique Saint-Andoche), 433
Semur-en-Auxois (Notre-Dame), 434
Souillac, 256, 268
Strasbourg (Saint-Thomas), 461
Tournus (La Madeleine), 426
Tournus (Saint-Philibert), 426
Troyes (Sainte-Madeleine), 440
Vence (Rosaire), 369
Verdun, 297
Vézelay (Sainte-Madeleine), 437, 439
votive offerings in, 147
Cimiez, 369, 371, 372
Cinq-Mars-la-Pile, 220
Ciotat, La, 356
Cirque de Baumes, 312
Cirque de Gavarnie, 291
Cirque de Navacelles, 310
civil servants, 119
Clermont-Ferrand, 302, 313, 315, 317-18
Clews, Henry, 361
climate, 23, 117, 142
Clos de Vougeot, 431
Club Méditerranée, 67
Cluny, 422, 425
Cluses, 412, 419
Cocteau, Jean, 373, 379
Coeur, Jacques, 232
Cognac, 240-43
Col d'Aubisque, 290
Col de Bavella, 398-99
Col de la Faucille, 445-46
Col de la Haute Croix, 403
Collioure, 287
Colmar, 450-53, 455
Colombières gardens, 379
Combloux, 406, 413
Compiègne, 466, 476
Condamine, La, 376
Confort, 186
Confrérie des Chevaliers du Tastevin, 431
Conques, 132, 275
Conquet, Le, 182
Contamines-Montjoie, 417
continental breakfasts, 73
cooking in France, 82
Corbusier, Le (*see* Le Corbusier)
Cordes, 255
Cordon, 412
Corneille, Pierre, 146
Corniche Inférieure, 372
(Moyenne Corniche, 372)
Corniche Sublime, 380
Corot, Camille Jean-Baptiste, 147, 474
Corsica, 382-401
climate of, 383
description of, 385
driving in, 385
food and wine of, 400-1
getting to, 383
population of, 385
costs, 35-38
reducing, 37
Côte d'Azur, 353
Côte de Beaune, 91
Côte de Nuits, 91
Côte-d'Or, 91, 422, 426-27, 430-31
Côte Fleurie, 141, 148
Côte-Rôtie, 339
Côte Sauvage, La, 198-200
Côte Vermeille, 302
Cotentin peninsula, 142, 156-57
Côtes du Rhône, 93
Count of Monte-Cristo, 350
Coursegoules, 369
Crécy, 481
credit cards, 41
crêpes, 185-86, 200
Cro-Magnon man, 259
Croisic, Le, 205
cromlechs, 193
croupiers, 377, 378
crusades, 22-23, 318, 323, 437, 438
Cubism, 367
Customs, U.S., 41-44
Courbet, Gustave, 147, 449, 484

Daniel, Glyn, 258
Dantès, Edmond, 350
Daubigny, Charles Pierre, 147
Daudet, Alphonse, 329, 332
Daumier, Honoré, 350
Deauville, 142, 148-50
departments, 208-9
names of, 26
Désert des Agriates, 388, 389
Devinière, La, 216
Diane of Poitiers, 226

Dieppe, 482, 483
diets, special, 82
Digne, 380, 403
Dijon, 430, 431, 442
Dinan, 171-72
Dinard, 171-72, 176
Disque Obligatoire (for parking), 111-12
Dives-sur-Mer, 150-51
Divonne, 445, 446
Dole, 444
dolmens, 193, 197, 201, 395
Domme, 265, 267
Domrémy, 145, 462-63, 464, 473
Donville-les-Bains, 156
Dordogne River, 253, 317
Douarnenez, 185, 187
drip-dry clothes, 53, 63
driving (*see* automobiles)
dry cleaning, 53
Dumas, Alexandre, 292, 350, 482
Dunkerque, 481, 482

Eden Roc, 365
Eleanor of Aquitaine, 215
electric current in France, 51, 69
Entre-Deux-Mers, 244
Entremont (plateau), 347
Entrèves, 418
Épernay, 92, 474, 475
Erbalunga, 387
Escoffier, Georges Auguste, 367
Estaque, 348
Esterel, 360-61
Esterel Mountains, 361
Étretat, 480, 483-84
Eugénie de Montijo (Empress of the French), 150, 249, 409-10
Evans, Dr. Thomas W., 150
Évian-les-Bains, 420
Évian water, 420
Evreux, 161
exchange rates, 39
Eyzies-de-Tayac, Les, 258-59, 264
Èze-Bord-de-Mer, 373
Èze-Village, 373

Falaise, 164
Falicon, 372
fault finding, 130-31
Fécamp, 484
Fénelon, François de Salignac de la Mothe, 274
Ferney-Voltaire, 445
fiche, 65
Figeac, 255, 275
Filitosa, 383, 393-95
fish, 80
fishing, 410
Fixin (wine), 426
Flanders, 480
flashlights, 55
Flaubert, Gustave, 146
Flavigny-sur-Ozerain, 434
Fleming, Ian, 377
Fogg Museum, 484
Foix, 286, 288, 295
Font-Romeu, 287, 298, 299
Fontaine de Vaucluse, 342-43
Fontaines-Salées, 436, 437
Fontanelle, Guy Eder de la, 185, 187
Fontenay, Abbey of, 434
Fontevrault, 215-16
Fontvielle, 329
food, 73-86, 300, 380-81, 420, 442-43, 464-65, 479
  bread, 74
  continental breakfasts, 73
  cost of, 36
  dinner, 78
  fish, 81
  lunch, 74, 78
  meat, 81
  in *pensions,* 70-71, 77
  shopping for, 76
  soup, 81
Forges-les-Eaux, 485
Formigny, 153
Fort de Douaumont, 468
Fort de la Pompelle, 470
Fort de Vaux, 468
Fort la Latte, 172-73
Foundation Marguerite and Aimé Maeght, 368
Fragonard, Jean Honoré, 364
France
  battles in, 115
  farms of, 117-18
  highlight areas of, 24
  people of, 17, 123-24
  postal system of, 119
  size of, 117, 118
  train service in, 121
Francis I, 220, 221, 224, 225, 227, 229
francs, 40, 136-37
Franklin, Benjamin, 114, 203
Fréjus, 353, 356, 360

French Government Tourist Offices
addresses of, 30
on camping, 72
on driving, 101
hotel lists of, 67
hotel reservation forms of, 62
information from, 57
French language, 17, 55
French people, 17, 123-24
Fulton, Robert, 449

Gap, 403
garages, 64
Garnier, Charles, 378
gasoline, 112, 122-23
Gauguin, Paul, 179, 189-90, 327, 328
Gaulle, Gen. Charles de, 187
Gavarni, 293
Geneva, 411, 412, 419, 420, 422, 445, 446
Geneva, Lake, 400, 445
resorts on, 419-20
Genoese towers in Corsica, 387, 391
Gérardmer, 450, 465
Géricault, Jean Louis, 146
German concentration camp (Natzweiler-Struthof), 455-56
Germany (West), driving in, 48
Giacometti, Alberto, 368
Gien, 210, 232
Gislebert, 433
Glacier de Bionnassay, 415
Glanum, 331-32
Glières, battle of, 411-12
Golfe-Juan, 364
Gordes, 343
Gothic architecture, 132-33, 472, 478
Gouffre de Padirac, 273
Gould, Frank Jay, 364
Gourdon, 369
Goya, Francisco José de, 307
Gradlon, King, 185, 188
Grand, 463-64
Grand-Chartreuse, 404
Grand Port, 406
Grandcamp, 154
Grande Corniche, 372
Granville, 156
Grasse, 363-64, 403
Gravelines, 481, 482
Graves (wine), 244, 246
green card (automobile insurance), 46, 111
Grenoble, 403, 404-6, 411, 412, 448
Greuze, Jean-Baptiste, 426
Grimaldi palace, 376
Grotte des Demoiselles, 310
Grünewald, Mathias, 451
Guehenno, 203
Guérande, 204
Guéthary, 250
guidebooks, 15, 30, 65-66, 135
guides, 135-36
Guise, Duc de 227, 228
gunpowder, 211
Gutenberg, Johann, 459
Gypsies, 324

Haras du Pin, 164-65
Havre, Le, 485
health, safeguards for travelers', 30
Heine, Alice, 376
Heine, Heinrich, 292
Hemingway, Ernest, 114
Hendaye, 248-51
Hennebont, 190
Henri III, 214, 228
Henri IV, 212, 228, 290, 301
Henry II (of England), 157, 164, 215, 217, 219, 272, 273, 440, 481
Hermitage, L', 339
hierarchy of the road, 104-5
Hohwald, Le, 455
holidays, legal, 25
Honarat, Saint, 362
Honfleur, 142, 147-48, 484
hors d'oeuvres, 80
Hospices de Beaune, 428
Hossegor, 248-49
hotels
central-base system, 13-14, 141
Châteaux-Hôtels, 67
children in, 68
costs of, 35, 61
country, 13, 61
fiche, 65
government ratings of, 67
Hôtels Silencieux, 67
names of, 69-70
noise in, 59, 67
odds and ends of information about, 68
Relais de Campagne, 67

reservations in, 62-64, 99
rooms in, 63, 68, 69
Hôtels Silencieux, 67
Huelgoat, 176, 177, 181, 183-84
Hugo, Victor, 499
Huguenots, 324
Huissier (bailiff), 111
Hundred Years War, 236
Hyères, 353, 357

Ile aux Moines, 202
Ile de Gavrinis, 202
Ile de Porquerolles, 357
Ile de Port-Cros, 357
Ile de Sein, 186-87
Ile du Levant, 357
Ile-Rousse, L', 382, 387-89
Iles de Lerins, 363-64
Iles Sanguinaires, 393
Ingres, J. A. D., 280, 347
insurance, 34
automobile, 45, 48
International Driving License, 48, 251, 299
International Reply Coupon for postage, 62
International Road Signs, 101
International Telegraph Hotel Code, 62
invasion beaches (1944), 152-56
Isle-sur-la-Sorgue, L', 342
itineraries, 24-29

Jefferson, Thomas, 114, 333
Joan of Arc, 144-45, 161, 209, 217-19, 223, 231, 232, 444, 462-63, 472-73
Johnson, Samuel, 388
Jongkind, Johann Barthold, 147
Josselin, 204
Jouffroy d'Abbans, Claude de, 449
Juan-les-Pins, 364
July 14th, 28
Jura, 95, 444-49
description of, 444
food and wine of, 464

Kandinsky, Vasily, 368
Kayersberg, 455
Kelly, Grace, 376
Kennedy, Jacqueline, 114
Kléber-Colombes guidebook, 66

Lac de Montriond, 420
Lac du Bourget, 403, 406
Lagatjar menhirs, 183
Lamartine, Alphonse de, 422
Landes, 248
Langeais, 144, 211, 212
langue d'oc, 255
langue d'oïl, 255
Lannion, 173
Laon, 466, 476
Larmor-Badeu, 202
Laroque-des-Arcs, 279
Lascaux, 253, 262-64, 278, 424
laundries, 53
Lausanne, 420
Lavandou, Le, 357
Lavezzi, 397
Lawrence, D. H., 369
Le Corbusier, 351, 449-50
Ledoux, Claude-Nicolas, 447
Léger, Fernand, 366, 413
Leonardo da Vinci, 224
Lesconil, 187
Leszczynski, Stanislas, 461
letters of credit, 39
Lille, 479
Limoges, 235, 243
liquor allowance when entering the U.S., 43-44
Lisieux, 161
Llivia (Spanish), 118, 298
Loches, 211, 212
Locmariaquer, 197
Locronau, 185
Logis de France, 67
Loire River, 209, 210
Loire Valley, 210, 211
wines of, 94
Lorient, 190
Lorraine, 461-64
description of, 444
food and wine of, 465
Lot River, 253
Loti, Pierre, 173
Louis VII, 437-38
Louis IX, 323
Louis XI, 212, 222, 223-24
Louis XII, 219, 228
Louis XIV, 229, 250, 308
Louis XV, 447
Louis XVI, 203, 230, 447
Louis-Philippe, 149-50
Lourdes, 161, 291
Luchon, 286
Luçon, 237
Lurçat, Jean, 244, 274, 413
Luxembourg, 461

Luz-Saint-Sauveur, 293
Lyon, 319, 411, 448

Macinaggio, 387
Maeght Foundation, 368
mail
  addressing, 29
  forwarding, 25
Maison Carrée (Nîmes), 333-35
malaria, 389, 398
Malène, La, 302, 312
Man in the Iron Mask, 350, 362
Mans, Le, 223
Mansart, J. H., 165
Mantegna, 222
maps, 30, 130
maquis, 383
Marcillac, 275, 276
Marius, Caius, 348
Marguerite of Navarre, 292
Marne River, 474
Marseillaise, the, 459
Marseille, 323, 346-51, 356, 382
Martel, Charles, 236, 273
Martin, Sainte-Thérèse, 161
Marvejols, 313
Massif des Maures, 357-58, 360
Matisse, Henri, 368, 369, 413
Matisse Chapel, 373
Matisse Museum, 371
meat, 81
Medici, Catherine de, 226, 228
Mediterranean, 355
Medoc (wine), 246
Meergeren, Hans van, 373
megaliths, 174-75, 183, 184, 191-97, 201-2
Megève, 403, 411, 412, 416, 417
memory aids, 128
Mende, 312, 313
menhirs, 191-92, 394-95
Menthon, 411
Menton, 353, 356, 372, 375, 379, 380
menus, 79, 80
Mer de Glace, 414, 415
Mérimée, Prosper, 219, 305, 384, 395
Merlin, the sorcerer, 204
Messery, 419
Metz, 461
Meung-sur-Loire, 230
Meursault (wine), 426
Michelin guides, 23, 30, 65-66
  on camping, 72
Michelin maps, 30
Milandes, Les, 265-66
mileage, daily, 106
milk, 68
Millau, 302, 309-11
Mirabeau, Count, 345
Miró, Joan, 368
Mistral, Frédéric, 328
Moissac, 132, 255, 268, 280-82, 437
Molière, (Jean-Baptiste Poquelin), 229, 309
Molitg-les-Bains, 287
Monaco, 375-79
Monet, Claude, 484
money, safeguarding, 38, 41
money belts, 41
Monpazier, 264
Mont Blanc, 403, 404, 406, 409, 412-13, 416, 417
Mont Blanc tunnel, 418
Mont-Dol, 171
Mont-Dore, Le, 302, 316-17
Mont-Louis, 299, 300
Mont-Saint-Michel, 156-59
Mont Ventoux, 342
Mont Veyrier, 409
Montauban, 255, 280
Montbard, 435
Montbenoît, 447
Monte Carlo, 374-79
Monte-Cristo, Count of, 350
Montenvers, 414, 415
Montesquieu (Charles de Secondat), 246
Montfort, Simon de, 308
Montmajour, Abbey of, 328
Montpellier, 302, 303, 309, 310
Montrachet (wine), 426
Montréal, 435
Montreux, 420
Montrond, 447
Montségur, 295, 308
Morbihan, Gulf of, 197, 201-2
Morez, 446
Morgat, 183
Morlaix, 176
Morny, Duc de, 149, 249
Mort-Homme, 469
Mortagne, 165
Morzine, 420
motels, 68
Mother Goddess, 193
Moulin-à-Vent (wine), 423
Moyenne Corniche, 372

Mozac, 318
Mulhouse, 450
Munster, 465
Muscadet (wine), 205
museums
  entry fees, 119-20
  when closed, 27, 120-21
mushrooms, 82
Mussy-la-Fosse, 434

Nadaud, Gustave, 303
Nancy, 444, 461
Nantes, 94, 204, 205-6
Nantes, Edict of, 324
Nantua, 422
Napoleon I, 163, 290, 357, 383, 392, 393, 404, 435, 440
Napoleon III, 434, 449
Napoleonic period, 365
Napoule, La, 356, 361
Narbonne, 303
nationality plaques for automobiles, 45
Natzweiler-Struthof concentration camp, 455
Nazis in France, 115-16, 136-37
  near Azron, 202
  Blois, 227
  Caen, 162
  Cap de la Chèvre, 183
  Chambord, 230
  Dieppe, 482
  Dordogne, 268
  Dunkerque, 481
  Étretat, 485
  Falaise, 164
  Fort Penthièvre, 199
  Gérardmer, 450
  Glières, 411
  Gordes, 343
  near Grenoble, 404
  Lorient, 190
  Marseille, 349
  Natzweiler-Struthof, 455
  Normandy, 142, 152-56, 160
  Oradour-sur-Glane, 268
  Paluel, 268
  Périgord, 254
  near Pointe du Raz, 186
  Pointe de Grave, 239
  Pointe de Hoc, 154
  Primel-Trégastel, 175
  Quiberón peninsula, 198
  Reims, 471
  Royan, 238
  Saint-Julien-de-Lampon, 268
  Saint-Malo, 172
  Saint-Nazaire, 205
  Saint-Raphael, 361
  Sainte-Mère-Église, 154-56
  Sarlat, 268
  near Tarascon, 296
  Tours, 222
  Trégastel peninsula, 174
Nelson, Horatio, 289
Nernier, 419
Nice, 346, 354, 356, 366, 369-72, 380, 382, 403
Niepce Nicéphore, 426
night driving, 112-13
Nîmes, 333-35
Nissan-lez-Ensérune, 307
Normandy, 141-66
  climate of, 142
  description of, 142
  food of, 165-66
  Second World War in, 160
North Channel Coast, the, 480-85
Noves, monster of (sculpture), 338
noyades, of Nantes, 206
Nuits-Saint-Georges (town), 430
Nuits Saint-Georges (wine), 426
Nyons, 340-41

Olmeto, 393
Omaha Beach, 153
Onassis, Aristotle, 378-79
Oppenheim E. Phillips, 377
Orange, 339-40
Orcines, 317
Orcival, 317
orientation of churches, 133
Orléans, 210, 211, 213
Ospedale Mountains, 398-99
Ostheim, 452
oysters, 201, 247

packing, 59
Padirac, Gouffre de, 273
Paimpont, forest of, 204
Palice, La, 237-38
Paoli, Pasquale de, 388
Paray-le-Monal, 425
parcels, sending home, 52
pardons in Brittany, 181, 183, 203,
Paris, 426, 476, 485
parking, 64
  Disque Obligatoire, 111-12
Passage Graves, 193, 197, 202
passports, 31-33, 39

Pasteur, Louis, 69, 447
Patrick, Saint, 363
Patton, Gen. George, 157
Pau, 288, 290
Peille, 380
Peïra-Cava, 380
Pèlerins, Les, 418
pelota, 287
Penmarc'h peninsula, 187
pensions, 70-71
  wines in, 96
Périgord, 253-85, 302
  central bases of, 255
  described, 253-55
  dialects in, 255
  food and wine of, 94, 284-85
  prehistoric caves in, 253-54, 256-64
Périgueux, 133, 235, 244, 253, 256, 477
Péronne, 477
Pérouges, 423
Perpignan, 288, 296, 299, 300, 302, 303
Perros-Guirec, 172, 173, 176
Petites-Dalles, Les, 483
Petrarch (Francesco Petrarca), 343
Peyrane, 344
Pézenas, 309
photography, 57, 128-30, 426
phylloxera (plant lice), 338
Pic du Midi de Biggore, 293
Picardy, 480
Picasso, Pablo, 364, 365
picnics, 74, 76
Pierrefonds, 466
Pink Granite Coast, 173-75
place names, spelling of, 22
Plateau d'Assy, 413
Plessis-Bourré, 214-15
Plessis-lès-Tours, 212, 222
Pleumeur-Bodou (Telecommunications Center), 175
Ploermel, 204
Ploumanac'h, 173-74
Plovau, 187
Pointe de Hoc, 154
Pointe de Raz, 186
Pointe de Saint-Mathieu, 182
Poitiers, 235, 236, 448
police, 109-11
Pommard (wine), 426
Pont-Audemer, 143, 147
Pont-Aven, 188-89
Pont-du-Gard (aqueduct), 335
Pont Valentré (Cahors), 279-80
Pontarlier, 447
Popes of Avignon, 336-38
Pornichet, 204
Port-Louis, 190
Port-Navalo, 202
Port-Vendres, 302
Porto, 382, 391, 392
Porto-Vecchio, 398, 399
Posidonius, 347
post offices, 25, 119
Poste Restante, 25
Pouilly-Fuissé (wine), 424
Pouldu, Le, 189
Pourriérs, 348
Prades, 287
Prades (Casals music festivals), 300
prehistoric caves (*see* caves)
Promenade des Anglais (Nice), 371
Propriano, 393-95, 401
Protestants, 135, 224, 231, 312, 315
Proust, Marcel, 151
Provence, 322-52
  centers to tour from in, 323
  food of, 351-52
  wine of, 339, 352
provinces and departments, 208-9
Puigcerda, 298
Puy de Dôme, 315, 316-17
Puy, Le, 313
Puys, 482
Pyrenées, the, 286-301, 445
  bases to stay in, 286
  Basque cooking in, 300
  prehistoric caves in, 294-95, 296-97

Quarré-les Tombes, 436
Quiberon, 198-99
Quilan, 288
Quimper, 187-88
Quimperlé, 190

Rabelais, François, 209, 216-17, 220
radios, 55
Rainier III, Prince of Monaco, 376, 378-79
razors, electric, 51, 69
reading lamps, 51
Reims, 92, 466, 471, 474
  battlefields around, 470
Relais de Campagne (hotels), 67
Rembrandt, 222, 347
Renau, Ernest, 173

René I, King of Anjou, 214, 345, 346
Renoir, Pierre Auguste, 347, 367, 474
reservations in hotels, 63, 99
  traveling without, 65
restaurants, 79-86
Restaurants Routiers, 80
Revolution, French, 135, 198, 203, 206, 208, 223, 231, 305, 314, 328, 338, 345, 408, 425, 435
Rhône Valley, 338-39
  wine of, 339
Ribeauvillé, 455
Richelieu, Cardinal, 217, 220, 237, 309, 332
Richelieu (town), 219-20
right-hand priority on the road, 103-4
Riquewihr, 455
Riom, 318
rites of passage, 133
Riva-Bella, 152
Riviera, the, 353-81
  airport on, 371
  bases to stay on, 356
  camping on, 354
  climate of, 355, 370
  food and wine of, 380-81
roads
  animals on, 109
  repairs to, 109
  types of, 106-7
Roanne, 319
Rocamadour, 270-71, 273
Rochefort-sur-Mer, 238
Rochelle, La, 217, 238
Roc'h Trévézel, 179
Rodez, 275
Roland, 288
Romagne-sous-Montfaucon, 469
Romanesque architecture, 132-35, 235, 253, 274, 280, 281-82, 297, 309, 317, 328, 433
Romanesque sculpture, 253, 268, 281-82, 300, 425
Romans in France, 131
Roncevaux, 288
Ronchamp, 449
Roquebrune, 372, 375
Roquefort, 310-11
Roquemartine, Castelas de, 332
Roquepertuse, 347, 351
Roscoff, 176
rosé (wine), 339
Rothschild, Ephrussi de, 355
Rouen, 143-47, 463, 485
Rouffignac, 256-58
Rouget de Lisle, Claude Joseph, 459
roulette, 378
Rousseau, Jean-Jacques, 406
Roussillon (region), 302
Roussillon (town), 343, 344
Royan, 236, 238-39
Royat, 317
Rozier, Le, 310, 312
Rudelle, 275

Sables-d'Olonne, 235, 237
Sables-d'Or-les-Pins, 173
Saché, 221
Sade, Marquis de, 330
Saint-Angulf, 360
Saint Bartholomew's Day, 228
Saint-Benoît-sur-Loire, 231-32
Saint-Bernard Pass, Little, 403
Saint-Brieuc, 173
Saint-Ceré, 274
Saint-Cirq-Lapopie, 278
Saint-Claude, 444-47
Saint-Duzec-en-Pleumeur, 175
Saint-Émilion (wine), 244, 246
Saint-Enimie, 311, 312, 320
Saint-Florent, 388-89
Saint-Gervais, 406, 412, 415, 417
Saint-Gilles-du-Gard, 325
Saint-Girons, 288
Saint-Guénolé, 187
Saint Honorat, 362
Saint James of Compostela, shrine of, 290
Saint-Jean-Cap-Ferrat, 373
Saint-Jean-de-Luz, 248-50
Saint-Jean-du-Gard, 315
Saint-Jean-les-Vignes, Abbey of, 476
Saint-Jean-Pied-de-Port, 288, 290, 291
Saint-Laurent, 447
Saint-Lô, 160
Saint Malo, 171-72
Saint-Michel-de-Cuxa, Abbey of, 300
Saint-Mihiel, 467, 468
Saint-Nazaire, 205, 206
Saint-Nectaire, 302, 316, 317
Saint-Paul de Vence, 368
Saint-Père-sous-Vézelay, 437
Saint-Pierre, 200

Saint-Pol-de-Léon, 176
Saint-Quentin, 477
Saint-Raphael, 357, 360
Saint-Rémy, 323, 330-31
Saint-Savin-sur-Gartempe, 235
Saint-Tropez, 357-59, 374, 390, 417
Saint-Valéry-en-Caux, 483
Sainte-Anne-la-Palud, 183-84
Sainte-Marguerite, 350, 362
Sainte-Marie-de-Campan, 294
Sainte-Maxime, 358, 359
Sainte-Odile, 456
Saintes, 240
Saintes-Maries-de-la-Mer, 324
Salins-les-Bains, 447, 448
Sallanches, 412, 419
Saorge, 380
Sarlat, 265, 267-68
Sartène, 395-96
Sassenage, 405
Saulieu, 426, 433-34
Saumur, 210, 215
Sauternes, 244, 246
Saxe, Marshal, 461
Schongauer, Martin, 451
Sélestat, 455
Sémillante (frigate), 397
Semur-en-Auxois, 434
Senlis, 466
Sens, 439, 440
Sète, 308
Sévigné, Madame de, 341
Shaw, Geroge Bernard, 145
ship, traveling by, 56
shoes, 54
Signac, Paul, 358
Sisteron, 403
sketches as memory aids, 128-29
Smollett, Tobias, 309, 354, 369, 372
Soissons, 476
Solenzara, 399
Solutré, 278, 422, 424
Somme River, 477
sommelier (wine steward), 96
Son et Lumière spectacles, 213, 284, 439
Sorel, Agnes, 223
Sospel, 380
Souillac, 256, 268
soup, 81
Soustons, 248
Spain, driving in, 48
speed on French roads, 105, 107-9
sports clothes, 54
Stein, Gertrude, 114
Stern, Isaac, 379
Stevenson, Robert Louis, 314
Stonewall, C.S.S. (ironclad), 198
storks of Alsace, 452-54
Strasbourg, 444, 450, 452, 456-61
Struthof (*see* Natzweiler-Struthof)
Sully-sur-Loire, 232
Superbagnères, 286
Super-Cannes, observatory of, 362
Syndicats d'Initiative, 30, 136

table manners in France, 84
Talleyrand, Duc de, 229
Talloires, 406, 408-9, 411, 412
Tancarville bridge, 146, 485
Taoulet, 293
Tarascon, 328, 332
Tarascon, Tartarin de, 332
Tarascon-sur-Ariège, 286, 296
Tarbes, 288, 290
Tarn, Gorges of the, 302, 307, 309, 311-12
Tarn River, 253
téléphérique, 409, 413, 415, 416
telephoning in France, 62, 119
Telstar, 175
Tende, 380
Thackeray, William Makepeace, 351
Thonon-les-Bains, 420
Tintinville, 369
tips and tipping, 63, 135
Tonnerre, 428
Toulon, 357
Toulouse, 253, 255, 282-83, 295, 308
Toulouse-Lautrec, Henri de, 284
Touquet-Paris-Plage, Le, 480, 482
Touraine, 209
Tourettes-sur-Loup, 369
tourism in France, 124-25
Tournus, 425-26
Tours, 209, 212, 213, 221-22, 448
towers, Genoese, in Corsica, 387, 391
traffic (*see* roads)
travel agents, 29
travelers checks, 38-39
traveling as an art, 127-31
Tréboul, 186
Trégastel, 174
Trench of the Bayonets, 469
Tréport, Le, 482
Trésor de Vix, 440-41

Trinité-sur-Mer, La, 190
Tristan and Isolde, 185
Trois-Épis, Les, 444, 455
Tronoën, 187
Trophée des Alpes, 372
Trouville, 148-50
Troyes, 440
truffles, 82
Tuck, Edward, 372
tumuli, 197, 202
Turbie, La, 372
Turckheim, 455
Twain, Mark, 114, 145

Ugine, 412
United States Aisne-Marne memorial, 457
U.S.A. automobile plaque, 45
United States Customs, 41-44
Ushant, 182
Ussé, 220
Utah Beach, 152-54

Vaccination, International Certificate of, 30
Vaison-la-Romaine, 341-42
Val d'Esquières, 357-58, 360
Val d'Isère, 403, 416
Valençay, 229
Valenciennes, 479
Valéry, Paul, 309
Vallauris, 364
Vallée Blanche, 416
Van Gogh, Vincent, 189, 322, 327, 328, 331, 347
Vauban, Sébastien, 300
Vaucouleurs, 463, 467
Vaunes, 204
Vence, 368-69, 373
Vendée, 237
vendettas, 384, 395, 397
Vendôme, 213
Ventimiglia, 379
Vercingetorix, 434
Vercors, Le, 404
Verdun, 466-70, 477
Versailles, 209, 210, 229
Veules-les-Roses, 483
Veulettes-sur-Mer, 483
Vézelay, 422, 435-39
Vézère River, 258
Vichy, 318
Vienne, 319
Vierville, 153
Vieux-Boucau, 248
Vigan, 310
Villandry, 212
Villard-de-Lans, 404
Villefranche, 373
Villefranche-de-Rouergue, 264, 275
Villeneuve-lès-Avignon, 336, 338
Villeneuve-Loubet, 367
Villon, François, 230-31
Vinci, Leonardo da, 224
Viollet-le-Duc, Eugène Emmanuel, 156, 305-6, 438-39
visas, 33
Vix, Trésor de, 127
Vizzavona, 390
Voie Sacrée, La, 467
Volnay (wine), 426
Voltaire (François Marie Arouet), 232, 421, 446
Vosne-Romanée (wine), 426
Vougeot (wine), 426

water, mineral, 77
Weiden, Roger van der, 429
Wellington, Duke of, 290
Werfel, Franz, 291
Wilhelm II, Kaiser, 455
William the Conqueror, 151, 162, 164
Windsor, Duke of, 358
wine, 87-100, 205, 207, 234, 244, 284-85, 339, 381, 420, 440, 442-43, 464-65, 479
  Appellation Contrôlée, 90
  buying, 95
  with food, 83, 88
  glasses for, 84
  harvesting, 99
  labels on, 89
  in *pensions,* 78
  regions and, 89-95, 99
  in restaurants, 95
  vintage years for, 97-98
  vintages of, 89
Wylie, Laurence, 343

Young, Arthur, 230, 280, 305, 308
Ys, 185, 188
Yvoire, 406, 419

Zola, Émile, 291, 348
Zonza, 399